KEN

The Ups and Downs of Ken Livingstone

Andrew Hosken is a senior reporter on BBC Radio 4's *Today* programme, investigating a wide range of stories at home and abroad. In 2003, he won the One World Media Award for a series on Algerian terrorism for *Today*. Hosken is also the author of *Nothing Like a Dame: The Scandals of Shirley Porter*. He lives in London.

ANDREW HOSKEN

KEN

The Ups and Downs of Ken Livingstone

ARCADIA BOOKS

Arcadia Books Ltd
15–16 Nassau Street
London W1W 7AB

www.arcadiabooks.co.uk

First published in the United Kingdom by Arcadia Books 2008
Copyright © Andrew Hosken 2008

Andrew Hosken has asserted his moral right to be identified as the author of this
work in accordance with the Copyright, Designs and Patents Act, 1988.

A catalogue record for this book is available from the British Library

ISBN 978-1-905147-72-4

Typeset in Minion by Discript Limited, London WC2N 4BN
Printed in Finland by WS Bookwell

Arcadia Books supports English PEN, the fellowship of writers who work together
to promote literature and its understanding. English PEN upholds writers'
freedoms in Britain and around the world, challenging political and cultural
limits on free expression. To find out more, visit www.englishpen.org or contact
English PEN, 6–8 Amwell Street, London EC1R 1UQ

Arcadia Books distributors are as follows:

in the UK and elsewhere in Europe:
Turnaround Publishers Services
Unit 3, Olympia Trading Estate
Coburg Road
London N22 6TZ

in the US and Canada:
Independent Publishers Group
814 N. Franklin Street
Chicago, IL 60610

in Australia:
Tower Books
PO Box 213
Brookvale, NSW 2100

in New Zealand:
Addenda
PO Box 78224
Grey Lynn
Auckland

in South Africa:
Quartet Sales and Marketing
PO Box 1218
Northcliffe
Johannesburg 2115

Arcadia Books is the *Sunday Times* Small Publisher of the Year

Contents

Foreword

It would be easy to take Ken Livingstone for granted. It is hard to think of another political figure as enduring as London's first directly-elected mayor. He first came to prominence in 1981 after an audacious coup to become leader of the Greater London Council and nearly 30 years on, he is still very much here; still setting the agenda and still getting up people's noses. Over the last three decades he has apparently been through a number of incarnations, from Red Ken, the 'most odious man in Britain', to 'cuddly Ken' of the chat show sofa. Now, he is just Ken. But he has always been the same man, and one of the most effective political operators in the country. Both Tony Blair and Margaret Thatcher tried and failed to destroy him and he may yet see out Gordon Brown and David Cameron.

Although Livingstone has spent the past 30 years in the full glare of publicity, he remains something of a mystery. He is extremely protective of his privacy and despite all the newspaper profiles, refuses to talk about aspects of his personal life. As a politician, he always seemed to be the lone guy against the Establishment whereas in reality, he has always been the head of a small tight-knit team of discreet political activists with which he now runs London. As with many of us, there are contradictions – the cold and ruthless politician who is not afraid to weep in public, the oppositionist who craved power, the modest and approachable man given to bouts of arrogance, the self-effacing wit who occasionally reveals how very seriously indeed he takes himself, and the naturally courteous figure that can offend and insult with the best of them. Above all, he is a phenomenon – a man both publicity-hungry and shy. He polarises public opinion like no other politician. He has been likened to the Plague.

He may be best remembered for all the controversies and the outrage he has caused, whether in his close relationship with Sinn Féin in the 1980s or his curious dealings with figures like Sheikh Yusuf al-Qaradawi and Hugo Chávez a quarter of a century later.

It is easy to forget that Livingstone is the man who introduced the congestion charge, the wheel clamp, the low emission zone, and the civil partnership for gay people to Britain. Alongside Tony Blair, he is credited with winning the bid for the 2012 Olympics for London, for some a mixed blessing, for others a wonderful opportunity.

He is a national figure whose parliamentary career never took off and who failed in his ambition to become prime minister. But he has played a unique role in the politics of London. He was blamed for the abolition of the Greater London Council but he can take credit for re-establishing government for the capital. Directly-elected mayors with executive powers are a new and novel concept for Britain, and the job has been likened to a feudal monarchy, not least by Livingstone himself. The experiment may well have failed with another personality, but under Livingstone, it has evolved into an important and influential role, described by some as one of the most powerful posts in the country.

His rise is a fascinating story about a man who emerged through the rough and tumble of street politics and the tedium of local government. It is an uneven story of ups and downs. It is the story of the rise and fall of the urban Left which took the Labour Party to the brink of extinction. In 1997 few people would have taken bets on Livingstone's re-emergence. But by 2000, despite the fiercest smear onslaught conjured up by New Labour at the height of its power and hubris, he was mayor; by popular acclaim, he was the 'people's Ken'.

In 2008, Livingstone faces his biggest threat in the shambling form of Boris Johnson, another political maverick. This has coincided with one of his greatest political crises resulting from a string of allegations of cronyism, incompetence and even corruption at City Hall. Martin Bright, the political editor of the left-wing *New Statesman,* even described him as a 'disgrace to his office' and called on Labour to drop him as its candidate.[1] But only a fool would write off Livingstone.

◆

I have conducted approximately 200 interviews for the book, including seven with Ken Livingstone, who was very generous with his time during what was clearly a fairly hectic period. It is an unauthorised biography but he was happy to go on the record. Only on a couple of occasions, on relatively minor matters, did he ask to speak off the record. I have tried to give as much information as possible about the sources of my information. To be fair, very few people said 'Don't quote me on this'. You will see that 'off-the-record briefings' increase in number as the book describes more recent events.

With quotations, I have differentiated between people who I have interviewed and those whose words have been recorded by others. If someone in the book *says* something, I have spoken directly to them; if they have *said* or *remembered* something, then their views are recorded reliably in print or elsewhere, or they have died.

I would also like to explain some of the terminology in the book, particularly that dealing with political views on the right and left wings of the Labour movement. *Far left* refers to Trotskyists and other communists. I know many Trotskyists resent this term because it sounds similar to *far right* which is used to refer to neo-Nazi groups. But I notice that the alternative, *ultra-left*, is often used as a term of abuse among Marxists during their arguments. Besides, *far left* appears to be the term favoured by many writers and journalists.

The term *hard left* refers to left activists like Ken Livingstone who are not revolutionaries. *Soft left*, sometimes also called the *Tribunite left* after the group of MPs organised around the *Tribune* paper, refers to traditional left-wing Labour politicians such as Michael Foot, Neil Kinnock and Aneurin Bevan.

I also refer to Trotskyists as Trots and the Stalinist communists who once supported the Soviet Union as Tankies, not as a form of abuse but because that is how they refer to each other and themselves.

The *Evening Standard* has been known as the *London Evening Standard* and at one time, even the *New Standard* following a merger with another paper in the 1980s. So I've just stuck to the *Evening Standard* or the *Standard*.

◆

The book would have been impossible without the help and support of many people. So apologies in advance if I have missed anyone out, but I would like to express my thanks for the staffs of the British Newspaper Library in Colindale, Warwick University, the London Metropolitan Museum, the London School of Economics, the Greater London Authority, the Mayor's Office,

Neale Coleman, Chris Mullen MP, Alan Meale MP, Professor Tony Travers, Harry Barlow, Eddie Lopez, Jonathan Rosenberg, Graham Bash, Keith Veness, Mira Bar-Hillel, Simon Harris, Ross Lydall, Ed Howker and everyone at *Private Eye*, particularly Tim Minogue. I would also like to thank my editor at the *Today* programme, Ceri Thomas, for allowing me to take unpaid leave to write the book. My love and thanks to Katrin and Freddie, my family and friends – once again – for their patience and understanding. If you wish to get in touch with any suggestions, or information for future editions, please contact me by email on andrewjhosken@yahoo.com.

Andrew Hosken
27 February 2008

Note
1 *Evening Standard*, 21.1.08

Chapter 1

Brockwell Park, 1945–1969

Disappointment was Ethel Livingstone's predominant feeling after giving birth to her son at home in her mother's flat on 17 June 1945. Not only had she hoped for a daughter but she thought her little boy looked unsightly, with his bald head and an eye infection which temporarily distorted his features. She soon changed her mind as the infection cleared up and dark curly hair began to appear. Kenneth Robert Livingstone was born in his grandmother's flat off Streatham High Road in a war-weary, bomb-pocked part of south London in the middle of Britain's first general election campaign for 10 years. Three weeks earlier, the Labour leader Clement Atlee had forced Winston Churchill to dissolve his grand war coalition government. For the next 41 years, this small area of south London, part of the borough of Lambeth, would provide Ken Livingstone with everything he would need to take him through the rest of his life and political career. It provided his home and family life, his education, his first start in politics and set him on the road to national prominence.

Livingstone's father, Robert Moffat Livingstone, and mother, Ethel Ada Kennard, or 'Eth' to her friends, had married at Wandsworth Register Office almost five years earlier on 27 June 1940 when France was all but defeated and overrun. They were only 24 and 25 years old respectively. Bob Livingstone met Ethel in April 1940 in the Cumbrian port of Workington at a music hall where she had been working with one of the country's best known illusionists, Cecil Lyle. According to John Carvel, Livingstone's early biographer, Bob, a merchant seaman, was in the audience on a run-a-shore with some leery and beery shipmates. They seemed less preoccupied with 'The Great Lyle' and more interested in winking and waving at Ethel and two other assistants. Bob Livingstone got to meet Ethel backstage and the two quickly became an item. 'We were really meant to meet,' she told Carvel years later.[1] They were a devoted couple. When Bob died aged only 56 in October 1971, Ethel Livingstone was bereft.

'He was wonderful,' she said in 1985.[2] 'We were perfectly compatible, Bob and I.'

Like many wartime couples, the Livingstones suffered high anxiety and long separations. Bob, a Scotsman from Dunoon on the Firth of Clyde in western Scotland, joined the Merchant Navy aged 17 in 1932 as a deck boy, the lowest of the low, and during the war he was promoted to master. He spent several days adrift at sea near Murmansk, an experience so harrowing that it compelled him to leave the Merchant Navy after the war and gave him nightmares for the rest of his life. Ethel stayed in London with her mother Zona Kennard at her flat off Streatham High Street, 21b Shrubbery Road. Ethel had trained as a ballet dancer. 'In a less class-ridden society she might have gone into ballet, I suppose,' says Ken Livingstone. 'But she ended up on the musical hall route.'[3] She had started as a dancer aged 14, and with two close friends formed a dancing trio called the Kenleigh Sisters and accompanied crooners like Donald Peers and entertainers including Tommy Trinder and Tessie O'Shea on tours around provincial theatres. But during most of the war, Ethel was bound to Shrubbery Road to look after Zona who was incapacitated following an operation to remove her knee. To make a living Ethel got jobs at armaments factories nearby.

Along with his parents, Zona Kennard was the most significant adult in Ken Livingstone's early life. He spent the first five years in her Shrubbery Road flat and later she came to live with the family elsewhere in the Norwood area of south London. Livingstone mentioned her rarely until asked years later by the psychiatrist Anthony Clare. Until then, Livingstone had always painted the picture of a contented family life with devoted parents and happy holidays in Butlins. But clearly Zona's behaviour helped cast a pall over his early years. She was 'tyrannical', Livingstone told Clare, adding, 'My grandmother was so manipulative it wasn't true. She was one of those women who actually orchestrate the situation if things aren't going their way… She would suddenly start to worry about how soon she was going to die and how.' It was, he said, 'a real classic study of manipulation within the family'. 'And of course,' he added, 'there was a lot of pain and anguish we didn't need to live with.'[4] He and his mother would often be reduced to tears as she repeatedly hurled vicious abuse at the gentle Bob Livingstone.

Livingstone is a sensitive man and was clearly traumatised by his grandmother's behaviour, particularly towards his father. Zona Kennard had been a widow for nearly 30 years by the time Ken Livingstone was born. Her own husband, Charles Kennard, died in World War One. Ken Livingstone did not know much about his maternal grandfather other than that he had been a 'bit of a lad' and he was sent to the Western Front to save on the costs of a court martial where 'he got blown to bits very rapidly with no surviving trace'.[5] But Charles Kennard's military record, although not remarkable by the astonishingly high standards of the time, was one of suffering and sacrifice. He enlisted with the Sixth Battalion of the Dorsetshire Regiment at Battersea on 14 August 1914, 10 days after Britain declared war on Germany. Certainly, he fell foul of the military authorities. The official records at the National Archives in Kew show how he was first posted to France on 3 July 1916, two days after the start of the Battle of the Somme in which the regiment fought, and that he was injured in the fighting in northern France. The records also demonstrate that Kennard was jailed twice by the military: first for 21 days after being found drunk in town on 16 July 1916, without a pass and then compounding the offence by lying to a superior officer. He received a seven-day sentence exactly two years later for being absent without leave for more than two and a half days and missing a military tattoo. Charles Kennard was killed in Flanders on 16 May 1917.

At the time, Zona was pregnant with her second child, Ken Livingstone's uncle, also called Kenneth. The child was born little more than two months later. Ethel, Livingstone's mother, was born in May 1915, shortly before Zona and Charles were married and could never remember her father. Zona Kennard never remarried and she had a difficult life, raising two children on her own and living precariously in one south London tenement after another, from the Oval to Shrubbery Road. 'She absolutely doted on me,' says Livingstone. 'It was only with hindsight I realised she was a nightmare to live with. She had these violent mood swings.' Zona resented newcomers to the tight family unit she had struggled against the odds to maintain.[6] In 1965, on her death bed, she apologised to the family for the pain she had caused them, particularly Livingstone's father Bob. Years later, Ethel saw a television programme about people's psychological disorders and recognised similar symptoms in her own mother.

◆

Streatham was a mainly white working-class area just south of the river; the mass immigration from the Caribbean would come later, in the 1950s, when the country desperately needed to fill jobs no one else seemed to want. In the post-war years, the area became a building site as the local council cleared the bomb sites and many of the slums to provide new homes. 21b Shrubbery Road was dangerously close to the bustle and traffic of Streatham High Road and so for the first five years of his life, Livingstone was forced to stay indoors all day, often gazing at the blue light of Streatham police station directly opposite, the officers beginning or finishing their beats and the large noisy pigs they kept behind the station to supplement their rations.

When Livingstone first came to public attention by taking over the Greater London Council in 1981, newspaper feature writers beat a path to his door and wrote thousands of words about his supposedly exotic background. But, it was a very ordinary upbringing for a working-class boy growing up in the hungry post-war years. After the war, Ethel earned money by working for the local baker and by picking up the occasional Saturday morning shift at the Freemans catalogue dispatch in Stockwell. She also worked as a cinema usherette, occasionally having to plonk a young Livingstone on the back seats during screenings when she could not get a babysitter. As an 11-year-old, he had to endure a week of Bill Haley's 'Rock Around the Clock' while his mother sold drinks and ice creams. For a time, Bob Livingstone worked at sea on cross Channel ferries. He took his family on one trip. They had no passports and could not disembark so sailed back. He also worked on fishing trawlers. 'I remember my mother hated it,' says Livingstone, 'because he would come back from the trawlers and his hands would be bleeding from these gashes from the hooks and the netting and things like that.'[7] Ethel was delighted when Bob left the Merchant Navy in January 1951. The reason given on the official form is terse: 'At own request.' But he had never really recovered from his terrible wartime experiences and returned home to a window-cleaning round along Streatham High Road as well as an evening job moving scenery at the Streatham Hill Theatre. By now the family had moved out of Shrubbery Road to a new estate in Tulse Hill built by the London County Council not far away at 23 Irby

House. Zona, who hated living on her own, virtually moved in with them soon after.

◆

Livingstone adored his father but always found him something of a mystery and missed him fiercely when he died unexpectedly and far too young; he had to piece together his father's past from others. Bob Livingstone never spoke much about anything that happened before he met Ethel. Bob grew to loathe his own father, also a former merchant seaman and also called Robert Moffat Livingstone. Bob was closer to his mother, Catherine, and was deeply hurt when his father conducted an affair while she lay dying of tuberculosis. Robert Livingstone senior later ran a ranch in Argentinia. At Catherine's funeral, Bob's father shook him by the hand and said, 'Good luck son.' The pair never saw each other again.

◆

Livingstone's early childhood meant holidays at Butlins, lazy Sundays by the lido in Brockwell Park and games on the precarious bomb sites in Norwood before they were cleared by the local council. He attended St Leonard's Primary school, attached to the church of the same name, where he was also christened, off Streatham High Road and almost directly opposite Shrubbery Road. Livingstone was raised amid the rubble and ration books of post-war Lambeth, and absorbed the ideals of its close-knit working-class community. As leader of the Greater London Council in the 1980s, Livingstone was often painted as something new and nasty, a bogey man from the sinister 'loony left'. But Lambeth taught Livingstone the importance of old-fashioned values of bobbies on the beat, politeness and compassion. In 2008, to the derision of his political candidates, he was still railing against the hallmarks of Thatcherism he saw as alien and evil: 'snouts in the trough', 'no such thing as society' and 'greed is good.'[8]

At 11, Livingstone failed the Eleven Plus, a controversial exam introduced in 1944 to separate what the educational establishment considered the wheat from the chaff. At St Leonard's, he had sat at the back of classes with around 45 pupils. 'At the back you tended to be ignored,' says Livingstone, 'and not surprisingly the teachers would invest time on pupils they felt had a reasonable chance of passing the exam.' Only a quarter got through and less stigma was attached to those children in areas which had dispensed with segregation in state education and introduced the comprehensives. In Livingstone's case, success meant the chance of getting into the local Strand Grammar School with its emphasis on academic studies and enhanced opportunities to go to university; failure meant going to the new comprehensive school built in Tulse Hill with its focus on technical training. As Labour's education spokesman, Neil Kinnock railed against the Eleven Plus based on his own school days in Tredegar. He observed how few schoolchildren were 'wreathed in smiles', but that there were 'floods of tears in many homes'.[9] Livingstone remembers that his own parents were disappointed but they had never entertained any great expectations.

Tulse Hill Comprehensive was a vast eight-floor rectangular block of tinted glass panels and concrete teeming with 2,300 boys. In 1990, after years of decline both in fabric and pupil numbers coupled with the expense involved in removing the asbestos widespread throughout the structure, the school was demolished to make way for social housing. But, on 11 September 1956, when Ken Livingstone first walked through the gates, it was a modern, state-of-the-art comprehensive drawing children from south London suburbs including Brixton, Streatham and Brockwell Park. Early on, when some boys accidentally put their feet through the wafer-thin cloakroom plasterboard walls, it was clear that speed rather than high building standards had been the priority in construction, but, according to former pupils and teachers interviewed for the book, the facilities were remarkable: six gymnasiums, 26 workshops for prospective carpenters, toolmakers and engineers, two floors containing laboratories and one for the arts.

There was the use of a boathouse near Putney, but for games, pupils had to take the bus south to the Priest Hill playing fields in the Surrey town of Ewell. In the Great Hall with its highly professional stage lighting system, there was a huge organ bought from the Rose Hill cinema which would belt out favourites like the Purcell 'Trumpet Voluntary' or the school song, *Ad Unum Omnes* (All for one and one for all), of which one verse:

> *With head and heart and voice,*
> *We strive to show our praise*
> *For the spirit of our school:*
> Ad Unum Omnes.[10]

The song reflected the faux public-school ethos which Tulse Hill's first head teacher Clifford Thomas attempted to impose on his boys. Thomas, a former deputy head teacher of Dulwich College, believed passionately in all the rigmarole he had helped maintain there: prefects and a system of eight houses named after great figures of British history like Sir Christopher Wren and Isambard Kingdom Brunel.

The uniform, which was compulsory, consisted of blue tie, blazer and cap, all adorned with the school badge depicting a lamb carrying a cross above a blue and white striped shield. All items could be bought at David J. Thomas men's and boys' outfitter in Hearne Hill, or the Co-op in Brixton.[11] For the younger and more modern teachers like the school's head of biology, Raymond Rivers, the whole set-up was absurd. 'I felt very strongly about it,' says Rivers, 'I always spoke up as I believed and I felt it was nonsense. I didn't put it that way but I spoke against it.'[12] Rivers joined the school in 1957, a year after Ken Livingstone, and quickly became one of the most popular and inspiring teachers at Tulse Hill, as well as an important influence on Ken Livingstone's life. The teacher gave Livingstone his enduring passion for amphibians including newts, frogs and salamanders. Livingstone remembers his first proper encounter with an amphibian, which took place as a 12- or 13-year-old while playing truant in Brockwell Park. He caught a newt in the ponds and took it home. The menagerie grew to include a South African bullfrog called Black Joe, salamanders, two long monitor lizards, a baby alligator and two poisonous Formosan vipers, along with the serum which had to be injected within two minutes of a bite to prevent death.[13]

◆

By his own admission, Ken Livingstone was a small and insecure schoolboy who struggled to cope at Tulse Hill School. 'Ken was a lively outgoing child,' his mother Ethel said later. But by the time he joined Tulse Hill, both she and Livingstone's father Bob were worried about their son who had become increasingly solitary.[14] She added, 'I remember saying to Bob "I don't know what will become of him" because he didn't like school. He wasn't interested in going out with girls, or going to football. He wasn't interested in anything except his pet lizards and friends – always wanted to be the boss. No, you couldn't say he was all that popular when young.'[15] Ethel Livingstone's comments could be aimed at many pre-pubescent and pubescent children. But at the risk of deploying cod psychology, many people interviewed for this book, including long-term friends and close advisors have remarked on Ken Livingstone's essential reserve, even shyness, which may surprise some observers of this controversial and outspoken politician. A common complaint about Livingstone, particularly when he was in Parliament, was that he was solitary and unclubbable, and protective of his private life to the 'point of secrecy'.[16] Many commentators have also remarked on Livingstone's easy charm and self-effacing manner, possible manifestations of shyness and qualities not often found in politicians.

Ethel Livingstone thought her son was like Bob. 'Everybody loved Bob,' she once said, 'and Ken's got a lot of his father's ways... the way he talks, that smile.'[17] It may be that he inherited his natural, although perhaps uneasy, showmanship from his music-hall mother. Livingstone's small stature and lack of self-confidence were sniffed out by the many school bullies with all the nous of a police blood hound. Despite the cap badges and rowing races on the Thames, the local catchment guaranteed a ready supply of rough and violent youths. 'They used to say that if you could survive Tulse Hill School, you could survive anywhere,' says John Land who was a contemporary of Livingstone.[18] Another former pupil, John Harris, remembers seeing some of the older boys hanging a science teacher out of the window of a first-floor laboratory by his braces. 'The cane was used quite readily in the school,' he says. 'Certainly bullying did happen and I learned to deal with that.'[19]

Pupils were streamed according to ability. Three classes were thought to be academic. But teacher shortages often forced the cancellation of lessons in subjects such as maths or history. Livingstone was placed in form six, the bottom of the middle category. Although he was promoted after two years at Tulse Hill, he never adjusted to the change. Some children did flourish. Alumni include the actors Tim Roth and Kenneth Cranham, the Jamaican-born poet, Linton Kwesi Johnson, and the *Guardian* investigative journalist, David Hencke. Hencke says that he also found the school 'too big'. 'I only really flourished when I got into the sixth form,' he says.[20]

Aside from Raymond Rivers, another big influence on Livingstone was the academic and poet, Philip Hobsbaum, who died in June 2005, and was his form teacher for his first year. Hobsbaum told Carvel that he thought Livingstone was 'highly articulate and very friendly' and thought his future lay in journalism or advertising rather than politics, which he often discussed with the young boy and his classmates. Livingstone thought Hobsbaum an inspiration and wistfully regrets he did not spend longer with him. 'He was incredibly charismatic,' says Livingstone. 'If I had more of an exposure to him I might have done better at school and gone on to university because he was very good at driving people.'

Livingstone stood out neither academically nor, perhaps oddly for the man who was instrumental in winning the 2012 Olympics for London, at sport. The reason he remains ambivalent about sport is that he was 'the weediest runt in the school'. Ian Scott, another contemporary, remembers Livingstone as one of those boys on Raymond Rivers' rota for looking after the laboratory animals. 'He really was one of those with a ball of string and an apple core half-covered with frog spawn in his pocket,' says Scott.[21] 'Rivers was a brilliant teacher, absolutely brilliant. He made learning fun.' Livingstone clearly thought the same but still dropped out of school aged 17 with four O-levels in English language, English literature, geography and art: 'the easy ones,' according to Livingstone. His last few years were marred by unhappiness and truancy. Later, at night school, he did an A-level in zoology, a fact which Raymond Rivers would not learn until years later. He remains loyal to his boys and is discreet about Livingstone, but he does remember meeting Livingstone's parents for a discussion at one stage 'which I doubt I would have done had I not thought there was a problem'. But he could find no domestic or personal reasons why Livingstone was not doing better at school. He failed to get the two extra O-levels he needed to get into sixth form despite two further attempts. Some of his closest advisors feel that Livingstone has an exaggerated respect for official qualifications which may stem from his failure at school.[22]

◆

Livingstone helped Bob on his window-cleaning round while applying for jobs as a keeper, first with London Zoo and then Gerald Durrell's zoo in Jersey, but without success. However he applied successfully to become an animal technician with the Chester Beatty cancer research clinic on the Fulham Road in

London. Livingstone says, 'My parents didn't have any expectations of my achieving anything. All they wanted was for me to get a job with a pension. And my first job had a pension so they relaxed after that and stopped worrying, because they had never had a pension.' Livingstone's main job was caring for the laboratory animals which included rabbits, mice and goats. The laboratory technicians had responsibility for the welfare of the animals, from feeding them and cleaning out their cages to preparing them for experiments. A former Chester Beatty technician, David Kulper, said many of his experiments involved giving laboratory animals cancer by forcing them to smoke cigarettes. 'I didn't smoke until I worked for Chester Beatty,' says Kulper, 'but there were all these free cigarettes donated by HM Customs and we all helped ourselves.'[23] Cancer-riddled rats would be put out of their misery by placing a pencil across the neck behind the ears and then pulling sharply on the tail. He and Livingstone shared an interest in herpetology and during breaks in the canteen room, would sometimes discuss African clawed frogs over tea and cake. He remembers a rather reserved youth. 'I thought he was a bit of a geek,' says Kulper. 'He wore a blue serge suit and brown shoes. On the Monday we would all discuss what we did at the weekend and I'd ask Ken and he'd say "Not much, I'm saving my money to get married."'

Livingstone's initial tasks included cleaning out the rats' cages and making sure they were watered and fed. Gradually, he worked his way up to assisting in the management of experiments. By the time Livingstone moved to Chester Beatty's laboratory in Carshalton, he was the deputy head of the animal unit. 'This meant I had a legal responsibility for the welfare of the animals,' says Livingstone. 'If a doctor or a professor was conducting an experiment and you felt that the level of pain caused did not justify prolonging the life of the animal, you had both the right and the duty to terminate the experiment.' However, one former Chester Beatty scientist later claimed that he could not remember Livingstone intervening in experiments. 'I don't remember him dancing up and down saying, I'm not going to stand for this,' Dr Christopher Grant told the Sunday Times in 2008. 'If something like that had caused trouble I'm certain I would have heard about it and I don't recollect it.'[24] But Livingstone insists he would sometimes exercise his right to terminate experiments, occasionally to the annoyance of some medics and that as a consequence, he was told that he did not have a bright future with Chester Beatty. Given Livingstone's established love of animals and his track record in annoying those in power, his version of events is by no means inconceivable. During this time, and until the age of 28, Livingstone lived with his parents at the house they bought in 1957, the first they had ever owned, at 66 Wolfington Road in Norwood.

Chester Beatty brought him into contact for the first time with socialists. 'There were about 14 of us technicians, all men,' he said later. 'I suddenly dropped into an environment where everyone in that room except me was a committed socialist from a committed socialist background.'[25] Other Chester Beatty employees often observed Livingstone increasingly poring over political biographies and books on contemporary history.[26]

◆

In late 1966, Livingstone and a friend from Chester Beatty, Mick Towns, started a six-month hitch-hiking tour through Africa, travelling in countries including Algeria, Nigeria, Ghana and Togo. It was the first time the pair had ever left the country and Livingstone said later it broadened his horizons in the same way as national service and university had for others.[27] Their initial destination was the Mountains of the Moon in Rwanda to see the gorillas being cared for by the zoologist Dian Fossey, but civil wars in Sudan and elsewhere barred their progress, so they decided to head south-west across Algeria and the Sahara before going through the jungles of Ghana on their way to Cameroon and the lowland gorilla.[28] On the trip, he met many radical young people in both the Voluntary Service Organisation and the American Peace Corps who liked to debate politics passionately and often. One was Ole Olsen, an anti-Vietnam campaigner, who Livingstone helped to get into the UK. Livingstone would later buy his first house in Brixton from Olsen. His imagination fired up by his trip, Livingstone returned home determined to become involved in politics.

Livingstone's parents had voted Conservative but he was propelled leftwards to the Labour Party by a combination of events and influences. His parents had been particularly important in moulding his attitudes on race and homosexuality. Bob Livingstone, who had spent 20 years on boats living cheek by jowl with people of all races, had always been clear that people were equal, an unusual perspective in the 1950s and 1960s. 'My mum had grown up in this music-hall world where sexual orientation was no great hock either,' says Livingstone. But he was no class warrior, a fact long realised by disappointed Trotskyist former colleagues. Livingstone argues that class was never an issue in his political formation: he had grown up in London where there was no problem getting a job. He says he never met an unemployed person until he was in his twenties. In February 1969, Livingstone walked to Chestnut Road[29] and the home of a Labour activist called Dennis Kelly where he joined the Norwood Labour Party.

Notes

1 John Carvel, *Citizen Ken*, Chatto and Windus, 1984, p27
2 *Woman*, 23.11.85
3 Interview, Ken Livingstone, 10.10.07
4 *In the Psychiatrist's Chair*, BBC Radio 4, presented by Anthony Clare, 28.8.88
5 Interview, Ken Livingstone, 10.10.07
6 Ibid.
7 Interview, Ken Livingstone, 11.10.07
8 Ken Livingstone, Weekly Press Conference, City Hall, 8.1.08
9 Robert Harris, *The Making of Neil Kinnock*, Faber and Faber, 1984, p126 (Kinnock speech on 19.6.79)
10 Supplied by former pupil John Land, and Tulse Hill School website
11 Ibid.
12 Interview, Raymond Rivers, 11.10.07
13 John Carvel, *Citizen Ken*, p36
14 *Woman*, 23.11.85
15 Ibid.
16 *Sunday Telegraph*, by Richard Croft, 30.8.87
17 *Woman*, 23.11.85
18 Interview, John Land, 24.7.07
19 Interview, John Harris, 31.7.07
20 Interview, David Hencke, 29.10.07
21 Interview, Ian Scott, 20.7.07
22 Off-the-record interview, 2007
23 Author interviews, 2007
24 *Sunday Times*, 17.2.08
25 *Guardian*, 28.4.84
26 Author interviews, 2007
27 John Carvel, *Citizen Ken*, p39
28 Interview, Ken Livingstone, 1.11.07
29 Interview, Ken Livingstone, 26.11.07

Chapter 2

'Rise like lions after slumber!' 1969–1973

Ken Livingstone joined the Labour Party at about the same time Neil Kinnock was thinking of leaving it. This fact was not lost on Kinnock later, in the 1980s, when he and Livingstone shared a mutual loathing, one of the few things the two men had in common. Livingstone joked that he was one of the few examples of a 'rat climbing on board a sinking ship'.[1] People were deserting the Labour Party at the time, not joining it. Before Kinnock became the new firebrand MP for Bedwellty in south Wales, he had despaired of Labour in government. Like many other members, he was convinced that Prime Minister Harold Wilson had been seriously wrong about the economy for years and he was depressed about his decision to devalue the pound on 18 November 1967, a result of rocketing oil prices in the wake of the Six Day War five months earlier. Like many on the left at the time, Kinnock also opposed Wilson's proposals to curb both union power and pay increases as articulated in the highly contentious but ultimately doomed White Paper, 'In Place of Strife'.

The Vietnam War was another source of anger particularly for the Left. Wilson had refused to send British troops to fight alongside the US but in 1968, as hundreds of thousands of British people took part in anti-Vietnam protests, the government's foreign secretary Michael Stewart spoke warmly of US military strategy. Kinnock said later, 'That was the moment I thought of leaving and that was the moment Ken Livingstone decided to bloody well join.'[2] Kinnock stayed but many left. And Livingstone did join. He felt the same betrayal as Kinnock about Labour in government, an anger which he and many others would feel with growing bitterness during the next decade with successive Labour governments. It would find expression following the election defeat of 1979 when it would bring the Labour Party close to political extinction. Livingstone's political career flourished in the 1970s and 1980s on the crest of this righteous anger and his political fortunes would go into gentle decline as it abated and the party gradually moved rightwards to evolve into New Labour. Livingstone had nearly joined the Labour Party a year earlier in 1968, but decided against it after the Wilson government restricted the immigration of Asians who had been expelled from Kenya by President Jomo Kenyatta. For Livingstone, it was just another betrayal by Wilson.

◆

Between the end of his Africa trip and joining the party, Livingstone did engage in relatively minor political activity. He had attended some of the anti-Vietnam protests held in London in 1968, the same year which saw the student protests in Paris. He had helped US Army draft dodgers like Ole Olsen and campaigned against redundancies at Chester Beatty. He also subscribed to a magazine called *Anarchy* which anarchists somehow managed to put together, but he shunned the temptation of many left-wingers to join up with one of the plethora of Trotskyist parties around then. Labour in London at that time was in a particularly bad state. The party had been virtually extirpated in the May 1968 elections for London's 32 boroughs. In the backlash following the Wilson devaluation and the higher prices it caused, Labour made a net loss of 747 seats, costing it control of 15 borough councils, mostly to the Tories. Labour fiefdoms including Haringey, Lewisham and Islington fell to the Tories, leaving the party in control of only four boroughs. One of those to fall was Livingstone's own borough, Lambeth, of which Norwood was part. Lambeth had always been considered a safe Labour borough but astoundingly in May 1968, the Tories won 57 seats out of 60. The future prime minister, John Major, was one of the victorious councillors. He was soon appointed chairman of the council's Housing Committee.

The carnage proved extremely helpful to ambitious left-wingers like Livingstone. It had effectively eradicated a whole generation of old, largely right-wing, councillors whose word held sway in the council chambers and the local parties. It also left the party vulnerable to the large number of bedsit revolutionaries from groups like Militant and the International Marxist Group, many of whom joined Labour while retaining their passion for revolutionary politics. When the shoots of Labour recovery did begin to appear in the early 1970s, more often than not, they were red rather than green. The advance of the Left through the 1970s gathered speed as the social democratic consensus in the Labour Party broke down aided by a deepening economic crisis and disillusionment at the response of Labour governments to it.

◆

A brief description of the Labour Party's structure will be useful because this was the ladder climbed by Livingstone. The basic building block of Labour is the ward, a small electoral district represented by a number of councillors. Wards are also used to form parliamentary constituencies and boroughs. Each ward has its own committee with a chairman and secretary, in common with both the constituency parties and an overall party organisation for the London borough. The constituency parties are run by members of the General Management Committee (GMC) and, in London, Labour candidates for the local council are chosen by a separate borough-wide body called the Local Government Committee, which is made up of local activists. The next two tiers above the boroughs are the powerful Greater London Labour Party, bringing together Labour representatives from the 32 boroughs and then the national party headquarters.

At this time, and until the triumph of Tony Blair and New Labour in 1997, the party's main instrument of administration, the National Executive Committee, or NEC, was extremely powerful. NEC membership bestowed enormous prestige and the committee was responsible for drawing up party policies and enforcing discipline, including the ultimate sanction of expulsion. NEC members are elected each year by the all-important Labour Party conference which brought together everyone in the Labour movement, particularly the trade unions which had created the party in the first place.

The sorry state of the Labour Party was obvious to Livingstone at that first meeting of the Leigham ward of the Norwood Labour Party. There were three other people at the meeting, including Pat Craven who was known to be one of the Trotskyists from Militant Tendency.[3] By his second meeting, Livingstone had become chairman and secretary of the Norwood constituency party's Young Socialists. He was also selected as a member of the Norwood General Management Committee and put on the Local Government Committee. He wrote later: 'My arrival had been rather like taking a bottle of gin into a room full of alcoholics. I was immediately passed round and consumed.'[4]

Brynley Heaven was a member of the Young Socialists. At 23, Livingstone was considered rather elderly to be chairman of the Young Socialists. The cut-off age was 25. Heaven remembers a rather fun and charismatic figure at the weekly meetings in Rosendale Road in Herne Hill near Brockwell Park. Early on, it was clear that Livingstone had an extraordinary emotional intelligence that was rare in politicians and that he would develop to engage or enchant almost any audience. 'You can imagine the usual rather tedious bill of fare,' says Heaven. 'There were the trade unionists talking about their strikes and so on. And then Ken decided he was going to talk about sex and instead of the usual awful meeting, there would be standing room only! It was then that Ken's talent as a crowd-puller really hit me. Most politicians have developed this crap way of speaking whereas Ken always said something that meant something.'

◆

Politics helped to give the young Livingstone self-confidence, which he clearly lacked. Later he said, 'The reason I didn't join the Labour Party until I was 23 was that working-class kids do not go out and join things they don't know. They become involved when you take them to it. My confidence came in my twenties and not in my teens, and that's the classic pattern for working-class kids.'[5] The late 1960s and early 1970s saw the rise of what academics like to describe as the 'new urban Left'.[6] Livingstone was an absolutely archetypal 'urban Lefty', straight out of central casting, and compounded when, in September 1970, he enrolled at one of the hot houses for this powerful and fast-growing movement, a teacher-training college. These young left-wing radicals were nurtured by the post-war education reforms introduced by Clement Atlee which opened their minds through the tertiary education often denied their parents, and then radicalised by the student protests of the late 1960s, the campaign against the war in Vietnam and the many perceived 'betrayals' of the Wilson government. The political commentator Peter Jenkins would dismissively describe this emerging political class as 'the Lumpenpolytechnic'.[7]

John Golding, an important right-wing union official and the former Labour MP for Newcastle under Lyme, would play a significant and unwelcome role in Ken Livingstone's career. Golding identified the type of young left-wing Labour activist who would fight tooth and nail during the ruinous 1979 to 1983 Labour Party civil war. 'While socialists were very rare among the electorate,' said Golding, 'there were many thousands of them to be found in the Labour Party. Until the late 1960s and early 1970s, when the old order started to change, these socialists had been kept in order by the Labour right who were entrenched on local councils and in the unions.'[8] He sniffed that this 'new generation of party members educated in the universities and polytechnics were more radical than their parents', adding: 'This generation persuaded themselves that their book learning was of far greater value than the experience and judgement of their working-class parents and that they knew all the answers.'[9]

◆

Ken Livingstone enrolled at the Philippa Fawcett teacher-training college in Leigham Court Road near Streatham Common. He was 25 and by leaving Chester Beatty he was abandoning a dead-end but relatively secure job with a ready income. He would not receive a proper salary again until 1987 when at the age of nearly 42, he was first elected as the MP for Brent East. In the meantime, he existed on the paltry expenses paid to elected members of councils and later received cheques for some writing and journalism. Livingstone attended Philippa Fawcett so infrequently during his three-year course that several former students interviewed for this book were convinced, wrongly, that Livingstone had dropped out after a year without obtaining his teacher-training certificate. In fact Livingstone did complete the course and passed his final exams, but he never qualified as a teacher because he failed to do the mandatory probationary year following the course. If he had qualified Livingstone had planned to teach science to remedial classes.[10] Now, he was less interested in pursuing a teaching career and became increasingly absorbed with politics and making his way as a politician. The student grant would have been the overwhelming factor, according to one former Norwood Labour activist. 'He was a lab technician, and then a trainee teacher,' says the activist. 'I don't seriously imagine for one moment that he saw it as anything other than a means to pay the rent.'[11]

A year before Livingstone's arrival, the college had been through the trauma of a grisly student suicide. A student had locked himself in the woodwork department and burned himself to death in protest at the Soviet occupation of Prague. Police found a banner amongst the debris which read 'In memory of Jan

Palach', the student who had died after setting fire to himself in Wenceslas Square. The college had a lively students' union which would send members on protests to campaign against the policies of the Tory education secretary, Margaret Thatcher, particularly her unpopular decision to cancel free milk in schools. By the time Livingstone arrived, the principal, Alison Shrubsole, had finally relented to student demands for a bar on campus, and afterwards college social life centred on what some wag named 'The Fawcett Inn'.

Livingstone was very dismissive about Philippa Fawcett later, telling John Carvel it was filled predominantly with naive young women from the Home Counties and that it was 'a complete waste of three years'.[12] But many students also came from normal backgrounds and went on to become successful teachers, including his future wife, Christine Chapman, whom he met at Philippa Fawcett. He had proposed before, to a woman he declines to name. He will only say that they are still friends and that she has two 'wonderful daughters'.[13] When they met, Christine Chapman was 24, a year younger than Livingstone but in the year ahead of him at Philippa Fawcett and an active member of the college students' union. Her contemporaries in the college and her comrades in the Norwood Labour Party, where she became active after meeting Livingstone, remember her as an intelligent, attractive and bubbly young woman, who was fun to be around. In 1971, she was also president of the college union, but former students remember how she had to stand aside for one particular meeting which had been called to discipline Livingstone over his political activities. Livingstone had been involved in organising politically aware school pupils, particularly members of a group of radical young students called the Schools' Action Union. Under his influence, the Norwood Labour Party infuriated some head teachers by voting radicalised youths on to the governing bodies of schools.[14] Jo Beveridge, a Philippa Fawcett trainee and a Norwood Young Socialist, is certain his activities politicising school pupils predated his enrolment at the college. 'That's when I first noticed him,' says Beveridge. 'He was very involved in politicising secondary school children.'[15]

Paul Moore and his brother Kevin were both in the sixth form of Battersea Grammar School in Streatham when they first met Livingstone. He helped them set up an Action Union at

Battersea, which he says was a 'repressive' school where teachers made liberal use of the cane. 'Brutality was the norm,' remembers Paul Moore, adding: 'The only thing it taught us was a bit of subversion really.' Paul Moore would follow Livingstone into the Norwood Young Socialists and formed a life-long friendship and association with him.[16] Livingstone was accused of allowing the young radicals to hold meetings at Philippa Fawcett which alarmed many of the trainee teachers. He was arraigned before a special meeting to discuss a motion of no confidence in him as the college union secretary. Approximately two hundred people attended the meeting. As president, Christine Chapman would have chaired the meeting but her obvious conflict of interests meant she could not, so her predecessor as president, Fred Corbett, was asked to step in. Corbett says, 'I remember a lot of anxiety, obviously, a teacher-training college having somebody who was encouraging school students, in effect, to unionise, caused quite a lot of concern. It was a big thing in our little world at the time. There was a lot of baying for blood and people wanted him out. There was a reasonably good debate about the issue and the thing really fell down.'[17] Livingstone was also able to point to procedural defects in the requisitioning of the meeting and there was no vote of confidence.

◆

The first important political influence on Livingstone was Eddie Lopez, the full-time constituency agent for Norwood. Lopez was a dynamic hard-working socialist whose parents had been refugees from the Spanish Civil War. He had trained to become a chartered accountant but dropped out, threw himself into politics and trained as a party agent. 'He did everything he could to push me forward as rapidly as possible,' Livingstone wrote later.[18] Lopez was the first person to suggest Livingstone stand as a candidate for Lambeth Council at the borough elections in 1971. Often, activists had to wait years for the opportunity but now there was a need for new young councillors to take the place of the old guard who had been largely culled at the previous poll in 1968. Lopez and Livingstone became close friends. 'When he joined, he was like a breath of fresh air,' says Lopez. 'He was somebody who was young and radical. He didn't seem to carry all the claptrap that was around Militant or some other Trotskyist organisations. I would describe him, as I would describe myself, as a libertarian socialist. It was that period in the late 60s and early 70s when a lot of young people were into alternative societies, a different way of life, trying to get out of the rut of capitalism that was apparent then.'

♦

In May 1971, Livingstone was elected to Lambeth Council. This time, as the Heath government battled economic crises and trade union militancy, it was Labour's turn to conquer in the local elections. Labour candidates won 51 out of a possible 60 seats to regain control of Lambeth Council. Both Christine Chapman and Livingstone were elected to the council. During the campaign, Livingstone had been helped by his fellow students. Ruth Holt says she was one of 'the groups of lefties' at Philippa Fawcett who helped Livingstone's campaign. 'I liked Ken, he was a nice guy,' says Holt. 'I felt he was a lot like me. What you see is what you get. That's what I told the voters.'[19] Holt is one of those who wrongly thought Livingstone had dropped out of college after his victory.

Immediately after the election, a pattern was set for the course of Livingstone's political career for the next 30 years, through his time on local councils, at the Greater London Council and Parliament, right up until he became the first directly-elected mayor of London in May 2000: his active participation in the never-ceasing ideological war over the soul of the Labour Party by its factions at its centre and both right and left wings. Participation in this war became second nature to him from the beginning. He became bilingual in the sectarian language of internal party feuding of caucus, purge and power. In countless articles and particularly in his 1987 autobiography, *If Voting Changed Anything, They'd Abolish It,* Ken Livingstone goes into great detail about the Left's bitter power struggles with the right. In Lambeth, three days following the election, Livingstone fulminates how he and his fellow left-wingers had been outflanked 'by our opponents' when it came to choosing which councillors would chair the important town hall committees responsible for the borough services like housing and social services.

The 'opponents' in question were, of course, fellow Labour comrades who had also been successfully elected on to Lambeth Council. But they were from the right or centre, and therefore hardly 'comrades' at all. The right-wing 'old guard' seized most of the important committee positions under their leader, Charles

Dryland. The Left's attempt to take senior positions failed after an intervention by the Labour Party's regional organiser, John Keys, who reappears later in the story. Keys threatened Eddie Lopez with disciplinary action for supporting the Left. 'We could not know then,' Livingstone wrote later, 'that within three years we would be completely defeated and isolated and that we had seven years ahead before a Left leadership would be elected.'[20]

Livingstone was elected as vice chairman of the Housing Committee, and for the first time, at the age of 25, tasted power. Initially, he found it quite terrifying. 'It was a real struggle,' says Livingstone. 'When I got on the council, I didn't know how to read a balance sheet. As vice chair of housing – we had 30,000 homes, a huge maintenance programme, a major capital investment programme – I really struggled for the first two years. It was only at the end of the second year when I wasn't just frantically trying to keep my head above water.'[21] Councillors received meagre allowances but the council's officers were salaried employees with pensions and years of experience in their specialist fields. Livingstone received invaluable help and guidance from the most senior officer responsible for Lambeth's council housing, the department director, Harry Simpson. Simpson was dynamic and lacked the pomposity of his senior colleagues in the council's management. He had proved invaluable to the 1968–71 Conservative administration and had persuaded the Housing Committee chairman, John Major, to turn his back on plans to cut back the house-building programme by showing him and his colleagues the disgraceful conditions in which black families were living. The Tories cracked down on rogue landlords and quadrupled the building programme inherited from Labour. Livingstone retained affection for Major, even during his premiership. In 1985, he wrote, more in disgust with the Labour right than out of admiration for the Conservative Party: 'What became clear was that the Tory administration was turning out to be more progressive when it came to building houses than previous Labour administrations.'

◆

Another important figure in Livingstone's political development and career also appeared at this time. Ted Knight was, and remained, a determined revolutionary Trotskyist. He had been expelled from the Labour Party in 1956 over his membership of the Trotskyist party, the Socialist Labour League, and after several attempts to rejoin Labour, he was finally allowed back shortly before Livingstone was elected to Lambeth. Knight benefited from a time when the Labour Party took a relaxed view to revolutionaries in its ranks. That would change in the 1980s. Knight swiftly became a serious force in the Norwood party shortly after being readmitted in 1970 at the age of 36. Livingstone wrote later: 'I misjudged Ted by assuming he had tired of revolutionary politics and had come back to the Labour Party in search of a parliamentary career. I was rapidly disabused of this notion.'[22] By the end of the 1970s, Knight was 'Red Ted' leading Lambeth Council to open conflict with the government. His career and that of Livingstone, a decade his senior, appeared entwined for years until a cataclysmic falling-out in the mid 1980s.

Knight is an immaculately-dressed, diminutive figure with impeccable manners, an old-style courtesy and a ready, if perhaps slightly chilling, smile. Brynley Heaven, formerly of Norwood Young Socialists, says, 'Ted was a very different kettle of fish from Ken; he was like something out of Chicago, and I certainly don't mean the musical! He was a significant figure in the south of Lambeth and a much more limited figure than Ken in every way. Ted had something of the Mayor Daley of Chicago about him in the sense that he would be good at stitching things up and pushing here and there with his followers.'[23]

Keith Veness, a close friend of Livingstone, often saw the future mayor of London and Knight together, one always quite scruffy in jeans and safari jacket, the other always prim and immaculate in a suit and tie. 'They were the odd couple,' says Veness. 'You couldn't find two people more different in lifestyle, behaviour, outlook and everything else. Ted's a nice guy once you batter down the defences. He's quite old-fashioned and gentlemanly in a way, and that's something you could certainly never accuse Ken of being!'[24]

Jo Beveridge, from her vantage point in the Young Socialists, thought Knight had enormous influence over Livingstone, particularly after the older man rapidly became top dog as chairman of the Norwood constituency. Increasingly, she thought the party was being run by a clique that included Knight, Livingstone, Livingstone's fiancée and future wife, Christine Chapman, Len Hammond and his wife Leslie. It was what Knight described as 'a very hard core of people that were able to challenge the right-wing control of the local Labour Party'.

It is undeniable that Knight had great influence over Livingstone and whether or not his nascent political career would flourish in Lambeth. Livingstone said that Knight managed to change his mind on two important issues dear to the heart of the true lefty: the 1972 Housing Finance Act and British troops in Northern Ireland. The 1972 Housing Finance Act had given the Tory government the power to force councils to put up the rents of their tenants. The Tories were convinced that Labour councillors often raised local taxes to subsidise what they saw as ridiculously low rents. After all, council tenants voted mainly for the Labour Party while those who had to pay higher local taxes were home owners and businessmen who tended to vote Conservative. Knight persuaded Livingstone that the new law should be opposed despite the possible risk of suffering a heavy financial penalty in the form of a surcharge imposed by the district auditor and a ban from public office. The government had the ultimate power of sending in a special commissioner to take control of the housing of any council which resisted. Livingstone had decided the law should be obeyed, until Knight 'persuaded' him. Knight says, 'We had to advise him that we would deselect him [as a councillor] if he persisted in that position. But Ken was very willing and happy to learn.' Knight concluded after later bitter experience that Livingstone would take doctrinal opposition to the government only so far. 'Ken always has a problem when it affects his possible future.'[25] However, the government-imposed rent increase of 50 pence a week for Lambeth in 1973 was agreed by the council thanks to the Labour right-wing members who were in the majority.

Knight also encouraged Livingstone to drop his support for the troops trying to keep the failing peace in Northern Ireland and join calls for their immediate withdrawal. Knight says, 'When they sent troops in, he defended it as most members of the Labour Party did at the time, saying you were taking it out of the hands of the maniac police over there [the Royal Ulster Constabulary] and the army would be a regulating force.' In a debate, Knight again persuaded Livingstone that the army was not a peacekeeping force but 'a body of oppression'.[26] Knight's most important role was to teach Livingstone about the nature of politics and how to defeat your opponents. 'At first, he was somewhat naive,' says Knight. 'What I was able to bring about was an understanding that if you are going to succeed, then you had to build a base; you had to build allies; and you had to organise to win.'

◆

In the early 1970s, there were also great changes in Livingstone's personal life, including one particularly tragic and unforeseen event. In October 1971, Bob Livingstone died of a heart attack while working on a cottage in Lincoln which he and Ethel were planning to retire to a month later. He was 56 and Ken Livingstone was only 26. 'It was devastating and incredibly painful,' says Livingstone. 'He had been incredibly fit and healthy and then died of this massive heart attack just as I got elected to Lambeth Council and he was really proud. And so I had been through the complicated bits young men have with their fathers and just as we should have settled into a comfortable relationship, he's gone. And 20 years later that was still painful.'[27] By then Livingstone had moved out of the parental home in Wolfington Road and into a flat near West Norwood railway station in Hennen Road. In December 1973, he married Christine Chapman at a small register office wedding at Market Bosworth in Leicestershire. His best man was Derek Prentice, a fellow Lambeth councillor and close friend, who drove Livingstone up to Leicestershire the night before the wedding. 'It was very much a small family wedding,' remembers Prentice. 'Apart from me, there were very few other political people at all. It was nothing special. I remember some funny speeches about him being some ultra left-wing politician coming from a right-wing family. It was all very nice and low key.'[28]

Derek Prentice was also Livingstone's next-door neighbour. Curiously, the Livingstones' first house, 80 Trinity Rise, had been sold by his old friend Eddie Lopez on his departure from London two years earlier in 1971. Lopez had sold the house to Ole Olsen, who then sold it to Livingstone. It had three bedrooms and a small north-facing garden where Livingstone immediately built his first-ever pond for his latest amphibians, including six tree frogs, which made so much noise that some neighbours thought they were geese. Prentice remembers questions being raised in a debate at Lambeth Council's Environment Committee. Livingstone gathered up the frogs from his garden and discreetly released them in Brockwell Park. There were other creatures of a political nature which usually made difficult pets, but would prove extremely useful to Ken Livingstone over the next 30 years.

Notes

1   Ken Livingstone, *If Voting Changed Anything, They'd Abolish It*, Harper-Collins, 1987, p11
2   Robert Harris, *The Making of Neil Kinnock*, p46
3   Interview, Ken Livingstone, 26.11.07
4   Ken Livingstone, *If Voting Changed Anything, They'd Abolish It*
5   *Guardian*, 'The Terry Coleman Interview', 21.12.81
6   John Gyford, *The New Urban Left; Origins, Style and Strategy*; Patrick Seyd, *The Rise and Fall of the Labour Left*, Macmillan Education, 1987, p140
7   *Guardian*, Peter Jenkins, 4.10.80; Patrick Seyd, *The Rise and Fall of the Labour Left*, p44
8   John Golding, *Hammer of the Left* (Edited by Paul Farrelly MP), Politico's, 2003, p29
9   Ibid., p29
10 Interview, Ken Livingstone, 3.1.08
11 Author interview, 2007
12 John Carvel, *Citizen Ken*, pp44-45
13 Interview, Ken Livingstone, 26.11.07
14 Ken Livingstone, *If Voting Changed Anything, They'd Abolish It*, p17
15 Interview, Jo Beveridge, 27.7.07
16 Interview, Paul Moore, 5.11.07
17 Interview, Fred Corbett, 16.8.07
18 Ken Livingstone, *If Voting Changed Anything, They'd Abolish It*, p16
19 Interview, Ruth Holt, 26.7.07
20 Ken Livingstone, *If Voting Changed Anything, They'd Abolish It*, p21
21 Interview, Ken Livingstone, 25.10.07
22 Ibid.
23 Interview, Brynley Heaven, 13.8.07
24 Interview, Keith Veness, 5.10.07
25 Interview, Ted Knight, 4.7.07
26 Ibid.
27 Interview, Ken Livingstone, 3.1.08
28 Interview, Derek Prentice

Chapter 3

The Young Chartists, 1970–1973

The history of the British far left is a bleak saga of split, purge and defeat. Hundreds of apparently normal adults have spent a lifetime, from a youth of wild-eyed fervour to a disappointed old age, selling newspapers few people wanted to buy and waiting for a revolution which never came, despite the exhortations of many false prophets. It is probably a case of 'the less said the better'; a tale 'full of sound and fury, signifying nothing', as Macbeth once said, and unlike Macbeth, not even the subject of a decent tragedy. But without a study of Britain's home-grown revolutionaries, the story of Ken Livingstone and his rise makes no sense. On the surface, there has always been the *Macro Ken* of the 'Big Picture', seeking to lead the debate on the economy, London, Ireland, Israel and global warming but this has always been underpinned by the *Micro Ken,* a politician who has never had any qualms about working with obsessive activists on the far left and getting mixed up in the politics of the street.

Livingstone's enemies would concede that he has charisma and formidable political gifts, but without the help of tight-knit and often secretive tiny groups of Trotskyists, and/or former Trots, it is difficult to see how Ken Livingstone would have become leader of the Greater London Council at the age of 36, the Member of Parliament for Brent East six years later, or how he would now be mayor of London looking for a third term in office. He may well have risen without their help, but he did not.

Later, it would be difficult to get too worked up about revolutionary Marxists. Despite their rarity value, they induce mainly feelings of indifference or contempt. But back in the 1970s and 1980s, they ran the Soviet Union, Eastern Europe and many other unhappy places; there was a Cold War on and the Western democracies were very concerned about them. By and large, they ruined the countries they ran and had to acquire many tanks and secret policemen to persuade their subjugated peoples to treat them seriously.

Of course, the Trot variety of revolutionary never got to run anything very much, leaving aside the odd council or student body here and there. Politically, they have always been considered to be a bit of a joke, particularly in Britain. British Trots can be friendly and perfectly civil, but they do not believe in parliamentary democracy; they say it is a system which only perpetuates the evil of capitalism and the exploitation of the proletariat. Leon Trotsky proposed revolutions in other nations to destroy their democratic institutions and replace them with instruments of workers' rule.[1] Like Lenin, he believed the permanence of the Revolution in the Soviet Union could only survive if revolutions took place elsewhere, particularly western Europe. However, Trotsky's great adversary, Stalin, believed there could only be 'socialism in one country', and as uprisings had failed elsewhere in Europe, the important thing was to strengthen the revolution internally. This was also the view of official communist parties, like the Communist Party of Great Britain, nicknamed 'Tankies' after the Soviet Union's habit of sending tanks into neighbouring countries.

The difference in ideology between socialists on the hard left, who still believed in parliamentary democracy, and the Trots on the *far left* has been analysed by an academic, David Webster: 'Modern British Trotskyism is a doctrine of conflict: struggle and violence are wholeheartedly accepted. It is believed that capitalism ... is bound to collapse sooner or later ... they (the Trotskyists) conclude that any intensification of class conflict is unequivocally good, in heightening the contradictions between capitalism and bringing about a "raising of consciousness" and mobilisation of the working class for revolution.'[2]

◆

Ken Livingstone has always worked very closely with Trots and former Trots. They have worked tirelessly for him and taught him much about how to organise, how to defeat his enemies and how to win power. Trots have always been the real outsiders of the Labour movement. Many would infiltrate the Labour Party in an attempt to change it into something it was never going to be – a movement hell-bent on a violent revolution. The party would hold periodic witch-hunts to root out the blatant Trots but let its guard down in the 1970s, with almost fatal results. Like the Trots, Livingstone has always craved acceptance. But the key difference has always been that where many Trots joined the Labour Party essentially to destroy it from within and change it into a revolutionary movement controlled by them, Livingstone really sought acceptance from the party so that one day he could rise to the top of it; he acted increasingly in isolation when denied the acceptance he craved.

Ken Livingstone never really understood the class struggle from a Marxist revolutionary perspective, despite his working-class origins. Doctrine left him cold; gut instinct was always what drove him. The Trots provided Livingstone with a network of political obsessives; he would eventually give them a powerful influence in the running of London. Essentially, Livingstone has always been a political loner and prefers to work closely and discreetly with like-minded activists he can trust. Trots, despite their splits and rows, are the same. When asked in interviews for this book about his close long-term connections to Trots, Ken Livingstone said, 'It's exactly the same as Churchill working with Stalin. You don't get to choose your allies but you know who the enemy is.'[3] But for the orthodox and more discerning of the Labour Party, associating closely with Trots was the political equivalent of being raised by wolves. Livingstone always knew how to get Trots working for him, but he was never one of them.

From the start of his involvement with the Labour Party, he was one of the multitudes of the shunned and neglected. He was simply one of the many activists initially on the wrong side of the void that opened up between the parliamentary leadership of the Labour Party – which took the big decisions – and the great unwashed in the constituencies, the unions and the council chambers. Background and education determined there would be no gilded path for Livingstone as there would be for a privileged few in the party, such as Tony Blair who advanced via Oxbridge and the Bar. Like another Labour rebel, Aneurin Bevan, Ken Livingstone would have to rely on instinct, talent and oppositionism as well as organised networks of Trots. 'You never have a party where all the good people are,' he says, 'it never works out like that. Shirley Williams ended up in a party with David Owen... and I ended up with some decidedly unsavoury leftists who didn't really believe in democracy. I never let them set the agenda.'[4] But he did let them get close.

◆

Ted Knight, a lifelong Trotskyist revolutionary, says, 'Ken never had a very clear political philosophy. Ken never read philosophical books from a political point of view. He had a gut feeling; he was opposed to exploitation and inequalities in a big way. He had a social conscience and wanted to do something about it. But he saw it within the existing parliamentary and political system. He didn't consider taking up arms against anybody as a way forward or changing dramatically the electoral system. He thought you could persuade and change the Labour Party.' Senior figures in the Labour Party would come to believe that Livingstone would use Trots to help his career. In 2000, Neil Kinnock said he never thought Livingstone was a Trot, adding: 'He's a "Kennist". He really is. "Red Ken" was always a bit of a joke. I don't think he's even a Red.'[5]

In the 1980s it was Livingstone's proud boast that he had never read the works of Karl Marx. Trotsky never figured. His political heroes included important figures from the 1960s including Robert Kennedy and strangely perhaps for an atheist, the reforming pope, John XXIII.[6] Trotskyists were not attracted to Ken Livingstone because they believed he was the next Lenin or Trotsky but because they thought he, like Tony Benn, would be a potential Alexander Kerensky, a transitional and transient pre-revolutionary figure, who could be pushed aside once the real revolution began. Naturally, they would take it from there. Some even hoped to find him on the right side of the barricades.

◆

British Marxists, both Tankies and Trots, were a source of fascination and irritation for both Lenin and Trotsky. In 1920, even before the establishment of the British Communist Party, Lenin had become exasperated by the division among the four separate communist groups. In his pamphlet, *Left-Wing Communism, an Infantile Disorder,* Lenin called on the four organisations to put aside their differences and unite. 'A "state of mind" alone would never bring off a successful revolution,' he said, adding: 'The cause of revolution may be harmed by certain errors that people who are most devoted to the cause of the Revolution are about to commit or are committing.'

The Communist Party of Great Britain was set up soon afterwards. The issue which divided the communists at the time and would divide them for decades afterwards was their relationship with the Labour Party. After all, it was the only mass party representing the workers. Lenin was clear that electoral success by Labour could eventually lead to revolution and that communists should vote for the party against the Liberals and Tories in constituencies where there was no communist candidate standing. The overall objective was to destroy the Labour Party; in the interim, Lenin said communists should support the Labour Party's general secretary Arthur Henderson 'as the rope supports a hanged man'. His disciple Trotsky went further. In his long years of exile, and before his assassination by a Stalin-sponsored ice pick in August 1940, Trotsky was a keen advocate of his followers joining the Labour Party. In 1936, he urged them: 'It is understood that, regardless of how we enter, we will have a secret faction from the very beginning. Our subsequent actions will depend on our progress within the Labour Party.' This policy of 'entryism' is practised by the far right as well as the far left. Essentially, it means members of one group infiltrating another with a variety of objectives from destroying it or taking it over to influencing policy or picking up recruits.

Secrecy and discretion were essential, as Trotsky made clear: 'It is very important we do not lay ourselves open at the beginning to attacks from the Labour Party bureaucracy which will result in our expulsion without having gained any appreciable strength.' Both Lenin and Trotsky dismissed Labour's leaders as 'social patriots' who put their country before the struggle of international socialism and the proletariat. Trotsky said his followers should oppose these 'patriots' inside the Labour Party and organise among themselves; that they should never lose the bigger picture of capturing the Labour Party from within: 'While it is necessary for the revolutionary party to maintain its independence at all times, a revolutionary group of a few colleagues is not a revolutionary party and can work most effectively at present by opposition to the social patriots within the mass parties.'[7]

The Soviet Union was the main issue which separated the Trots and the Tankies. Trots dismissed the Soviet Union as 'state capitalist' whereas the Tankies in the Communist Party supported it regardless of the atrocities committed in its name. Following the death of Stalin in 1953, a leading British communist, Rajani Palme Dutt, wrote: 'The genius and will of Stalin, the architect of the rising world of free humanity, lives on forever in the imperishable monument of his creation.'[8] After the old monster was denounced as a mass murderer by his successor Nikita Khrushchev in the famous Secret Speech of March 1956, Palme Dutt was heard to reflect that 'if Comrade Stalin was wrong, then he was right to be wrong,' adding: 'That there should be spots on the sun would only startle an inveterate Mithras worshipper.'[9] But many of his comrades did leave their party in disgust over the revelation; more left following the Soviet Union's invasion of Hungary later that year. Many leapt from their tanks and became Trots.

By 1956, the small parties making up the revolutionary Trotskyist movement in Britain were political plankton. Some Trots rested harmlessly in the gut of the Labour Party; the rest were completely at sea, drifting in search of a revolution. Most of them had made a superhuman attempt at unity by belonging to the Revolutionary Communist Party. It lasted five years until 1950 when its general secretary, Jock Haston, renounced revolutionary politics and joined the Labour Party, taking some senior colleagues with him.[10] In his book, *Militant*, on the Trotskyist Militant Tendency, the journalist and author Michael Crick observes that Trots habitually select the names of their parties from a 'holy list of words' including: Workers, Labour, Socialist, International, Revolutionary, Marxist, Communist, Militant, Group, Party, Tendency and League. 'According to the rules of the game "Select a Sect",' wrote Crick, 'you can pick any two or three from the above list.'[11]

By the end of the 1960s, there were four main Trotskyist parties, each with their own bite-size Lenins: the Militant Tendency led by Ted Grant; the Socialist Workers Party led by Tony Cliff; the International Marxist Group founded by Pat Jordan and Ken Coates; and the Workers Revolutionary Party led by Gerry Healy. By the early 1970s, both the SWP and WRP had rejected entryism, mainly to keep their doctrine clean of contamination from the social patriots within the Labour Party but partly because they had long been rumbled. Members of the IMG never seemed to make up their minds, joining the Labour Party and then leaving again a few years later on at least two separate occasions.[12] Militant grew to be a force within the Labour Party by disingenuously claiming their name referred only to a newspaper, and not a political organisation. Periodically, Labour would purge Trots, particularly in the mid 1950s and again in the mid 1980s. The single thing which bound these groups together, aside from revolutionary politics, was deep contempt for one another. This intersect rivalry over who should emerge as the leaders of the struggle has congealed into a deep hatred far exceeding that reserved for capitalism, 'revisionists' and the ruling class. Personality clashes are difficult to avoid in groups of politically obsessive activists and often rows break out over the interpretation of Trotsky's creed: what is or what is not a degenerated or deformed workers' state? Which group is the true representative of Trotsky and the Fourth International? As with the old jokes involving the true purpose of double ledger bookkeeping and the Schleswig-Holstein question, it is probable that they were only completely understood by three men: one mad, one dead and a third who has forgotten the question.

Down the years, the disputes have resulted in expulsions, splits and denunciations. As many Trots recognise, these disputes are not the cause of defeat, but the consequence. Their attempts over the decades to woo the proletariat have reminded some observers of a woman being fought over by a number of suitors of whom she is barely conscious and probably would not find attractive if she met. It is not uncommon – during the course of a political career – for some Trots to be members of half a dozen or more different parties, often of diminishing numbers. Some in the Labour movement recount the story of John Archer, who led a thousand Trots in the 1930s, with high hopes of successful revolution, ending his days in December 2000 as the leader of a group of which he personally constituted precisely 50 per cent of the total membership.[13] To a greater or lesser extent, the four main Trotskyist groups all play a role in Ken Livingstone's story, particularly the Workers Revolutionary Party and the International Marxist Group. But for the first 15 years of his political career, a fifth much smaller group would play the essential part.

◆

In *If Voting Changed Anything, They'd Abolish It* Ken Livingstone makes several references to the Chartists.[14] At first glance, you could be forgiven for thinking that this was the group of radicals who led a mass movement for social and political reform in early Victorian Britain, including universal suffrage for all men aged over 21 and the introduction of a secret ballot at parliamentary elections. But the organisation Livingstone wrote about was a group of young Trots and its real name – among its tiny group of members – was the Revolutionary Communist League. At the risk of labouring an earlier analogy, if groups like the Socialist Workers Party (SWP) and Workers Revolutionary Party (WRP) were mega plankton, the Revolutionary Communist League would be micro plankton. The SWP and WRP boasted approximately 500 to 1,000 members each, while it is unlikely that the membership of the Chartists/RCL ever exceeded 30. During the period of the early to mid 1980s, at the time of their crucial significance to Ken Livingstone, their number may just have reached double figures.

The Revolutionary Communist League was formed at 154 Pemdevon Road in Croydon on 11 April 1970, the day Chelsea played Leeds United in the FA Cup final. The first debate among those who gathered there concerned the match itself – should the television be on or off? It was decided that the cause of the revolution and the plight of the proletariat would not be hindered or harmed, or at risk from 'revisionist elements', by having the television on, so a discussion about forming the Revolutionary Communist League went ahead, with the game, resulting in a 2–2 draw, in the background. The Pemdevon Road house was home to a young revolutionary, Keith Veness, a burly, friendly bear of a man, who would later become close friends with Ken Livingstone. Others gathered there included his friends, the anthropologist Christopher Knight, and Graham Bash, a young lawyer from Leyton in east London.

Bash says, 'In those days, every Trot group had a real name and an open name. Among ourselves, we were the Revolutionary Communist League; for public consumption we were the Young Chartists.'[15] Veness had been in the WRP and the International Marxist Group; Chris Knight was in Militant Tendency; Bash was an unaffiliated Trot. All three men were members of the Labour Party. They had also joined an organisation called Socialist Charter, comprising a small number of Labour Party members, including a few MPs campaigning for a mishmash of left-wing causes. Bash says, 'We thought it had a useful name because it related to the Chartists in Labour history and we felt that name would be a useful launch pad with the Labour Party and the unions. All 10 of us! My God, we had illusions! The objective was to essentially destroy the Chartists' organisation by making life uncomfortable for the existing members, forcing them out and then using the name "the Chartists" as cover.'

'It was wrong,' says Bash. 'We'd never do it these days. But that's what we did in those days. It was a nasty thing to do. These days, I think if the means are nasty then it usually has an effect on what you are trying to create.' The RCL group found it absurdly easy to rid the Socialist Charter of non Trots. 'What we did was to call an Annual General Meeting,' recalls Bash. 'We got a majority; it was so small you could have a majority with about 15 people and we just decided that we should get everybody to pay so much of their income, about six per cent of gross income, I think, and that got rid of all the ones we didn't want.'

Vladimir Derer, an important Labour Party activist, was a victim of this purge. He never took seriously the Young Chartists, as the RCL now styled themselves in public. He described the group as 'a bit of a joke'. 'Socialist Charter which started as a rather ambitious movement was reduced to a small group,' says Derer. 'It was rather farcical. In the end, there were just seven members of the Socialist Charter executive committee of which four were the so-called Young Chartists and the other three were MPs. There was a vote and the MPs lost by three votes to four! The Young Chartists took over and people who supported Socialist Charter like myself, and the MPs, left.'[16]

It is difficult to say for sure exactly when Livingstone first came into contact with the group, but from all accounts, it was probably in 1971 or 1972, shortly after he was elected to Lambeth Council. One Young Chartist, Paul Moore, had taken over the Norwood Young Socialists in 1971 after Livingstone became a councillor. He had also been active with Livingstone in the Schools' Action Union.[17] His fellow Chartist, Keith Veness, remembers meeting Livingstone at a football tournament for the Labour Young Socialists in Brockwell Park. He and the other RCL members were much younger than Livingstone; some were in their teens. Veness was approaching 20 and Livingstone would have been 27 or 28. Veness remembers: 'Paul Moore said to me, "He's an *old* bastard, but he's all right. He's a left-winger; he supports Young Socialists and what we're trying to do." So I decided to give him the benefit of the doubt.'[18]

It was clear to Veness and his friends that Livingstone wanted to get to the top as quickly as possible. 'We used to talk to Ken and he always used to say "Be open about your ambition. If you want to be prime minister, say yes",' says Veness. 'He wanted to be those things; he never kept it a secret and so people had more respect. We also thought that the only reason to be in politics is power, if you really want to change things.'[19]

Like most of the Young Chartists, Veness liked a drink and a laugh and a kick about in the park, and he despised 'Old Testament' lefties like the Trots in Militant whose lives revolved around selling as many copies as possible of their paper *Militant* and attending tedious meetings. The Young Chartists warmed to Livingstone because he did not seem to take life too seriously. 'The worst "crime" was being unserious,' says Veness about the Left, 'and that was what was so attractive about Ken. He actually had a sense of humour and thought there was no harm in having a joke in politics even at your own expense and no harm in being self-deprecating.'[20]

Livingstone did not join the RCL. In around 1973, the Trotskyist Socialist Labour League also attempted to recruit him as he started to grow in influence, but he kept out.[21] Livingstone understood that a lot of the hard-line Trots had a very focused view about 'discipline and class'. 'But I was both flaky and undisciplined,' says Livingstone, 'I saw nothing attractive in being in a disciplined little group that told me what to think.'[22] He thought deep down that those people advocating a revolution were 'completely mad', but nevertheless, from an early stage in his career, he made common cause with revolutionaries. They had their use.

As a Lambeth councillor, Livingstone was able to help the Young Chartists find a headquarters at 9 Loughborough Road in Brixton, not far from the town hall. There, the group started a paper called the *Chartist*, described by Bash as 'blood-curdlingly revolutionary'. The front page carried the famous Trotsky cry: 'Labour – take the power!' Livingstone says: 'I helped them rent a rather squalid basement in Loughborough Road where sewage appeared whenever it rained. And they were unlike all the other Trot groups. Chris Knight, Graham Bash and Keith Veness were heavily into personal politics, and I was much closer to those than any of the other left groups I worked with. I liked them. Chris Knight's interest was anthropology so we would discuss the evolution of language, how sex evolved and sexual customs. So in no sense were they a normal hard left group. They were a really nice bunch. If you had to spend the rest of your life with a Trotskyist group, it's the only one you could put up with.'[23]

Although Bash and Knight knew that Livingstone was ideologically light on his feet, they were pitilessly pragmatic. 'The crucial thing was "an ounce of action was worth a ton of theory,"' says Bash. 'To strengthen the workers' movement and weaken the Tories was what we were after.' He adds: 'I thought at that time that Ken lacked a strategic view. Ken was always weak on the class issues and trade union issues... The irony is that he has never been a Trotskyist at all but he has linked up over the years with Trotskyist groups who are uncritical mouthpieces.'[24]

One Chartist campaign was its tiny offshoot The Soldiers' Charter, a blatant and failed attempt by Trots to politicise and organise members of the armed services. The Chartists also helped Livingstone in his campaigns to prevent cuts in council housing budgets. In 1973, the Chartists split, in keeping with Trotskyist traditions. The majority, no more than a dozen people, had moved to the right. They abandoned Trotskyism and devoted their energies to working wholly within the Labour Party. They took the *Chartist* with them.[25] The few original remaining Trots, including Bash and Knight, then formed an even smaller group, called publicly and accurately, the Chartist Minority. It was this group which continued to be hugely important to Ken Livingstone, who became increasingly significant to the Chartists as his power grew within the London Labour Party during the 1970s. They began to see him as one of the leaders of a struggle 'which would strengthen the workers' movement'.[26] In return, Livingstone could call on help from the Chartists who were clever, organised and politically ruthless. Their help would always prove critical at a time Livingstone needed them most, particularly when he decided to seize control of County Hall.

Notes

1   Leon Trotsky, *The Permanent Revolution, Results and Prospects*
2   David Webster, 'The Labour Party and the New Left' (Fabian paper, 1981); David and Maurice Kogan, *The Battle for the Labour Party,* Fontana, 1982, p74
3   Interview, Ken Livingstone, 1.11.07
4   Interview, Ken Livingstone, 25.10.07
5   *Guardian*, 19.1.00

6 Interview, Ken Livingstone, 1.11.07

7 Michael Crick, *Militant*, Faber and Faber, 1984, pp30-31, based on Leon Trotsky, 'Interview with Collins' (1936), *Writings of Leon Trotsky, 1935-36*, Pathfinder, New York, 1977, pp 379-382

8 Rajani Palme Dutt, 'Stalin and the future', *Labour Monthly*, Volume 35, 4.4.53

9 Duncan Hallas, 'The Shyster lawyer', *Socialist Review*, September 1993, pp29-30

10 Michael Crick, *Militant*, p38

11 Ibid., p27

12 John Marston, 'Letter of resignation from the IMG', 9.12.82, University of Warwick File no. mss128.212

13 Mike Calvert, 'John Archer, 1909 to 2000: A Personal Tribute to a Revolutionary Life', (http://www.whatnextjournal.co.uk/pages/Back/Wnext18/Calvert.html); Interview, Pete Willsman, 29.9.07

14 Ken Livingstone, *If Voting Changed Anything, They'd Abolish It*, pp71, 74, 89, 90, 93, 210-211

15 Interview, Graham Bash, 9.10.07

16 Interview, Vladimir Derer, 29.9.07

17 Interview, Paul Moore, 5.11.07 – see Chapter 2

18 Interview, Keith Veness, 24.8.04

19 Ibid.

20 Ibid.

21 Interview, Ken Livingstone, 28.12.07

22 Interview, Ken Livingstone, 10.10.07

23 Ibid.

24 Interview, Graham Bash, 15.8.07

25 *Guardian*, obituary of Al Richardson, by John McIlroy, 24.1.07; Interview, Graham Bash, 9.10.07

26 Interview, Graham Bash, 15.8.07

Chapter 4

The South Bank Show, 1973–1977

The London Marriott County Hall combines luxury and style with one of the best locations money can buy. Why not enjoy 'extreme comfort' in the Westminster Suite, situated directly on the River Thames with marvellous views opposite? The hotel's website boasts: 'Some of our luxurious and opulent bedrooms offer breathtaking views of London's South Bank, Big Ben and the Houses of Parliament.'[1] All you have to do is stick your head out of the window and look east in the other direction and enjoy the splendid view of the Millennium Wheel. There is also the spa, the pool and the aquarium, brimming with at least four varieties of shark. The 'London Marriot County Hall' was designed by a 29-year-old architect called Ralph Knott in the belief that he was expressing democracy rather than five-star graded ostentation complete with minibar and trouser press. In 1908, Knott had set up a practice with another architect, E. Stone Collins, when he won a competition to build a grand new headquarters for the London County Council.

By 1906, the LCC had decided that its premises in Spring Gardens near Trafalgar Square may have been adequate for its predecessor, the Metropolitan Board of Works, but was no longer big enough for the biggest local authority the world had yet seen, and so it bought three adjoining plots of land just to the east of the south side of Westminster Bridge. Knott had designed such a leviathan of bricks, mortar and Portland stone, not to mention marble and oak, that it took 11 years to build, with work starting five years before the First World War and being completed in 1922 shortly after Hitler took over the Nazi party and started planning the Second. The scale of the building was extraordinary: 1.2 million square feet, 1,200 rooms, 3,000 windows and 12 miles of corridor, often wide enough for a car to drive through.[2] The edifice proclaimed the importance of London as the hub of a world empire with imperial exuberance. But, despite its stolid permanence, County Hall would be the home for London-wide government for just a little more than half a century. The principal reason for its change of use from public service to room service would be Ken Livingstone.

◆

A traveller in time could do worse than arrive in County Hall one evening in 1934 in the hope of seeing the LCC's greatest leader, the predatory Herbert Morrison, prowling the corridors in his pyjamas looking for an unsuspecting secretary, or during the day, drawing up huge slum-clearance and house-building programmes. Seven years later, the traveller would step from his machine to observe the LCC war effort, how officers and councillors organised the evacuation of children and the emergency services during the Blitz. Fast-forward 25 years to 31 March 1965, and he would witness Morrison's ashes being cast into the Thames by mourners on a tug alongside Westminster Bridge and a ceremony marking the replacement of the LCC with the Greater London Council. Again, by travelling to the end of March 1986, he would see a weeping Ken Livingstone waving to a vast crowd for the last rites of the GLC. The traveller might have missed the significance of 12 April 1973 when voters threw out the Conservative administration and put Labour back in control of County Hall for the first time in eight years. Among the victors was Ken Livingstone, at 27, the new Labour member for Norwood. His 11,622 votes meant a majority of just 3,615 over his Conservative rival in what was always a GLC marginal seat.[3]

Livingstone's friend and local agent Eddie Lopez had helped engineer his selection as a GLC candidate, which happened in June 1972, 10 months before the elections.[4] But his Chartist friend, Keith Veness, says a seat on the GLC was not considered a great prize at the time. He says: 'When Ken said, "I've put myself on the [selection] panel for the GLC" I said, "What the fucking hell did you do that for?" He said, "I just think we should stand for everything that comes up". In those days, you could give away a seat on the GLC with Green Shield stamps! People didn't understand the importance of the GLC.'[5]

Two things aided Livingstone's victory in what would always be a marginal GLC seat – the unpopularity of the Heath government and plans by the outgoing Tory administration at County Hall to build a vast motorway network in and around London, including four orbital routes known as 'ringways'. Thousands of homes would have to be destroyed to clear the way for the so-called Motorway Box. In the years before the elections, there had been a fierce 'homes before roads' campaign in those areas affected, particularly in south London areas like Lambeth and Lewisham where the protests were led by the local borough councils. Labour's manifesto for the GLC, *A Socialist Strategy for London*, rejected what it described as 'motorway madness' and 'reckless and irrelevant'. The Tories had been forced to moderate the proposals in the run-up to the 1973 election, but it still meant the destruction of 5,000 homes, affecting 50,000 people, and roads which would only 'attract more traffic and add to the congestion' at a cost of £2 billion. Labour's manifesto said the money would be better spent on improved public transport.[6]

Livingstone's Lambeth faced severe disruption under the proposals, with the loss of 1,100 homes and the blight of another 1,200. According to Livingstone, his Tory opponent and sitting Norwood member, Peter Malynn, did himself no good by supporting the GLC road plan drawn up by his party bosses at County Hall despite the fact it meant rerouting part of a motorway through Norwood. Livingstone made sure the note of the meeting which proved Malynn's compliance with the plans was published by the local press. Livingstone wrote: 'It is an indication of the rigid [Conservative] party discipline inside County Hall that members were prepared to vote to devastate their own constituency rather than vote against the party whip.'[7] The new Labour member for Norwood would never be bound by such pettifogging rules on party loyalty. The aura emanating from County Hall was one of self-confidence and self-importance; the GLC aped, and often exceeded what was on offer at the other end of the bridge in Westminster. The constituency for a GLC member was coterminous with that of an MP. You were not a mere councillor at the Greater London Council, but a member, and often your facilities would be much better than those of a back-bench Member of Parliament, as many MPs bitterly observed. GLC members traipsed into 'divisions' to cast their 'ayes' or 'noes', as in Parliament, and many had designs on getting a berth across the Thames. A joke of sorts went that GLC really stood for 'Gone to Look for a Constituency.'[8]

There were eight floors in the main building of County Hall fronting the river, but the best appointed and furnished was unquestionably the first, the members' floor, complete with vast oak-panelled offices, the elegant council debating chamber, acres of marble, secretaries and drinking cabinets. Poorly-executed oils of former holders of the honorary position of chairman of the GLC in their ceremonial garb glowered self-consciously from the walls. The chairman's ceremonial throne in the chamber was carved from a piece of petrified oak discovered, along with a Roman boat, by the workmen who built County Hall. There was the members' bar with vast veranda and even a grand piano. Access was reached first by the granite steps in front of County Hall and then through the heavy bronze doors before reaching the staircase which went up to the floor.[9] Most of the council's 35,000 employees or officers were barred from entry to the members' floor, unless they had special permission. Many had to make do with lunch in the canteen in the basement or a drink in their bar named appropriately after a type of internal memo, the Service Circular.

When it came to hiring staff, the GLC claimed to have the pick of the crop and its recruiters could often be seen on the milk round at graduate fairs alongside those from Whitehall on the hunt for new civil servants. The future foreign secretary, David Miliband, was once a GLC management trainee under Ken Livingstone's leadership although he no longer mentions the fact in his official CV.[10] Other local authorities had to make do with a bog-standard chief executive or town clerk for a manager and a finance director to look after the books; but the GLC was headed by the director general, who was paid more than the head of the civil service,[11] and the comptroller of finance in charge of the money. One former comptroller claims his old office, vast and complete with bar and bathroom, would have satisfied Benito Mussolini.[12] By the early 70s when Livingstone joined, many senior officials claimed good war records and could be seen in pinstripe suit and bowler hat, umbrella tucked under the arm rifle-fashion, striding down the corridors as the Blakey metal protectors on their well-worn shoes click-clacked on the highly polished parquet. The GLC replaced not one huge local authority but two; Middlesex County Council also passed into oblivion with the LCC. The GLC's area now not only included inner London, but all of Middlesex and parts of the Home Counties in Surrey, Essex and Kent which had been absorbed by the growing metropolis.

◆

By 1973, only eight years after coming into being, there were some discordant voices calling for GLC abolition. As a strategic body, it seemed to have lost its way. Many of its big projects, like the Motorway Box or the proposed redevelopment of Covent Garden had to be fought tooth and nail and were eventually defeated by campaigners who could see them for the grotesque acts of vandalism they were. Too often the GLC's services seemed to replicate those provided by the 32 constituent London boroughs. Both tiers were municipal landlords and had responsibilities for planning and roads. But the GLC was responsible for things which the boroughs clearly could not do: the fire brigade, the Tube and buses, and building the Thames Barrier and the Blackwall Tunnel.

The new Labour leader of the GLC was a 64-year-old party workhorse from Bermondsey in south London called Sir Reg Goodwin. Goodwin was a deeply reserved Christian with calm so monastic that one journalist felt on meeting him, he was seeing 'a monk welcoming one to his retreat'.[13] By a strange twist of fate, Goodwin was also born in Streatham and went to the same primary school as Ken Livingstone, St Leonard's. Unlike Livingstone, Goodwin passed the Eleven Plus and got into the local Strand Grammar School which later yielded some of its playing fields for the siting of Tulse Hill Comprehensive. Goodwin left school to start working for his father's tea brokerage firm and developed a tea palate so discerning that the murky brew from the GLC's canteen was said to merit 'an expert's wince'.[14] By the time of his very unassuming assumption of power at County Hall, he was coming to the end of a 28-year stint as the general secretary of the National Association of Boys' Clubs. An opponent of the motorcar and a determined non-driver, Sir Reg Goodwin spurned the leader's official limo and when necessary would consent to being driven about by his wife, Penelope, or 'Lady Pen', in the couple's battered Ford Prefect.[15]

On election, he was taken in hand by Peter Walker, a 27-year-old Labour Party employee and activist, about to be appointed as his aide. Walker describes his old boss as a 'man from the 1930s living in the 1970s'. He gently persuaded Goodwin to put aside his waistcoat and old-style vests with hard white collars and studs and don modern cotton shirts. 'He even started getting a bit of fan mail from women,' says Walker. 'Reg Goodwin was a modest and self-effacing man; he was very honest but he was not a strong man and this is why a lot of people didn't like him and criticised him."[16] David Cowling, who worked alongside Walker in Goodwin's office, says: 'It strikes some people as quite surprising that somebody who could be the leader of the largest local authority in western Europe could be intensely shy, but he was. He was very laconic; he had a sense of humour... I was a great fan of him. He wasn't a man who was easy to warm to but he was, in my experience, somebody for whom you reserved respect, not because he demanded it but because he deserved it."[17]

Peter Walker did his best to shield Goodwin from three forceful women in his administration – Gladys Dimson and Dame Evelyn Dennington who respectively chaired the powerful Housing and Transport Committees. Peggy Middleton, the diminutive chair of a finance subcommittee, was the third. Like Sir Reg, the three could chart their County Hall careers back to previous Labour administrations of the old London County Council, particularly those led by Sir Isaac Hayward, who ruled with a rod of iron and brooked little dissent. The three women sensed Goodwin's vulnerability. On one occasion, Walker was virtually floored by Middleton when he tried to bar her entry to the leader's office, while Goodwin fled to the County Hall chapel.[18] Illtyd Harrington, Goodwin's extrovert former deputy, also remembers the many visits to the chapel. 'In fact, he found it very difficult to get off his knees and come upstairs to make a few decisions,' he says. 'You could never get an opinion out of him; he would always smile. He looked rather like someone who would have made second deacon in a Methodist church."[19]

Setting aside his timid demeanour, Goodwin's manifesto was both radical and ahead of its time, as well as being surprisingly Green. As promised, Labour swiftly dumped the Motorway Box and decided instead to tackle mounting congestion by investing more in buses and the Tube. Fare reductions were promised and free bus travel for pensioners. The Goodwin manifesto also promised to end the housing crisis. 'One million Londoners are today without a place to call home,' it stated.[20] But only 200,000 had made their way on to waiting lists for housing, provided either by the GLC or the 32 London boroughs. At the same time, London's supply of uninhabitable slums seemed to be growing exponentially. There were a total of 199,000 official slums, growing at

4,000 a year. The previous Tory house-building programme was inadequate, not to say 'lamentable'. In 1972, the Tories had set themselves a target of building 5,000 new homes a year. But this was less than half the number of slums being demolished annually. Besides, even then the GLC had failed to reach its own modest target. 'These facts are not just a disgrace but a disaster,' said the manifesto. 'They represent the biggest single sign of poverty and squalor in the midst of an apparently affluent London.'[21] Astonishingly, Goodwin pledged his GLC would buy up all of London's privately rented housing and renovate it for people in housing need. 'It was a very radical manifesto,' says Maurice Stonefrost, the GLC's finance comptroller general in 1973. 'It was far more radical than the later manifesto of Ken Livingstone in 1981. The sums involved in purchasing the property were huge.'[22]

But within a year, Goodwin's plans were effectively destroyed by the economic crisis precipitated by the decision of Arab-dominated OPEC, the Organisation of Petroleum Exporting Countries. OPEC decided to penalise the West for its support of Israel in the Yom Kippur War earlier that year with a lethal combination of increasing the price of crude oil, cutting back production and in the case of the US, an embargo lasting several months. In 1974, the price of oil quadrupled and inflation started to rise. Maurice Stonefrost says: 'The oil crisis was a lot more frightening than people now realise. There was an underlying feeling that we were no longer in control of what was going to happen. It led to a huge outflow of money from Britain to the Middle East. There was much less certainty over credit. There had always been the assumption built up over half a lifetime that everybody would go on improving and the public sector would be improving even faster than the private sector. That went with the oil crisis.'[23]

The worldwide economic crisis blew many manifestos and hopes off course: the Wilson government which took power in 1974 would also be badly hit. For those on the Left, like Ken Livingstone, the response to this crisis by Labour both at County Hall and Downing Street amounted to treachery. The 'traitors' would have to be removed and excoriated and Ken Livingstone would be in the forefront of those doing the purging. The 'betrayal' of *A Socialist Strategy for London* would define Livingstone's first term as a GLC member as he fought in vain to preserve the promises contained within it. However, it would also provide him with the impetus he needed to take over the GLC as leader in 1981. *A Socialist Strategy for London* was blown away by an ill wind but one that eventually did Ken Livingstone a great deal of good. Livingstone made up what was then a tiny group of three or four left-wingers in the ruling Labour administration. Another was Tony Banks. The two young activists swiftly became friends as well as comrades. Peter Walker often saw the two together.

Livingstone, as photos of the period show, was fairly scruffy with wild hair and a beard. 'He was a political obsessive,' says Walker. 'Politics was a cult for him as it would have been for me if I hadn't had kids! He didn't come from great wealth; he was working class. He had a good feeling for [making] coalitions but it didn't mean to say he was as confident as a lot of people.' Walker also thought that Livingstone was 'under the shadow of Ted Knight'.[24] Illtyd Harrington, Goodwin's deputy, remembers his first impressions of Livingstone at County Hall. 'He was a strange character,' says Harrington, 'he sort of loped around; that's how he worked. He was rather hesitant. I wouldn't say shy, but he wasn't abrasive either. He had a rather nice, rather vicious south London sense of humour, which is quite different from a north London sense of humour. I knew his great mentor was Ted Knight. He was an interesting character. He was on the hard left which was very much in the ascendancy even then.'[25]

Banks, two years Livingstone's senior, was brash, hyperactive and witty, with a dapper, not to say, dandyish appearance.[26] His father was an army sergeant major and engineering fitter who became a senior diplomat in Warsaw. Like Livingstone, he was also a Lambeth boy who had been educated at Archbishop Tenison's Grammar School in Kennington. Banks did badly at school after falling out with his teachers but gained the exams necessary to get into university. In 1973, he was head of research for the Amalgamated Union of Engineering Workers (AUEW). He would later become assistant general secretary for the Association of Broadcasting Staff, a union which represented BBC employees among others. Banks would become better known as the MP for both Newham North West and West Ham and a passionate animal rights campaigner.[27] He had also been a Lambeth Labour councillor since 1971, like Livingstone, and became a GLC member in 1970. Like Livingstone, some people would write off Banks as a 'cheeky chappie' but, again like Livingstone, he became one of the most astute political operators and remarkable characters produced by County Hall.

◆

By 1973, Livingstone had decided to devote himself full-time to politics. Apart from the fact that he had 'fallen in love with local government',[28] and was clearly politically ambitious, there were several pragmatic reasons for this. Unlike London boroughs, GLC meetings were mainly held during the day, explaining the high preponderance of members who were either retired or wealthy. In 1972, the government introduced a system of allowances and expenses for elected representatives of local authorities which gave Livingstone, in conjunction with his wife's income, something to live on. Livingstone swiftly developed contempt for the predominantly middle-class bias of the GLC members. He also concluded that for many of the richer members, the GLC was 'a pastime in an otherwise leisured world – somewhere to visit during the week before returning to the country for a long weekend'. He added: 'Too often working-class Labour members seemed to feel the need to mimic class attitudes that were not their own and some of them slipped into intolerable behaviour towards typists, restaurant staff, chauffeurs and messengers.'[29]

Livingstone was made vice chairman of the Film Viewing Board, a GLC body with the power to censor mainly soft porn movies. He had already been identified by the leadership as a 'tricky little bastard',[30] and Livingstone thought at the time that his new role was a way of pushing him into relatively uncontroversial siding. He formed a good relationship with his chairman, Enid Wistrich, the new Labour member for Hampstead. Like Livingstone, and most other members of the Board, she opposed censorship. In January 1975, a report based on widespread consultation recommended that the GLC should stop censoring films for adults aged over 18.[31] When the proposal was defeated in January 1975, she resigned. Livingstone found many of the films he was forced to watch boring and stupid, including *The Porn Brokers, Snow White and the Seven Perverts, Sex Farm* and *Is there Sex after Death?* One Tory member for Bromley, Frank Smith, took such a light-hearted attitude to the job of censor that he wore a dirty raincoat to viewings and sometimes saw the same film twice. But Livingstone would change his view on censorship as he observed how films began to change from the silly but relatively harmless variety of *Oh! Calcutta!* to 'a disturbing mixture of violence linked with the degradation of women'. Ten years later, he would support calls for scenes of violence against women to be cut from films. [32]

◆

Labour had won 57 GLC constituencies compared to 33 for the Conservatives and two for the Liberals from a total of 92 seats. There were approximately 16 left-wing Labour members, including the smattering of hard left-wingers like Livingstone and Banks. Increasingly, the Left began to work together as a caucus within the main Labour group as the manifesto commitments crumbled during the financial crisis. Before the oil crisis, Goodwin's GLC had started to build the homes and cut the fares it had promised. It had even carried out its promise to provide free bus travel for London's nearly 1.25 million pensioners. But, as former GLC press officer, Wes Whitehouse, revealed in his book, *GLC –The Inside Story*, the Transport Committee chairman, Dame Evelyn Dennington, was actually upset when so many applied for a free pass, adding: 'She monitored the scheme closely and became angry when told of couples garaging their car and travelling free on the buses.'

Within six months, thanks to the inflation caused by OPEC, the interest on the GLC's huge £1.6 billion debt was running at £7,000 a day. Until 1990, local councils raised money with a form of taxation based on property values known as rates. In London, the borough councils collected these taxes both on their own behalf and for the GLC. After one year of the Goodwin administration, the GLC's share of the rates bill increased by 46 per cent. If Goodwin stuck to his manifesto commitments, he would have to increase the County Hall share of the rates bill by a ruinous 200 per cent over the next four years. Instead, Goodwin and his deputy Illtyd Harrington decided to jettison the manifesto.

With the support of the right-wing and centre members, the two Labour leaders cancelled key elements of *A Socialist Strategy for London*. Livingstone and the small left-wing contingent pressed for rate rises to pay for the manifesto, arguing that the burden would fall mainly on business and the rich. Instead, time and again, Goodwin's administration decided to penalise the less well-off through more indirect forms of taxation such as big increases in fares and rents. This strategy was agreed by Goodwin and his cronies at a secret meeting in Aldermaston in May 1974. The Left was furious, claiming Goodwin was effectively robbing the poor to pay the rich at a time when they were already suffering from high inflation. Livingstone says, 'What I demonstrated at every Labour group meeting was that the impact on the average family's budget was worse if you held the rates down but put the fares and rents up... On the buses and Tubes you affected every family in London and you could demonstrate what it would cost the family if you put up the fares by x amount and what it would cost the family to put up the rates. And it was a factor of about three to one in favour of a rent increase. It wasn't even rational; it was part of the thinking that, well, you can't put up taxes – but you can put up fares. Some things had become totemic.'[33]

As the economy plunged deeper into crisis, with inflation peaking at 26.9 per cent in August 1975,[34] the GLC was forced to put up its share of the rates bill by a staggering 80 per cent as well as putting up the rents for its 230,000 tenants by 10 per cent. Fares on the Tube and buses were increased first by 25 per cent and then a further 20 per cent.[35] One of Goodwin's aides, David Cowling, attended many meetings of the GLC Labour group as it disintegrated into warring factions. He says, 'Sir Reg Goodwin was confronted by this Labour group which comprised people of his own generation and background who were themselves ambitious and full of their own sorts of plans and weren't backward in coming forward when it came to plotting, sitting side by side with this set of Young Turks, the Ken Livingstones and Tony Banks of this world, who were representing a new sort of politics which I think he probably struggled to understand. It's not that he had not met left-wingers before: of course he had. But I think that generation probably caused him a bit of confusion, with its personal mindset and motivations.'[36]

♦

By April 1975, two years into the Goodwin administration, there was the final 'betrayal' of the manifesto: £50 million was cut from the council's house-building budget. Ken Livingstone, now the vice chairman of the GLC's Housing Management Committee, opposed the cuts. Goodwin sacked him after he refused to support the package. Livingstone said later, 'I told him not to worry... I would not be prepared to have him in any administration I was leader of, either.'[37]

With the Chartists' help, Livingstone led an ultimately unsuccessful 'Labour Against the Housing Cuts' campaign. Margaret Morgan, one of the moderate Labour members, says, 'Ken was a lousy vice chairman [of housing management]. When he resigned we thought he couldn't hack it – that he couldn't do the business, as it were. In that position, you've got to work hard and think about what you're doing, and that wasn't the way he presented himself. He was always oppositional in the Labour group.'[38] Cowling remembers Livingstone as a 'backbench voice without any great following within the group'. 'He was clearly someone who increasingly got up the nose of the traditionalists and the real right-wingers,' says Cowling. 'Ken was a complex mixture; he could be irritating and not only irritating, but difficult and dangerous, from our perspective, as the leader's office trying to defend the leader. But he's also highly personable.'

◆

By May 1975, the Labour administration was tearing itself apart as County Hall was submerged in crisis. Goodwin's right wing was also playing up, insisting that not enough was being done either to balance the books or to deal with the group's left-wing trouble-makers like Livingstone. Goodwin fired his Housing Committee chairman, Gladys Dimson. Two other right-wingers, Dr Stephen Haseler and Douglas Eden, resigned their senior committee roles. They complained that the council was 'on the financial rack', and that it should stop dithering and cut spending before it ran out of money. They also warned about the danger posed by the new breed of hard left-wingers at County Hall. The *Daily Telegraph* reported that the two men had resigned 'largely because they have been unable to persuade the majority of their colleagues to wake up to the dark influences of the extreme-Left within the GLC.'[39] Later that month, the GLC abandoned its annual reception to save a meagre £15,000.[40] For Livingstone and the Left, the Labour government was also guilty of treachery. In October 1976, it was forced to borrow £1 billion from the International Monetary Fund (IMF). The humiliation came at a price: cuts in public spending of £1 billion, handed down in part to local government which was responsible for about a quarter of it.

◆

By late 1976, it was obvious to many, particularly Livingstone, that Labour would lose control of the Greater London Council in the elections, due to take place on 5 May 1977 during the height of the Queen's Silver Jubilee. Livingstone's Norwood seat looked vulnerable and before the election, he looked across the river towards the safe Labour constituency of Hackney North. Again the Chartists helped secure him this safe berth following the retirement of the first black man to be voted on to the GLC, Dr David Pitt, ennobled by Harold Wilson as Baron Pitt of Hampstead. 'It was my old friends in the Chartist group who helped me get selected in Hackney North,' Livingstone wrote in 1987.[41] He rebutted charges that he switched horses to save himself, by claiming this was part of a strategy to make way for another left-winger to stand in Norwood and so increase the Left representation of the GLC Labour group. But Keith Veness, the Chartist who was instrumental in securing Hackney North for Livingstone, says the main reason was Livingstone's vulnerability in Norwood. 'In Hackney North it was a case of someone's got to do it!' says Veness. 'Ken was not a good GLC constituency representative. Ken's joke was that whenever he made a victory speech at elections, he would thank the "people of wherever he was" for returning him!'[42]

Livingstone was right to jump ship; Norwood was recaptured by the Tories on polling day by a slim majority of 1,352. In Hackney North, Livingstone was comparatively home and dry with 9,548 votes to his name, a majority of 3,921. But Labour was routed at County Hall, losing 29 of the 57 seats it held, ushering in a hard right-wing Conservative administration. Livingstone had survived but the election had wiped out many of his right-wing opponents and a few competing left-wingers. Standing among the ruins of Goodwin's administration, few could look ahead to the next election four years away, and predict that the conditions would be perfect for Livingstone to lead a dramatic takeover of County Hall.

Notes

1   www.marriott.com/hotels
2   *Independent*, 6.4.95 and 6.12.95
3   GLC election, 12.4.73, compiled by Intelligence Unit, Greater London Council, supplied by David Cowling, BBC Research
4   Interview, Eddie Lopez, 16.10.07; Ken Livingstone, *If Voting Changed Anything, They'd Abolish It*, p40
5   Interview, Keith Veness, 5.10.07

6   *A Socialist Strategy for London*, Labour Party manifesto, GLC Election 1973, pp4, 10-11
7   Ken Livingstone, *If Voting Changed Anything, They'd Abolish It*, p42
8   Interview, Mair Garside, relating joke by Frank Dobson MP, 17.8.07
9   Wes Whitehouse, *GLC – The Inside Story*, James Lester Publishers, 2000, pp32-33; Author interviews
10 www.number10.gov.uk/output/Page7463.asp
11 *Guardian*, 'Survivor at the other South Bank show', profile of Sir James Swaffield, 13.7.81
12 Interview, Maurice Stonefrost, 21.11.07
13 Profile, Sir Reg Goodwin, *South London Press*, 3.3.70
14 Ibid.
15 Wes Whitehouse, *GLC – The Inside Story*, p74; Professor Tony Travers, 'GLC Leaders, 1965-1986', London School of Economics (www.lse.ac.uk)
16 Interview, Peter Walker, 15.9.07
17 Interview, David Cowling, 29.8.07
18 Ibid.
19 Interview, Illtyd Harrington, 4.7.07
20 *A Socialist Strategy for London*, Labour Party manifesto, p1, claim based on a 1966 census
21 Ibid., p13
22 Interview, Maurice Stonefrost, 21.11.07
23 Ibid.
24 Interview, Peter Walker, 15.9.07
25 Interview, Illtyd Harrington, 4.7.07
26 *Daily Telegraph,* obituary of Tony Banks, 10.1.06
27 *Guardian,* obituary of Tony Banks, 10.1.06
28 Interview, Ken Livingstone, 11.10.07
29 Ken Livingstone, *If Voting Changed Anything, They'd Abolish It*, p51
30 Author interviews, 2007
31 *Daily Telegraph*, 30.1.75
32 Ken Livingstone, *If Voting Changed Anything, They'd Abolish It*, pp52-55
33 Interview, Ken Livingstone, 25.10.07
34 Denis Healey, *The Time of My Life*, Penguin, 1990, p396
35 Wes Whitehouse, *GLC – The Inside Story*, p90; John Carvel, *Citizen Ken*, pp56-60; Author interviews
36 Interview, David Cowling, 29.8.07
37 Ken Livingstone, *If Voting Changed Anything, They'd Abolish It*, pp66-67
38 Interview, Margaret Morgan, 16.8.08
39 *Daily Telegraph*, 1.5.75
40 *Guardian*, 28.5.75
41 Ken Livingstone, *If Voting Changed Anything, They'd Abolish It*, p74
42 Interview, Keith Veness, 5.10.07

Chapter 5

A gathering storm, 1973–May 1979

The causes of conflicts are often easy to identify although they can appear increasingly baffling as they recede in the collective memory. The seeds for the civil war which tore apart the Labour Party between 1979 and 1983, and helped make it unelectable for nearly a generation, had been liberally sprinkled by the successive Labour governments of Harold Wilson and James Callaghan over the best part of a decade; they fell on the fertile ground neglected by the right and centre of the party, but tilled by the Left and the betrayed.

In the public mind, battle commenced shortly after the defeat of the Callaghan government in May 1979 when the former Labour cabinet minister Tony Benn rallied the Left to his standard and tried to take control of the party in the cause of socialism. But Ken Livingstone and others had already been fighting the phoney war on picket lines or protest marches and in smoky pubs or meeting rooms at County Hall and elsewhere for years. Everywhere, the sense of disillusionment and betrayal by Labour administrations at a national and local level deepened to the extent that it became a network of trenches. A vast 'No Man's Land' formed between the Parliamentary Labour Party and many of the activists who had worked hard in elections on its behalf only to feel ignored and treated like dirt. This grassroots fury was articulated most clearly back in 1973 with the creation of a very important organisation called the Campaign for Labour Party Democracy, or CLPD. This was an organisation which sought to make Labour MPs and Labour governments accountable to the rank and file party members.

John Golding was the Labour MP for Newcastle under Lyme and an important right-wing combatant in the fight to come; he was convinced, as were many others, that the CLPD marked 'the beginning of Labour's civil war,' adding, '... [the] CLPD issued a clarion call for the Left, demanding that the NEC [National Executive Committee] ultimately wrested control of the manifesto from the leadership and put through every mad, half-baked or self-congratulatory policy passed by the barmies, and for that matter the misguided, but well-meaning at [the annual Labour Party] conference.'[1] The *casus belli*, or the straw that broke the camel's back for the CLPD, was Harold Wilson's refusal in 1973 to honour an amendment passed by an annual party conference insisting that a future Labour government took into public ownership 25 of Britain's largest manufacturing companies 'covering the major sectors of the economy'.[2] The patriarchal leader of the CLPD was Vladimir Derer, a 61-year-old Czech socialist who fled from the Nazis to Britain in 1939. He joined the Labour Party in north London and his house in Golders Green essentially provided the HQ for the CLPD.[3] He was the same Vladimir Derer who was forced from Socialist Charter by the Young Chartists three years prior to the formation of the CLPD.

◆

As with many extremely important events, the formation of the Campaign for Labour Party Democracy on 25 June 1973 went largely unnoticed. On the face of it, not much happened. Arthur Latham, the left-wing MP for Paddington North, booked a room in the House of Commons for the meeting but did not even turn up. Some party activists arrived and started moaning that Labour MPs did not take much notice of volunteer activists like them who did all the hard work out in the constituencies on their behalf. The CLPD had identified a dichotomy at the heart of Labour. Elections were supposed to be an expression of democracy but in reality the voters, and particularly the Labour voters, had little choice over who would represent them. Once selected to represent a safe seat, there was no way to sack a Labour MP, unless they were spectacularly incompetent and even then it was almost impossible. The few deselections which had taken place had been messy and bitter divorces. The MPs were not only virtually unassailable but they alone had the privilege of choosing the party leader and the party leader decided what was in the election manifesto. For the rank and file, it was a closed shop and they were on the outside.

This small group of activists made two main demands:

- The mandatory reselection of MPs after every general election so they would be accountable to local volunteer activists in the constituencies and under pressure to carry out the policies of the rank and file agreed at the annual Labour Party conferences.

- The election of the leader of the Labour Party by all the members of the Labour movement by means of an 'electoral college', a voting system by which individual Labour Party members, trade unionists and members of Parliament would all have a say.

For years the CLPD laboured in relative obscurity, but following the 1979 defeat, it swiftly achieved both objectives. Not bad for a tiny group of political obsessives whose total income at the time of the 1979 election was £941.96 and net assets in the bank were £176.26.[4] In bringing about the changes, the CLPD helped break the power of the parliamentary party. As Denis Healey, former Chancellor of the Exchequer and party leader, would ruefully observe later: 'It was all too easy for the Labour Party leadership to dismiss these little groups as no more than alphabet soup. Yet they succeeded in achieving most of their constitutional objectives within two years of our defeat. Thereby they condemned the Labour Party to defeat in the next two general elections as well.'[5]

The CLPD and other groups which joined its cause were not after constitutional change for the sake of it but because it would help propel the party to the hard left. The CLPD demanded a strong role for the unions in forming social and economic policy, unilateral nuclear disarmament, withdrawal from NATO and the EEC. It resented the failure of Labour governments to remove discrimination against women and minority and ethnic groups.[6] These were all the hard left positions shared by Ken Livingstone. As a result of the constitutional changes, many of these demands became enshrined in Labour's disastrous 1983 election manifesto. The Left had everything to gain from 'increasing democracy' within the party. Up to 1979, it was gradually gaining ascendancy in the constituencies, among Labour councillors and several trade unions. There is little doubt that, as John Golding observed, the Left gained sway over some of the unions, most constituency Labour parties and certainly over the ruling National Executive Committee.[7] The CLPD worked hard to become as affiliated with as many constituencies as possible and also targeted powerful unions which had 40 per cent of the votes at the annual party conference.[8]

During the 1970s, Ken Livingstone was at the vanguard of this struggle. His rapid rise in London politics in the 1970s was largely thanks to the advances made by the Left. There was scarcely a sectarian battle between right and left in London in which he was not actively involved. His seizure of power at County Hall in May 1981 was a part of this wider ideological struggle and represented the most spectacular gain of the Left – its high-water mark. Afterwards, highlighted by the narrow defeat of Tony Benn at the September 1981 Labour Party conference, the influence of the Left began to fade and by June 1983, it was in full flight.

◆

In 1973, by the time he captured Norwood for Labour, Livingstone was still a Lambeth councillor and the vice chairman of the Housing Committee. As with the GLC, he was embroiled in battles with the right and centre forces then in control at Brixton town hall. At one stage, he and a number of other left-wing councillors were expelled from the Labour group, not the party itself, and only readmitted following an inquiry by the National Executive Committee,[9] against the wishes of the council leader David Stimpson. Livingstone wrote proudly that 'during the period of our exclusion we had operated a more effective opposition than the Tories'. He added: 'We now enjoyed working as a team against an administration whose growing incompetence earned ridicule in meeting after meeting.'[10] Nowhere was this ineptitude more visible than in Livingstone's field – housing. There was a homelessness crisis in the borough, exacerbated by the council's decision to compulsorily purchase hundreds of houses so they could be demolished and replaced with ugly tower blocks. Livingstone complained that 'perfectly good homes' also went under the wrecker's ball. He also discovered that Lambeth's housing officials were operating a secret racist letting's system by which white working-class families appeared to get first pick of the good council housing. On the race issue, the 1970s were still relatively unenlightened times, as demonstrated by unofficial posters which appeared at an election in Clapham and elsewhere in south London:

> FACE THE FACTS: If you desire a coloured for your neigh-
> bour – VOTE LABOUR! If you're already burdened with
> one – VOTE TORY! The Conservatives in office will bring

up to date the Ministry of Repatriation [sic], to speed up the return of home-going and expelled immigrants.[11]

The council's officers denied there was a bias in favour of white tenants, despite Livingstone's good intelligence. The evidence was eventually published by the *South London Press*. He concentrated his campaign on getting housing for families, including many black families, stuck in the council's halfway housing.

◆

In August 1973, the *South London Press* reported how Livingstone threatened to resign 'if the council fails to honour longstanding promises' to rehouse 76 families ensconced at the council's half-way accommodation, Edward Henry House in Waterloo, by 13 November 1973. Livingstone told the paper: 'Short of an earth-quake we can start moving the families out in that period... although I cannot give them a specific promise, they have been let down by the council in the past, so as a reassurance, to make them feel better, I will resign if the council don't get moving this time.'[12] The conditions at Edward Henry House had become squalid. Families on the ground floor were flooded out during storms that month. In a speech to homeless families in another halfway house, the former police flats making up Ferndale Court in Brixton, Livingstone said the council had 'completely misled' its tenants for the last 10 years. Some families had been there for six years and conditions for the 500 children were dire, with boys and girls having to sleep four to a room up to the age of 13. Baths were in the kitchens and there was damp everywhere.[13] Conditions were not much better at the third accommodation in Black Prince Road, Vauxhall. Livingstone refused to continue the 'policy of making idle promises' and told the families that it would be at least two years before they could all move into decent permanent homes. In December 1973, out of frustration over the council's failure to provide housing for the tenants, he resigned but stayed as a backbench member of Lambeth council until 1978, by which time he had left the borough. According to Tony Bird, the senior housing officer for central Lambeth, Livingstone's resignation did force the council to move the families out of the halfway houses. 'Once out of the halfway homes and into decent housing, the tenants' lives were transformed,' says Bird, 'and that was all to his credit.'[14]

◆

By the end of 1973, Livingstone had decided his future lay with the GLC and using County Hall as a springboard to getting into Parliament. In March 1974, he was elected on to the powerful executive of the Greater London Labour Party, or GLLP, which had responsibility for drawing up the manifesto for the GLC Labour group and drawing up lists of candidates for council and parliamentary seats. Here, he would make contacts across the capital that would prove vital in his later campaign to capture the GLC. Already by March 1976, he had built up a 'small, loose left wing' in constituency Labour parties and trade unions. Through the GLLP Livingstone was able to exert increasing external pressure on the Goodwin administration to stick by the manifesto but the cuts in services and the fare and rent rises went ahead in any event. Livingstone says he could see power ebbing away from local government in the mid 1970s as successive central governments moved to control spending. 'That's when I started looking for a parliamentary seat,' he says, 'once I got on to the regional executive [of the GLLP] I started meeting MPs in good numbers and watching them perform. I realised I could do that.' He charts his ambition to lead the Labour Party back to his time on the London party executive. 'I wanted to be prime minister,' he adds.[15]

◆

In June 1977 Livingstone was selected as the Labour parliamentary candidate for Hampstead, which was something of a shock for some of the wealthy, liberal intellectuals there. By 24 votes to 22, he beat their preferred candidate, who was an economist and Foreign Office diplomat called Vincent Cable, who later became the Liberal Democrat MP for Twickenham in 1997, and for a short period in 2007, the acting leader of his party following the resignation of Sir Menzies Campbell. Cable was a former president of the Cambridge Union and held a PhD from Glasgow University. Some in the local area thought Cable was the 'right stuff' and reacted poorly to Livingstone's selection. Livingstone later published the following letter written to the Labour National Executive Committee by an angry member who wanted the decision overturned:

His [Livingstone's] education is sketchy. I understand he went to a College of Education and well know how low the standard is at some such places which I think I would describe as a school for nannies. This is a great pity when one thinks that there were in the running candidature two PhDs, a QC and several other graduates of reputable universities such as Oxford.

I am not suggesting every Labour candidate should be a graduate: merely that to win a constituency with as sophisticated an electorate as Hampstead we need a candidate of clear intellectual ability... this selection has been a clear use of Ovid's line: 'Video meliora, proboque; deteriora sequor...'[16] *('I see the better things, I follow the worse.')*[17]

Livingstone suffered further embarrassment at his first Hampstead dinner party when he made the mistake of chewing his way through the bouquet garni, a bundle of herbs used for flavouring soups and stews. He said later that he compounded the error with the excuse that 'bouquets garni were not standard fare in Lambeth'.[18]

◆

Livingstone and his wife Christine sold 80 Trinity Rise to the then general secretary of the Union of Communication Workers, Tom Jackson, who was best known for his magnificent handlebar moustache, and moved for the first time to the other side of the Thames. The couple bought a house in Lymington Road in West Hampstead at the edge of his constituency. However, he could not escape Lambeth completely; his old comrade and mentor, Ted Knight, was selected to fight Hornsey, next door to Hampstead. Both constituencies were Tory marginals and the two men had high hopes of winning. Geoffrey Finsberg, the Tory MP for Hampstead, was defending a majority of only 1,725 and in Hornsey the margin had been 782 at the last general election in October 1974. His new home and constituency lay within the borough of Camden. Livingstone won selection as a Labour candidate for the Kilburn ward and was voted on to the council in the borough elections of May 1978. He also won the internal Labour Party group vote to be the chairman of the council's Housing Committee, alongside his other positions as the GLC member for Hackney North and a parliamentary candidate.

Livingstone is not remembered fondly by some of his former senior colleagues at Camden who say he was intensely ambitious and not a particularly competent housing chairman. As at Lambeth, County Hall and on the Greater London Labour Party executive, Livingstone threw himself wholeheartedly into sectarian battle between the right and the left. The controlling group of Camden Labour councillors were split down the middle between right and left, with the right, under the leadership of Roy Shaw, clinging on to power by their fingertips. Phil Turner, a former Camden councillor, said the left-wing councillors, including Livingstone used to meet up before important council meetings in an unofficial group, or caucus. Turner knew Roy Shaw had little time for Livingstone, who had been appointed not by the leader but by his fellow councillors, according to Camden Council rules at the time. 'I think Roy grew to detest him actually. I think Roy regarded Ken as a big chancer and a bit ruthless with it. I think Ken can be very ruthless in political terms.'[19] Turner says Livingstone was an outstanding public speaker; that was how he had got people to choose him as housing chairman, despite the fact 'they had never heard of him'. He adds: 'I used to sit alongside him in council and group meetings and marvelled at him. He always made very good speeches.'

Shaw's deputy was John Mills, against whom Livingstone once stood for the deputy leadership of the council. Mills says, 'Ken Livingstone was always very entertaining and very good value. To go out for a drink with Ken was a pleasure really. He was always full of stories and jokes and things. He was inclined to lose his temper if crossed. Certainly a bit of a tactic for those of us who opposed him was to get him to lose his temper and then he tended to lose support. He has got a relatively short fuse. It wasn't that difficult to wind him up to catch him out.'[20]

As in Lambeth and elsewhere, there were serious housing problems in Camden. Ken Livingstone shocked many of his fellow Labour councillors on the left and right by setting up his own office in the housing department to keep an eye on the officers, a move frowned upon by his colleagues. Many councillors were part-timers and decided policy, but left it to the full-time officials working for the council to implement the decisions. John Mills says, 'I have to say my experience of getting public sector organisations to function efficiently is not to stand over the shoulders of the people who are supposed to be getting it all done. You give them a clear framework within which to work and deadlines and what the political choices are and let the officers get on with what the officers are paid to accomplish.'[21] The Camden Labour leadership thought Livingstone was failing to tackle the housing problems, including the delays in repairs to housing stock. Roy Shaw, who was unable to give an interview for this book through illness, told Livingstone's first biographer John Carvel: 'He was a lousy chairman of housing... He was totally in the pocket of the officers... His main concern was using the position to get publicity for himself.'[22]

As he attempted to wrestle with politics and housing in Camden, Livingstone did have his eye on the bigger picture. By 1978, the next general election was imminent. Many people expected Prime Minister Jim Callaghan to call it that October. Livingstone and the rest of the Left were fixated on controlling the Labour Party, in defeat or victory. Ken Livingstone raised his standard for the Left in this early phoney stage of the Labour Party civil war at Hampstead Town Hall on 15 July 1978, with the setting up of an obscure campaign called the Socialist Campaign for a Labour Victory, or SCLV. In retrospect, this was a smaller and ultimately less successful version of the Campaign for Labour Party Democracy, CLPD. In his book, Livingstone says the SCLV campaign brought together 'various left-wing factions'.[23] But according to key Chartist, Graham Bash, and others, the SCLV was essentially a coming together of two small Trotskyist groups under the figurehead leadership of Ted Knight and Ken Livingstone.[24] This included a group of Trots headed by an Irish revolutionary called Sean Matgamna, and naturally Livingstone's old friends, the Chartists. To Vladimir Derer, founder of the CLPD, the SCLV was a 'Trot thing' of little particular significance. 'There were several groups participating in it,' says Derer, 'they were of a Trotskyist orientation and there were disagreements amongst them.'[25]

The group organised around a publication which appeared sporadically called *Socialist Organiser*. Priced at 10 pence, it first appeared in October 1978, shortly after Jim Callaghan had made the fateful decision not to declare a general election that year. The *Organiser's* first salvo went: 'Every struggle will face attempts to stifle it with cries of "Don't rock the boat, or you'll let the Tories in!" The Socialist Campaign for a Labour Victory says that is no way to attack the Tories. We fight to keep the Tories out but also to build and prepare a socialist fightback against the present government's second string Tory policies and against the next government, *Tory or Labour*.'[Author's italics][26]

Aside from the Chartists and the Matgamna Trots, the support of three parliamentary constituencies was also cited by *Socialist Organiser,* but these were also largely Chartists from Brent East, Ilford South and Hackney North.[27] To be frank, the SCLV made a negligible impact on the history of the Labour Party and politics at this time. Predictably, what was in essence a Trotskyist set-up split within a year over tactics on how to deal with the new Tory government-imposed cuts on council spending. But *Socialist Organiser* does provide a valuable insight into Livingstone's views of Labour and strategy at this time. The paper provided him with a platform to express for the first time the way in which the GLC could be seized by the Left; it also shines a bright light on the political contacts, notably in Brent East, that he had established by this time. The SCLV was as much a declaration of war against the leadership of the Labour Party by Livingstone and the two hundred other activists who turned up in Hampstead in July 1978 as it was against the Tories. With a year to go before the crucial 1979 election, one Callaghan policy above all would be the focus of the attack, although ironically, it was the defeat of this policy, and the circumstances of the defeat, which would help condemn Labour to 18 years in opposition.

◆

By late 1978, the government was still committed to using wage restraint to control inflation in both public and private sectors and had set the limit of annual pay rises for everyone at five per cent. Livingstone and the rest of SCLV were bitterly opposed to the policy, as an editorial in *Socialist Organiser* made clear: 'In deferring election until the New Year, James Callaghan and the rest of the Labour cabinet have made their intentions abundantly clear. The barricades for the general election are to be built around defence of the five per cent pay limit and the wretched battery of anti-working-class policies from the last four years. The Socialist Campaign for a Labour Victory says the Tories are much better at winning elections on Tory policies than the Labour Party! The SCLV aims for a massive Labour vote, but a vote with a difference. We want to keep the Tories out, but to do so, [by] campaigning for socialist policies and against the pro capitalist "record" of the Labour government, which has consistently bitten the hands [of those] that voted us into office in 1974.'[28]

By Christmas 1978, the government pay limit of five per cent was crumbling as big companies faced down strike threats with pay increases way in excess. 'The going rate was 15 per cent and there seemed nothing the government could do,' wrote John Golding, the MP for Newcastle under Lyme.[29] Workers at the Ford Motor Company settled for 17 per cent and the government felt unable to impose sanctions against the firm after five left-wing MPs abstained during a vote in the Commons. The road-haulage and oil-tanker drivers went on strike for pay increases well above five per cent.

By early January 1979, the 'Winter of Discontent' had arrived. Public sector workers also struck. Uncollected rubbish piled up in the streets, and, notoriously, in Liverpool, gravediggers refused to work and the city council had to hire a factory in Speke to store the dead. By 1 February, when school caretakers went on strike, Callaghan realised during a cabinet meeting that the situation had slipped from his control. According to the diaries of Tony Benn, then energy secretary, 'Jim asked how the cabinet was going to survive. We had got to the point where indiscipline was threatening the life of the community and the government must have a clear line. The situation was extremely grave and the Tories could win, giving Mrs Thatcher a mandate for the most violent anti-trade-union policy.'[30]

In Camden, as elsewhere, council manual workers were demanding a working week limited to 35 hours and a weekly pay packet of £60, which in some cases represented a 50 per cent increase. According to former Camden Labour councillors the question of whether to settle became another ideological battle between the left and right. The council's Labour leadership had initially resolved to leave the issue in the hands of the national government and union negotiators and were caught out when a resolution came from party activists in Hampstead to settle locally and give in to the workers' demands.[31] The council's leadership under Roy Shaw had no strategy about how to deal with this proposal when it came before the group of Camden Labour councillors. Neighbouring Conservative-controlled Westminster hired private contractors to clean the streets and collect the rubbish, but in Camden, in line with SCLV policy, Livingstone argued forcefully in favour of agreeing the workers' terms.

John Mills, former deputy leader, says, 'Ken Livingstone got up and made a speech saying, "No, we shouldn't stick with national negotiations; we should have a Camden view on it." That was passed and the only other resolution on the agenda that was pertinent to all this was one from Hampstead, which was an extremely left-wing party at that stage, saying we should pay the whole lot and then there was another vote, which was very narrowly carried by one or two votes. I was chairman of the Finance Committee at the time, and I voted against this, but once the vote had been carried [in favour], there was no going back.'[32] But chaos reigned in the wake of the decision. Mills, who had to sort out the finances, was not sure whether the deal applied to all workers or included overtime pay. The answer was that it did and it did not. The deal became known as the 'Camden Surplus' because the Left, led by Livingstone, advocated not an increase in the basic rates of pay but instead, as a device, a 'supplement' to the wages of every worker earning up to the minimum of £60 a week. That would be a greater hike for those on £35 than those on £45. But for Livingstone and the other councillors who supported it, the surplus very nearly ended in personal bankruptcy and the destruction of their political careers. Council finances were policed by a government-appointed accountant called the district auditor, who had the power to force councillors to pay back personally – a 'surcharge' – any money lost as a result of illegality.

In 1981, by which time Livingstone was leader of the GLC, the district auditor for Camden, Ian Pickwell, did find against Livingstone and the others and applied to the High Court to force them to pay up and have them disqualified from public office for five years. But the court threw out the case and Livingstone survived.

Mills says, 'The fact we avoided surcharge wasn't because of Ken Livingstone, it was because the council did consist of some luminaries in the local authority world who had fairly strong reputations for being reasonable and sensible. It was decided that what we had done had been just about within the bounds of reasonableness.'[33] Roy Shaw was convinced that it was a case of Livingstone gesture politics which nearly proved disastrous. Shaw concluded that Livingstone proposed the big wage rises to discredit the right-wing leadership and display his left-wing credentials but that he would have privately hoped it would fail.[34] It would be a recurring charge levelled against Livingstone, and denied by him, down the years.

On 3 May 1979, there was a 5.3 per cent swing from Labour to the Conservatives and Margaret Thatcher became prime minister.[35] In Hampstead, Livingstone was defeated as the sitting Tory MP Geoffrey Finsberg increased his majority to 3,681; there was a similar story for Ted Knight in neighbouring Hornsey. Labour would be out of power for 18 years. But in the immediate aftermath, the well of bitter recrimination and blame, accumulated over the last decade, would overflow; the result would be a full-blown conflagration. For Livingstone and the Left, their hour had arrived.

Notes

1   John Golding, *Hammer of the Left*, p32
2   Website of the CLPD, the Campaign for Labour Party Democracy, www.clpd.org.uk; Interview, Vladimir Derer, 29.9.07
3   David and Maurice Kogan, *The Battle for the Labour Party*, p45
4   Ibid., p48
5   Denis Healey, *The Time of My Life*, p469
6   David and Maurice Kogan, *The Battle for the Labour Party*, p49
7   John Golding, *Hammer of the Left*, p29
8   David and Maurice Kogan, *The Battle for the Labour Party*, pp41-43
9   Ken Livingstone, *If Voting Changed Anything, They'd Abolish It*, p35, and author interviews
10 Ibid., p36
11 *South London Press*, 26.6.70
12 Ibid., 31.8.73
13 Ibid., 5.10.73
14 Interview, Tony Bird, 1.12.07
15 Interview, Ken Livingstone, 25.10.07
16 Ovid, *Metamorphoses*, VII, 20
17 Ken Livingstone, *If Voting Changed Anything, They'd Abolish It*, pp84-85
18 Ibid.
19 Interview, Phil Turner, 11.7.07
20 Interview, John Mills, 30.7.07
21 Ibid.
22 John Carvel, *Citizen Ken*, p65
23 Ken Livingstone, *If Voting Changed Anything, They'd Abolish It*, p89
24 Interview, Graham Bash, 7.9.07
25 Interview, Vladimir Derer, 29.9.07
26 *Socialist Organiser*, p1, October 1978

27 Ibid., October 1978 and December 1979
28 Ibid.
29 John Golding, *Hammer of the Left*, p69
30 Tony Benn, *The End of an Era, Diaries 1980-1990*, Arrow Books, 1994, (see 1.2.79)
31 Interview, John Mills, 30.7.07
32 Ibid.
33 Ibid.
34 John Carvel, *Citizen Ken*, p66
35 Peter Joyce, *Guide to UK General Elections 1832-2001*, Politico's, 2004, p348

Chapter 6

'Labour, take the power!' May 1979–May 1981

Ken Livingstone's favourite movies include *The Godfather, Parts One* and *Two*, and he is such a student of both masterpieces that he insists that the main reason for the third in the series being such a dud in comparison was the failure to persuade the film star Robert Duvall to repeat his performance as *consigliere*.[1] The first two films would be in some people's top 10, but for Ken Livingstone, the movies, and the novel about the Corleone mob by Mario Puzo on which they are based, have long been a point of political reference and a source of philosophy. As far back as 1986/87, he wrote: 'I have often thought that Mario Puzo's *The Godfather* is a much more honest account of how politicians operate than any self-justifying rubbish spewed out in political biographies and repeated in academic textbooks. One sentence in that book typifies the way most politicians deal with each other. Tessio, the longest-serving of the Corleone mob, has switched his allegiance and betrayed the family by setting up Michael Corleone for assassination. His treachery is uncovered, he is led away to his death, and as he goes he sends Michael Corleone a final message, "Tell Mike it was only business," he says, "I always liked him."'[2]

Livingstone would still be quoting from the book and the films two decades later. It is safe to assume that he sees himself more in the role of Michael Corleone than that of his treacherous underling, Sal Tessio. To use a Puzo metaphor, many obscure local politicians would end up 'sleeping with the fishes' by the time Ken Livingstone was done. Many people find Livingstone personally amiable and approachable but he has always been capable of great ruthlessness and it is pointless to deny it. It is a trait which most successful politicians have and it was this aspect of his personality which first came to public attention two years after the defeat of the Callaghan government when he and his comrades seized power at County Hall. 'I love meetings and plotting,' Livingstone once said. 'I didn't get where I am today without plotting.'[3]

Other more senior political players at that time took advantage of the collapse in the Labour Party's post-election confidence. Within a week of the election results, Tony Benn put out a press statement saying he would not stand for a frontline opposition spokesman post in the shadow cabinet, and moved ominously to the backbenches. Within weeks, the mass forces of the Left rallied to his causes of socialism and Labour Party democracy. 'Blame for the defeat lies solidly on the Labour government's policies,' Livingstone told *Socialist Organiser* in May 1979.[4] 'The Left has got to make sure that people don't forget the record of the Labour government. We've got to ensure that the blame of defeat is pinned on the leaders and the policies responsible. People will flood into the party as they did in 1970–74. They must be reminded of the disastrous record of Callaghan. We must revive the question of reselection [of Labour MPs] at this year's Labour Party conference. As long as the PLP [Parliamentary Labour Party] elect leaders, they're going to be pretty rubbishy.'

This was the view of many of the constituency parties up and down the country which had long fallen under the Left's control. As Livingstone demanded, the blame came crashing down on the Parliamentary Labour Party and the former cabinet ministers. Tony Benn made it clear early on that he would lead the Left out of the darkness and on a crusade to capture the Labour Party. The extent to which the hard left, allied to the massed ranks of the betrayed, now ruled the roost was vividly demonstrated in September 1981, when 225 parliamentary constituencies, a remarkable 81 per cent of those taking part, voted for Benn to be deputy leader of the party.[5] The so-called 'Bennite left' was a loose coalition gathered from the Labour movement: a number of hard left MPs, several union bosses, the majority of constituency Labour Party activists, important organisations like the Campaign for Labour Party Democracy (CLPD), and of course, with the odd exception here and there, the Trots. Curiously, Benn's own record as a member of the Wilson and Callaghan governments was brushed under the carpet in the euphoria at the emergence of a credible leader who would lead everyone to the Promised Land. If God can forgive the sinner that repenteth, then who were the comrades of the CLPD and the Institute for Workers' Control to disagree? Benn's stated objectives of making the Labour leadership and parliamentary party accountable to the local activists through the annual conference and compulsory reselection of MPs hit the right chord at absolutely the right time.

As *Socialist Organiser* put it in October 1979: 'Tony Benn will undoubtedly become a very significant figure on Labour's left. When he makes pronouncements about defending working-class interests, turning Labour into a mass party, making [annual] Conference sovereign and leaders accountable, we will take up the fight to turn these pronouncements into reality.' There was a note of caution for Benn from *Socialist Organiser*: 'Working-class militancy can't be switched off and on at the convenience of parliamentarians. When Labour leaders start speaking in left-wing terms after years of servility to right-wing policies, we should note it carefully. For as easily as that left-wing talk is switched on, it can be switched off again when the struggle heats up.'[6] Many of Benn's old former cabinet colleagues and MPs on the centre and right of the party were convinced he was simply an opportunist taking advantage of the unstoppable leftward march of Labour. They were also convinced he wanted the party leadership for himself and they were right.

◆

To John Golding, the Labour MP for Newcastle under Lyme, his fellow NEC member Tony Benn had, at the advanced age of 54, developed a 'genetically determined characteristic to move from the centre to the left with age, which is quite at odds with human nature'. In his waspish and compulsive memoir, *Hammer of the Left*, Golding pointed out that Benn had once been better known as the second Viscount Stansgate, Anthony Wedgewood Benn. 'In a vain attempt to identify himself with the working class, however,' said Golding, 'he had adopted the name "Tony Benn" and had started drinking tea from a mug and visiting fish and chip shops.'[7] Golding did concede that Benn was 'exceedingly bright, attractive, hail-fellow-well met... with remarkable charisma', but pointed out that he was extremely ambitious. Benn rid himself of his inherited title which he hated 'because it was thought impossible for a lord to become prime minister'.[8] Golding's view of Benn accords with many on the right and centre of the party at the time, as well as influential figures on the soft left. In his book, *Loyalists and Loners,* written in 1986, Michael Foot showed what his biographer Kenneth O. Morgan described as a 'controlled bitterness towards one whom he regards as very much a wilful "loner", and not a team player at all'.[9] The same criticisms were repeatedly made of Ken Livingstone, for whom Tony Benn was an inspiration and a prophet. Livingstone wrote: 'Audiences of hundreds and often thousands listened as he analysed, examined, predicted and gave confidence that we could achieve socialism and, yes, it did involve the very people in that particular audience. Not only did every speech seem to produce a new idea or policy, but each one was crafted with a care and a beauty the movement had not heard since the death of Nye Bevan nearly two decades before. After the windy rhetoric of the Wilson/Callaghan years, Benn's speeches stood out like paintings of a great artist hung amidst a display of painting by numbers.'[10]

Graham Bash, Livingstone's Chartist colleague, says Benn was a 'messianic figure, a prophet,' adding: 'He spoke in a language that hadn't been heard until after the First World War. Nothing had been heard of this for 60 years and there was a vision of a Labour Party that really encompassed not only its traditional base but could go beyond it to women, to black people and to all those fighting on the fringes of traditional politics, who for the first time could begin to see a home.'[11] The key issue for Livingstone and the Left was how to take the fight to Margaret Thatcher; her monetarist policies to deal with the deep recession of the time demanded drastic cuts in public spending coupled with both the control of public sector pay and trade union power. By the end of 1979, inflation was forecast to rise to 18 per cent and the minimum lending rate was set at 17 per cent.[12] In her first budget in June 1979, Thatcher announced immediate cuts of £3.5 billion in public spending and started planning to cut a further £6.5 billion for the following year.[13]

Before the election, Thatcher had long come to believe that the post-war political consensus of the Conservatives and Labour was dead, as she revealed in a conversation with the British ambassador to Iran in May 1978. She told him that people who believed in consensus politics were 'traitors'.[14] Livingstone and Benn did not believe in it either. While the moderate Labour leadership appeared to flounder in its response to Thatcher's challenge, the Left saw it as a fight to the death. They recognised it for what it was – a declaration of war on the left-wing militants in the trade unions, local government and the Labour movement. Where the Left and Thatcher came together was in their relish for the collapse of the wider political post-war consensus that had begun a decade earlier. 'Following the defeat in the general election,' wrote John Golding, 'we should have picked ourselves up and sorted ourselves out. Instead we stayed on the floor, kicking hell out of each other, while Thatcher walked all over us.'[15] He accurately described the strategy of the Left as 'Leave Thatcher, we'll get Callaghan first'.[16]

Chris Mullin, later elected as Labour MP for Sunderland South, was a close associate of Tony Benn and edited his 1979 book *Arguments for Socialism*. He was also a leading light in the Campaign for Labour Party Democracy, the CLPD. He says, 'A large divide had grown up in the 1960s and 1970s between the leaders and the led. What we felt was that the Parliamentary Labour Party didn't take the blindest bit of notice of the members. Once you were in Parliament in a safe seat, you tended to get a stiff neck looking up towards those in power rather than backwards over your shoulder to the people who put you there. Our intention was to give MPs a reason to look over their shoulder at those who put them there.'[17] The Left was also helped by a catastrophic drop in Labour Party membership following the election defeat. More than half of party members, mainly moderates, left in two years, from more than 660,000 in 1979 to 276,000 in 1981.[18]

Livingstone once joked that the Left was 'never a threat to anyone,' adding: 'Most of us have trouble getting out of bed in the morning.'[19] But it achieved its major objectives with bewildering ease and speed following the election. At the acrimonious Labour Party conference in Brighton in October 1979, the mood was summed up by the party's own general secretary, Ron Hayward, who pronounced, 'I come not to praise Callaghan but to bury him.'[20] By large majorities, the left-controlled conference agreed proposals for the mandatory reselection or deselection of all MPs before each general election. The delegates also voted to take away from the Labour leadership the sole power to draw up the manifesto and to hand it over to the party's NEC, which was now controlled by the Left.

The Left's campaign was as much about power as democratisation. As the Left was in control of both the constituency parties and the NEC, these changes gave it the whip hand in dictating party policy as well as influencing who would become Labour

MPs. Denis Healey described this period as an 'arid wasteland in which hollow men went round and round the prickly pears of constitutional reform', adding: 'But on the outcome of these arcane rituals depended the future of the Labour Party as a force in British politics.'[21] The last key objective of Benn and the CLPD was to take away the MPs' power to choose the party leader and hand it over to the Labour movement, giving the unions and party activists a much greater say. This goal was largely achieved in principle at a special Committee of Enquiry which held its final meeting in Bishop's Stortford on 15 June 1980. In the teeth of fierce opposition from MPs like Shirley Williams and David Owen, soon to leave and form the Social Democratic Party, the committee agreed that future leaders of the Labour Party should be chosen by an electoral college, giving 50 per cent of the votes to MPs, 25 per cent to trade unionists, 20 per cent to constituency activists and five per cent to affiliated bodies like the Fabian Society. A special conference would be held in Wembley in early 1981 to decide the issue.

On 30 May 1980 two weeks before the Bishop's Stortford decision, Tony Benn held a party at his west London home. There was, he wrote, 'a sort of new left gathering'. This included representatives of CLPD and other hard left groups including the avowedly Trotskyist Socialist Campaign for a Labour Victory, established by Ken Livingstone and others in Hampstead two years previously. Another guest was 'Ken Livingstone of the GLC'. Benn said: 'These people have formed the Rank and File Mobilising Committee and, when the time comes, they will be the people who organise the Benn election campaign.'[22] But by May 1980, Livingstone was much more involved with his own leadership prospects than Tony Benn's. He never played a role in the Rank and File Mobilising Committee, the CLPD or the other important left-wing causes. He had his own project – to make himself leader of the GLC on the back of this insurrection; he was already working with the Chartists to purge the GLC Labour group of right and centre opponents and take over County Hall.

Livingstone had to fight to get the Left interested in County Hall, for years considered a tedious and irrelevant side-show. Back in 1976, he told his fellow left-wing GLC member Tony Banks that the GLC was 'the single most important elective body in the UK after Parliament and that the Left should see its potential'.

Banks replied that the GLC 'had about as much prestige as a regional committee of the engineering workers' union'.[23] Shortly before Thatcher's victory, Livingstone attempted to interest the Left again by portraying County Hall as a potent weapon to use against a Thatcher government. Writing in *Socialist Organiser*, he urged the Left to prevent candidates from the right and centre being selected for the GLC elections in May 1981: 'Those who have a commitment to a socialist GLC need to start organising now if this motley crew are to be prevented from discrediting the Labour Party in the eyes of the electorate for a second time in a decade.' He added: 'There must be a major effort to get ordinary rank and file party members to stand for the GLC and ensure that it is more representative of the party as a whole than previous Labour GLCs.'[24]

Livingstone returned to the theme in the following month, telling the Left the biggest obstacle to regaining control of the GLC would be the record of its last administration under Sir Reg Goodwin, 'which hangs around the neck of the party like a rotting albatross'.[25] With some foresight Livingstone predicted the following: Labour would be defeated at the 1979 general election; the Tory government would rapidly become unpopular; Labour would win control of the GLC at the next County Hall elections scheduled for May 1981. His proposed policies for this future Labour administration included: axing road-building programmes, introducing substantial cuts in bus and Tube fares and providing greater investment in housing. He added: 'Clearly the above policies would set the GLC on a collision course with the Tory government and the London Labour movement must be mobilised in support of a Labour GLC.' A month before Thatcher's victory, Livingstone concluded that 'the GLC is a body which must be used in the fight to bring down the Thatcher government and to show what can be achieved by a fighting socialist council'.[26] Livingstone called a meeting in Hampstead Town Hall to discuss 'taking over the GLC.' 'I was the only person who turned up,' says Livingstone.[27]

The Socialist Campaign for a Labour Victory was clearly not the vehicle Livingstone needed to seize County Hall. The Trots in the group had already split over the tactics dealing with the Thatcher-imposed cuts in council budgets. Some said councils must neither raise local taxation in the form of rates nor cut local services to meet government spending limits. Others advocated raising taxes, which would have a greater impact on business and the well-off. It was yet another replay of the arguments which tore apart the Goodwin administration at County Hall. The Chartists of the tiny Revolutionary Communist League now intervened crucially to salvage Livingstone's bid for power. Chris Knight and Keith Veness visited Livingstone at Camden Town Hall in the summer of 1979, shortly after Thatcher's victory. Discussion turned to the GLC elections more than 20 months away. Veness says, 'I remember saying to him we should do something about the GLC because it's got a lot of money and a lot of power.' The three decided to put out a circular to every ward and constituency party, calling on Labour Party members to meet at County Hall to plot a left-wing takeover of the GLC.

The note infuriated the Labour Party's full-time official for London, John Keys, who Veness describes as a 'right-wing bastard, absolutely dreadful'.[28] Keys sent out a note aimed at Livingstone, a member of the party's executive committee, warning that it was wrong for any executive member to participate 'in factional meetings that could undermine the executive committee'.[29] Livingstone ignored the note and went to the 1979 conference at the height of the Benn-CLPD insurrection to drum up support for his own crusade.

◆

On 18 October 1979, Livingstone called the first meeting on 'Taking over the GLC' and described it, tongue firmly in cheek, as 'The John Keys Annual Memorial Lecture' in honour of the man whose overreaction had guaranteed its success.[30] At the end of 1979 came the next stage in the campaign. Keith Veness and his wife Valerie held a meeting with fellow Chartists like Graham Bash and Chris Knight, along with Livingstone, at their home in Dalmeny Road near Tufnell Park. They decided to publish a monthly news sheet called *London Labour Briefing*, also known as *Briefing*.

Briefing would play a crucial role in the Left's seizure of power. It kept left-wing members informed about what was going on across London as Labour selected its candidates for the GLC elections of 1981. Information about potential right-wing traitors was regularly supplied to the left-wing activists controlling most of London's constituency Labour parties. But *Briefing* would become more than just a left-wing weekly which played an instrumental role in itself. People referred to it as an organisation, almost a force within the Labour movement: for some, necessary; for others, malignant and divisive. A former Livingstone advisor would describe *Briefing* '…as a vitriolic, sectarian grouping that drove Labour in London to the brink of extinction, the distillation of all that turned the public off about Labour in the eighties.'[31] The Chartists, now the 'Chartist Minority', of the Revolutionary Communist League were always at the heart of *Briefing*, and despite the odd spat, so was Ken Livingstone.

Livingstone's takeover of the GLC in May 1981 has often been called a coup: the Labour Party won the election under a moderate leader who was then deposed within 24 hours by Livingstone. But Livingstone guaranteed his success in the year running up to the polls. His strategy was to purge right-wing candidates and get as many left-wingers as possible selected in winnable seats and marginal seats. Livingstone had learned at the feet of a master. He had helped Ted Knight do exactly the same thing before the local borough elections of 1978, allowing 'Red Ted' and his comrades to seize the leadership at Lambeth Town Hall from the old right and centre coalition.[32]

Essentially, much of this work had already been done for Livingstone. In the 1977 defeat, 29 out of a total of 57 GLC Labour members had lost their seats and many of those who survived were too old or too fed up to stand again. By the beginning of 1980, a third of the existing Labour opposition members at the GLC were planning to retire. The Left did all the organising while the activists on the right and centre appear to have stuck their heads in the sand. At Chris Knight's insistence, *Briefing*'s slogan was one of Trotsky's favourites: 'Labour, take the power!'[33] Although the Chartists were the main players, there were contributors and fellow travellers from other sections of the Labour movement. *Briefing*'s first trial issue in February 1980 was headlined: 'Taking over the GLC. Labour must win in 1981.' Thereafter, *Briefing* supplied a regular diet of acts of betrayal by the right and centre, as well as gossip and news about impending selections across the capital. In its March 1980 edition, it named all the Labour members of the Inner London Education Authority who had voted for cuts in schools' budgets as opposed to those real left-wingers who voted against. Time and again, the message went out to those left-wingers in control of selecting candidates for the GLC: deselect those who oppose us; select those who support us.

Livingstone had done more than most to lay the foundation stones for his putsch. From his vantage point on the regional executive, he had been one of those to successfully fight for mandatory reselection of GLC candidates long before it became national policy for MPs. The power for drawing up the GLC manifesto had been transferred from the executive to the Labour leadership. Livingstone personally persuaded many of the successful candidates to stand for selection. Both Dave Wetzel and Paul Moore, his old friend from the Chartists and Norwood Young Socialists, say they stood successfully for GLC seats after being lobbied by Livingstone. At first, Wetzel had no interest in County Hall, telling Livingstone: 'You've got to be joking! They're all pinstripe suits waiting to die! What do I want to join that lot for?' Livingstone replied: 'No, it's going to be different. You've got to get involved.'[34] Wetzel relented after several more phone calls from Livingstone and was selected for the Tory-held marginal of Hammersmith North, which he would win. Paul Moore stood successfully for selection as Labour candidate in Lambeth Central. He says: 'By 1980, Ken was openly going around the London Labour Party to activists and saying "Have you thought about standing for the GLC?" He was trying to encourage anybody – who might be left, or centre-left, or a young radical of any kind – to have a punt at it. In the run-up, we were meeting in the Jubilee Tavern opposite County Hall one evening a week for what seemed like about two years before the bloody election!'[35]

Meetings were also held in the Barbican flat of the Bennite hard left-winger Audrey Wise, who had lost her parliamentary seat for Coventry South West in the '79 general election. Livingstone had met her daughter, Valerie, and encouraged her to stand for selection. Valerie Wise was only 25 and then the political education officer for the Westminster South Labour Party, as well as being involved in the CLPD. She had invited Livingstone to give a speech to her local party and afterwards they went for a drink. 'I was making some criticism about the GLC,' says Wise, 'and he turned round to me and said, "Why aren't you standing?" Because, obviously he was going around trying to encourage people to stand because, let's face it, he wanted to be leader.'[36]

With the help of Mike Ward, a close colleague of Livingstone's in the regional London Labour Party, Wise was selected for Battersea South. Wise adds: 'We knew, because Ken had all these figures, which seats we had to win for us to have a Labour GLC.' Wise says she became part of Livingstone's inner circle and held parties for the Left candidates in her mother's flat. 'This was so Ken and the rest could get to know each other as the Left candidates. And we invited anybody who was anywhere near the Left. He wanted to be leader so he'd worked out he needed people like me but he also needed others who weren't quite as on the Left as us but maybe he could bring them over and maybe offer them something.'[37]

Sir Reg Goodwin was one victim of the Left's advance on the GLC. As the Left gathered strength, his days were numbered. He was still leader of the GLC Labour group when he lost the selection vote to be candidate for Bermondsey to a young left-wing activist called George Nicholson. Goodwin was almost 71 years old. 'He had to go,' says Nicholson, 'he had had his time; he was tired. People like Reg who have been in political power for a long time never know when to give up. It was a hell of a thing for me to do to stand against Reg Goodwin. People in the Bermondsey Labour Party hated me for doing it.'[38] When the vote was announced, Goodwin quietly said to Nicholson, 'You've got it.' Goodwin died six years later. 'Reg would not have had those years with his family,' says Nicholson, 'if he had been reselected to the GLC.' In Mario Puzo speak, it had not been a directly orchestrated hit by the *Briefing* Mob; Bermondsey had been taken over by left-wingers like Nicholson and Peter Tatchell who were crying out for change. But it was one less traitor for Livingstone to worry about.

Goodwin had one last card up his sleeve following his deselection. During 1980, it seemed certain that there would soon be a Labour administration at County Hall due to Mrs Thatcher's unpopularity, but who would lead it? It was obvious to Goodwin that the Left was making significant advances in the selection of candidates, so on 15 April 1980 he unexpectedly resigned, hoping his moderate heir apparent, Andrew McIntosh, a 47-year-old business consultant, would become the Labour leader. The two main contenders to replace Goodwin were McIntosh and Goodwin's deputy, Illtyd Harrington. Livingstone was caught out. It was a leadership poll a year earlier than expected or desired. But he flew back from his holiday in Italy and immediately started campaigning for the job among the tiny electorate of 28 GLC members.

The leadership election was on Monday, 28 April 1980, and the result caught most people by surprise. On the first ballot, Livingstone polled 10, ahead of Harrington and McIntosh on nine each. Harrington was defeated in a run-off ballot. There was a final head-to-head vote. McIntosh beat Livingstone by 14 votes to 13. It was pretty clear that McIntosh would be in serious trouble if there were another leadership election, as expected, after the GLC election in 12 months' time. Goodwin may have convinced himself that he had outwitted Livingstone, but immediately after the vote Illtyd Harrington told McIntosh, 'You've got a year.'[39] Livingstone continued plotting. Leonard Vigars, a reporter on the *Evening News,* had his finger on the pulse: 'If there is a left-wing "takeover" of the GLC after next year's elections, as has been forecast in some quarters, the new leader could be ousted when extremists come to power.'[40]

The journalist John Evans observed that McIntosh won 'because his colleagues thought he was less likely to frighten the ratepayers than his rivals, Ken Livingstone, an austere and frightening-looking left-winger and Illtyd Harrington, one of London's best-known politicians but also regarded by many as one of the most erratic.'[41] Livingstone decided that there was no point in being on the GLC if Labour did not win control, and so he decided to abandon the safe pastures of Hackney North for a marginal inner-London seat. Neale Coleman, a leading Labour activist in Paddington, remembers: 'In the selection period for the '81 GLC there was an immense political battle in every constituency and particularly in every constituency Labour might win.'[42] Jean Merriton had been the Labour GLC member for Paddington until the defeat of 1977. Now the left-wingers controlling the party did not want her and were keen to know who on the Left to approach. 'Essentially we didn't think she'd vote for Ken if it came to a leadership election,' says Coleman, 'and we didn't trust her on policy issues.'

A group of activists from the Paddington party gathered at Coleman's flat in Castlemayne Mansions and spotted the name of Livingstone's wife, Christine Chapman, on the *Briefing* lists of possible candidates. Someone rang Chapman who said she wasn't interested but suggested her husband could be. Livingstone eventually defeated Merriton in the selection process and was chosen for his third different GLC constituency in eight years.

Mair Garside managed to fend off an attempt by the Left to capture selection in her Woolwich East seat. One hot sultry Thursday evening during the summer of 1980, she was working late at County Hall. She noticed an intense meeting taking place directly opposite in Room 168 and because it was being used informally, there was no air conditioning. The door was left open and she could hear every word. Ken Livingstone was doing most of the talking but the others, mostly potential candidates, would occasionally have their say. She says, 'Ken was saying there would be 30 odd of us, out of a total of 50 or so members. They were all substantially the new people and the people were being promised that they would have [committee] chairmanships. I don't think I took it all that seriously, to be honest. It took me a while to realise who some of the people were. They weren't people I had seen around in much of the Labour Party.'[43]

◆

By September 1980, with half of the 92 selections made, left candidates had already unseated seven former Labour members and had been chosen to fight 16 winnable seats.[44] By February 1981, all bar one of the 92 Labour candidates had been selected: 10 former Labour members had been replaced and candidates who were obviously from the Left had been selected to fight 23 of the 54 most winnable seats.[45] Livingstone calculated that McIntosh could rely on the votes of only eight other candidates.[46] 'The major gains by the Left in the summer have continued throughout the autumn,' he wrote at the time. By this stage, the Labour Party was sinking faster into conflict and chaos. In October 1980, Jim Callaghan took a leaf from Sir Reg Goodwin's book by resigning the party leadership to make way for a moderate replacement before new rules made it likely that a candidate from the Left would win. The Bishop's Stortford Enquiry made it certain that party leaders would soon be elected by party activists and unions and so he resigned while that power still remained solely with MPs. In November 1980, Michael Foot, the soft left candidate, beat Denis Healey by 10 votes to take charge.

◆

On 24 January 1981, the party held its special conference at

Wembley to debate the proposed election changes for future leaders and deputy leaders. The author and humorist John O'Farrell would accurately describe the conference as 'an attempt to lose the remaining voters it had failed to alienate the previous autumn'.[47] The CLPD achieved its third great objective: an electoral college to pick future leaders, with 40 per cent of the votes going to the unions and 30 per cent each to the constituency parties and MPs. On the following day, 25 January 1981, four senior Labour politicians, Dr David Owen, Shirley Williams, Bill Rodgers and Roy Jenkins held a press conference in Limehouse, east London, to announce their departure from the Labour Party and their intent to establish a Council for Social Democracy which formed the basis of the Social Democratic Party (SDP). Others swiftly followed.

On 1 April 1981, Tony Benn announced he would fight to replace Denis Healey as deputy leader of the Labour Party, a decision which caused a media frenzy and led to six months of bitter infighting between right and left. With the searchlights from the media watchtower fixated on the bloody battlefield, few noticed that the Left under Ken Livingstone was about to deliver one of its most spectacular blows.

Notes

1   Interview, Ken Livingstone, 1.11.07
2   Ken Livingstone, *If Voting Changed Anything, They'd Abolish It,* p115
3   *Guardian,* 19.1.00
4   *Socialist Organiser,* May 1979, article by Ken Livingstone
5   Patrick Seyd, *The Rise and Fall of the Labour Left,* p134; *Labour Party Annual Conference Records,* p26
6   *Socialist Organiser,* October 1979
7   John Golding, *Hammer of the Left,* p17
8   Ibid.
9   Kenneth O. Morgan, *Michael Foot, A Life*, HarperCollins, 2007, p401
10 Ken Livingstone, *If Voting Changed Anything, They'd Abolish It,* p92
11 Interview, Graham Bash, 15.8.07
12 Hugo Young, *One of Us,* Pan Books, 1993, pp193-208
13 John Campbell, *Margaret Thatcher, Volume Two: The Iron Lady*, Pimlico, 2004, pp46 -53; Margaret Thatcher, *The Downing Street Years,* HarperCollins, 1995, pp38-59
14 Hugo Young, *One of Us,* p223
15 John Golding, *Hammer of the Left,* p97
16 Ibid.
17 Interview, Chris Mullin, 3.10.07

18 Patrick Seyd, *The Rise and Fall of the Labour Left*, p41; NEC Report, 1986, p49
19 *Guardian*, Terry Coleman, 3.6.87
20 Kenneth O. Morgan, *Michael Foot, A Life*, p373
21 Denis Healey, *The Time of My Life*, p473
22 Tony Benn, *The End of an Era, Diaries 1980-1990*, (see 30.5.80)
23 Ken Livingstone, *If Voting Changed Anything, They'd Abolish It*, p75
24 Ken Livingstone, 'Labour's left must organise', *Socialist Organiser*, March 1979
25 Ken Livingstone, 'A Socialist Manifesto for London', *Socialist Organiser*, April 1979
26 Ibid.
27 Interview, Ken Livingstone, 25.10.07
28 Interview, Keith Veness, 24.8.04
29 John Carvel, *Citizen Ken*, p71
30 Interview, Keith Veness, 24.8.07
31 *Evening Standard*, article by Nita Clarke, Livingstone's GLC press officer (1983-1986), 18.4.00
32 Interview, Ted Knight, 4.7.07
33 *London Labour Briefing* (supplement), February 1984, quote attributed to Trotsky, 'The Transitional Program', p16
34 Interview, Dave Wetzel, 5.11.07
35 Interview, Paul Moore, 5.11.07
36 Interview, Valerie Wise, 19.7.07
37 Ibid.
38 Interview, George Nicholson, 21.8.07
39 Interview, Illtyd Harrington, 4.7.07
40 *Evening News*, 16.4.80
41 *Evening News*, 'Are Labour's Plans for London too Left for its Leader?' by John Evans, 22.5.80
42 Interview, Neale Coleman, 31.10.07
43 Interview, Mair Garside, 17.8.07
44 *London Labour Briefing*, September 1980, p4
45 My calculations based on interviews and *London Labour Briefing*, February 1981, pp6-7
46 *London Labour Briefing*, February 1981, pp6-7
47 John O'Farrell, *Things can only get better: Eighteen Miserable Years in the Life of a Labour Supporter, 1970-1997*, Doubleday, 1998, p45

Chapter 7

'London's ours!' May 1981

Illtyd Harrington was working quietly at his desk in County Hall being ignored as usual by his long-suffering former leader, Sir Reg Goodwin, in another part of the office when the door opened and in walked Ken Livingstone in his habitual safari jacket, open-necked shirt and slacks. It was 1 May 1981, just six days before the GLC elections. Livingstone peered at Harrington, and with a curious grin said, 'What's wrong with you, you miserable old git?' Harrington replied, 'There's nothing wrong with me and there'd better not be after you're elected leader of this council next Thursday.'[1] 'Nah,' mocked Livingstone, as he turned on his heel, 'we need you as the acceptable face of extremism.' Goodwin, eking out his last days as a political force at County Hall, sat mute.

Aged 63 in May 1981, Illtyd Harrington was still one of the most boisterous and charismatic characters at County Hall. An imposing Falstaffian character with white beard, lilting Welsh accent and acid wit, Harrington had once been considered to be a dangerous left-winger whose selection for the Dover parliamentary seat in 1960 had been vetoed by senior Labour Party officials on the advice of the security services. But the hard left members at County Hall, including Ken Livingstone, had always treated Harrington with suspicion, particularly during the Goodwin administration when, as finance chairman, he had to put up fares and cut housing programmes. 'I wasn't quite the devil incarnate to them,' says Harrington, 'but I didn't obey their rules and ideology or have the doctrinal certainties they had.'

Harrington and his long-term partner Christopher Downes, a theatre dresser, were well-known figures in the worlds of politics and the stage, hosting parties at their Marylebone flat for friends as diverse as Peter Mandelson and Alastair Campbell to famous actors including Maggie Smith and Robert Stephens.[2] Harrington had never been under any illusions when it came to how ruthless Livingstone could be. In the late 1970s, he was out walking in the

Chilterns with the former Labour cabinet minister Barbara Castle, whose husband Ted had been a GLC alderman, when the topic came up about how to get ahead in politics. Castle said, 'Illtyd, you'll never get anywhere like Ken because they'll knock you into the mud and you won't get up. You haven't got the killer instinct. But he's got it, Ken Livingstone's got it and you haven't.'[3]

During the Livingstone purge of 1980 and early 1981, the Left had made a failed attempt to deselect Harrington in his Brent South constituency and replace him with one of its own. His guard was up after the attempt. He says, 'I had let it be known in the run-up to the election that I was not to be fucked with and that I was quite capable of breaking somebody's legs if it came to it!' Livingstone had clearly received the message.

◆

Ken Livingstone seemed certain to command the biggest bloc of supporters in the Labour group, but to clinch it he needed the support of the two significant power brokers, Harrington and Harvey Hinds. Through them, he could persuade the centre to support him against McIntosh. Hinds had been the chief whip of the Labour group for as long as anyone could remember and knew where all the bodies were buried. He had been a canon at Southwark Cathedral and entered politics after doing youth work, particularly for the London Union of Youth Clubs.[4] He later told a Tory GLC member that he started to devote more time to the Labour Party after realising he no longer believed in God.[5] 'He should have been a Jesuit,' says one former Tory member of the GLC and a friend of Hinds. 'Harvey was such a devious little shit!'[6] Hinds proved crucially important, and in 1987 he received a free copy of Livingstone's memoir *If Voting Changed Anything, They'd Abolish It* inscribed by the author: 'To Harvey – who made it all possible.'[7]

There had been an attempt by the Left to kick Hinds out of his safe berth in Peckham and install Ted Knight in his place. But Livingstone intervened to prevent this particular assassination attempt because he needed Hinds to win so he could command the centre, even if that meant denying Knight a safe seat. 'There was an effort by Peckham to get rid of Harvey Hinds,' says Livingstone, 'but I didn't support that because Harvey was crucial in delivering the centre bloc. We had actually insisted on reselection and everyone had to go through reselection and a lot of people tried to get rid of him and failed, but I didn't do anything to help them.'[8] Hinds was considered an excellent chief whip with all the necessary attributes of patronage, discretion, menace and flattery. 'A good chief whip is worth their weight in gold,' says Livingstone. 'He knew everybody. He knew whose marriage was in trouble and who had money problems. People would go in there and cry on his shoulder and I really didn't want people doing that to me.'

'Effectively,' concedes Livingstone, 'who won that leadership election was in the hands of Harvey and Illtyd.'[9] The two men had come to believe their own survival depended on Livingstone; certainly they had long stopped believing it could depend on McIntosh. Astonishingly, the only person who thought he was safe was McIntosh himself. In interviews for this book, former GLC members including Valerie Wise, George Nicholson and Dave Wetzel, all say that McIntosh made no attempt to court their votes, but they concede that it would have made no difference even if he had. Livingstone had been so convinced that he would emerge as leader after the elections that he approached McIntosh early in 1981 and told him: 'Look Andrew, I am going to beat you, however many seats we win; if there is a Labour administration, it will elect me leader.'[10] Andrew McIntosh had rearranged his business life to free up the time necessary to be leader of the GLC, and that probably involved turning down work. He clearly expected victory at the polls to provide the balm necessary to soothe away any doubts about his suitability for the job. But everyone at County Hall, particularly the Tories, knew that Livingstone would take over there in the event of a Labour victory.

A Tory member, Bernard Brook-Partridge, was chairman of the GLC at the time of the 1981 election. He says, 'During the election campaign, I received in my office weekly an A4 buff envelope just addressed to me and I don't know to this day who sent it me. It contained the minutes and reports of this extreme left-wing group within the Labour Party that was then scheming to get Ken in and McIntosh out. I did try to warn McIntosh about this in a way.' Brook-Partridge's warning may have seemed rather obtuse. He once asked McIntosh 'if everything was alright,' and received a cheery but baffled affirmation. Brook-Partridge decided to leave it at that.[11]

The news of the plot reached high levels in the Tory Party. In a debate on 13 March 1981, less than two months before the poll, Geoffrey Finsberg, MP for Hampstead and a junior environment minister, told the House of Commons that the left-wingers currently running the London Labour Party 'would not be fit to clean the boots of people like Herbert Morrison'. 'I would be less uneasy if I thought there was going to be a Labour council after 7 May,' he said. 'What scares me to death is that it will be not a Labour council, but a Marxist council.'[12] In the weeks before the election, Sir Horace Cutler, the GLC's Thatcherite Tory leader, had run a campaign warning that left-wing extremists were lurking in the shadows waiting to take over. He claimed 47 of the 92 Labour candidates, including Livingstone, were 'Marxists' plotting to oust McIntosh. Cutler's 16-page manifesto made 17 references to 'Marxists' and laboured under the heavy pun, 'KEEP LONDON OUT OF THE RED'. For the press, but not the thousands of GLC staff he laid off, Cutler was a comical figure that with his bow tie and pointy beard resembled a Ruritanian squire from *The Prisoner of Zenda*. But he was in deadly earnest as he grumbled, 'We don't want a lot of little Benns trotting around London.'[13]

Livingstone's Conservative opponent in Paddington, Patricia Kirwan, has always believed that the Tories wanted Livingstone to win and helped engineer it because they believed he was bound to do enormous damage to the Labour Party if he pulled off his coup. She was defending the most marginal Conservative seat in London, but had felt so abandoned by her own party that her husband Peter had to draft in his mates from the City to help him hand out leaflets and glad-hand the voters. Livingstone seemed able to field an army of left-wingers who descended on Paddington and went among the electorate. 'The people he was working with were quite frankly disgraceful,' says Patricia Kirwan. 'He was working with all the minority revolutionary-type groups. He was terribly in with bits of the Socialist Workers Party and the Workers Revolutionary Party and the troublesome anti-racism groups. Anything that was anti-Establishment, he was in with. And when you've got an election with say a 30 per cent turnout, out of 25,000 people, all you need is five per cent of that, and you're home and dry.'[14]

Andrew McIntosh has been a member of the House of Lords since 1983 and has also served as a junior government minister.

Clearly he does not just want be remembered as the man who was ousted by Ken Livingstone, and he remains reluctant to talk about him. McIntosh was obviously outmanoeuvred but he also fell victim to a mixture of wishful thinking and complacency. His wife Naomi was a friend of Jill Craigie, the wife of the Labour leader Michael Foot. McIntosh was an Oxbridge man with links to the most senior figures in the party. What was Ken Livingstone from Tulse Hill and his band of Trots compared to that? He could not bring himself to believe that he would be dumped within hours of leading his party to victory. It was wishful thinking. For Michael Foot, the GLC election was the first real test of public opinion about his leadership and he had thrown himself into the campaign, launching the manifesto with McIntosh and railing against the misery and unemployment created by Thatcher's monetarist policies.

♦

The sun shone on the morning of 7 May 1981 and then came the drizzle, followed by thunderstorms in the evening.[15] Everyone anticipated that County Hall would fall to Labour. Nationally, the party was in a terrible plight but with deepening recession, high interest rates and rising unemployment, the Thatcher government was also deeply unpopular. Besides, in four of the five previous GLC elections, the party in power at Westminster had failed to take over County Hall. Livingstone's result in Paddington was one of the earliest declarations of the evening. Ken Livingstone benefited by a 12.6 per cent swing in Paddington and polled 11,864 votes, with a majority of 3,397[16] over Patricia Kirwan, who fled the count in tears. As the seats fell to Labour across London, Michael Foot, McIntosh, their wives and other revellers took to the GLC bar to celebrate on the spectacular veranda overlooking the river and the Houses of Parliament as the thunder rumbled in the distance. According to Illtyd Harrington, Foot told McIntosh: 'It's going to be fine, because you, Andrew, are in charge and you know the machine.'[17]

In an interview for this book, Michael Foot said this was the first time he learned of the impending coup by Livingstone, planned for the following day. One of his secretaries had heard about it and warned him. 'I didn't agree with what he was doing,' says Foot, 'I was on Andrew McIntosh's side and still am in a kind of way! I still think it was the wrong thing to do. I didn't think it was right because we had fought the election with McIntosh as our leader and McIntosh had every right to be angry about it.'[18] Ken Livingstone had deliberately stayed away from the celebrations at County Hall because he did not want to be faced down by Foot. Livingstone says, 'I knew if I went to the victory party, Michael Foot would get me in a corner and say, "I don't want you to stand [for the leadership]." And I couldn't face having a row with Michael Foot because I like him so much. I was about the only person who didn't go to the victory party; I knew what Michael would do and I wasn't going to get into that position.'[19]

McIntosh had planned to diffuse Livingstone's challenge by the simple tactic of catching everyone on the hop by holding a meeting at 9 a.m. the following morning, 8 May 1981, to confirm his leadership. Livingstone simply outplayed him by deploying his muscle on the Greater London Labour Party executive which decreed the postponement of the meeting until 5 p.m. As Livingstone admitted later, 'The left-dominated Executive agreed to call the first meeting at 5 p.m. on Friday [8 May 1981]. The rather weak justification for this was that we might face protracted recounts which could take most of Friday. The real reason was that it would allow me to convene a left caucus for 3 p.m.'[20] In an attempt to protect McIntosh, Michael Foot wrote a note expressing his strong support for him and gave it to George Page,[21] who had succeeded John Keys as the party's London regional general secretary. What greater demonstration of the leadership's weakness was there that Page did not summon the energy to read out Foot's note because he knew few would take any notice of it?

The two camps turned up at County Hall the following day to decide who would get the key posts in the new Labour administration. Labour had won 50 seats, a nine-seat majority over the Tories but 10 fewer than Livingstone had hoped.[22] The party had failed to take a number of key marginals, including Hampstead and Hendon North. The biggest blow to Livingstone's confidence came from his former Norwood seat which everyone was expecting Livingstone's old comrade Ted Knight to win. But Knight, who had been leader of Lambeth Council since 1978, had not endeared himself to the electorate by a recent local tax hike of 50 per cent. The candidate for the Social Democratic Alliance (SDA) got 3,709 votes, allowing the Tory to beat Knight by a fairly comfortable margin of 2,593. The SDA candidate was Dr Stephen

Haseler, the former Labour GLC member who had resigned his chairmanship in 1975 in protest at Sir Reg Goodwin's failure to deal with the antics of 'extreme left-wingers' like Livingstone. In March 1980, Haseler had warned that 'left-wing extremists'[23] were planning to take over the GLC under the leadership of Ted Knight. Certainly Knight would have been in a strong position to replace Livingstone given the right circumstances. Some on the Left thought Haseler may have done Livingstone a favour by keeping out Knight. 'Knight was going to be the chair of finance,' says Bryn Davies, another left supporter of Livingstone, 'but we always assumed he would end up being leader.'[24]

'It was like the gunfight at the O.K. Corral,' says Livingstone's Chartist comrade, Keith Veness. 'McIntosh was down there with his minders and people were being offered all sorts of things to vote for him. We also had minders at County Hall. I was told to sit next to one GLC member called Simon Turney and keep an eye on him.'[25] As the rumours circulated, the *Evening Standard*'s County Hall reporter Mike King had heard Livingstone was about to oust McIntosh but he did not want to queer his pitch with the new administration, so the paper sent another journalist, Keith Dovkants, down to County Hall to confront Livingstone. Dovkants found Livingstone in his room and said, 'Ken, there's a rumour that you're going to do a putsch and that McIntosh is going to be booted out.'

'He was his usual evasive self,' says Dovkants. 'He wasn't quite as polished in those days but he was evasive and said, "We'll have to wait and see what happens." We certainly knew it was going to happen.'[26]

But Livingstone did trust a few journalists and had sat down shortly before the election with John Grigsby, the local government correspondent of the *Daily Telegraph*, and went through the numbers. 'He was really not a very organised man at that stage,' says Grigsby, 'but he sat down and he had a list of all the candidates and said "He's for me; he's against me; he's for me; he's against me" and so on down the list. And it appeared he was very accurate when the election came. And it was clear he had done a lot of work.'[27] As a result, the *Daily Telegraph* was able to make the acute observation: 'The triumph of the Left in London, already substantially accomplished in the boroughs and constituencies, will then be crowned in glory.'[28]

During the morning, Andrew McIntosh did a round of interviews for television and radio and even allowed himself to be photographed with Livingstone on the steps of County Hall. The photo shows both men smiling and a confident-looking McIntosh, hands thrust into his pockets. According to Livingstone's own calculations, 22 members were on the left and 18 on the right. Harvey Hinds and Illtyd Harrington worked hard to persuade eight of the 10 centrists to vote for Livingstone. The key event was the Left caucus meeting in Committee Room 166 at 3 p.m.

Mair Garside, the right-wing Labour member for Woolwich East, had not been invited to the 3 p.m. meeting and only realised that something was up while having lunch in the members' dining room with her back to the diners. Her friend asked, 'Do you have a meeting to go to?' Garside replied there was a Labour group meeting but that was not until 5 p.m. 'But the dining room is absolutely empty,' said her friend. Garside turned round. 'I saw it was absolutely true,' she said, 'everybody who had been in for lunch had gone and they had gone to the caucus meeting.'[29]

◆

'Caucusing' is frowned upon in political circles because it is a way for a significant minority to decide what line to take at meetings and organise to get their own way. Of course, this was absolutely what Ken Livingstone intended but it made a mockery of the official group meeting later that afternoon.

Paul Moore, who Livingstone had persuaded to run in Lambeth Central, says, 'There were 30 people there out of a total of 50. I was thinking, "Bloody hell!" Some of the people who were there weren't even left-wingers. Harvey Hinds was there; Illtyd Harrington was there so it was pretty obvious that something was going on and that people were jumping ship already.'[30] Dave Wetzel, who won Hammersmith North, says, 'That was McIntosh's mistake again because in the same way he wasn't talking to me, he couldn't have been talking to those other people.'[31] The group then decided which of them would get the senior posts in the administration. 'Ken for leader came up first,' remembers Wetzel, 'that went through on the nod. Next up was deputy leader – Illtyd Harrington was nominated. That was no contest. Then we went through every chairmanship and vice chairmanship.' By contrast, there was no comparable gathering by the members on the right. They had not organised as a group and had drawn up no lists for any senior position. McIntosh had told his supporters he would supply a list of nominations for the senior posts once he had been confirmed as leader.[32]

The 5 p.m. group meeting in room 143 was chaired by the former hard left MP for Paddington, Arthur Latham. George Page kept Foot's note in his pocket. Latham announced there were two leadership contenders. Livingstone won, as planned, by 30 votes to 20. There followed a vote for every committee chairmanship and vice chairmanship. McIntosh was out so there were no right-wing nominations. Again as planned, the Left's preferred candidate won. 'I sat there in total disbelief,' says Livingstone, 'and there were no other nominations. Arthur Latham, who was in the chair, called nominations, I would nominate someone. There would be deathly silence and we would move on to the next one.'[33] Within a few minutes, McIntosh's fate was sealed. 'It was a fait accompli,' says Margaret Morgan, a former right-wing GLC member. 'Those of us on the right had no opportunity. Whoever the Left decided, won. I think it was disgraceful because it denied a substantial minority of the group a say in who became leader or a committee chairman.'

Even though she had been aware of the plotting, Mair Garside insists she was stunned. 'We sat there and of course the first shock was Ken being elected instead of Andrew,' says Garside. 'I do remember the "shock-horror", there was no doubt about it. The other 15 or 20 of us were absolutely shocked.

'They then made a nomination for every single position. Ken told me later he thought we would have had our own nominations for posts but we didn't and as a consequence he ended up with people he'd rather he didn't have. But we just sat there, absolutely stunned. You may say we were an innocent bloody lot... I used to hear of caucuses, and although no one would ever believe me, I don't think I was ever a member of a caucus. But caucuses would be four or five people. A caucus which would have 30 well-disciplined people was something quite new.'[34]

Then there followed a limp attempt by the right to postpone a similar meeting planned the following day to decide the top jobs at the powerful semi-autonomous Inner London Education Authority (ILEA) to give them time to organise. Before the suggestion was rejected by Ken Livingstone and his cadres, there was a slight kerfuffle over new dates for the ILEA meeting. 'Don't bother about dates in your diary,' snarled Tony Banks, the new chairman of arts and recreation, at the right-wingers. 'You won't have anything in your diary!'[35] According to Illtyd Harrington, Andrew McIntosh left the room in tears and refused to talk to him because he considered him to be '...part of the conspiracy.' Harrington watched as McIntosh gathered up his books from the office and left by a back entrance.[36] 'Ken made no effort to mollify Andrew,' says Harrington, 'the left held to their guns and the right just gave in.'

Later that evening, Dave Bayliss, the GLC's chief transport planner, saw McIntosh and his wife standing in the car park, both 'in a state of great distress and in tears'. Bayliss asked what the matter was. McIntosh replied, 'That so and so Ken Livingstone has become the leader; there's just been a coup.'

'I found it a little bit surprising for an experienced politician [like McIntosh].' says Bayliss. 'These things happen in politics. But it was a tremendous shock for Andrew. I had a lot of time for Andrew; I thought he was a decent man. He was badly let down. I don't think he was surprised about Ken Livingstone because Ken was a very ambitious and determined individual, but I think what he was most upset about was that the people he counted on as friends had turned on him and let him down.'[37]

'People always laugh when I tell them this,' says Livingstone, 'but I really felt sorry for Andrew.'[38]

◆

All but five of the 29 who voted for Livingstone got senior positions. '...not a single person who voted for Andrew held a position,' wrote Livingstone later. 'That was a recipe for disaster.'[39] You can be too successful and Livingstone recognised this later. The overweening success of the purge proved gratuitous and counterproductive, leading sections of the press to treat the new left-wing administration as somehow disreputable. Livingstone wrote later that he wanted to appease the right-wingers by giving them some senior positions on the ILEA, whose members were made up mainly by new GLC members and therefore the Left. But the overall aggressive nature of the putsch intimidated the moderates at County Hall. Harvey Hinds estimated at the time that seven of the new GLC members were potential defectors to the Social Democratic Party, then at the height of its short-lived popularity. Had they defected Labour would have lost overall control of the

GLC. Some did go in the months following the takeover, but not enough to rob Livingstone of power. But Livingstone's alleged conciliation over the ILEA appears somewhat bogus. Following a 'celebratory piss-up'[40] to mark its victory, the Left staged a copy-cat coup in County Hall the following morning to take over the ILEA and its £700 million budget. Bryn Davies supplanted his highly-respected Labour colleague, Sir Ashley Bramall, as chairman of the ILEA. The right-winger Mair Garside was replaced as deputy chairman by Frances Morrell, another key left-winger. Among the three Left members to be co-opted on to this powerful body were Stephen Benn, Tony Benn's son who had failed to win the safe Tory seat of Chelsea, and Keith Veness who failed to be selected in Brent East.

Keith Veness accompanied Livingstone on a tour of County Hall shortly after the election. They were attended by several senior officers. Veness remembers Livingstone's irritation when he discovered that officers in the planning department were still working on contingency plans for sections of the wretched Motorway Box which he and many others thought had long been consigned to the dustbin of history by Goodwin. Veness says, 'Some arsehole had decided that it was best to keep people working on it as a contingency in case the Tories revived it, and there were all these people working on maps and compulsory purchase orders.' He remembers Livingstone telling a senior manager, 'Get them working on something else!'

Then the touring party came across a strange room, secured by a padlock and chain. Veness, who worked as a housing estate manager in Hackney, threatened to cut the chain open with the bolt croppers he carried around with him unless the door was opened. 'I'd already been told it was a Masonic temple,' says Veness. 'After all this humming and hawing, about 20 blokes turned up looking worried. Finally the door opened and they said, "There we are, sir, nothing to worry about." Then I saw a painting of this big eye and said, "What are we doing paying for a Masonic temple?" They said, "Well it's hardly ever used." So we turned it over to be a meeting room.'

Livingstone also started to tackle the traditional privileges of GLC members and senior officers. 'As each chauffeur left, we didn't replace them,' says Livingstone. 'A lot of the Left said, "There must be no free booze for the committee chairs," and that was one thing on which the centre bloc wasn't going to budge so that was one thing I had to concede on.' Livingstone told the Left, 'Look we get to run the GLC, you'll just have to live with the fact that we're going to have to buy in £1,000 worth of booze a year.'[41]

◆

'London's ours!' announced *London Labour Briefing*. 'After the most vicious GLC election of all time, the Labour Party has won a working majority on a radical socialist programme.' Writing in *Briefing*, Ken Livingstone added: 'We must ensure that we plan the way ahead rather than just respond to the government's attacks as they occur. Part of our task will be to sustain a holding operation until such time as the Tory government can be brought down and replaced by a left-wing Labour government.'[42] The triumphalism soon died. Over the next six months, the government, the judiciary, the Labour Party and the media would descend with all their power on Ken Livingstone. Far from bringing down the Tory government, he would spend the next five years struggling for his own political survival.

Notes

1   Interview, Illtyd Harrington, 4.7.07
2   Ibid.; *Camden New Journal*, obituary of Chris Downes, 27.11.03
3   Interview, Illtyd Harrington, 4.7.07
4   Interview, Lin Hinds, 15.8.07
5   Interview, Patricia Kirwan, 16.8.07
6   Ibid.
7   Ibid.
8   Interview, Ken Livingstone, 25.10.07
9   Interview, Ken Livingstone, 25.10.07
10 Ibid.
11 Interview, Bernard Brook-Partridge, 28.6.07
12 *The Times*, 14.3.81
13 *Guardian*, 8.4.81
14 Interview, Patricia Kirwan, 16.8.07
15 Met Office archives
16 *Guardian,* Results, 8.5.81
17 John Carvel, *Citizen Ken*, p16
18 Interview, Michael Foot, 15.7.07
19 Interview, Ken Livingstone, 25.10.07
20 Ken Livingstone, *If Voting Changed Anything, They'd Abolish It*, p136
21 Ibid.; John Carvel, *Citizen Ken*, p18
22 Interview, Ken Livingstone, 25.10.07
23 *The Times*, March 1980
24 Interview, Bryn Davies, 16.7.07

25 Interview, Keith Veness, 24.8.04
26 Interview, Keith Dovkants, 14.11.07
27 Interview, John Grigsby, 13.7.07
28 *Daily Telegraph*, 30.4.81
29 Interview, Mair Garside, 17.8.07
30 Interview, Paul Moore, 5.11.07
31 Interview, Dave Wetzel, 5.11.07
32 Author interviews
33 Interview, Ken Livingstone, 25.10.07
34 Interview, Mair Garside, 17.8.07
35 Interview, Margaret Morgan, 16.8.07
36 Interview, Illtyd Harrington, 4.7.07
37 Interview, Dave Bayliss, 10.7.07
38 Interview, Ken Livingstone, 25.10.07
39 Ken Livingstone, *If Voting Changed Anything, They'd Abolish It,* pp140-141
40 Interview, Keith Veness, 24.8.04
41 Interview, Ken Livingstone, 25.10.07
42 *London Labour Briefing*, article by Ken Livingstone, June 1981

Chapter 8

The Robespierre of Randolph Avenue, May–October 1981

Ken Livingstone's first six months as leader of the Greater London Council were so catastrophic that his reputation probably never really recovered from the intense battering it received in these first few months. By the end of 1981, the powerful and dark forces he had galvanised were not so much revolutionary left-wing with the power to smash Thatcher but vituperatively right-wing and hell-bent on getting rid of the Greater London Council and Ken Livingstone's gang with it. By the time of the coup, the Fleet Street press had declared war on the hard and far left. Tony Benn and 'Red Ted' Knight had long since been labelled as dangerous loony lefties bent on the destruction of everything the country stood for. Benn's challenge for the deputy leadership was seen widely as the defining moment in the battle against the great threat from the Left. But in May 1981, that contest would not be held until the Labour Party conference at the end of September, almost five months away. According to John Mortimer, the author and barrister, who interviewed him shortly after he took over the GLC, Livingstone was 'perhaps the first genuinely left-wing leader to achieve real power in England,' adding: 'He has entered into his kingdom long before his mentor Tony Benn, so he is the forerunner as well as the disciple, the Huxley to Benn's Darwin, the John the Baptist to Benn's... but the comparisons should go no further.'

Overnight, Ken Livingstone went from being an obscure local politician to being one of the best-known hate figures produced by Fleet Street for decades. On 8 May 1981, Margaret Thatcher reacted to the news of the coup. Speaking at the Scottish Conservative conference in Perth City Hall, she said, 'Others have more sinister ambitions. They have no time for parliamentary democracy. They look to the manipulators of the block vote: the tiny caucuses which plot and scheme to win power through apathy,' adding that the extremists' object was power and, 'power for one purpose only – to impose upon this nation a tyranny which the peoples of Eastern Europe yearn to cast aside.'[2]

Right-wing newspapers including the *Sun* and particularly the *Daily Mail* made the running immediately. On 9 May 1981, the *Mail* reported how 'a left-wing extremist was installed as leader of the Greater London Council'. The *Sun* described Livingstone as 'Red Ken' and the title stuck. Livingstone became so synonymous with his new Fleet Street handle that not long after becoming leader he was invited to open a new Sikh temple, the Shri Guru Ravidass, in Southall, west London. He pulled open the curtain to reveal the plaque which announced that the temple had been opened by 'Mr Red Ken Livingstone'. Virendra Sharma, an Ealing Labour councillor who was present at the ceremony, says, 'They thought it was the general term for him; it was innocently done. Ken saw the funny side of it. If he had taken it negatively he could have asked them to remove it. But it's still there and we laugh about it today.'[3] The paranoia spread even to the *Financial Times*, which stated: 'WARNING: If the Labour Left can pour out of a "moderate" Trojan Horse and capture London it might use the same tactic to capture Britain. If it does, and succeeds, the erosion of our democracy will surely begin. None of this need take place, but only a change of the rules necessarily initiated by the present government can make certain it does not.'[4]

The new intake at County Hall made no attempt to douse the flames. Steve Bundred, the new vice chairman of the Police Committee, had written: 'Our manifesto will bring us into direct conflict with the government. There's no doubt about that. The role of the GLC, in my view, will be to tackle the government head-on and lead the political struggle within London.'[5]

◆

On Monday, 11 May 1981, the first working day after the putsch, the 40,000 GLC and ILEA employees went about their business as usual. The bus and Tube drivers turned up for their shifts as did the workmen building the Thames Barrier. The teachers were there to ring the school bell and the road gangs arrived after their fry-ups and mugs of tea to dig up the roads. But something seismic had happened. The way in which the GLC was perceived had changed completely and that change of perception would kill it. There was a clear sense in press and government circles that there was something illegitimate about the new administration. Others

felt it too. Writing from Brasenose College in Oxford, the constitutional expert Vernon Bogdanor observed that Labour had
polled only 41.8 per cent of the vote, two per cent more than the
Tories, adding: 'The representation of the left and right factions
of the Labour Party in the GLC depends not upon the degree of
support for them amongst the electorate but upon the attitudes
of a small number of the majority of Labour voters. There is no
reason, therefore, to suppose that Mr Livingstone represents the
views of the majority of Labour voters.'[6]

Within a week of the putsch, the journalist Robin Pauley
observed that Livingstone 'may have made a crucial misjudgement
by giving so many committees to their [*sic*] own faction', adding,
'Mr Livingstone has ignored the lesson so well understood by Mr
James Callaghan and Sir Harold Wilson; tiny majorities require
the widest possible spread of jobs and responsibilities to hold
them together.'[7] In 1981, spin doctors had been heard about but
certainly had reached nowhere near the epidemic levels needed
to make an impact on public consciousness. The only thing that
stood between the wrath of Fleet Street and Ken Livingstone was
the press office of the GLC. It proved to be out of its depth.

In the early days, Livingstone was an unknown quantity and
it would be the newspaper feature writers, rather than the news
reporters and leader writers, who would lead the way in explaining him to a baffled nation. The tone was set by Max Hastings of
the *Evening Standard*. The press office[8] arranged for Hastings to
interview Ken Livingstone at his Paddington flat, 195 Randolph
Avenue in Maida Vale. In Hastings' article, Livingstone emerges
literally as the bedsit revolutionary. He even irons his own clothes
during the interview. Hastings set the scene: 'He is separated
from his wife and says that everything he owns is in the bedsit: a
portable snooker table, a tank of salamanders, a wardrobe, a bed,
a suitcase, a couple of chairs and a portable TV. He had spent the
afternoon doing his ironing, with which he persisted through the
early stages of our interview.'

With characteristic frankness, and not a little naivety,
Livingstone told Hastings that up until his successful leadership
bid, he had been subsisting on £70 a week. 'Last night,' reported
Hastings, 'he was talking on the telephone to a friend about the
prospect of drawing an additional £4,000 a year as leader, which
he hoped to achieve without arousing the ire of the puritans of

the Left.' It is hard to argue against Hastings' description of a man 'consumingly dedicated to politics. And to power'. Hastings was fair enough to point out Livingstone's affability but over-whelmingly the image he paints is of the ruthless and ascetic revolutionary clown, a character from a strange political ghost story essentially lacking in humanity. One senior Labour GLC member told Hastings that Livingstone was 'utterly ambitious, mean, ruthless, a brilliant organiser of caucuses'. Allegedly, when he split from his wife, Livingstone told a colleague: 'I don't need anybody. I can cope.' This colleague told Hastings: 'He's not interested in ordinary human relations – simply in getting to the top of the greasy pole.'[9]

'That one piece set the tone,' says Livingstone. 'Food and drink I've always liked, but Robespierre? Someone who eats a bowl of gruel and dies a virgin? You want to be Danton! No one in their right mind wants to be Robespierre.'[10]

Brian Silk of the *Daily Telegraph* elaborated on the theme a lit-tle later: 'The harsh realities of life confront Kenneth Livingstone soon after he crawls from under his pink patterned duvet in the simple bed-sitting room, which shakes every time a train passes on the Bakerloo line below.'[11] Silk dispenses much cool mockery as he talks about the £20 a week rent for Randolph Avenue and the lavatory shared with other tenants: 'To the neighbours he is the bizarre character who spends his free time searching the local terrain for slugs and woodlice to feed his seven pet lizards.' Like Hastings, he struggled to reconcile Livingstone's charm and openness with the circumstances of the coup and the Trotskyist company he kept. 'All that matters to him is his Socialist dream for London,' wrote Silk, 'and the power to make the dream a reality.'[12]

But when you scoured the piece for evidence of revolution, the only item that sprang to attention was a plan to reduce the cost of travel on the Tube. Silk was enough of a professional not to forget Livingstone's snooker table, 'which provides the central feature of the room'. Livingstone struck Silk as a solitary man: 'It is close to midnight when Livingstone comes up the steps at Maida Vale Station and stops to buy a bag of chips on the way to his room and his seven cold-blooded friends.'

If Brian Silk or Max Hastings had called on Livingstone a year earlier, they would not have found him in his grotty bedsit but the flat he shared with his wife Christine Chapman in Lymington Road, West Hampstead. Hastings may then have observed a scene of innocuous domesticity. Livingstone could have shown Hastings the pond he had built for his newts. Livingstone had separated from Christine Chapman in September 1980 and he moved out of their home, taking his reptiles with him; the couple tried to remain on amicable terms.[13] 'I got the salamanders,' says Livingstone, 'and Christine got the flat.'[14] She had reverted to her maiden name because she was 'fed up with living in Ken's shadow',[15] and was reported to say the split happened because 'Ken was never, ever, at home'.[16] Clearly ambition and the coup had taken its toll on the marriage. She told reporters that the pressure of work was to blame. The couple tried to resolve their differences during a holiday to Hong Kong, Bangkok and Canton in August 1981.[17] He had moved out of their home and into the flat in Randolph Avenue.

In October 1982, Livingstone would be divorced on the grounds of his adultery with an attractive brunette called Kate Allen, who worked as a policy officer with the GLC and became a long-serving Labour member on Camden Council; she would one day be the director of Amnesty International UK. More details about the break-up were given later by Livingstone's mother Ethel in the interview she gave for the magazine *Woman*. 'I liked Chris a lot,' she said. 'But I knew it would never last. I compared them to me and Bob and they argued too much.'[18]

The *Sun*, under the editorship of the aggressive maverick Kelvin MacKenzie, was fascinated by Livingstone and established a reporting team to dig up the dirt. According to the writers Peter Chippindale and Chris Horrie, 'A minute scrutiny of his lifestyle for clues to deviancy disappointingly revealed only that he kept newts and lived extremely modestly.'[19] 'Fucking newts!' MacKenzie raged at his hit squad. 'All you can find is newts?'[20] The team was sent out again but 'Red Ken's private life was relentlessly dull'. Like the rest of Fleet Street, the *Sun* found what it was looking for in Livingstone's public statements and activities.[21]

◆

Ken Livingstone did little to dampen the flames of paranoia which had broken out in newsrooms up and down Fleet Street. Every statement and action in those early days was seen as a provocation. Before long, Livingstone's honesty, integrity and even sanity would be issues for public debate. One of his first acts was to turn down an invitation to the Royal wedding of Prince Charles and Lady Diana Spencer at Westminster Abbey on 29 July 1981. Livingstone insisted that it was not a deliberate insult but simply a decision 'to pull back from ceremonial functions in order to concentrate on the work for which the group had been elected'. Livingstone wished the couple a happy life and said the Labour group would dispatch a gift, a £250 painting[22] already bought by the previous Tory administration, adding: 'I would like politely to reply and decline the offer and I hope that the ticket can go to someone happier in that sort of setting.' The Tories failed by 42 votes to 38 to compel Livingstone's acceptance. The Liberal member Adrian Slade described it as a 'petty and political decision'. Two Labour members abstained.[23] But, Livingstone would insist: 'No one has elected us to go to weddings. We were elected to run the buses.'[24] But he never confined himself strictly to the business of running County Hall and made frequent forays into controversial issues over which the GLC had no jurisdiction, a key factor in hastening if not necessitating its abolition.

On Saturday, 28 May, Livingstone was on the outskirts of north London to welcome the 500-strong People's March for Jobs, protestors against rising unemployment who had set off from Liverpool, Llanelli and Huddersfield 28 days earlier. The GLC's emergency civil defence camp beds were brought out of storage and the marchers were put up at County Hall for two nights with food and drink thrown in at a cost of £19,000.[25]

Not for the last time, Livingstone had to contend with the tight laws forbidding the use of taxpayers' money for overtly political campaigns. Agreement for the use of County Hall for the marchers had to be confirmed properly by an authorised GLC committee, but officers blocked Livingstone's desire to give GLC and ILEA employees, including teachers, the day off to attend the final rally at County Hall on 1 June. Maurice Stonefrost, comptroller general in charge of the GLC's finances, said the decision would be unreasonable in law because it meant closing down schools and other public services. There were heated exchanges. And Livingstone was forced to back down.

Revenge was swift. Stonefrost received an order from Livingstone requisitioning his palatial office as sleeping quarters for some of the marchers. Stonefrost left behind fresh towels and crates of Newcastle Brown Ale and returned to work after the weekend to find the office spick and span with a thank-you note and an invitation to attend a Durham miners' rally later that year.[26]

The ambiance at County Hall changed dramatically following Livingstone's takeover. It swiftly became known as 'the People's Palace'.[27] Now it seemed any old Tom, Dick and Harry could get on to the members' floor. Gone were the avuncular certainties of past years and in came the insecurities brought by media and government hostility. As the second most important official at the GLC, Maurice Stonefrost experienced the change immediately. 'Whereas before you might have had a one-to-one meeting with somebody,' says Stonefrost, 'there now tended to be about 30 or 40 people in the room at any one time, most of whom you didn't know and who weren't even on the council. There were very large meetings and lots of note-taking and lots of people watching each others' backs.'[28]

There was shock at one committee meeting when a GLC member plonked her baby on the table during a debate and started to change his nappy. When another brought her baby into the plush surroundings of the GLC chamber at a council discussion, David Avery, the Tory GLC member for Westminster and the City of London, proposed that 'it be removed'. 'All hell broke out,' remembers Stonefrost.[29] Illtyd Harrington, a member of the GLC since its inception in 1964, also witnessed the changes. The GLC had always been like a 'Rolls Royce engine' but after the putsch, standards went down. 'When the rebels arrived,' remembers Harrington, 'they were the rag tag and bobtail of this world! Meetings didn't start on time. There wasn't much discipline in some of the meetings. The old Herbert Morrisonian traditions were no longer observed.'[30]

◆

The new GLC administration under Livingstone looked across the Thames at the leadership of Michael Foot and had nothing but contempt for the loyal opposition he led. Harrington says, 'They really believed at one stage that they were the end of Thatcherism and they saw themselves with some justification as the coherent political opposition in the country.'[31]

Valerie Wise, one of Livingstone's inner coterie, says, 'We were the opposition to Thatcher. Labour was absolutely inept in Parliament at doing anything and of course, we were there right opposite. We couldn't have been better located, could we!? What a great thing to do – to put the unemployment figures right opposite Parliament! We thought we could bring down Thatcher, but of course, we learned she's got more power as prime minister.'[32] The contrast between Livingstone's domestic arrangements and his working conditions could not be starker. He now occupied a vast office on the principal floor and in an adjoining room were several secretaries tackling an ever increasing correspondence. Most of the junior or senior people who have worked for Livingstone either at the GLC or as mayor of London say he is an excellent boss: a good delegator, decisive and supportive as well as being a friendly and modest colleague.

A former GLC secretary remembers his sense of fun and love of animals. She says, 'Ken offered pretty girls – like me at the time – chocolates out of a lovely large chocolate box and when you put your hand in there was a salamander! Once he chewed food for starving chicks in Africa, which had been orphaned, so that they would not die. Unfortunately, he got terrible indigestion as a result. He once suffered a whole day with twin kittens in his office, because my cat Doughnut had given birth again, and one of his secretaries wanted a couple. All visitors were greeted with mewing and a pretty oppressive smell.'[33] Livingstone could often be seen lolloping along the corridors of County Hall in what *Time Out* once described as his 'distinctive apelike stride... permanently surrounded by an entourage of aides, hacks and sycophants'.[34]

◆

The manifesto drawn up by the Greater London Labour Party, and influenced as much by Andrew McIntosh as Ken Livingstone, promised London Underground fare reductions and job creation schemes. The Greater London Enterprise Board, or GLEB, was established to invest in schemes which would get thousands of people back to work. But in those first critical months, Livingstone and his administration would be sucked into the mire on issues for which the GLC had never held any responsibility.

Elsewhere in England, the funding and priorities of police services, or police forces as they were known, were the responsibilities of local authorities. But in London, the Metropolitan Police was considered too important to be anything but the responsibility of the home secretary. Livingstone's manifesto demanded that the Met be brought under the control of the GLC. In July 1981, Livingstone established a Police Committee to monitor the activities of the Met. Other left-wing Labour councils in London, also concerned at the activities and what they were convinced were the blatant racist attitudes of the police, followed suit. The appointment of Paul Boateng to chair the new committee outraged the *Daily Telegraph* which spluttered that Livingstone 'had appointed a black man to chair the Police Committee'.[35]

In 1999, an inquiry by a retired High Court judge called Sir William Macpherson would allege that the Metropolitan Police Service suffered from 'institutional racism,' but in 1981, it was considered disgraceful for politicians to criticise the police. The Police Committee first met on 13 July 1981, as did the new Ethnic Minorities Committee under the chairmanship of Ken Livingstone.[36] At the inaugural Police Committee meeting, Boateng was conciliatory and insisted that he did not see his job as 'knocking the police'.[37] But by then Livingstone had already upset the applecart. Three days earlier, on 10 July 1981, Livingstone stood in Brixton beside Ted Knight, the Lambeth Council leader and an old comrade, and launched a vitriolic attack on the Met. He blamed the police for exacerbating the problems which caused the Brixton riots in April 1981 and alleged that Lambeth's police had a 'reputation for violence' describing the Special Patrol Group, a highly controversial police squad set up to deal with disorder, as a 'Clint Eastwood gung-ho, World War Two elite'.[38]

Gaining less attention were Livingstone's remarks largely blaming the disorder on 'the inevitable consequences of government-induced mass unemployment'.[39] Lord Scarman who chaired the government inquiry also identified social and economic problems, as well as 'racial disadvantage,' but did not call for the resignation of the Metropolitan Police commissioner, Sir Kenneth Newman. But Ken Livingstone and 20 other GLC members did demand Newman's resignation. Twenty-six years later, Mayor Livingstone would defend the commissioner, Sir Ian Blair, against calls for his resignation in the wake of the inquiries into the killing by the police of the innocent electrician Jean Charles de Menezes. His argument for defending Blair was that it would set a bad precedent. It was not something which appears to have concerned him in 1981.

◆

Occasionally, Livingstone's outpourings were greeted more with disbelief than fury. But in particular his views on Northern Ireland would cause the most disgust. When Livingstone took power in May 1981, few people could look forward to May 2007 and predict that former arch-enemies Ian Paisley, leader of the Democratic Unionists, and Martin McGuiness, of Sinn Féin, would sit side by side at Stormont Castle as first and deputy first ministers of the Northern Ireland Assembly while peace took root across Ulster. The default position of most of the British press was to express outrage, mainly at atrocities committed by republican paramilitaries in the Provisional IRA and the Irish National Liberation Army, the INLA, and its belief that British troops were helping to prevent an all-out civil war breaking out between the two communities. The Thatcher government's public position was not to negotiate with terrorists. On the hard left, there was widespread sympathy for the republican movement and the belief that the British Army, supported by the Unionist community and the Royal Ulster Constabulary, was an imperialist occupying force. One new long-haired Labour left-wing member of the GLC, Stephen Bundred, was a key figure in the Troops Out campaign with strong links to Sinn Féin leaders like Danny Morrison.[40]

By May 1981, tensions were running extremely high in Northern Ireland. On 5 May, three days before the Livingstone coup the republican prisoner Bobby Sands died in the H-Block of the Maze prison at Long Kesh outside Belfast after a hunger strike lasting 66 days. Riots broke out in Northern Ireland and 100,000 people attended Sands' funeral. Nine other republicans would starve themselves to death during the spring and summer of 1981, a turbulent and fetid period in Ireland and on the streets of Brixton, Toxteth and Handsworth. On 13 June, Livingstone addressed a rally at the start of a demonstration organised by the London branch of the H-Block/Armagh Committee with relatives of the H-Block hunger strikers. On 21 July 1981, he stood on the steps of County Hall to welcome Alice McElwee, the mother of 23-year-old Thomas McElwee, a H-Block prisoner who would die of starvation 18 days later on 8 August. Thomas McElwee was convicted for a firebomb attack on a shop in a small town in County Antrim called Ballymena, in which a 27-year-old woman,

Yvonne Dunlop, burned to death in front of her nine-year-old son, Geoffrey.

In a speech, Livingstone said: 'The H-block protest is part of the struggle to bring about a free united Ireland. They have my support and the support of the majority of the Labour Party rank and file.'[41] Condemnation came from all sides. An opinion piece in the *Sun* stated: 'The British troops went to Ulster to protect the Catholics and cannot leave without risking an unparalleled bloodbath,' adding: 'In his brief spell on the stage, the insufferable Mr Livingstone has proved himself a menace to stability in public life.'[42] According to the journalist Mark Hollingsworth, some Labour GLC members believed that Livingstone's views had become 'diversions from the GLC's mainstream policies'. At a meeting of the Labour group on 27 July, the minutes show there was a discussion about 'public relations' and the cryptic comment that 'the group had a responsibility to the party to show that the programme on which all are agreed can be put into practice and made to work.'[43]

On 29 July, the day of the Royal wedding, Livingstone released black balloons over the city as the couple travelled along their route to St Paul's Cathedral. At the same time, County Hall was the scene of a sponsored fast in support of the hunger strikers by about 20 teenagers holding banners declaring 'Royalty is celebrating – Irish prisoners are dying.'[44] It became increasingly clear that the Labour Party's national leadership was becoming fed up with what it believed was a vote-losing stream of verbal diarrhoea. When Livingstone urged Labour MPs to disrupt Parliament to block local government legislation, it was a bridge too far for Stanley Clinton Davis MP, Labour's trade spokesman, who said that 'his infantile leftism was making him a recruiting sergeant for the Social Democrats'.[45] Clinton Davis was merely expressing the party's growing concern at the negative electoral impact Livingstone had started to make.

Livingstone's welcome for the hunger strikers backfired with an astonishing counter stunt. On 21 August 1981, exactly one month after Alice McElwee had been greeted by Ken Livingstone, a sad little delegation from Ballymena arrived at County Hall: the three sons of Yvonne Dunlop, the woman murdered by Alice McElwee's son. The Dunlop sons, Denis, aged 13, Terry, 12 and Geoffrey, the nine-year-old boy who had watched his mother burn to death in Thomas McElwee's firebombing, were accompanied by their grandfather, Stanley Spence, who happened to be the mayor of Ballymena. The boys became political footballs. When the Tory chief whip, Geoffrey Seaton, heard that Livingstone was to send a delegation to greet the boys at Victoria Station, he dispatched his colleague Joan Wykes to intercept them at Gatwick Airport and, after a trip on a boat down the Thames, bring them to County Hall for lunch. Wykes says, 'Livingstone had got wind of the fact that the press was gathering around and said he wanted the boys to go and meet him. The boys sadly didn't eat any lunch because they were so nervous about meeting Livingstone. Livingstone was out there on the veranda of the dining room with the press.'[46]

With breathtaking aplomb, Livingstone agreed to pose for pictures with the three boys and gave them a hug. There were heart-rending scenes as the children broke down in tears during the photo call; Livingstone told the Unionist politicians, including Stanley Spence, who accompanied the delegation that they should not have raised the issue of the mother's death in front of the boys. But Denis Dunlop, the eldest boy, told the media: 'We have just come to show Mr Livingstone how we are left without a mum. The hunger strikers have a choice, but my mum did not.'[47] Livingstone 'deplored' every death in Northern Ireland but, according to the Guardian, specifically refused to condemn the actions of the IRA. The paper quoted him as saying, 'I am not going to condemn violence only by one section of the community.'[48] But he was clearly furious at being dragged into a tasteless political game.

Afterwards, Wykes took the boys to Hamleys toy shop for the afternoon and then back to County Hall for tea in the members' room so they could watch the television news report of the visit. Wykes says, 'We had one programme on because we heard the boys were going to be on that station. Livingstone walked in, ignored the grandparents, the boys and just switched over to another channel without so much as a "by your leave" or "excuse me", sat down and watched it and when it was over, he walked out and ignored them all again.'[49] The following day, Wykes took the boys on a trip to HMS Belfast and St Paul's Cathedral where the wedding decorations were still up. In Trafalgar Square, the woman selling pigeon seed organised a quick whip round and gave each of them £5. 'We took the family back to Victoria Station,' says Wykes, 'and they were so thrilled that London was on their side and they had such a good reception and I thought, well, eat your heart out, Livingstone!'[50]

◆

Also that August, a poll for Capital Radio revealed 54 per cent of the people interviewed thought that Ken Livingstone was a disaster and only 24 per cent would vote Labour, 18 per cent less than it polled in May.[51] In an astonishing piece of character assassination, the *Daily Mail* interviewed three psychologists to assess Livingstone's mental state. Dr Robert Shields opined, 'When he makes his extreme iconoclastic comments on bisexuality or politics, it is his way of saying "I'm not like my father or my mother". There is a tendency for people who feel they have not made their mark competitively in adolescence to become aggressive in attitude and become extremist.' An anonymous woman psychologist concurred with her learned friend, 'He certainly appears to have all the determination to be a fanatic.' A third psychologist continued in a similar vein.[52]

According to the journalist Mark Hollingsworth, one psychologist who refused to cooperate did the decent thing and wrote to the *Daily Mail*'s editor, Sir David English, to dissuade him from running the piece. Dr Frank McPherson, chairman of the British Psychological Society, said no reputable psychologist would participate in such a project. The paper ran the article. A complaint made by a freelance journalist about the *Mail* to the Press Council was rejected.[53]

By the end of August, rumours circulated of a plot to mount an internal coup against Livingstone. The *Sunday Times* claimed that party officials 'are seriously worried by Labour's poor showing in recent London council by-elections'.[54] The nameless officials were concerned about losing more council seats in future polls 'and a main cause, they believe, is Livingstone'. The paper added that he 'would have to fend off challenges from every quarter'. A dozen Labour moderates on the GLC, including the spurned McIntosh, were holding weekly meetings to discuss tactics. Even Steve Bundred, a left-winger, expressed concern at Livingstone's 'peripatetic punditry', and said that 'a more reflective style is needed'.[55] After only four months in power, Ken Livingstone was in danger of returning to the obscurity which had cloaked his ascent.

Notes

1   *Sunday Times*, the John Mortimer interview, 19.7.81
2   Speech by Margaret Thatcher to Scottish Conservative conference, 8.5.81, Thatcher Archive: CCOPR 413/81
3   Interview, Virendra Sharma MP, 28.11.07
4   *Financial Times*, 'Now is the time to change the rules', 13.5.81
5   *Socialist Organiser*, 'How the left won North Islington', by Steve Bundred, 4.4.81
6   *The Times*, letter by Vernon Bogdanor, 15.5.81
7   *Financial Times*, Robin Pauley, 15.5.81
8   Interview, Ken Livingstone, 25.10.07
9   *Evening Standard*, 'I see no tanks, Mr Livingstone', May 1981
10 Interview, Ken Livingstone, 25.10.07
11 *Daily Telegraph*, 'Bed-sitter vision of the Socialists' Mr London', by Brian Silk, 15.6.81
12 Ibid.
13 Interview, Ken Livingstone, 25.10.07
14 Interview, Ken Livingstone, 26.11.07
15 *Evening Standard*, 30.7.81
16 Ibid.
17 John Carvel, *Citizen Ken*, p91
18 *Woman*, 23.11.85
19 Peter Chippindale and Chris Horrie, *Stick It Up Your Punter, The Rise And Fall of the 'Sun'*, Mandarin Paperbacks, 1992, p131
20 Ibid.
21 Ibid.
22 *The Times*, 20.5.81
23 *The Times*, 29.5.81
24 *The Times*, 30.7.81
25 Ibid.
26 Interview, Maurice Stonefrost, 21.11.07
27 *Guardian*, 30.7.81
28 Interview, Maurice Stonefrost, 21.11.07
29 Ibid.
30 Ibid.
31 Interview, Illtyd Harrington, 4.7.07
32 Interview, Valerie Wise, 21.7.07
33 Interview, 24.7.07
34 *Time Out*, 'In the Public Interest', by David Rose, 22.1.82
35 *Daily Telegraph*, 27.5.81
36 *Guardian*, 14.7.81
37 Ibid.
38 *Evening Standard*, 17.7.81
39 Ibid.
40 Interview, Danny Morrison, 19.7.07
41 *Daily Telegraph*, 22.7.81
42 *Sun*, 23.7.81

43 Mark Hollingsworth, *The Press and Political Dissent: A Question of Censorship*, Pluto Press, 1986, pp80-81
44 Author interviews and *Daily Telegraph*, 29.7.81
45 *Guardian*, 31.7.81
46 Interview, Joan Wykes, 26.6.07
47 *The Times*, 22.8.81
48 Ibid.
49 Interview, Joan Wykes, 26.6.07
50 Ibid.
51 *Daily Mail*, 12.8.07
52 *Daily Mail*, 20.8.81
53 Mark Hollingsworth, *The Press and Political Dissent: A Question of Censorship*, pp81-83
54 *Sunday Times*, 30.8.81
55 Ibid.

Chapter 9

Get Leninspart! October 1981–May 1982

The one person who could have destroyed Ken Livingstone with a few public words was the Labour leader Michael Foot, as his successor Neil Kinnock would one day do so brutally to the Militant Liverpool councillors. Foot himself effectively ended the political career of Peter Tatchell, the left-wing parliamentary candidate for Bermondsey, with a few choice words in the House of Commons in December 1981, but with Livingstone, he stayed his hand.[1]

Livingstone never knew that he had a mystery benefactor who persuaded Foot to be tolerant and merciful. In 1981, Una Cooze was a 51-year-old Trot with 'very strong socialist principles', a member of the Westminster Labour Party and a cat lover, with two cats, including one named after the communist Rosa Luxemburg.[2] She was also Michael Foot's secretary and was described by Foot in an interview for this book as 'one of the closest friends I ever had in my life'.[3] To Foot's biographer, Kenneth O. Morgan, she was not only 'endlessly loyal' to Foot but also 'Michael's conscience'.[4]

Michael Foot says, 'All the way through that time, Una was putting Ken's case well and I came round to supporting Ken later very largely because of her influence which I trusted throughout and which I still trust, by the way.

'She was a really wonderful supporter of Ken and it was his kind of socialist ideas which she liked best. She was herself a very strong left-wing socialist; you might call her a Trotskyite. She understood what was happening. Una kept me informed about what was happening at County Hall.'[5] Cooze did not entirely prevent Foot lashing out at Livingstone in those early months, particularly after disastrous London by-elections.[6] But she clearly did temper his reaction, despite the growing anger in the Labour Party over Livingstone's behaviour. The GLC was the last thing the Labour movement needed while it was tearing itself apart over the Benn deputy leadership challenge. When commentators and politicians talked about 'the London Effect' on the electoral chances of the Labour Party, they were talking about something negative and the names always mentioned were Ken Livingstone and Ted Knight.

A few did see the funny side. For *Private Eye*, Livingstone provided a rich seam of satire. He swiftly became Ken Leninspart, whose daily routine went as follows: '09.30: Get up, feed newts, read Council minutes; 10.30: Cycle to work; 11.00: Attend meeting of Labour group to discuss tactics vis-à-vis "the right to work" sit-in which all GLC employees will be paid to take part in on 3 August; 13.00: visit to squat in Camden as gesture of solidarity with London's growing army of 8 million homeless.' The day culminated at 5 p.m. when he cycled home 'to feed newts, study agenda prior to tomorrow's vital General Purposes Committee to allocate £20 million for building special bus shelters for disabled gays.'[7]

◆

John Mortimer, on assignment with the *Sunday Times*, also struggled to get worked up into too much of a lather over the latest red menace, particularly after being told by Livingstone: 'For the first time we've got an army trained to subdue a civilian population, and the whole of the serious Left could be executed in half a day. Who knows what's going to happen in a year or two?

'We could have a radical socialist government under attack from the army or the police like in Spain or Chile. Or it might be the banks. That's one of the reasons why the police must be answerable to us.'

Over the next few years, Livingstone would repeatedly express his fears of a military coup. It played well with those on the hard and far left, and it was this fear which transmogrified into the novel published in 1982, Chris Mullin's *A Very British Coup*, which depicted the sabotage of a left-wing Labour government by the security services. But the idea that *Coronation Street* would be interrupted one day by the chief of the defence staff in full uniform announcing the arrest of Benn, Livingstone, Knight and so on struck Mortimer, and many others, as plain potty.

Mortimer had a sudden vision of the left-wing MP for Liverpool Walton, Eric Heffer, 'being led blindfold to the wall,' or the newly appointed Met commissioner Sir David McNee 'forming an unholy alliance with NatWest to take over the BBC'.[8] Mortimer recognised that 'Livingstone's coup has, on the face of it, and once you've forgotten about the firing squads in Whitehall, fairly modest aims'.

◆

With most of the press attention focused on Livingstone as the 'chief people's commissar', it was easy to ignore the new left-wing inner circle, many of whom were extraordinary people in their own right and who operated with considerable freedom from Livingstone. He later described his crew as 'a farmyard of bizarre personalities' and often claimed that no 'loner' could have assembled them and kept them together for so long.[9]

Illtyd Harrington and Harvey Hinds had cut a deal to remain deputy leader and chief whip. Both men were close to 60 but most of Livingstone's powerful new comrades were in their thirties and forties, symbolising the ascension of a new generation.

John McDonnell was an intense and wiry hard left-winger representing the Hayes and Harlington constituency on the western extremity of London. McDonnell was the son of Irish immigrants; his mother was a shopkeeper and his father, a bus driver and former docker.[10] At the time of his election to the GLC, he was an official for the National Union of Mineworkers. He would later become the MP for Hayes and Harlington and in 2007, following the resignation of Tony Blair, he failed to get enough support to field himself as the Left's candidate for the Labour leadership.[11] He struck many of his colleagues as serious and doctrinaire. He described himself as a 'fairly hardnosed administrator'.[12] McDonnell became finance chairman and was in regular contact with Maurice Stonefrost, who remembers very little small talk or many social exchanges.[13] Livingstone was thought to be in awe of McDonnell, according to his former GLC colleagues.[14] The two men were close until a cataclysmic falling out in 1985.

Paul Boateng was a solicitor and Methodist lay preacher of mixed Ghanaian and Scottish parentage. Boateng later became the first black man to sit in a British cabinet as chief secretary to the Treasury before going on to become the high commissioner to South Africa.[15] His Police Committee monitored the Met, and repeatedly attacked it for racism and lack of accountability.

As chairman of arts and recreation, Tony Banks was determined to take the ideological battle to the arts by switching resources from centres of cultural excellence and elitism including the National Ballet to street theatres and community arts events.

He wanted to cut funding to the National Theatre, the Royal Opera House in Covent Garden and the English National Opera. He thought few Londoners liked ballet and the opera or could not afford them if they did, so why should they pay to support them? He thought orchestras should get off their trombones and double bases and perform for the workers at Ford in Dagenham. The new commissars did prefer 'steel bands in Woolwich to Donizetti in Bow Street'.[16] The *Financial Times* reported: 'The problem with the Banks approach is that he sees the arts serving his constituency.

'He does not believe that the arts can be separated from politics. He would reckon he would be falling down on his job if every decision he makes was not a political decision.'[17]

The putschists had planned for Banks to chair the Transport Committee but he decided against it at the last moment on the grounds that it would be too time-consuming so the job went almost by default to Dave Wetzel. Over the years, Wetzel did various jobs after training as an electrical engineer, including making tools for Wilkinson's Sword. But he was best known for having followed his father on to the London buses to become first a conductor and then a driver. For years, he maintained a necessarily discreet collection of old bus tickets and was passionate about Esperanto,[18] an invented language which no country had adopted or was ever likely to. With his trademark mutton chop sideburns and his habit of signing off letters 'Yours in socialism', Wetzel was one of the most colourful and enduring of Livingstone's comrades. His deputy in charge of the GLC's roads and public transport was Paul Moore, Livingstone's old friend from Lambeth and the Chartists. Moore, a cheerful and reflective man, worked as a telephone engineer and a union official.

Another important figure in Livingstone's firmament was Frances Morrell, a newcomer to the GLC and already elected by her peers to be deputy chairman of the ILEA. A tall Amazonian woman, Morrell had impeccable left-wing credentials. For years, she had acted as Tony Benn's political advisor and was a key figure in both the Campaign for Labour Party Democracy and Benn's own struggle for power. A ruthless political operator, Morrell would replace as chairman Bryn Davies, another left-winger and a former Lambeth councillor, two years later. Livingstone could not stand her.[19]

At 25, Valerie Wise was the youngest of Livingstone's inner circle and one of the most influential. She was married to an optician, and in Illtyd Harrington's eyes 'nothing could be blander than that'.[20] She wore huge glasses and was considered by some to be rather earnest and serious. Her mother Audrey Wise, a close associate of Tony Benn, guaranteed Wise a seat at the Left's top table. 'She became known as Val,' says Harrington. 'Now she was a "Valerie"; she was never a "Val". She would sit there for hours gazing at Ken and looking at me as if I was Eliza Doolittle's father. I would occasionally get a wintry smile out of her.' She spoke with a warm Lancashire accent and despite perceptions, she could laugh at herself. Livingstone could always rely on her to dress up in funny costumes for his many publicity stunts. She would be put in charge of the GLC's most controversial new body, the Women's Committee and its support group, the Women's Unit. Livingstone himself would chair the new ethnic minorities sub-committee which mainly handed out grants to bodies representing London's many diverse communities.

The manifesto was built around a desire to redistribute wealth from rich Londoners to poor Londoners, whether by using rate-payers' money to cut the cost of Tube travel and school dinners or by giving grants to groups representing minorities and the poorer London boroughs.

The GLC was a 'precepting authority' which meant the unpopular job of collecting the money it needed fell on the lower tier of 32 London borough councils and they mainly drew the flak for higher bills. A quarter of the GLC's revenue was collected by the country's richest council, the Tory-controlled City of Westminster, which would later campaign the hardest for the abolition of the GLC.

◆

In 1973, Reg Goodwin's administration had been blown off course by the oil crisis; Livingstone's was blown off course just as quickly, partly by his behaviour and the antagonism caused by his policies. Whatever the long-term achievements of Livingstone's administration, there is no question that its aggression towards the government and the Establishment ultimately spelled doom for the GLC. In the eyes of the government and the media, Livingstone started badly and got worse. Within eight months, he was in deep crisis and within two years, Margaret Thatcher started the wheels in motion for abolition. Such was the backlash by judges, civil servants, politicians and journalists that Livingstone failed not only in the key objective of bringing down Thatcher but also in implementing many of his policies. It would lay Livingstone open to the allegation that he had laid the GLC at the sacrificial altar of his ambition.

For senior officers and those on the right, Livingstone's decision to post the latest unemployment figures on County Hall directly opposite the Houses of Parliament for everyone to see proved a persistent irritation. 'That undoubtedly antagonised the government,' says the former director general of the GLC, Maurice Stonefrost. 'You could imagine Margaret Thatcher being out on the veranda of the Commons opposite with President Mitterrand and looking across the river furiously at the latest unemployment banner.'[21]

But rising unemployment was the greatest social scandal during the years of Livingstone's GLC, rising to more than three million. In May 1979, when Thatcher came to power, there were 132,000 registered unemployed in Greater London. By September 1982, this figure had trebled to 390,107. One in six people were unemployed in inner London; in Stepney in east London, the figure was one in three.[22] The decision to post the figures on County Hall was taken by Livingstone after receiving a letter suggesting the idea arrived from the Ealing Trades Council.[23] Livingstone's only regret was that he did not go for the more expensive electronic version to allow the figures to be updated on an hourly basis. 'At that stage I was trying to keep the rates down so I went for the cheaper option and thereafter regretted it,' says Livingstone. 'You could have had lots of cheeky messages aimed at the House of Commons.'[24]

But the Left started to suffer a series of defeats shortly after gaining power from a combination of forces. With a majority of only six, the disenfranchised dozen or so right-wing Labour GLC members were able to check some of Livingstone's 'excesses'. Tony Banks failed to convince the GLC, which he imagined the Left now controlled, to deprive the privileged of funding for their favoured institutions; the right-wing GLC Labour members combined forces with the Tories to defeat his proposal to withhold £575,000 promised to the Covent Garden re-building fund. According to *Private Eye*, Banks was furious, turning on two of the moderate female GLC members who had voted against him with the words: 'You pair of fucking bitches!'[25] One was Anne Sofer who resigned from Labour and her St Pancras North seat shortly afterwards.[26] She stood successfully in the ensuing by-election for the Social Democratic Party (SDP) cutting Livingstone's majority by eight to six.

◆

In July 1981, the left-wingers controlling the ILEA failed to implement a manifesto commitment to cut the cost of school meals. According to *London Labour Briefing*, 'a rat bag of right-wing defectors were to blame'. 'A shameful day for London Labour,' declared *Briefing* under the headline 'SCHOOL MEALS SELL-OUT'.[27] The right-wing Labour members collapsed through fear of surcharge by the district auditor. One member, Gladys Dimson, said, 'But my husband owns half a house. He shouldn't have to live under the stress and strain of the district auditor threatening to take this away!'[28] Another ILEA and GLC member, Charlie Rossi, the thickset left-wing rat catcher from Camden, replied, 'Then you should bloody well resign!' Frances Morrell, the ILEA deputy chair, asked, 'Who rules – the electors or the judges?'[29]

The answer to Morrell's question would be given emphatically at the end of the year by three elderly judges in what would be a devastating reverse for Livingstone's administration. Throughout the plot to takeover the GLC, Livingstone had been the party's transport spokesman and instrumental in composing the radical new 'Fares Fair' policy. The manifesto promised cuts in the price of travel on the Underground of between 25 and 32 per cent. 'Clearly fares cuts will be the major issue,' stated Livingstone, adding, 'we must negotiate wages and conditions of LT [London Transport] staff in order to get more use from the existing bus and Tube stock in order to provide the extra capacity needed when fares are cut.'[30]

But there was a catch; Livingstone, his comrades and senior officials had overlooked an obscure clause in the 1969 Transport (London) Act, the Act of Parliament which laid down the rules of how the GLC should run the London Underground.

The Act stipulated that the GLC had the power to make grants for the Tube through its executive 'for any purpose'. But Section 7.3 of the Act stated that the GLC – through the London Transport

Executive – had a duty to ensure that the Tube would 'break even' as far as possible. The Section would prove Livingstone's Achilles' heel.

Thirteen years previously on 17 December 1968, Richard Marsh, the Labour transport minister, told the House of Commons that the most significant thing about the new Act was 'the new financial and service obligations which will be placed on the executive,' adding, '…the overriding duty will be the financial onus to break even and to meet financial objectives.' Later, in March 1969, Marsh said grants could be used to subsidise a particular loss-making service 'where the cost of closing might be considerably higher'.[31] After all, the simple fact remained: the London Underground had run at a loss since 1973.[32] But the iceberg of Section 7.3 still lay submerged from view waiting for a socialist administration to strike it.

◆

The GLC cut the fares on Sunday, 4 October 1981 and by the middle of the week, thousands of new passengers were flooding back on to the Underground. 'Cheaper fares turned rush hour into crush hour,' reported the *Daily Express*, adding, 'Staff had to work overtime to cope with long queues for season tickets.'[33] Fares Fair looked a runaway success, bringing new life to the Tube and cutting congestion. It would not last.

Few at the GLC sensed any danger. After a meeting with the Tory transport secretary Norman Fowler to discuss the policy, Livingstone joked, 'The minister wants to see me again. I think he must want me for my body.'[34] The GLC announced an additional local tax called a 'supplementary rate' to raise the £125 million needed to pay for the Tube fare reductions.

This would have to be collected by the London boroughs which were being worked into a lather by the press including the *Evening Standard* which announced, 'RATES – THE FARES FAIR TIME BOMB', claiming that Londoners faced an extra bill of £385 million.[35] Businesses in London, which bore the brunt of the increase, also feared the impact of the supplementary rate. At a time of chronic and rising unemployment, the London Chamber of Commerce and Industry claimed that it would cost 25,000 jobs. Six months previously, a survey by the Chamber showed that 40 per cent of firms said they would move out of the capital if there was another substantial rates rise. For them, despite his unemployment banners, Livingstone was exacerbating jobless-ness, not solving it.[36]

Fares Fair represented a huge redistribution of wealth. This fact was not lost on Tory-controlled Westminster City Council, which started to campaign for the abolition of the GLC from mid-October 1981. Westminster had to pay more than 20 per cent of the bill for Fares Fair; £351 million of the £411 million collected by Westminster went to the socialist strongholds of the ILEA and GLC.[37] 'Fares Fair may have been controversial,' wrote the author and transport writer Christian Wolmar, 'but it revitalised the Underground turning it into a popular political cause as well as increasing passenger numbers.'[38]

The fate of the GLC and its flagship Fares Fair policy was effec-tively decided over a Sunday pre-lunch drink in the late summer of 1981 on the south-east extremity of London. Dennis Barkway, Tory leader of Bromley Council, arrived at the Bird in the Hand pub on Gravel Road near Bromley Common for his weekly tipple with three fellow councillors, Fred David, chairman of the coun-cil's Finance Committee, Philip Jones and Simon Randall, who was also a GLC member, as a well as a lawyer. Inevitably, the sub-ject of the evil Livingstone came up.

Randall thought the GLC was legally vulnerable on Fares Fair: that Livingstone and his transport chairman Dave Wetzel had neither taken the policy through the proper procedures nor taken proper external legal advice. Barkway said: 'I'll have a look into it,' and got the council's solicitors to examine the position. They agreed there was a legal case and a challenge could be made.[39]

There is no doubt that the hysteria whipped up about and by Livingstone contributed to Bromley's decision to fight. Barkway remembers attending a public meeting about the unpopular sup-plementary rate in Bromley before his legal challenge. 'There was almost mass hysteria,' says Barkway. 'I remember my anxiety about how irate these people were about what was being done to them because of this potential charge that was going to be levied on them – this extra financial burden. They were literally in the mood to go out and do something silly and I recall having to calm the whole meeting down.'[40]

Bromley challenged the legality of the supplementary rate on the following grounds: it was procedurally flawed, so the GLC lacked authority; there was no attempt to 'break even'; and that the London Underground did not extend to Bromley. 'This omitted two key arguments,' suggested Wolmar, '...many Bromley residents did travel into central London and use the facilities and that even those who did not were likely to benefit from the reduction in traffic congestion.'[41]

Barkway's first challenge was rejected by the High Court on 3 November 1981; the two judges, Lord Justice Dunn and Mr Justice Phillips were clearly reluctant to become embroiled in political controversy, but Bromley Council's solicitor Simon Pugh felt there were grounds for a further challenge to the next highest court, the Court of Appeal.

The case was heard on 10 November by the land's most famous judge, the Master of the Rolls, Lord Denning, sitting with Lord Justice Watkins and Lord Justice Oliver. All three Appeal Court judges found in Bromley's favour, destroying the central manifesto policy of Livingstone's administration.

For Oliver, Section 7.3 of the 1969 Transport Act was the clincher: the London Underground had to be run as far as practicable on business lines. For Watkins and Denning, the decision to cut fares was 'a bad case of an abuse of power, which totally disregarded the interests of the ratepayers'. The judges agreed that by breeching Section 7.3, the GLC was breeching its 'fiduciary duty' to the ratepayer, in other words, its duty to try to balance the books.

Denning suggested that Labour should have disregarded its own election manifesto and muddled along like everyone else in power: 'When a party was returned to power, it should consider what it was best to do and what was practical and fair.'[42] On 17 December 1981, five Law Lords sitting in the House of Lords, the highest court in the land, rejected the GLC's appeal to overturn the ruling of Denning and the others. For Livingstone, it was game over.

After the Lords' judgment, Dennis Barkway, the cause of the calamity, received a call from Michael Heseltine, the government's environment secretary. 'Mr Heseltine was so pleased with the outcome,' remembers Barkway, 'that [he told me] if I was ever in the House of Commons, he would put me on his shoulders and carry me through!'[43] Barkway also recalls the reaction of several taxi drivers: '"You're the bloke who done Ken Livingstone, aren't you? Well, all London is cheering for you!"'[44]

Mrs Thatcher was also clearly delighted, telling the House on 17 December 1981: 'I welcome the clear and unanimous judgment from the House of Lords and congratulate Bromley on having taken steps that have clarified the position for London's ratepayers.

'The judgment runs to about 100 pages. We shall need time carefully to consider what it says, but it is already clear that the GLC's action was a breach of the duty that it owed to ratepayers and wrong in law.'[45]

◆

It was a catastrophe from which Livingstone's administration never recovered. For all the bluff and bluster emanating from County Hall over the next few months, the People's Palace buckled under the law and did what the judges told them. It was forced to abandon Fares Fair and double the cost of travel on the Underground. The Lords' judgment meant the GLC had to recoup the £125 million spent on the unlawful policy. On 4 October 1981, a 40 pence Tube ticket had been reduced to 30 pence under Fares Fair. After the Lords' judgment, it went up to 60 pence. Fares Fair became 'Fares Very Unfair'.

The default position of many on the Left was to blame Denning, who at 82, was considered to be well past his prime, expressed best by the *New Statesman*, which lamented: 'The proper casualty of the London Transport dispute should be the reputation of Lord Denning: a once-great judge who over-estimated his capacity to resist the eccentricities of age.'[46] The anger was felt not only on the Left but also by experienced County Hall civil servants like Maurice Stonefrost. He says, 'The Law Lords were really obviously concerned about the nature of the left-wing GLC. There they were saying, "We're going to do this; we're going to do that." And that seemed to them to be wrong. I also think they were concerned to maintain proper balanced methods of decision-taking and they regarded this one as not properly balanced. The GLC had decided to do it and they did it regardless of the fact.'[47]

Also overlooked is the fact that of the 10 senior judges who studied Fares Fair, eight concluded it was unlawful and two others had expressed reservations about it, before passing the buck upwards. Not all these judges could really be described as 'capitalist running dogs' bent on the destruction of Red Ken. The GLC was not sovereign like Parliament. It was created by Parliament and could be abolished by it. In any event, it had to abide by the laws set down by it.

Tony McBrearty, a Labour GLC member on the right who became housing chairman, blames the fiasco on the naivety of Ken Livingstone, his transport chairman Dave Wetzel and the others on the Left. He argues there was no proper debate of the policy and therefore it lacked the proper authority. 'It was blown by Dave Wetzel,' says McBrearty. '[It was] total inexperience. That's my firm belief. Dave went to the Transport Committee and said, "We've won the election, here's our manifesto and this is what we're going to do." That's what lost it in the [House of] Lords, instead of saying we're now going to have a debate on something which is going to cost millions and millions of pounds and we're going to have a vote.

'If we'd done that we'd never have lost the case... but Dave in his naivety just said, "That's what we're going to do."'[48]

It is unfair simply to blame Wetzel; it was a collective failure by Livingstone's administration. Even if the judiciary was looking for an excuse to slap down Livingstone, he had provided it. But the idea that any public transport system could be made to break even or run without huge public subsidy was risible elsewhere in the civilised world.

The episode ended in chaos and farce. At a full meeting of the GLC on 12 January 1982, Livingstone voted against a resolution to obey the law. To disobey would have meant certain surcharge and disqualification. But unless he was very stupid, and he was not, he must have known that he would be defeated and that the Lords' judgment would be upheld by the law-abiding majority of GLC members. The Tories joined forces with the moderates in the Labour group to prevent the council acting illegally. In the end a significant number of Labour GLC members voted with the opposition to bite the bullet and uphold the law. The Tories had contemplated the tactic of abstaining to leave Livingstone skewered on the pike of illegality but a number balked at the risk of surcharge, disqualification and impoverishment, and voted to put up the fares by 100 per cent as the courts demanded. Finally, the result was 27 to 24 votes in favour of legality.[49] After the vote Livingstone was asked a tongue-in-cheek question by his deputy Illtyd Harrington: 'Well, what do we do now, leader?' Livingstone replied furiously: 'We fucking carry on.' 'Fancy a drink?' scoffed

Harrington as Livingstone slammed his office door behind him.[50]

Not for the last time, Livingstone would be accused of playing to the crowd on the Left when he knew it was safe. As Illtyd Harrington later told Livingstone's early biographer John Carvel, 'I think Ken was opportunistic because he knew the law had to be obeyed, but he knew other people would see to it that it was done.'[51] Despite the gestures and threats, the GLC would always obey the law when it came to the crunch during the five years of Livingstone's leadership.

◆

Following the meeting, there was the short-lived 'Can't pay, won't pay' campaign led by Dave Wetzel, whose offer to resign following the Lords' judgment had been rejected by Livingstone.[52] Wetzel encouraged travellers to refuse to pay the court-imposed fare increases.

On one occasion, Wetzel boarded a number 12 double-decker bus bound for County Hall and as the bus stopped in Trafalgar Square he was approached by the conductor. Wetzel handed over a County Hall-produced 'Can't Pay, won't pay' ticket in lieu of the fare. The conductor refused the chit and threatened to call the police. Wetzel says, 'So I stood up and explained to everybody downstairs why I was refusing to pay the fare.' He asked the travellers: 'Do you want me to get off the bus or do I stay?' Wetzel took a vote; downstairs voted for him to stay but upstairs, where there were more passengers, voted to eject him. 'The moral of the story?' says Wetzel, 'Never trust the smokers on the top deck of a Routemaster!'[53]

Pragmatic as ever, Livingstone stopped supporting 'Can't pay, won't pay' because it did not have popular support[54] and, as Wetzel proved, it put bus conductors and the ticket collectors on the Underground in an invidious position. The GLC decided to raise the £125 million it needed to repay the Underground's debts by putting up the rates. The same amount was withdrawn in a central government grant by Heseltine, but it did leave County Hall with that massive extra amount of money in recurring years.

◆

In the following two years, Livingstone was desperate to reduce the fares at least to the level he had inherited from the Tories.

County Hall spent a great deal of money on lawyers to achieve essentially the status quo. According to the senior officer responsible, Dave Bayliss, the GLC's former head of transport, the process used to lower the fares a second time was much more rigorous. Even then, it was a pyrrhic victory. He says: 'Firstly, ticket prices went down a third for the first time with Fares Fair; then we went up a half after the Lords' judgment and then went down a half. With the intervening inflation, fare levels stayed pretty well where they had started out.'[55]

There was widespread dismay about the courts' decision. At a meeting of the Queensbridge ward Labour Party in late spring 1982, a young barrister called Tony Blair moved a motion for that year's party conference condemning the judges' political interference. The motion, seconded by his wife Cherie Booth and carried by 11 votes to nil reads: 'Conference reaffirms its belief that democratically elected politicians should be answerable to their electorate and that political decisions should not be subject to the interference of the courts.' It called on Conference to 'abolish the judge-invented doctrine of fiduciary duty (which means that the duty to ratepayers takes precedence over manifesto pledges) and restrict councillors' liability to surcharge or disqualification to cases of serious crime.'[56] It is one of the few recorded instances of Blair registering his support for Ken Livingstone.

The howls of anguish by the Left were expressed loudest in *London Labour Briefing*. '...the GLC is now being forced to tear up the main plank of our manifesto,' wrote Livingstone's old Chartist friend Keith Veness, who urged Livingstone and his Labour comrades to resign power and let the Tories run the GLC with the SDP and Liberals. He added, 'This is the acid test to distinguish socialists from social administrators. It cannot be ducked.'[57] But Livingstone's pragmatism and ambition had allowed him to duck it or at least keep his head while all about him were losing theirs. There was still a lot to play for.

Livingstone could lose his temper but by and large retained his composure during this stressful period. On 11 May 1982, Livingstone and his mother Ethel met the *Carry On* film star Kenneth Williams who was being wined and dined by Illtyd Harrington and his partner Chris Downes at County Hall. Williams later recorded in his diary that Livingstone and his mother had both been 'charming', adding, 'Ken is v. attractive

I must say.'[58] Harrington observed Livingstone and his mother interacting with Williams. 'The rapport between the three was really quite extraordinary,' remembers Harrington. 'You could see that he [Livingstone] obviously adored his mother, a pretty little woman, and that she had worked hard as a dancer. And I realised that he was a natural performer, a very good timer. Like all musical artists, he was very good at dealing with hecklers. But I noticed that there was something in Ken's relationship with his mother that he had to be performing and demonstrating. But no one, including me, appreciated how ruthless he was.'[59]

The final humiliation over Fares Fair came a little more than two years afterwards when Mrs Thatcher essentially renational-ised the Tube by taking it away from County Hall and turning it over to a government-run quango as an appetiser to the abolition of the GLC. Over the next few years, in his fight with Thatcher and others, Livingstone would have to deploy his qualities of ruthlessness and showmanship to survive.

Notes

1   Kenneth O. Morgan, *A Life, Michael Foot,* pp420-423
2   Biography, Una Cooze, www.geo.ed.ac.uk/~brucebak/tree/01060107.htm
3   Interview, Michael Foot, 15.7.07
4   Kenneth O. Morgan, *A Life, Michael Foot,* p386
5   Interview, Michael Foot, 15.7.07
6   Ken Livingstone, *If Voting Changed Anything, They'd Abolish It,* pp178-180
7   *Private Eye,* Issue 508, 5.6.81, p14
8   *Sunday Times,* the John Mortimer interview, 19.7.81
9   *Evening Standard,* the Andrew Billen interview, 10.6.98
10 John McDonnell biography, www.john-mcdonnell.net/about.htm
11 *Guardian,* 'Honest John', (profile of John McDonnell), by Ronan Bennett, 26.9.06
12 Ibid.
13 Interview, Maurice Stonefrost, 21.11.07
14 Author interviews
15 Paul Boateng biography, British High Commission, South Africa, www.britishhighcommission.gov.uk
16 *Sunday Times,* the John Mortimer interview, 19.7.81
17 *Financial Times,* 'London faces an arts revolution', by Antony Thorncroft, 11.7.81
18 Interview, George Nicholson, 21.8.07
19 Author interviews, 2007
20 Interview, Illtyd Harrington, 4.7.07
21 Interview, Maurice Stonefrost, 21.11.07
22 GLC Report to Industry and Employment Committee, 12.10.82

23 Interview, Ken Livingstone, 8.11.07
24 Ibid., 8.11.07
25 *Private Eye*, Issue 517, 9.10.81
26 Greater London Council minutes, 13.10.81
27 *London Labour Briefing*, Issue 13, August 1981, p1
28 Ibid.
29 Ibid.
30 Ken Livingstone, 'The Struggle for Power', *London Labour Briefing*, Issue 9, March 1981, p4
31 Hansard HC and *Guardian*, article by Michael Zander, 13.11.81
32 *Evening Standard*, 'GLC "is uncaring" over cheap fares', statement by Peter Weitzman QC, 29.10.81
33 *Daily Express*, 8.10.81
34 *Daily Telegraph*, 17.7.85
35 *Evening Standard*, 8.10.81
36 *Evening Standard*, '25,000 London jobs at risk on rates, say businessmen', 12.10.81
37 Andrew Hosken, *Nothing Like a Dame, The Scandals of Shirley Porter*, Granta, p58
38 Christian Wolmar, *The Subterranean Railway, How the London Underground was Built and How It Changed London Forever*, Atlantic Books, 2004, pp303-304
39 Interview, Dennis Barkway, 17.8.07
40 Ibid.
41 Christian Wolmar, *The Subterranean Railway, How the London Underground was Built and How It Changed London Forever*, pp303-304
42 Judgment, Lord Denning, Bromley LBC vs. GLC, 13.11. 81
43 Interview, Dennis Barkway, 17.8.81
44 Ibid.
45 Prime Minister's Questions, Hansard HC [15/446-50], 17.12.81
46 *New Statesman*, 'The cost of national incompetence', 13.11.81
47 Interview, Maurice Stonefrost, 21.11.07
48 Interview, Tony McBrearty, 25.7.07
49 Ken Livingstone, *If Voting Changed Anything, They'd Abolish It,* p208
50 Interview, Illtyd Harrington, 4.7.07
51 John Carvel, *Citizen Ken*, p146
52 Interview, Dave Wetzel, 5.11.07
53 Ibid.
54 *London Labour Briefing*, p8, June 1982
55 Interview, Dave Bayliss, 10.7.07
56 John Rentoul, *Tony Blair, Prime Minister*, Time Warner Paperbacks, 2001, p89
57 Ken Livingstone, *If Voting Changed Anything, They'd Abolish It,* pp211-212
58 Russell Davies (Ed.), *The Kenneth William Diaries*, HarperCollins, 1994, (see 11.5.82)
59 Interview, Illtyd Harrington, 4.7.07

Chapter 10

Dangerous liaisons: Comrade Gerry, 1981–1985

Lord Denning cannot take the credit for the first momentous defeat of the hard left. With hindsight, that happened on Sunday, 27 September 1981, six weeks before the Fares Fair judgment, when Tony Benn was defeated by Denis Healey for the deputy leadership of the Labour Party at the annual conference in Brighton. It had been a close-run thing, down to the nearest of a hundredth of a decimal point: Healey got 50.426 per cent and Benn 49.547 per cent. At the time, the Benn/Healey contest was seen by all as a totemic joust between the left and right for control of the party. The Left saw Michael Foot as a temporary figure; Benn as deputy would have been his natural successor.

It had taken a superhuman effort to rescue the Labour Party from itself, and particularly its grassroots. Foot and Healey had managed to throw back the barbarians at the gate by the narrowest of margins, despite the Left's formidable control of most of the Labour constituency parties. But the constituencies constituted only 30 per cent of the total number of votes in the electoral college designed ironically by Benn's friends in the Campaign for Labour Party Democracy (CLPD). MPs also made up a third of the votes and here, crucially, a small number of soft left MPs, particularly Neil Kinnock, Foot's successor and close friend, abstained in the second ballot. It swung the result. Ken Livingstone was filmed at the conference, his exasperation clearly visible on a BBC *Panorama* programme broadcast shortly afterwards,[1] when he insisted any MPs considering defecting to the Social Democratic Party should be ineligible to vote.[2] The fightback from the right continued as four left-wingers were voted off the National Executive Committee and replaced with moderates.[3]

Following the vote, Tony Benn and his wife Caroline attended a meeting at the Queen's Hotel in Brighton arranged by Livingstone's old friends in *London Labour Briefing*.[4] The last words of Benn's diary entry that night read '…it has been far more successful than anything else I could possibly have dreamed of at the beginning.'⁵ But neither Benn nor anyone else on the left, particularly Ken Livingstone, ever again posed as serious a threat to the party 'establishment'.

Graham Bash, Chartist and a key figure in *Briefing*, says, 'The critical moment in the history of the Labour movement was the defeat of Benn for the deputy leadership; it was the pivotal moment. It was absolute rubbish for anyone to claim it was a victory. It was a decisive moment.'⁶ John Golding, the Labour MP for Newcastle under Lyme and a prominent NEC right-winger, started to hope the civil war was going his way. When asked about his strategy, he would reply 'playing for time'.⁷

Shortly before that conference in Brighton, Ken Livingstone launched a new weekly newspaper. At a press conference on 4 September 1981, Livingstone announced that along with two Lambeth Labour councillors, the ubiquitous 'Red' Ted Knight and Knight's deputy on Lambeth Council, Matthew Warburton, he was now 'joint editor' of a new left-wing weekly newspaper, the *Labour Herald*. The paper would argue for hard left policies and chart the decline of the Left's influence through a series of reverses over the next four years. Aside from the odd reference, here and there, there has been little mention of the *Labour Herald* when people write about Ken Livingstone, which is a pity, because therein lies an extraordinary saga.

◆

The *Labour Herald* was a weekly newspaper with its own reporters, photographers, colour page spreads and cartoonist. Astonishingly for its time, the *Herald* carried colour photographs more than four years before the arrival of the country's first national colour daily paper, Eddie Shah's *Today*. The *Labour Herald* was printed by a company called Astmoor Litho Ltd at 21–22 Arkwright Road in the Cheshire town of Runcorn. The press belonged to the Workers Revolutionary Party (WRP), a the Trotskyist organisation. Livingstone's decision to form a close commercial and political relationship with the WRP was dangerous, conceivably reckless and could have destroyed him politically and financially. Ultimately, he survived thanks to a combination of luck and sloppy journalism. It was a relationship which highlighted the wisdom of the old warning about the dangers of lying down with dogs.

Livingstone's introduction to the WRP was through Ted Knight who had been a member of its Trot predecessor, the

Socialist Labour League. The leader of both the WRP and the Socialist Labour League was Gerry Healy. In his heyday, Healy was the secretary of the international Trotskyist movement[8] and in the early 1950s, fought ideological battles alongside giants of the Labour movement including Michael Foot and Aneurin Bevan. At the end of his life, he was a reviled irrelevance with a tiny following, namely the actor siblings Vanessa and Corin Redgrave. The rest, you might say, is a footnote in history, and a deeply unpleasant one at that. Bob Pitt, one of Gerry Healy's biographers, wrote that by the end of Healy's life 'his ambition to establish himself as a figure of world-historic significance lay in ruins'.[9] That is some understatement. Healy died in December 1989 at the age of 76 and his funeral at Highgate was attended by Ken Livingstone who, along with other mourners, was surprised to encounter an angry picket at the cemetery gates, not of striking gravediggers but of Healy's former followers. Even in death, the old revolutionary managed to provoke feelings of betrayal and blind fury.[10]

It is easy to speak ill of the dead because they cannot sue for defamation, so it is important to stress that the allegations against Gerry Healy, that he was a serial rapist and abuser of vulnerable young women, a violent drunken oaf, a celebrity-obsessed syco-phant, a sectarian demagogue, a vindictive bully, a political joke, a blatant anti-Semite, a traitor to the World Socialist Revolution, a possible accessory to torture and murder, a professional liar and a fraud as well as a pathetic stooge for sinister Middle East regimes, were made when he was still alive and had access to enough money, but insufficient inclination, to go to a good libel lawyer. It is also important to point out that these things were not said by the 'fascist reactionary press,' 'Bonapartist imperialists' or 'revisionist scum', but by his most loyal cadres and comrades.

Brian Behan, the playwright and one-time disciple of Healy, described his former leader as 'bald, with the little sore eyes of a newborn pig'.[11] Illtyd Harrington, Livingstone's former deputy, says, 'Healy was quite a frightening looking creature; he had the head of the archetypal Broadmoor psychopath – a big bullet head. But he controlled them all through a series [sic] of moral and intellectual blackmail.'[12] But Healy did have charisma. According to Tony Benn's wife Caroline, who saw him speak, Healy had 'an electric personality'.[13]

As for the Workers Revolutionary Party under Healy, it is hard to fault a description by the leading Trot theorist Sean Matgamna in the *Socialist Organiser*, founded by Ken Livingstone and others in 1978, '…the WRP is no laughing matter. It is a pseudo-Marxist gobbledegook-spouting cross between the Moonies, the Scientologists and the Jones Cult which committed mass suicide in the Guyana jungle three years ago. It recruits and exploits mainly raw, inexperienced, politically, socially and psychologically defenceless young people. It employs psychological terror and physical violence against its own members (and occasionally against others).'[14]

But that was clearly not what Livingstone saw in Gerry Healy. Writing in March 1994, long after Healy's atrocities had been publicly exposed, Livingstone stated: 'It was a privilege to have worked with Gerry Healy.'[15] He added, 'I first met Gerry Healy in 1981, shortly after I became leader of the Greater London Council and was immediately captivated by his vivid recollection of events and personalities on the left. He had recognised the changed political climate which enabled Labour to take control of County Hall, and that we were using the immense resources of the Greater London Council to support those struggling for jobs and other rights. Gerry Healy saw that it was possible to use the GLC as a rallying fortress for Londoners who were opposed to Thatcher's hard-line monetarism.'[16]

The two men worked very closely indeed. Not only was Healy Livingstone's printer, but Livingstone became Healy's staunch defender and supporter, even to the point of regularly attending WRP annual conferences. At the time, not many people took any notice of Livingstone's foreword or the book in which it appeared, *Gerry Healy: A Revolutionary Life*, by two Healy supporters, Corrine Lotz and Paul Feldman. His contribution to this hagiography was surprising because it came nearly a decade after the exposure of Healy's misdeeds. In short, there were enough horror stories about Gerry Healy to equal the total output of both M.R. James and Bram Stoker.

It is not only remarkable that Healy had about five hundred followers when he first met Livingstone but that he had any at all. It was not uncommon for Healy to beat up senior cadres of the WRP at meetings of the central committee including Stuart Carter who had dared question one of his decisions.[17] On another occasion,

Healy repeatedly interrupted the speech of one of his comrades who carried on regardless. An exasperated Healy snapped: 'Stop speaking when I am interrupting.'[18] What ultimately destroyed Healy were not his dealings with Middle Eastern mass murderers but his serious sexual assaults on dozens of WRP female cadres.

◆

Livingstone's old Chartist friend Keith Veness was in the WRP between 1965 and 1968 and recalls a desolate period of whisky-fuelled violence, denunciations, purges and a daily grind of listening to Healy's rants. Evenings were taken up with selling Healy's daily newspaper, the *News Line,* which often carried articles written in the turgid Healyite style, once compared to a 'sandbag dragged through a puddle of glue'.[19]

'Members were worked to death,' remembers Veness, 'basically you had to give all your wages to the organisation and then you had to get out selling the paper every night. And if you didn't turn up for a paper sale one night, you'd get three people around your door asking where you were.'[20] Veness describes Healy as a man 'with a huge head out of proportion with his body,' never very far from a bottle of whisky from his native Ireland. Veness adds: 'Apparently Healy had been around the republican movement in Ireland but the rumour was that he had stolen money from them and he couldn't go back there, otherwise his knee caps would have parted company from the rest of him.'[21]

Veness remembers the case of one member, Geoff Pilling, a quiet self-effacing polytechnic lecturer in Marxism, who made a tactical error in resigning at the start of one of Healy's notorious summer camps for the party's youth wing, the Young Socialists. 'If you wanted the holiday from hell,' says Veness, 'then you could have done worse than go on one of Gerry Healy's summer camps. 'They used to hire a field from some farmer outside Arundel down in Sussex and all four hundred of us were down there under canvas. In the afternoon, there'd be these sessions on "materialist dialectics" by some fucking bloke who didn't know what he was talking about.'

At night, Healy's goons patrolled the grounds to prevent young cadres from making nocturnal assignations to keep them pure for the class struggle. Naturally, Healy himself did not feel bound by such restrictions when it came to 'the youth,' as would be dramatically revealed years later. Healy ordered Veness and three others into his presence. 'That bastard Pilling's resigned,' Healy said, 'he's got to be called to account. He must answer for his actions in front of the working class.' Banging the table, as was his habit, Healy screeched, 'Get Pilling!' The four men drove immediately to Pilling's home in Leeds and arrived at 8 a.m. They snatched Pilling outside his local newsagent's and bundled him into the car and drove back to Arundel at 90 mph. 'Pilling was screaming all the time,' remembers Veness, 'so we had to hit him occasionally to keep him quiet. It was like some really bad American gangster movie.'

They arrived back at the Arundel camp in time for Healy's 'afternoon denunciation session'. 'It was absolutely appalling,' says Veness, who was only in his teens at the time, 'we were then treated to an hour and a half of Healy foaming at the mouth and screaming at Pilling, "You've sold out! You're a Menshevik! Get up here and admit it!" We all yelled out, "Admit it!" Healy didn't demand the death penalty but he did virtually. It was like one of Stalin's show trials in the thirties. It was a lesson to everyone else: "Don't you try and leave."' As Pilling gibbered plaintively into the microphone, he was grabbed by the scruff of the neck by Healy and frogmarched off the field and left to make his own way home.

By the age of 18, Veness had had enough and tendered his resignation to Healy in his offices above a butcher's shop at 186a Clapham High Street. Healy lost his temper and swung a punch; Veness, a tall man, whacked him hard in the face. 'I picked up the metal chair to hit him with it,' says Veness, 'then I hesitated because I thought I might kill him and three or four blokes busted into the room and grabbed hold of me and threw me out.'[22] Some managed to quit a little less dramatically; a former WRP member Jan Pallis left Healy a simple note, 'Goodbye, it has been very unpleasant knowing you.'[23]

◆

Livingstone was assiduously courted by Healy. The old rogue recognised in such a high profile and charismatic left politician, as had other Trots, a conduit to possible revolution, or at least a relationship which might add lustre to the grubby and discredited WRP. Livingstone's relationship with Healy's revolutionary sect went largely unnoticed by the mainstream media, which was more obsessed with the GLC's so-called loony policies and outrages, as well as the scandal of Livingstone's relationship with Sinn Féin.

As GLC leader, Livingstone attended three successive WRP annual conferences from 1982 to 1984,[24] invariably accompanied by Ted Knight. The 1984 conference at the Dominion Theatre in London's West End took place on 18 November at the height of the miners' strike. Livingstone was guest speaker. Some of Livingstone's senior colleagues at the GLC saw the potential dangers of mixing with Healy. Before the 1982 WRP conference, John Carr, chairman of the Staff Committee wrote to Livingstone: 'Quite what pleasure you will get out of going to such a meeting or quite what purpose would be served, I cannot imagine. However I am sure you will be mindful of the Peckham by-election...'[25]

The *News Line* reported: 'Ken Livingstone, the leader of the Greater London Council, said, "We could be on the point of the most major breakthrough in socialism in international terms since the October Revolution of 1917."'[26] The speech provided proof, if it were needed, that Livingstone always knew exactly what buttons to press when it came to rousing Trots to his cause. Veness remembers talking to Livingstone about the WRP. 'I know who they are,' said Livingstone, 'and I know what they're like.'[27] Many WRP hardliners were clearly sickened by what they saw as their leader sucking up to the faux left.[28] But by the autumn of 1981, Livingstone's relationship with the Trots and others who made up the *London Labour Briefing* group had become estranged. Veness says, 'Ken's view was that the problem with *Briefing* was that it was a maverick organisation.'

According to Graham Bash, co-editor of *Briefing*, Livingstone was becoming fed up with the occasional attacks on his administration by the open-minded and eclectic *Briefing* bunch. 'We worked with Ken for a couple of years until he went into *Labour Herald*,' says Bash, 'because although we were supportive we've always been independent and I think he probably preferred uncritical mouthpieces and we were never that.'[29]

◆

Livingstone and his two other *Labour Herald* joint editors Matthew Warburton[30] and Ted Knight insisted that the WRP got the printing contract because it offered good rates. But Knight concedes: 'It was good for them [the WRP]; it gave them work for their presses and it gave them a certain credibility I suppose, but that didn't worry Ken or I or anybody else. Of course, they didn't make the profits. They certainly made no profits out of us; there's no doubt about that.'[31] But Graham Bash and Keith Veness remain convinced that without considerable WRP funds and support, the paper would not have got off the ground. The fact remains that the real editor, Steven Miller, who worked full-time on the paper was a member of the WRP's central committee. The *Herald*'s views on a number of important issues, including Ireland, Palestine and the great social issues of the day were virtually indistinguishable from the WRP's.

◆

Briefing was primitively typeset and gave every appearance of being run off a photocopier. Graham Bash says, '*Briefing* was brilliant for our resources with lots and lots of supporters and 80 to 100 sellers in London and that's what we produce. Compare that with the beautiful colour of the *Labour Herald* and we couldn't compete. It was like someone in the Fourth Division playing against Chelsea. It was unfair. I thought, "This is being funded."'[32] After all, Livingstone was receiving just £70 a week in councillor allowances plus a further £4,000 a year as GLC leader. As leader and deputy leader of Lambeth Council, Knight and Warburton were hardly any better off. A weekly colour newspaper would have been an expensive hobby for three busy men with little obvious access to great wealth. Livingstone says it was 'subsidised' and that 'a friend of Ted Knight's put up about, I'm guessing here, several thousand pounds'.[33]

The WRP had astonishing resources for such a tiny party. It had a 'College of Marxist Education' at White Meadows in the beautiful Derbyshire village of Parwich. There was the state-of-the-art printing press, and most extraordinary of all, a daily colour newspaper with photographers and reporters, the *News Line*. Clues to the mysterious sources of the WRP's cash came in the remorselessly pro-Arab and anti-Semitic content of the *News Line*. The Iraqi and Libyan governments of the dictators Saddam Hussein and Colonel Muammar al-Gaddafi in particular could do no wrong, even when they murdered innocent people, which they frequently did. Shortly before Saddam Hussein became president, the *News Line* expressed support for the Ba'ath Party's nasty takeover of Iraq, or 'revolution' as described by Healy and others. On 1 July 1979, there was a conference in London of the All Trades

Union Alliance (ATUA), a meeting of WRP trade unionists. The following day, the *News Line* reported: 'The ATUA conference gave a hearty welcome to Talib Suwailh, an executive member of the Central Bureau of the Trade Union Federation of Iraq. He brought fraternal greetings from the Iraqi trade union movement to ATUA and stressed the bonds which unite them. Hands off the Arab Ba'ath Socialist Party and the National Union of Iraqi Students! Full support for the trade unions and their revolution! Victory to the Arab revolution! Forward to the World Socialist Revolution!'[34]

Shortly after his return to Iraq, Talib Suwailh was arrested with other communists and trade unionists. On 28 July 1979, Hussein's government claimed to have discovered a 'treason conspiracy'[35] supported allegedly by neighbouring Syria. Suwailh and 21 others were sentenced to death, after torture and a show trial, before being shot. The *News Line* made no criticism.

Five months earlier, Healy's paper had supported the decision by the Ba'athists to execute members of the Iraqi Communist Party, as Saddam Hussein continued to liquidate the opposition. 'From a historical point of view,' wrote Healy, 'the Ba'ath Socialist party of Iraq has played a hundred-fold more progressive role in the Middle East than Stalinism.' Healy then excused the summary murders of his fellow communists: 'The fact is that the Communist Party members were executed according to military codes which the Iraqi Communist Party discussed, approved and agreed to implement. To this day the Iraqi Communist Party has not called for the repeal of the military laws which ban the formation of secret cells in the army. It has never contested the fact that the arrested officials were guilty of the charges brought against them.'[36]

◆

When the WRP collapsed in October 1985, Healy's former senior comrades held an inquiry into his corruption. The report, which was kept confidential for more than a decade, had the dramatic title: 'CORRUPTION OF THE WORKERS REVOLUTIONARY PARTY, Interim Report of the International Committee Commission.'

The inquiry team recovered seven documents which showed that Healy had received secret donations from Iraq apparently in return for photos of London-based Ba'athist opponents. Healy had ordered a photographer from the *News Line* to take the pictures so he could hand them over to the embassy. The inquiry stated the sums may have been greater than the £19,697 known to have been received. The report says: 'The Commission has not yet been able to establish all the facts relating in [sic] the case of the photographs that were handed over to the Iraqi embassy. We do know the two WRP members were instructed to take photos of demonstrations of opponents of Saddam Hussein. One of the members, Comrade x [name suppressed], refused the order. A receipt for £1,600 for 16 minutes of documentary footage of a demonstration is in the possession of the Commission.'[37] The evidence suggests that the Iraqi money may have dried up at about the time of the outbreak of the Iran–Iraq War in September 1980. But the money certainly explains Healy's enthusiastic support for the torture and murder of Hussein's opponents.

There is no suggestion or a scintilla of evidence that Ken Livingstone or his two joint editor colleagues knew that Healy was in receipt of funds from Iraq or that they would not have condemned such activity had they found out. But they certainly were aware that Healy was accused of accepting money from another Middle East pariah, Colonel Gaddafi, because all three were sucked into the scandal at a time when the allegations of Healy's own dealings could not be proved. The WRP inquiry extracted a further 28 documents[38] from Gerry Healy's office which revealed the astonishingly close financial relationship between Healy and Gaddafi's government. The papers also show that not only is it probable that Libya bought the state-of-the-art Runcorn printing press used to publish both the *News Line* and the *Labour Herald* but also gave the WRP at least half a million pounds. According to the Commission of Inquiry, Healy signed a secret agreement with the Libyan government with the knowledge of only his closest WRP cronies.

The inquiry interim report adds: 'This agreement includes providing of intelligence information on the "activities, names and positions held in finance, politics, business, the communications media and elsewhere" by "Zionists". It has strongly anti-Semitic undertones, as no distinction is made between Jews and Zionists and the term Zionist could actually include every Jew in a leading position.' The report also states: 'This agreement was connected with a demand for money. The report given by the WRP delegation while staying in Libya included a demand for £50,000 to purchase a web offset press for the daily *News Line*, which was to be launched in May 1976.The Commission was not able to establish if any of this money was received.'

In August 1977, Healy went out to Libya to demand a further £100,000 needed to invest in the *News Line*.[39] The inquiry found that Healy's claim of support for the Palestinian people was simply a way of getting cash out of gullible sheikhs from Kuwait to Qatar. It was a cynical attempt 'to make the PLO an instrument for obtaining money from the Arab bourgeoisie'.[40] In October 1979, a WRP delegation went to Libya for a third time, and demanded £500,000 towards the WRP's plans for seven 'youth training centres'. Around £300,000 was raised, but the actual sum needed as of 21 May 1982, according to the inquiry commission, was £152,539.[41]

Healy sent begging letters to either Colonel Gaddafi directly or his contact on the People's Committee in the Libyan People's Bureau. Such was his reliance on Libya that on 28 August 1981, a few days before the launch of the *Labour Herald*, he wrote to Libya complaining that the non-arrival of the latest cheque had forced him to raise the price of the *News Line*. The Libyans already paid Healy to print Gaddafi's *The Green Book* outlining the colonel's views on democracy and according to the WRP inquiry, Healy received the money via huge overpayments for the work. The Libyans received information not only about their UK-based enemies and leading British Jews, but also the unflinching support of Healy's mighty organ. However, it seems likely that the Libyans greatly overestimated Healy's importance and got very little in return. Where many people saw a military dictatorship which sponsored international terrorism, the *News Line* paid tribute to Gaddafi's 'republic ruled by the masses', or Jamahiriya, as it did shortly after the launch of Livingstone's *Labour Herald*.

◆

On 12 December 1981, under the front page banner headline 'HANDS OFF LIBYA AND BROTHER GADDAFI,' the WRP announced: 'We say hands off Libya and Brother Gaddafi! Down with imperialism! Forward to the PLO! Forward to the World Socialist revolution! The Workers Revolutionary Party declares its complete solidarity with the Libyan Jamahiriya under the leadership of Brother Muammar al-Gaddafi against the terrorist threats of President Reagan and American imperialism.' As ever,

Healy attacked Israel as America's 'Zionist nuclear outpost'.[42] The money had started to dry up following the Israeli invasion of Lebanon in June 1982. There seems little evidence that the WRP continued to get more Tripoli cash following the murder in April 1984 of WPC Yvonne Fletcher by someone in the Libyan embassy in London. This was presumably because, as a result of the killing, all Gaddafi's diplomats were expelled and therefore, there would have been little more need of the WRP's intelligence on leading Jews. The WRP inquiry team was convinced that many documents were destroyed by Healy and that 'frequently cash was brought to the centre which would not be immediately banked', adding, 'therefore, it was possible for large sums of cash to come and go without being recorded.'

The list by year shows the following proven sums of money flowing into the WRP from the Middle East:

1977	£46,208
1978	£47,784
1979	£347,755
1980	£173,671
1981	£185,128
1982	£271,217
1983	£3,400
1984	£0
1985	£0
TOTAL	£1,075,163

Analysed by country, where it is possible to distinguish, the amounts are:

Libya	£542,267
Kuwait	£156,500
Qatar	£50,000
Abu Dhabi	£25,000
PLO	£19,997
Iraq	£19,697
Unidentified or other sources	£261,702
TOTAL	£1,075,163[43]

The question remains: What did Livingstone know and when did he know it? The first allegations about Healy's mysterious sources of money were voiced in January 1981 in *Socialist Organiser* by the Trot theorist and later Livingstone opponent, Sean Matgamna. Writing nine months before the launch of the *Labour Herald*, Matgamna claimed: 'It [the WRP] is very widely believed to be in receipt of subsidies from one or more Arab governments, from Gaddafi's Libya at least. Of course, there is no public proof of this.

'But for years during which its membership has not been more than four or five hundred, it has published a very glossy daily paper, the *News Line*, which has survived despite having only a tiny circulation. Its relationship to Gaddafi was and is that of a mercenary Hollywood publicity agent to his client… it also supports and shamelessly justifies the widespread murder of Communist Party members by the Hussein dictatorship in Iraq.'[44] If Livingstone no longer received the *Socialist Organiser* which he had helped establish, he was brought up short by *Private Eye* within weeks of the *Labour Herald*'s launch. A throwaway 35-word piece by the columnist 'Backbiter' on 9 October 1981 reported: 'Update on the financing of *Labour Herald*, the organ of Red Ted, and Ken Leninspart. The Libyan Colonel, he of the flashing eyes, has so far financed it to the tune of 200,000 petrodollars.'[45]

Up until then, Livingstone had tried not to rise to the many libels and smears emanating from Fleet Street. But he felt he could not ignore this tiny item in *Private Eye*. He wrote later: 'It was very damaging to have a rumour that I was being privately funded by a foreign power that was in the habit of murdering people.'[46] Along with Ted Knight, and Matthew Warburton, Livingstone issued his first ever writ for libel against the *Eye*.

The story was not true. Livingstone, Knight and Warburton had not received money directly from Colonel Gaddafi nor did they believe that they were benefiting directly or indirectly as a result. But they had entered into a political and commercial arrangement with Gerry Healy, a corrupt man who was in receipt of Libyan cash and could offer good commercial rates for printing work as a result. According to Livingstone, he was approached by Healy with the deal. Following the self-destruction of the WRP and the exposure of Healy's secret finances, *Labour Herald* collapsed immediately, as did Healy's vituperative rag, the *News Line*, printed on the same press. The defamation action was an enormous financial risk for Livingstone, scraping by on his councillor's expenses. He admitted that the case 'might very well have bankrupted Ted and me'.[47]

◆

More than two years later, in November 1983, *Private Eye* apologised, accepted there was 'no truth in these allegations' and paid damages of approximately £15,000 in an out-of-court settlement, as well as the three men's costs. A second magazine called *Event* which had made similar allegations had already gone bust. The joint editors promised that 'the money will be used in its entirety to ensure the continued publication and development of the *Labour Herald*'.[48] But, certain facts are puzzling. Livingstone himself cannot remember whether he ever asked Healy if the allegations were true.[49] At the time, he stuck by the WRP when Healy was accused of taking money from the Libyans. On 20 March 1983, the BBC *Money Programme* accused Healy of receiving money from Libya, provoking this outburst of Healyite anti-Semitism in the *News Line*:

'A powerful Zionist connection runs from the so-called left of the Labour Party right into the centre of Thatcher's government in Downing Street. There is no difficulty whatever in proving this. Top of the list, we have the most recent appointment of Mr Stuart Young, a director of the *Jewish Chronicle*, as youngest-ever chairman of the BBC, having been a governor only since 1981. He is the brother of Mr David Young, another Thatcher appointee who is chairman of the Manpower Services Commission.'[50] Accompanying this rant in the *News Line* was an article by Livingstone, who supported Healy's denial: 'There is certainly a case for suspecting the hand of the forces opposed to the Palestinians. The Zionists were particularly upset by the role the *Labour Herald* played in winning the Labour Party to an official policy to support the recognition of the PLO. The fact that smear [*sic*-smears] about me are being led [*sic*-fed] to the *Jewish Chronicle* on a fairly regular basis suggests that agents of the Begin government are active in the British Labour movement and press at present.'[51]

Asked about this opinion piece, Livingstone says: 'I have no recollection of it.'[52] When asked about the WRP Commission's findings into Healy's dealings with Hussein and Gaddafi, Livingstone replies, 'All I saw, because I'd never met Healy before I became leader [of the GLC] was somebody saying, "We think what you're doing with the Labour Party is right and you're going in the right direction and you could use our presses to produce a paper and we won't exercise any editorial control," and they never did.'[53] He adds: 'I'm sure he might have been quite a monster in earlier days and there was a fair amount of violence, no doubt, but all we had was a deal, a straightforward deal about production of the paper.'

Livingstone says: 'I didn't know there'd been a control commission and oddly enough I haven't seen it! I wouldn't have been at all surprised if he had been receiving money from Gaddafi. But we didn't [receive money from Gaddafi] and we had a straightforward commercial relationship. We flogged ourselves around the country selling the paper.' He concedes the *Herald* was printed at a good rate. 'Healy's position was absolutely clear,' says Livingstone, 'he thought the direction that Knight and I were travelling in the Labour Party was the right one. And there'd be points of disagreement. But they were quite happy to not make a profit, whether they subsidised it or not, I wouldn't know.' In 1984, Livingstone also said in an interview that Healy's printing company Astmoor Litho was in an assisted area with a large regional government grant.[54] It seems odd that Thatcher's government, not known for its generosity, was happy to fund one of Britain's most sinister Trotskyist organisations at the same time it was rolling in cash from Libya.

To be fair to Livingstone, Healy kept tight control of the finances and most of his senior WRP comrades remained in the dark about what was going on, including, apparently, even his deputy Mike Banda. But in light of the allegations, which imperilled his own career and finances, Livingstone's decision to stand by Healy and apparently not ask too many questions about whether or how he was subsiding the *Labour Herald* appears now to have been naive. There can be no doubt that the *Herald*'s fortunes were wrapped up in Healy's. On 23 October 1985, the WRP announced the expulsion of Gerry Healy for his crimes against the party.[55] The *Labour Herald* appeared for the last time,[56] after a month of disrupted production, on 4 December 1985, precisely 42 days later.

Notes

1   *Panorama*, programme number LCAE139W, 28.9.81
2   Ibid.
3   John Golding, *Hammer of the Left*, pp196-197
4   Tony Benn, *The End of an Era, Diaries, 1980-1990*, (see 27.9.81)
5   Ibid.
6   Interview, Graham Bash, 15.8.07
7   John Golding, *Hammer of the Left*, p199
8   Corrina Lotz and Paul Feldman, *Gerry Healy, A Revolutionary Life*, Lupus Books, 1994, (Foreword by Ken Livingstone)
9   Bob Pitt, *The Rise and fall of Gerry Healy*, (Foreword)
10 Interview, Illtyd Harrington, 4.7.07
11 *Belfast Telegraph*, obituary of Brian Behan, 3.11.02
12 Interview, Illtyd Harrington, 4.7.07
13 Tony Benn, *Free at Last, Diaries, 1990-2001* Arrow Books, 1994, (see 9.3.96)
14 *Socialist Organiser*, by Sean Matgamna, p10, 24.1.81, misdated 24.1.80
15 Corrine Lotz and Paul Feldman, *Gerry Healy, A Revolutionary Life*, (Foreword)
16 Ibid.
17 Bob Pitt, *The Rise and Fall of Gerry Healy*, Chapter 11, Gerry Healy's assault on Stuart Carter on 27.4.85
18 *Spectator*, 'The Fall of the Mekon', by Jim Higgins, 9.11.85
19 Ibid.
20 Interview, Keith Veness, 5.10.07
21 Ibid.
22 Ibid.
23 *Spectator*, 'The Fall of the Mekon', by Jim Higgins, 9.11.85
24 *News Line*, 25.10.82; *News Line*, 21.11.83; *News Line*, 20.11.84
25 Letter, John Carr to Ken Livingstone 18.10.82, London Metropolitan Archives, file no. GLC xx/01/29
26 *News Line,* 20.11.84
27 Interview, Keith Veness, 5.10.07
28 *News Line*, 'Build the WRP and its paper', 13.11.85
29 Interview, Graham Bash, 15.8.07
30 Interviews, Matthew Warburton, 19.7.07 and Ted Knight, 4.7.07
31 Interview, Ted Knight, 4.7.07
32 Interview, Graham Bash, 15.8.07
33 Interview, Ken Livingstone, 25.10.07
34 *News Line*, 2.7.79
35 *News Line*, 22.8.79
36 *News Line*, 8.3.79, p10
37 'The Corruption of the Workers Revolutionary Party', Interim Report of the International Committee Commission, 16.12.85
38 Ibid.
39 Ibid.
40 Ibid.
41 Ibid.
42 *News Line*, 12.11.81, pp 1, 8-9

43 Ibid.
44 *Socialist Organiser*, article by Sean Matgamna, p10, 24.1.81, misdated 24.1.80
45 *Private Eye*, Issue 517, 9.10.81, p5
46 Ken Livingstone, *If Voting Changed Anything, They'd Abolish it*, pp161-162
47 Ibid.
48 *Labour Herald*, p3, 25.11.83
49 Interview, Ken Livingstone, 25.10.07
50 *News Line*, 9.4.83
51 Ken Livingstone, 'The Zionist Connection', *News Line*, 9.4.83 (article accompanying *News Line* editorial)
52 Interview, Ken Livingstone, 25.10.07
53 Ibid.
54 John Carvel, *Citizen Ken*, p183
55 *News Line*, p1, 23.10.85
56 *Labour Herald*, 4.12.85

Chapter 11

Loony tunes, 1981–1984

GLC documents were little different from most official papers – stuffy, censorious and often unintelligible except to the select few. Very rarely was there any poetry, particularly any supplied by 'feminist publishers' and included at the behest of the Conservative Party. Item 25 of the GLC's Finance and General Purposes Committee paper on 25 November 1981 included the following verses:

> *I once knew a man*
> *Whose penis led his everywhere,*
> *A merry dance. [Sic]*
> *I knew another,*
> *Who had to take his out daily,*
> *Rain or shine.*
>
> *Today, two million pricks*
> *Are riding, meek as lap dogs,*
> *The Motorways One to Six.*[1]

The poem, 'Heavy Luggage', has five other verses, published again by the GLC at the Tories' insistence, and concludes

> *The Ms One to Six*
> *Snake and insist and*
> *Come again and again*
> *On the belly of Britain.*[2]

Never before at County Hall had the Tories insisted on the publication of the same poem twice, not even one by Shelley or Wilfred Owen. But the Tories came not to praise 'Heavy Luggage' but to revile it and all its kind, as they made clear in a statement above the poem: '…the Socialists confirmed the outrageous decision taken by their colleagues… to loan £12,000 of ratepayers' money to the Sheba Feminist Publishers.' Citing 'Heavy Luggage' as an example of Sheba's output, the Tories continued,

'The Conservative group is unreservedly opposed to a loan being secured by means of the publishers' books; books which at best could be described as erotic and at worst pornographic or even blasphemous.'[3] The loan went ahead.

The Sheba grant was simply another instalment in the long-running battle of the loony left versus Fleet Street, ex parte the Conservative Party and others in the High Court of Public Opinion. During the 1980s, there is little doubt that right-wing and even moderate sections of the press used the Sheba grant and other examples of left-wing 'loonyism' to demonise Labour councils, including the GLC, and by extension the Labour Party and its ability to govern. Ken Livingstone and his policies on women, ethnic minorities, the police and homosexuality bore the brunt of this onslaught, and he seemed to go out of his way to provoke it.

◆

At the start of his administration, these policies were side issues, accounting for a miniscule fraction of County Hall's total expenditure. The idea to give money to groups like Sheba came from Livingstone's bright chief of staff, Bill Bush, who spotted that the law allowed councils a little discretion about what they could spend money on. It was called the 'Two penny rate,' that part of the local taxation on which local authorities were allowed latitude. Despite being a GLC employee and not a politician, Bush had managed to get inserted into the 1981 manifesto commitments to fund community groups and campaigns as an effective way of delivering money to people who were affecting change on the ground.[4] This aspect of the GLC grew in importance as the government stripped the GLC of other powers and the tabloid press focused attention on it. By the time it was abolished, the GLC had no fewer than 13 different units handing out grants.[5]

In June 2007, few people raised an eyebrow when the gay Conservative Westminster Council leader Sir Simon Milton confirmed his commitment to his partner[6] at a civil partnership ceremony, first introduced to Britain by Mayor Livingstone nearly six years previously.[7] A lot has changed since 1981 when talented comic actors like John Inman had to parody their homosexuality for laughs and black and Irish people were often the butt of 'jokes' on mainstream television by comedians like Bernard Manning and Jim Davidson.

◆

An early campaigner for GLC abolition was Aims of Industry, a Thatcherite think tank based at 40 Doughty Street, London, headed by the part-time poet, Michael Ivens. In December 1981, Ivens promoted his 'Keep London Free Campaign'. He said, 'Aims of Industry's "Keep London Free Campaign" is concerned with the present threats to London, its business and its people, by the administration of Mr Ken Livingstone and his colleagues. The threat is not merely of extremist economic policies. Mr Livingstone has made it clear that his approach is a consistent one; he has deplored that it is not possible to turn London into an arena of close conflict – but that he has to back minority conflict: sexual, racial and so on.'[8]

For socialists like Livingstone, these minorities were the victims of conflict, but a conflict waged with ceaseless determination by the British Establishment to maintain its own status, wealth and privileges. Many Londoners happened to be gay, black, Irish, Asian, disabled and women, and possibly a combination of some or all of the above. Reg Race, a former advisor at the GLC, said Livingstone realised the importance of minorities in building a 'rainbow coalition', in which together minorities form a substantial bloc.

'Ken does have some very odd views about things,' says Race. 'He does follow this rainbow coalition stuff which in London is not an implausible way to political power because it's the only part of the country that has got a significant 35 to 40 per cent section of the population that's from a minority, plus others who are fantastically interested in Green or sexuality issues.'[9] But Livingstone had long concluded that the GLC was very good at supporting Establishment causes like opera and the orchestras. 'The established power structure got all sorts of subsidies in all sorts of ways,' says Livingstone. 'Those groups which were excluded were inevitably ones we wanted to help: women's groups, or lesbian and gay groups and they got a very small amount of money, dwarfed by the sums of money poured by the government into the established arts. Or into defence or agriculture.'[10]

But by giving minority groups a voice, and copious amounts of money, Livingstone seemed to touch a raw nerve in some Fleet Street editors and the Tory Party. In late 1981, the GLC's new policies on minorities were excoriated by Patricia Kirwan, Livingstone's Conservative candidate in Paddington, in her pamphlet for Aims of Industry, *Londoners and the Rates*. 'Money is being scattered like water [*sic*] on highly political campaigns and dubious fringe groups,' she wrote.[11] The grants and the 'dubious fringe groups' included: £1,000 to the London Gay Teenage Group; £7,600 to the English Collective of Prostitutes, £8,600 to Women against Rape; £750 to Lesbian Line for 'social activities'; £3,000 and £1,500 respectively to A Woman's Place and Rights of Women, both 'militant feminist organisations'.[12]

Advice to worried gay teenagers? Help for rape victims and prostitutes? Was not this the type of activity the GLC should be funding? If these groups were operating with people on 'the fringe' of society, then was it not about time to ask who had pushed them there? From a cursory glance at some of the press reaction to Livingstone's policies in the 1980s, you might conclude that a great many senior Tory politicians and a few tabloid newspaper editors were half-crazed, sexist, homophobic racists, hopefully a minority in their own right and therefore possibly eligible for a GLC subsidy.

◆

In the months after Livingstone came to power, it became hard to separate fact from fiction as newspapers vied with each other for which could get the barmier loony left stories. Soon, wonderful urban myths grew up, and continue to this day thanks to conflation, repetition and hazy memories. A favourite myth concerned coffee grown in Nicaragua; the country was ruled by those Central American sweethearts of the Left, the Sandinistas, who were struggling against 'the forces of imperialism', in the form of US-backed brigands known as the Contras.

In an interview for this book, a former GLC Tory member said he remembered how a large number of his Labour opponents became incapacitated by diarrhoea during Livingstone's administration after drinking Nicaraguan coffee at a County Hall event in support of Sandinistas. 'You could wander outside,' he continues, 'and there was the Labour deputy chief whip outside the khazi banging on the door because the coffee had given all this poor lot the trots. The Tories and Lib Dems started voting together and they lost about four or five divisions on the trot. And as I recall it, they convened a special council meeting to put back together all the business that they had lost.'[13]

The GLC did enter London into a 'twinning arrangement'

with the Nicaraguan capital, Managua, in July 1985,[14] but no other former member can remember the story and no special meeting was held because of coffee-induced diarrhoea. The story sounds not a million miles away from claims involving another favourite loony left hate figure, the former Haringey Council leader Bernie Grant. The *Sun* would claim that Grant ordered his workers to 'show "solidarity" with Nicaragua… by drinking the Marxist country's grotty coffee.'[15] Haringey Council denied the story not because it was embarrassing but because it was entirely false. That did not prevent it being repeated by some of the tabloids, including the *Daily Mirror*.[16]

Another loony coffee story which refused to die in the face of the facts also concerned the GLC. A diary item in *The Times* claimed that County Hall commissars had instructed staff they could no longer ask for black coffee because it was racist; instead, they should demand 'coffee without milk'. The tale ran and ran despite denials, forcing an exasperated John Carr, chairman of the GLC Staff Committee, to issue a statement, complaining, 'This story is quite untrue and I am surprised that one newspaper after another, from Yorkshire to London, has run the story without checking the truth of it. This kind of ridiculous story is extremely damaging to the work the GLC is trying to do to improve race relations and equal opportunities.'[17]

These myths swirled around with other hardy perennials, like the one about 'Barmy Bernie' Grant banning both black bin liners and the singing of the nursery rhyme 'Baa Baa Black Sheep' because they were racist; or the one about the equally loony Hackney Council banning the use of the word 'manhole cover' on sexism grounds. All were completely invented, usually by mischievous news agency hacks after one gallon too many in some smelly drinking hole. All were completely refuted at the time, to no avail.[18]

♦

Chris Mitchell, a former deputy head of the GLC's Grants Unit, says reporters were always trying to get grants for absurd spoof organisations so they could expose the latest 'Red Ken' lunacy. He says, 'Somebody put in an application for a grant to form a disposal squad to pick up the body parts of DHSS claimants who had been victims of [mass murderer] Denis Nielsen. The assumption by us cynics in the Grants Unit was that it was some bloody reporter from the *Daily Mail* who had nothing better to do.' Mitchell's suspicions turned out to be right.[19] The GLC's systems for checking out the bona fides of applicants were, despite claims to the contrary, extremely rigorous.[20] Some senior civil servants working for the government thought many of the GLC grants condemned by sections of the press actually went to perfectly respectable causes.[21]

Grants to gays caused the most fuss and this led to much prurient interest in Ken Livingstone's sex life. On 17 August 1981, he told the Harrow Gay Unity Group, 'Everyone is bisexual... almost everyone has the sexual potential for anything. It is only the pressures of society which make us conform in one direction or another.' The gay audience cheered Livingstone to the rafters particularly when he said the GLC would 'look favourably' on applications for grants from gay groups.[22] Journalists were dispatched to find out what they could about the lonely bachelor with the salamanders and the crummy snooker table. One persistent source of irritation for Livingstone was Anthony Doran, then home affairs correspondent for the *Daily Mail*. His editor, the legendary Sir David English, took a particular interest in the new GLC leader.

'The stories actually fell out of the trees,' remembers Doran, 'you had to be a pretty bad reporter not to pick up stories.'[23] He thought there were better stories elsewhere in the loony left strongholds of Lambeth under 'Red Ted' Knight and Liverpool in the grip of Derek Hatton and the Militant Tendency. Doran adds, 'The only reason why Livingstone was a good story was because he made himself so high profile and he was a bit of a cheeky chappie kind of character. Livingstone and I come from similar backgrounds, so I always liked him personally. I don't think he likes me but I can understand that. At a Brent by-election, I turned up, and he said to me, "I'd hoped you were dead."'[24] Doran swiftly concluded that Livingstone was not gay and was sent to find out more about his personal life. He was on a Sunday shift, and having received a tip-off, arrived outside a flat in north London when out walked Livingstone hand-in-hand with a woman who was not his then wife, Christine Chapman. Although the photographer failed to turn up thanks to a cock-up on the paper's picture desk, Doran had enough evidence to run a story about Livingstone's adultery with Kate Allen.

Doran claims that English did not think Livingstone's affair was that big a deal and was not prepared to pay Chapman a great deal of money for her story. 'I went from his girlfriend's flat to Christine's house,' says Doran. 'It was a quiet day; not many stories about and I had my doubts about doing the story.' He remembers Chapman's fury about Livingstone on the doorstep; she did not appear to Doran to be reluctant to talk. 'The editor just didn't think it was worth a lot of money,' says Doran. 'He didn't think she would have anything great to say and neither did the rest of us. It certainly wasn't true that she was pressurised [into telling her story.]' Encouraged by her reaction, he offered Chapman approximately £10,000 for her story. She rejected the offer. Livingstone says he and Chapman had considered taking the money. 'We discussed afterwards taking the money and splitting it,' says Livingstone. 'They said, "Don't worry about writing it, we'll write it. Ten grand was a lot of money in those days." I said to Christine, "Why don't you write about this really bizarre sex life we had and cash the cheque?" and then we'd appear and say it was all bollocks but we've got the money.'[25] If Livingstone had been caught hand-in-hand with a man, doubtless the cheque would have been much bigger.

◆

Under Livingstone, the GLC became essentially a powerful campaigning tool, whether for women's rights or the unemployed. With ever-increasing advertising budgets, County Hall became one of the most sophisticated campaigners around. From 1980 to 1984, the annual funding of voluntary organisations by the GLC rose from £6 million to £50 million.[26] Livingstone gave the GLC the strong sense of identity it had lacked for so long; it just happened to be the wrong sense of identity as far as the government and Fleet Street were concerned.

In July 1981, Livingstone introduced the Ethnic Minorities Committee and gave it a budget of around £2.9 million, much of it dispensed in grants under his chairmanship. The Police Committee was established the same month under the chairmanship of Paul Boateng, and the gay and lesbian working party. In June 1982, the Women's Committee held its first meeting.[27]

The Women's Committee, under the chairmanship, sorry, chairpersonship of Valerie Wise, questioned and exposed rampant sexism and inequality. In 1986, only four per cent of MPs and 17 per cent of councillors were women. At the GLC itself, only five per cent of senior officers were women, yet they made up 52 per cent of the population.[28] There was systematic discrimination against women when it came to jobs, and the women's unit was correct to claim that women were 'disproportionately represented in low status, low-paid jobs usually in non-unionised places of work with few rights and poor working conditions.'[29]

Along with gays and ethnic minorities, every GLC decision maker had to take into account the needs of women and how they would be affected by a particular course of action. Livingstone had established the Greater London Enterprise Board (GLEB) to invest in business ideas and generate jobs 'with particular emphasis on breaking down discrimination against various groups, namely ethnic minorities and women'.[30] Other Women's Committees sprouted all over London. Kate Allen, Livingstone's partner, chaired the one in Camden.[31] But the Women's Committee proved by far the most controversial and provided a steady supply of scandals. The 96 or so feminists who eventually ended up working in the Women's Committee support unit quickly proved to be easily the most unmanageable crew in County Hall and swiftly gained a reputation for being men-hating harpies in boots and boiler suits.[32]

For *Private Eye*, Val Wise's committee became the Wimmin's Committee; she became Valerie 'Olive Oyl' Wise. The committee provided a wealth of stories for the *Eye*'s new column, 'London Calling', which reported the antics in County Hall. Occasionally, genuine loony behaviour was identified. One edition of the *Eye* reported on an open meeting of the committee: 'Several hundred screaming wimmin conspired to wreck the proceedings when the photographer requested by Ms Wise to record the proceedings for posterity turned out to be a MIN! The poor chap entered the hall to a torrent of abuse, shouted insults and digital signs.' The *Eye* reported how the photographer waited outside while there was a 'democratic vote of the sisters'.[33] The stories of boiler-suited bellicosity were many and varied.

Several former GLC officials and Tory members interviewed for this book tell the story of how some Women's Unit employees objected to the portraits of former male GLC chairmen 'looking down on them' from the wood-panelled walls on the principal floor and demanded their removal or at least that they be turned to face the wall. The claim is also made by former County Hall press officer Wes Whitehouse in his book, *GLC – The Inside Story*.[34] Whitehouse's former colleague, Doreen King, who handled the committee's press arrangements, described the employees of the Women's Unit: 'They were dreary, humourless girls and like peas in a pod. All were in their twenties. They wore dungarees, lots of badges and Doc Martens boots. There wasn't a lick of make-up to be seen. I remember a security man opening the door for them and saying, "This way, ladies." They rounded on him and said, "We're not ladies."'[35] Some men did try their hardest. In June 1982, *Briefing* advertised an ANTI-SEXIST MEN'S WEEKEND. Those interested had to give their name and address and state whether they needed 'sleeping space, crèche facilities and/or vegetarian food.'[36]

◆

As the second most senior GLC official at the time, and soon to be promoted to the top spot as director general, Maurice Stonefrost identified two main problems with the Women's Committee and the other bodies established by Livingstone to address injustice: 'The first problem is the understandable passion of any new movement. By definition, the women's movement, like any new crusade has more passion and commitment than any established concern. And so difference of opinion on how to proceed became much more contentious and argumentative.'[37] The Women's Unit had no desire to be 'subsumed into the machine of County Hall'. Maurice Stonefrost says, 'They wanted to operate as a cooperative and wanted no men to be involved in it. I facilitated that.'[38] Even when he succeeded Sir James Swaffield as director general of the GLC, Stonefrost made sure that the women's unit did not have to report to him and instead appointed as the unit's overseer a senior woman official manager, whom he instructed to be discreet. But Stonefrost always considered the Women's Unit a 'hothouse for problems,'[39] and so it proved.

In the summer of 1984, the chaos that the Women's Unit had become was exposed to the world. In a bizarre twist for an organisation devoted to equality, this dysfunctional body was found guilty of 'institutionalised racism' by an internal GLC inquiry.[40] Louise Pankhurst, the GLC's women's rights advisor who ran the unit and had expressed concern about the problem, left halfway through her four-year contract. She received a £30,000 pay-off while describing her job as having been 'nightmarish'.[41] Pankhurst was reported to have said of Women's Unit workers: 'When charges of racism were made it was as frequently between Asian and Afro-Caribbean as between black and white.'[42] The *Telegraph* pointed out that 1984 was the GLC's Anti-Racism Year, adding, 'The Tories who last ran the GLC were an inestimable band of brothers-in-law; Mr Livingstone's charm notwithstanding, the present rulers are simply grotesque.'[43]

Valerie Wise's attempts to sort out the problems by taking the Women's Unit on a morale-raising trip to Brighton also backfired. The 31-strong team were spotted at the four-star Bedford Hotel. According to the *Daily Telegraph*, 'Spiky hair, boiler suits and sandals were *de rigueur*.'[44] During its four-year existence, the Women's Committee handed out £29 million to women's centres and playgroups, but by far the most contentious grant concerned a cheque of £800 given to a tiny organisation of women peace campaigners called 'Babies against the Bomb' in February 1983.[45]

There was already 'Families against the Bomb', established in north London in June 1981. One of the group's founders wrote: 'We have been criticised by feminists for using the word *families*. It is a reactionary title we have been told. This is because it has been presupposed that by families we mean "nuclear" families, i.e. husband, wife and two point whatever kids, presumably called the nuclear family because it is a potentially explosive combination.'[46] Families against the Bomb would encompass 'everyone from single parent families, the dreaded "nuclear family", extended families, groups of people, men and/or women caring for children communally, lesbian households with children etc.'[47]

Babies against the Bomb was formed by a 33-year-old mother called Tamar Swade, whose son Dario was two. 'I had my child in 1980,' says Swade, 'and that made me very aware of life and death and I wanted to protect my child and the whole nuclear issue was bubbling up.'[48] She was a member of the Campaign for Nuclear Disarmament which was then protesting alongside the Women's Peace Camp against the siting of 96 nuclear cruise missiles by the US at the Greenham Common airbase in Berkshire. But Swade found it difficult to attend CND meetings because she had to look after her child. She hit upon the idea of getting together with other like-minded mothers in her north London neighbourhood of Gospel Oak so they could all share childcare duties by keeping an eye on each others' children. They also wanted money to pay for the banners, stickers and badges for anti-nuclear marches and stalls. 'It started as a bit of a joke,' remembers Swade, 'we were lying around wondering what we should call ourselves. And it just came out. It was all so ridiculous. We all had visions of babies throwing their dirty nappies at Thatcher!'[49]

The £800 was a drop in the ocean not only compared to the GLC's annual £1 billion budget but also the £38 million given by Labour to more than a thousand community groups. 'It was a fraction of a fraction,' says Maurice Stonefrost.[50] Other groups which also received grants from the Women's Committee on 15 February 1983 included the Southall Black Sisters (£6,815) and the Black Women's Radio Group (£1,680). But it was the Babies against the Bomb which riled sections of the press and the Thatcher government which was already in the process of sharpening its axe.[51]

The Babies against the Bomb brought together two elements most despised by the Tories and their friends in the press: Livingstone's grants policy and the GLC's campaign on nuclear weapons and civil defence. Livingstone committed the GLC to rejecting its legal obligations to plan for the possibility of a nuclear attack on London by the Soviet Union. Instead money would be used to establish London as a 'nuclear-free zone' and to campaign for unilateral nuclear disarmament. At the time, this was seen as yet another futile gesture by Livingstone, but documents released years later by the government revealed the real angst the measure caused in Whitehall. The GLC had to prepare for a nuclear holocaust, just as its predecessor, the London County Council, had to plan for the eventual aerial bombardment by the Luftwaffe. This was not something a small borough could manage on its own; only a capital-wide strategic body would do. Sixty volunteer scientists and a large number of expert emergency planners depended on the GLC for funding and training. In 1981, there were still no signs of a thaw in the Cold War and civil defence planning was an integral part of Britain's defence policy.

Britain's derisory civil defence programme was best expressed by the Home Office leaflet 'Protect and Survive', which included advice on how to rid your house of combustible materials before an attack, including 'old newspapers and magazines', as well as advising: 'If you have a fire extinguisher, keep it handy' and 'Keep buckets of water on each floor.' 'After a nuclear attack,' the leaflet suggested, 'there will be a short period before fallout descends. Use this time to do essential tasks.' This included 'do not smoke' and 'go around the house and put out any small fires using mains water if you can'.[52] Meanwhile, Britain's 3,000 top people, including Livingstone, if he chose, would be safe and snug in deep underground bunkers dusting off plans to turn London's parks and open spaces into mass graveyards.

Livingstone wrote later: 'The thought of spending my last days locked in a bunker with Mrs Thatcher's cabinet while all my friends died held little appeal.'[53]

◆

On 20 May 1981, the GLC announced an immediate halt to the annual spending of £1 million on plans for nuclear war civil defence. Illtyd Harrington, Livingstone's deputy, said the government plans were 'a farce, a cruel deception and a waste of money'. He added: 'What we are challenging is the absurd cosmetic approach to Armageddon.'[54] Psychologically and politically, the GLC was also highlighting the folly of nuclear war and therefore by extension nuclear weapons, bolstering the growing calls within the Labour Party to support unilateral disarmament. The GLC abandoned its commitment to provide a total of 759 individual plans, most relating to post-attack survival. The four command posts in West Norwood, North Cheam, Southall and Wanstead were told to concentrate on planning for emergencies such as flood and fire. Nuclear defence training was scrapped and maintenance of the three main nuclear bunkers would cease. For three years, the bunkers were abandoned before being thrown open to a curious public every Sunday afternoon as part of a CND campaign.[55] The GLC also published the names of the 3,000 officials and politicians earmarked for survival.

'We are challenging the nuclear defence strategy,' announced Harrington. Again the GLC was acting in line with the core sentiment of the rebellious Labour movement. The party itself was about to adopt unilateral nuclear disarmament as the flagstone of its defence policy. By May 1981, 82 British local authorities with responsibilities for roughly 16 million people had declared themselves to be 'nuclear-free zones'. By March 1982, 170 local councils had passed motions calling on the government 'to refrain from the manufacture or positioning of any nuclear weapons of any kind' within their boundaries.[56]

But, as the civil defence authority for the capital, the GLC's announcement presented the government with a particular dilemma. In a confidential memo 11 days after the GLC decision, J.A. Howard, a civil servant in the F6 Division of the Home Office, wrote: '...any reversal now of the declared policy would depend on the moderate unease and chagrin about the leftward tendency of the new [GLC] leadership.'[57]

According to a second memo that day, one official revealed: 'The home secretary [Willie Whitelaw] in an aside today foresaw great difficulty in dealing effectively with the GLC revolt.' The memo proposed a discreet approach to Sir James Swaffield, the director general of the GLC. The official went on, 'My feeling is that he and his staff will be feeling very vulnerable, and may welcome our throwing a lifeline chance to talk to us on the quiet.'[58] Swaffield wrote back and said he would appreciate an 'informal talk.'[59]

The government explored the possibility of using the district auditor's power of surcharge to bully the GLC Labour members into submission. There was a theory that the GLC could be acting illegally if it was using public money for civil defence purposes other than that for which it was intended – nuclear war contingency planning. Therefore, the auditor could surcharge them and ban them from office for unlawful spending. There could be a possibility of sending in a government commissioner to undertake the work. There was a precedent. In 1956, the St Pancras Metropolitan Borough refused to carry out its statutory duties by building a new civil defence headquarters. A government commissioner was appointed and arranged for the HQ to be built at 16-21 Camden High Street, after which the bill was sent to the councillors.[60] This argument was rapidly rejected by two Home Office lawyers. A Mr Morris said, 'I cannot myself see any basis for the suggestion that a policy decision to limit emergency planning to civil emergencies and disasters might lead to surcharge, let alone disqualification.'[61] His colleague, a Mr Howard, agreed, adding: '...but let the GLC frighten itself out of the proposal if it wants to.'

The GLC nearly did frighten itself out of it. Newly released papers reveal that there was a government mole inside the GLC who was handing over confidential documents about civil defence to the Home Office. One note refers to papers 'passed to us in confidence by a GLC official'. The document revealed critical intelligence that a QC hired by the GLC had expressed concern that the district auditor 'could intervene'.[62]

But Harrington had set the public tone for defiance: 'If the government chooses to confront us we will have to face that challenge.' Instead the government assumed more responsibility for civil defence. The GLC also appointed as 'civil defence advisor', the *New Statesman* investigative journalist Duncan Campbell [not to be confused with Duncan Campbell of the *Guardian*] who had broken a number of security services stories that had embarrassed the government.

Soon, Campbell was able to secure from reluctant GLC officials documents showing how troops would ring the capital shortly before an attack to prevent the flight of seven million Londoners, six million of whom would die in the conflagration.[63] The GLC would declare 1983 as 'Peace Year' and forge a close working relationship with the Campaign for Nuclear Disarmament (CND). Anti-nuclear campaigning groups received grants and the GLC held propaganda exhibitions stressing both the destructive force of nuclear weapons and the folly of deploying them.[64] It would be a rare government defeat. According to the GLC's Tory spokesman on civil defence, Neville Beale, Livingstone and his comrades led 'an extremely able and active campaign to thwart the Home Office'.[65]

The government decided against deploying the district auditor and instead attempted to counter the propaganda with some of its own. In newspaper adverts, Thatcher's armed forces minister, Peter Blaker, stated rather pompously: 'Organisations spring up mushroom-like, calling themselves this group or that group against nuclear war. The implication is that there are actually people for nuclear war.' As for nuclear-free zones, Blaker asked: 'Would you ever dream of trying to protect your home from a thunderstorm by putting up a sign saying "storm-free zone"?'[66]

By turning the GLC into a campaigning weapon, Livingstone and his cohorts ensured that it would soon be campaigning for its own survival. Most of Livingstone's achievements at County Hall – along with the GLC itself – were largely forgotten not long after the smell of fireworks had cleared the air at the party to mark its abolition on the South Bank in 1986. Who really remembers Fares Fair or cares who built the Thames Barrier? But the GLC had proved important in helping to change attitudes on some of the most important social issues of the day. In many ways, that is its enduring legacy. Perhaps shock and provocation were the only effective instruments at its disposal.

Notes

1 GLC Council Agenda, Minority Party Report, Grant to Sheba Publishers, 24.11.81, p26
2 Ibid., 15.12.81, p36
3 Ibid., 24.11.81, p26
4 Interview, Ken Livingstone, 1.11.07
5 Interview, Chris Mitchell, former senior GLC grants officer, 12.9.07
6 *New Statesman*, article by Brian Coleman, 25.6.07
7 http://news.bbc.co.uk/1/hi/uk/1525205.stm
8 Patricia Kirwan, 'Londoners and the Rates', an Aims of Industry pamphlet, in the introduction by Michael Ivens
9 Interview, Reg Race, 23.8.07
10 Interview, Ken Livingstone, 1.11.07
11 Patricia Kirwan, 'Londoners and the Rates', pp5-6
12 Ibid.
13 Interview, former GLC Conservative member, 26.11.07
14 GLC Agenda paper 4, 'The Council's Relations With Managua', Nicaragua, 15.7.85
15 James Curran, Ivor Gaber and Julian Petley, *Culture Wars, The Media and the British Left*, Edinburgh University Press, 2005, pp90-91
16 Ibid., pp50-51
17 GLC Press release, Number 58, 'GLC Coffee Story Leaves Bitter Taste', statement by John Carr, 1.2.84
18 James Curran, Ivor Gaber and Julian Petley, *Culture Wars, The Media and the British Left*, pp92-107
19 Interview, Chris Mitchell, 12.9.07
20 Ibid.
21 Private briefing, former civil servant for Department of the Environment, 8.1.08
22 *Evening Standard*, 18.8.81
23 Interview, Anthony Doran, 13.7.07
24 Ibid.
25 Interview, Ken Livingstone, 25.10.07
26 Andrew Forrester, Stewart Lansley and Robin Pauley, *Beyond our Ken, A Guide to the Battle for London*, Fourth Estate, 1985, p47
27 Ibid., pp48-49
28 GLC booklet, 'The GLC Women's Committee 1982-1986, A record of change and achievement for women in London', p3
29 Ibid., pp30-31
30 Ibid.
31 *Labour Herald*, article by Kate Allen, pp6-7, 26.8.83

32 GLC booklet, 'The GLC Women's Committee 1982-1986, A record of change and achievement for women in London', p13

33 *Private Eye*, 'London Calling', issue 569, p7, 7.10.83

34 Wes White*house*, *GLC – The Inside Story*, p124

35 Ibid., pp124-125

36 *London Labour Briefing*, June 1982, p30

37 Interview, Maurice Stonefrost, 21.11.07

38 Ibid.

39 Ibid.

40 Andrew Forrester, Stewart Lansley and Robin Pauley, *Beyond our Ken, A Guide to the Battle for London,* pp45-46

41 *Evening Standard*, 'Nightmare battle by GLC woman', 10.8.84

42 Ibid.

43 *Daily Telegraph*, 'Editorial-Soap Bubbles', 11.8.84

44 *Daily Telegraph*, 'GLC women's £2,250 seaside trip "a fiasco"', 25.7.84

45 GLC press release, 'Grants made by Women's Committee', 21.2.83, London Metropolitan Museum

46 *London Labour Briefing*, 'Don't take MY children with you! – Families Against the Bomb', June 1982

47 Ibid.

48 Interview, Tamar Swade, 29.6.07

49 Ibid.

50 Interview, Maurice Stonefrost, 21.11.07

51 GLC press release, 'Grants made by Women's Committee', 21.2.83, London Metropolitan Museum

52 'Protect and survive', prepared for Home Office by Central Office of Information, 1976

53 Ken Livingstone, *If Voting Changed Anything, They'd Abolish it*, pp231-233

54 *The Times*, 21.5.81

55 *Guardian*, 18.9.84

56 GLC agenda paper, Joint Report of the Public Services and Fire Brigade Committee, Planning Committee and the Transport Committee, 9.3.82, p1

57 Memo, by JA Howard, F6 Division, reference CDP/73 86/11/36, 1.6.81

58 Memo, by Home Office official, reference CDP/73 86/11, 1.6.81

59 Letter, Sir James Swaffield to Robert Andrew of the Home Office, 5.6.81

60 Report by Air Commodore George Innes, Controller of Operational Services, GLC Emergency Planning Policy Review, August 1981, p3

61 Memos by Mr Morris and Mr Howard, Home Office solicitors, 15.6.81, reference CDP/73 86/11/36

62 Report by Air Commodore George Innes, Controller of Operational Services, GLC Emergency Planning Policy Review, August 1981, p8

63 Ken Livingstone, *If Voting Changed Anything, They'd Abolish It*, pp231-233

64 Speech by Neville Beale, former GLC member for Finchley, 'The Anti-Nuclear Policy', 12.9.86

65 Ibid.

66 *Willesden and Brent Chronicle*, article by Peter Blaker, minister of armed forces, 19.11.82, p15

Chapter 12

Green Ken, October 1981–May 1983

On 10 October 1981, the provisional IRA detonated a remote-controlled nail bomb placed in a van parked outside the Irish Guards Barracks in Chelsea as a bus full of soldiers drove past. Two civilians died: Nora Field, a 59-year-old widow, and John Breslin, aged 18. Thirty-eight others, including 22 soldiers and 16 civilians suffered injuries. It had been exactly a week since six hunger strikers at the Maze prison had called off their fast. Two days later, Ken Livingstone travelled to Cambridge to deliver a speech to the Conservative Reform Group on the dusty subject of rates. Someone from the audience asked him for his reaction to the latest IRA outrage, the worst on mainland Britain since a bombing campaign in London during 1975. According to *The Times*, Livingstone answered that the terrorists who carried out the attack were 'not criminals or lunatics running about,' adding: 'That is to misunderstand them.'[1]

The reaction was instant and savage. Memorably, the *Sun* splashed his comment on the front page under the headline: 'This damn fool says the bombers aren't criminals,' and said, 'This morning the *Sun* presents the most odious man in Britain. Take a bow, Mr Livingstone, socialist leader of the Greater London Council. In just a few months since he appeared on the national scene, he has quickly become a joke. But no one can laugh at him any longer. The joke has turned sour, sick and obscene. For Mr Livingstone steps forward as the defender and the apologist of the criminal, murderous activities of the IRA.'[2]

The *Evening Standard* registered a resigned contempt: 'Perhaps we should, by now, have become hardened to the fact that the man who runs London can be by turns sinister, unpleasant or merely foolish in his public comments. But this, coming at a time when an IRA active service unit is still at large in the capital and with more bombings threatened before Christmas, is worse than folly. It is criminal.'[3] This was the third row in just four months involving Livingstone and the dark, dangerous politics of Northern Ireland. Fleet Street had registered its distaste at his open support for the hunger strikers on the day of the Royal wedding and shock at the unseemly Dunlop boys' imbroglio the following month.[4] But now Livingstone appeared to be condoning the murderers of innocent people on streets of London.

Livingstone moved as fast to qualify his remarks in a letter to *The Times*: 'I abhor all violence. Murder on London's streets is shocking, and it is unacceptable. The bomb attack on Saturday emphasises that a permanent solution to the troubles of Ireland is essential, not just for Ireland itself, but for all parts of Britain. The point I was trying to make was that to crush the IRA as if they were simply criminals or lunatics will not work. It is the policy that has been tried for generations and still the killing persists. The IRA bombers and their supporters believe they have strong political motives. For this reason, if one is caught others come forward to take his place. This is not the case with individually motivated psychopaths; once arrested, the crimes cease.'[5]

But on the day he wrote to *The Times*, Monday, 13 October 1981, Livingstone appeared to throw fuel on the fire. His senior colleague John McDonnell tried to get the Labour group to enter into talks with the bombers of the republican IRA and Irish National Liberation Army (INLA).[6] According to the *Daily Telegraph*'s well informed local government correspondent, John Grigsby, there were 'angry scenes' when the proposal was made. Grigsby reported: 'There were cries of "disgraceful" from Labour moderates.'[7] By a majority of only 16 to 14, the group rejected the proposal.

'Naturally we welcome this decision,' said the *Telegraph*, 'it preserves our capital city from the disgrace of appearing to have been frightened out of its wits by a bomb outrage.' It added: 'For the present Mr Livingstone's London is a bad joke; when will it be recognised as a real menace?'[8]

Also on 14 October 1981, Livingstone was attacked on his way to give a talk to the City of London Junior Chamber of Commerce. A man with an aerosol sprayed red paint in his face. An organisation calling itself 'The Friends of Ulster' later claimed responsibility.[9] In a further incident, at the Three Horseshoes pub in Hampstead, Livingstone and some friends were attacked by a bunch of skinheads shouting 'commie bastard'. 'I didn't realise I could run so fast until that point,' says Livingstone. 'I should have done more sport at school.'[10] The *Daily Mail* later reported that Livingstone's estranged wife Christine Chapman was 'fed up with abusive phone calls directed at her controversial husband', packed her bags and 'headed for an address in north London'.[11]

◆

Ken Livingstone has often been accused of sticking his nose into issues which were not his concern. Even as mayor of London more than 20 years later, he would be mocked and criticised for opening up embassies abroad and forging links with dubious rulers like Fidel Castro and Hugo Chávez. But by wading into the quagmire of Irish sectarian politics, he did real political damage to the Labour Party and the Greater London Council. His critics argued that there was nothing in legislation which authorised the GLC to enter into negotiations with paramilitaries. The parliamentary draughtsmen hoped it would have enough on its plate building homes, motorways, Thames Barriers and so on, leaving the really big stuff like policy on Northern Ireland to the government. There is another point which tends to be overlooked: Ken Livingstone had never even been to Ireland by that stage to study the situation on the ground.

He may have abhorred violence but with every word and gesture he seemed to indicate his clear sympathy for the republican cause. He saw Northern Ireland as a part of the island of Ireland occupied by the British troops in the cause of imperialism. Some of his senior colleagues at the GLC would refer to the IRA – behind closed doors naturally – as 'freedom fighters'.[12] Livingstone was convinced that Britain would have to withdraw and allow a united Ireland. In an interview for the *Independent*, he said: 'It won't be perceived as a victory for the IRA because the IRA hasn't got majority support, but there will eventually be a united Ireland and the IRA will claim a victory for that. Many forces will have played a part in bringing that about, not least of which will be the exhaustion of the British public who don't want to carry on the slaughter year after year.'

Eventually, the British always abandon their colonial possessions, he said, adding: 'It's in line with other experiences whether in Vietnam or Algeria or Cyprus or Kenya or Aden. Tell me one that wasn't.'[13]

He also considered Northern Ireland a bogus state, as he made clear in the Labour Party weekly paper *Tribune*: 'I think that a united Ireland is absolutely inevitable. It was inevitable back in 1921 when the British government of the day gerrymandered Northern Ireland. The North has never been a viable body, and it has never been accepted by the majority of the Irish people. Those acts of violence are a reflection of the existence of Northern Ireland. While it exists, that violence will continue. It might die down, for a decade or more, but it will always flare up again.'[14]

It is true that the Labour Party's manifesto for 1983 called for a united Ireland but on the basis of a majority consensus in the North. Livingstone was way out of line, even for many of those on the left of the Labour Party, as were his views that the British were guilty of genocide against the Irish. 'If it had not been for the impact of British imperialism,' Livingstone told the *Irish Times*, 'there would have been a population of 15 to 20 million now. It would have been a European country on a par with Holland.'[15]

By 2006, the population of the Republic of Ireland was a little more than 4.2 million[16]; in Northern Ireland, the latest census shows a population of a little below 1.7 million.[17] Seemingly, Britain was responsible for blotting out the lives of at least nine million people before conception. Livingstone's view that Northern Ireland was a colonial province held down by a foreign power was shared by many Trotskyist groups including the Workers Revolutionary Party and the International Marxist Group.[18]

Livingstone's views on Ireland cast him in the role as a national hate figure and would later nearly cost him his life when Unionist paramilitaries seriously contemplated murdering him.[19] Hardline loyalists dubbed Livingstone 'Green Ken.'[20]

Livingstone's opinions were clearly sincere and they also helped advance his political career. He would not have been chosen as the Labour candidate for Brent East if his views on Ireland had been different, and there is no secret about that. His brutal battle to become the MP for Brent East is dealt with in the next chapter, but Livingstone had no doubt that his stance on Ireland was critical to securing the candidacy from the far left activists who helped control the constituency. The Irish made up approximately 12 per cent of Brent East. Livingstone admitted to the *Irish Times* after securing the seat: 'The reason I got selected for Brent East was because of my position on Ireland. It was the first constituency to make its policy Troops Out.'[21] This was also confirmed by the chair of Brent East Labour Party Emma Tait, who emphasised the importance of Livingstone's 'republican views', adding: 'If Ken Livingstone bottles out of this issue [Ireland], then it is likely that this party would cease to support him.'[22]

By the time of the Chelsea Barracks bombing, Livingstone's supporters had already set their sights on Brent East, but that would not become public for another year.[23] He was repeatedly accused by the Tories and others of promoting his high profile republican sympathy to win support and votes in Brent East.[24] Sir Horace Cutler, the aggressive Thatcherite builder from Harrow who led the Tory group, called for Livingstone to be officially censured by the GLC when it met on 21 October 1981. Cutler's motion read: 'That the Council do censure the leader of the Council (Mr Livingstone) for misusing his position to further his extreme views on subjects over many of which [sic] of the Council has no jurisdiction and, particularly, for his outrageous remarks reported on 12 and 13 October 1981 concerning the bombing in London on 10 October 1981.'[25]

Livingstone used his majority to defeat the motion with some ease, by 45 votes to 39. Cutler told the meeting that Livingstone had 'generally abused his position as leader of the council', adding: 'He is the worst thing to hit London since the plague, and in some ways akin to it. He must go now.'[26]

By all accounts, the censure meeting was a nasty, tedious affair. According to a sketch by Roland Freeman in *Time Out*, there was 'perpetual baying' from the Tories and various people threw abuse at each other or said things like 'shut up' or 'sit down' or 'hear hear'. 'There were dark mutterings about the future of the GLC,' murmured Freeman. 'Some councillors said things could not go on like this. The government would have to intervene and close the whole show down... perhaps the Tory tactics in the council chamber were a calculated plot to bring down Livingstone and, if necessary, the GLC with him.'[27]

For the Tories, tactics were helpful but not nearly as good as having Ken Livingstone. On 22 October 1981, the day after the GLC meeting, the voters delivered their verdict. Bill Pitt, the Liberal candidate, won the Conservative-held parliamentary seat of Croydon North West. At a time when the Thatcher government was unpopular, Labour should have won the seat, having come a close second in the 1979 general election. But Labour's support dropped by a catastrophic 14 per cent to let in the Liberals.[28] Much of that blame should have fallen on Tony Benn and his divisive attempt to take the deputy leadership from Denis Healey which ended in failure a month before the by-election. But Livingstone took the brunt of the blame. The damage was caused not only by his remarks on Ireland but also the levying of the additional supplementary rate needed to pay for Fares Fair which had been launched six days before the IRA attack. Livingstone claimed that the local Tory-controlled council for Croydon 'helpfully arranged for the rate demand to be delivered at the beginning of the [by-election] campaign.'[29] But other councils sent out the demand at the same time. Not only that, claimed Livingstone later, but the Liberal candidate Bill Pitt 'immediately pushed the issue of my remarks [on the IRA] to the forefront of the campaign.'[30] But is that not politics? His comments read like a man complaining about the rain after seeding the clouds.

◆

During Livingstone's first year in office, there would be a series of disastrous by-election results from Croydon North West to Glasgow Hillhead. 'The internal feuding was bleeding us dry,' wrote John Golding, Labour MP for Newcastle under Lyme. 'On the doorsteps, Benn was cursed and candidates [were] asked which side they were on... I found Ken Livingstone's name constantly linked with Benn.'[31] As a prominent right-wing member of the Labour NEC, Golding would play a critical role in the fortunes of Ken Livingstone.[32]

At the GLC censure meeting, Illtyd Harrington, Livingstone's deputy, had played the role of the elder statesman putting Livingstone back in his box: 'Today the GLC is extricating itself from Northern Ireland. It is beyond any doubt that the leadership of this council is now going to concentrate on the constitutional problems coming from central government. This meeting today is a watershed. We have taken a decision that we are going to get the GLC back on to a sane and sensible line.' That was a forlorn expectation. Harrington and other moderates had overplayed their hand if they thought they had brought Livingstone under control.

◆

By the time he became leader of the GLC, Livingstone already enjoyed close links to Sinn Féin. Andy Harris, the new member for Putney in south London, was a member of an obscure hard left group, the Labour Committee on Ireland. In July, it was Harris who had invited over Alice McElwee, whose son had murdered the mother of the three Dunlop brothers.[33]

Livingstone's most important conduit to Sinn Féin, the political wing of the Provisional IRA, was Steven Bundred, the left-wing GLC member for Islington North.[34] Along with his wife Kathy, Bundred was an important figure in the Troops Out movement. Troops Out was not 'politically affiliated' to Sinn Féin, but both organisations were very close. For Gerry Adams of Sinn Féin, Troops Out played an important role in raising awareness in Britain about the situation in Ireland.'[35] Members of Sinn Féin and Troops Out took part in regular exchange visits and held joint meetings to 'break down the wall of disinformation which successive British governments have constructed around Britain's war in Ireland'.[36] From 1972 onwards, a Troops Out delegation would visit Belfast every August for the Sinn Féin anti-internment march.[37]

Livingstone's key Sinn Féin contact through Bundred was its national publicity director, Danny Morrison, a former member of the IRA. 'There was a simple formula,' says Morrison, 'that one bomb in London was worth a hundred in Belfast. The whole purpose of the IRA campaign – and this was the purpose of the Troops Out movement as well – was that the IRA wanted a solidarity movement in England which would capitalise on public disillusionment on government policy over Ireland, so the IRA was trying to replicate the anti-Vietnam war movement which existed in the States and put pressure on the government there. Their attacks on soldiers in the North and the bombing campaign in England were part and parcel of the same strategy and that was to get the British public to put pressure on the government to say there's an alternative.'[38]

The bombing campaign continued. On 26 October 1981, a bomb disposals officer died trying to defuse a device at a Wimpy Bar in Oxford Street. On 20 July 1982, London witnessed two devastating attacks. In Hyde Park, four members of the Household Cavalry and seven of their horses were killed in a nail bomb attack. Another device exploded almost simultaneously beneath a bandstand in Regent's Park killing seven bandsmen from the Royal Green Jackets who were performing hits from the musical 'Oliver!'

On 20 October 1982, five members of Sinn Féin were elected to the Northern Ireland Assembly at Stormont Castle after polling 10.1 per cent of the popular vote.[39] They included Gerry Adams, Martin McGuiness, Owen Carron, Jim McAllister and Danny Morrison. It was a major coup for Sinn Féin although they refused to participate in the Assembly, along with the other main nationalist party, the Social Democratic and Labour Party, the SDLP, reducing it to the status of a meaningless Unionist talking shop. Winning elections had also become part of the strategy of Sinn Féin/IRA. Morrison had told Sinn Féin's conference in 1981: 'Who here really believes we can win the war through the ballot box? But will anyone here object if, with a ballot paper in this hand and an Armalite [rifle], we take power in Ireland.'[40]

The elections gave Sinn Féin a popular mandate and for Livingstone a reason to proffer an invitation. 'The British government usually got off the hook by saying sure these people don't have a mandate, they don't even stand for election,' says Morrison. 'But the government still wouldn't talk to us; they wouldn't allow the civil service to talk to us. We were still excluded from political life even though now we had a mandate. So here we had stood for election only to be snubbed, except for Livingstone who at this stage invited myself and Gerry Adams for what was popularly billed as peace talks in London.'[41]

Steve Bundred of Troops Out circulated among his fellow Labour GLC members a letter of invitation to Morrison and Adams to come to London on 14 December 1982. Twenty-six of the 50 Labour GLC members signed the letter and Bundred announced the fact on Monday, 6 December 1982. The letter began 'Dear Gerry' and ended 'Yours fraternally'.[42] It said: 'Your success and that of other Sinn Féin candidates in the recent Northern Ireland Assembly elections has clearly surprised many commentators in Britain.' The note said that this highlighted appalling ignorance on the mainland about Northern Ireland, adding: 'Members of the GLC do not claim to be exempt from this ignorance, but many of us share a general desire to see a speedy solution to the problems of Ulster, involving British withdrawal and a reunited Ireland.'

That same night a bomb exploded at a small disco bar called the Droppin' Well in the small Northern Irish town of Ballykelly in County Londonderry. It brought down the solid concrete roof on top of the people inside. Eleven soldiers died, including eight from the First Battalion, the Cheshire Regiment. Six civilians also died; the oldest was 26.

◆

It would be hard to find an example of another group of politicians as completely out of their depth as Livingstone, Bundred and the others on Tuesday, 7 December 1982. Yet again, County Hall was plunged into crisis by Ireland. They had learned nothing from the row of the previous year. There was a problem about dealing with paramilitaries and their representatives: they were unlikely to stop killing people on the strength of an invitation.

The Droppin' Well bomb was detonated not by the Provisional IRA but by the republican Irish National Liberation Army, the INLA. The reaction of the GLC Labour members seemed to be a combination of naivety and moral destitution. For the victims of the attack and their relatives, identifying the organisation responsible for the outrage would not have been an immediate priority. But not for Charlie Rossi, the Camden pest control officer, who said: 'If this does prove to be an IRA bomb, I will withdraw my support from the invitation. My original support was to try to prevent the bombing, to save London from getting walloped, to save things like the Hyde Park incident.'[43]

Of course, the IRA, supported by its political arm – Sinn Féin – had been responsible for the 'Hyde Park incident', which had occurred only five months previously and involved the murder of 11 British soldiers, the same number who lost their lives in Ballykelly. Initially, Livingstone was as ignorant as everyone else about which of the two main republican terrorist groups were responsible for the latest mass murder, the IRA or the INLA. His relief was palpable as the news filtered through, that on this occasion, the INLA could claim 'responsibility'. Livingstone's struggle to keep the show on the road as everyone tried to figure out who was responsible for the massacre was recorded during the day by the *Evening Standard* reporters Robert Carvel and Dick Murray. Livingstone told them: 'I find it incredible that Sinn Féin would actually support, or welcome, this sort of thing – I don't think they would.'[44] Would that include the Hyde Park incident of 20 July 1982?

When the INLA's involvement was confirmed, Livingstone and Bundred issued a joint press release: 'We are horrified at last night's violence, which adds, even more unnecessary deaths to the 2,500 killed since the present troubles began. We will make it clear at our next meeting with Sinn Féin next Tuesday – and Michael Foot asked us – that the Labour Party is absolutely opposed to violence.'[45] Such was his disgust at Livingstone's initiative that the Tory MP for Bury St Edmunds, Eldon Griffiths, obtained remnants of the Droppin' Well bomb and personally delivered them to Livingstone's office. Livingstone was not there so his deputy Illtyd Harrington took delivery of a girl's white dancing shoe, the sleeve of the record which had been playing at the time of the explosion and a smashed disco light.[46]

Livingstone's decision to persist with the invitation to Sinn Féin on the grounds that it was not responsible for the latest massacre was not only a disaster for the Labour Party, already crippled by the internecine sectarian scrap between right and left, but for Michael Foot's own quiet peace initiative.

The Labour Party conference of September 1981 had passed a motion calling for a united Ireland through consent. Clive Soley, then MP for Hammersmith North and a Labour spokesman on Northern Ireland, had secured Michael Foot's agreement to hold discreet talks with both sides of Ulster's divided community. Soley says, 'They agreed I could do it because I was seeing the elected representatives of both the Unionist and republican paramilitaries and I wasn't going to see anyone wanted for terrorist charges or criminal charges of any kind.

'I was quite close to going over when suddenly, without talking to me or anything, Ken invites Sinn Féin over to London. It blew that [Soley's initiative] out of the water so it actually slowed down the process of the party making contact.

'I just wouldn't have done something like that in his position. I don't think he did it deliberately. I think he did it because it would be a good thing to do. This was him really trying to be prime minister, leader of the party and mayor of London. He plays it as an individual, not as a team player.'[47]

Throughout out Wednesday and Thursday, 8 and 9 December 1982, the media pressure piled on Livingstone. Foot asked Livingstone to withdraw the invitation. 'We were trying to get a discussion going in Northern Ireland,' says Michael Foot. 'At one time Ken seemed to be saying that he didn't have any criticisms at all of the IRA, people who were doing the killing in Ireland. Some of us were very strongly against what they were doing although we wanted to see a united Ireland. We thought that Ken didn't condemn the terrorists there as strongly as he should and in the way the party did generally.'[48]

Livingstone agreed to report Foot's views to the GLC Labour group and admits he was facing a humiliating defeat when Margaret Thatcher came to his rescue. On the evening of 9 December, her home secretary, Willie Whitelaw signed exclusion orders under the 1976 Prevention of Terrorism (Temporary Provisions) Act banning Danny Morrison and Gerry Adams from entering mainland Britain.

In the Commons, Mrs Thatcher explained her reasons: '...in the aftermath of the hideous events at Ballykelly, I can also understand that no one, including the home secretary, could be sure that lives might not be at risk if the visit went ahead... If the House will permit me half a minute, I will come to the question – and directly to Mr Livingstone. Yes, because I believed that the paramount necessity was to try to get the invitation called off, particularly after the events that had occurred at Ballykelly. I believe that that was the right approach from the point of view of the whole.'[49]

'I think the Labour group would have forced me to withdraw the invitation,' says Livingstone. 'Then I would have been faced with: do I resign or live with it? The moment Whitelaw banned them – the issue ceased to exist. It wasn't even raised at the group meeting. So I was saved by Willie Whitelaw! The number of times I have been saved by the incompetence of my enemies is legion!'

But again the damage was done. The *Telegraph* reported ominously that the invitation was 'another nail in the coffin of the GLC'. Ministers now believed that 'so-called super authorities have encouraged meddling in affairs that do not concern them, political irresponsibility and a platform for critics of the government'.[50] Calls for the abolition of the GLC began to mount over the following months. By February, the government had received 50 separate representations in favour of getting rid of the GLC.[51]

◆

1983 was GLC Peace Year, although someone kept stealing the brass dove held by the angel of peace statue erected outside County Hall.[52] It was the year that the GLC banned a march by the Territorial Army at County Hall because, as Livingstone's chief whip Harvey Hinds acknowledged: 'A number of members felt strongly that a parade of a military nature within the environs of this building [County Hall] would not be appropriate in this year.'[53] However, closer contacts with Sinn Féin were not considered inappropriate.

In early 1983, Michael Foot was provoked into another intervention, this time to prevent the Police Committee whose vice chairman was Steve Bundred, giving a grant of £53,000 to Troops Out. The money, 'to monitor the Prevention of Terrorism Act', would have been more than seven times the organisation's annual income. Figures released at the time showed that Troops Out had an income of only £6,928 and a debt of £71.[54] The *Telegraph* referred to Livingstone's 'moral myopia' but again it was the Livingstone GLC acting in complete isolation to events elsewhere.[55] The story of the grant broke just two days before the Bermondsey by-election where the gay Labour candidate Peter Tatchell was the target of one of the most virulent and vicious political and media smear campaigns of modern times. He lost by a margin of more than 9,300 to the Liberal candidate Simon Hughes, in what had once been a safe Labour seat. Livingstone could not be blamed totally for the fiasco but his timing, yet again, as with the Croydon North West by-election in 1981, was believed to have caused substantial damage to Labour's prospects.

◆

Under the headline FOOT KICKS RED KEN INTO LINE, the *Evening Standard* reported details of the Labour leader's terse exchange with Livingstone. Foot, a former *Evening Standard* editor, said, 'I told him [Livingstone] how strong is my opposition to any idea of his council making a grant to the Troops Out movement in any form whatsoever.' He said of Troops Out: 'It is committed to policies which could cause immense suffering in Northern Ireland – policies which the Labour Party conference has rejected.'[56] Livingstone agreed that the grant was 'controversial and should be withdrawn so it can be considered by the full Labour group.'[57] That was the last anyone heard of it again. But the press could still have fun with the Babies against the Bomb grant which was announced at the same time.[58]

The following weekend, 26 and 27 February 1983, Livingstone and Bundred flew to Belfast for the first time as the guest of Gerry Adams and Danny Morrison. Sinn Féin took Livingstone on a tour of republican Belfast. He saw some of the bad housing conditions suffered by poor Catholics and was taken to several bars down the Falls Road, including the Broadway Bar and Walsh's, where the publican gave him a bottle of Black Bush whisky. On the Saturday evening, he was taken to the totemic Andersonstown Social Club in nationalist West Belfast. 'It was a club established as a shebeen [illicit drinking club] after the British government introduced internment on 9 August 1971,' says Danny Morrison. 'As far as the British Army was concerned, it was a real symbol of republican resistance. republican groups played pro-IRA songs in it or traditional republican laments. There were history lessons in the club and Irish language lessons. And two of the club's managers had been shot dead by the British Army.'[59]

As he entered, Livingstone won a round of applause. 'We went into the club rooms,' said Morrison, 'and people came over and asked for his autograph.' Gerry Fitt, the Independent MP for West Belfast soon to be displaced by Gerry Adams, said that Livingstone 'had allowed himself to be used for propaganda purposes by the IRA', adding: 'He has not met a real cross section of the people in Northern Ireland.'[60] Morrison remembers being told by Livingstone that bombing London was the wrong strategy and that it would 'put back the day when one can see a united Ireland'. 'The IRA would have needed something from the government to stop [bombing],' says Morrison, 'not the head of the GLC. But he was bringing to attention that there was another alternative.'

So, for Sinn Féin Livingstone's visit was significant. 'It was certainly very helpful in showing people the power of politics,' says Morrison, 'a lot of our community believed that with the armed struggle, people wouldn't talk to you unless you forced them to and so here was a person demonstrating that dialogue was possible. Ken was dealing with elected representatives and respecting their mandate and he was showing that the way forward to conflict resolution was dialogue. There was no doubt about it, the visit was a fillip for us and helped boost morale.'[61]

◆

On 26 July 1983, Gerry Adams finally arrived at County Hall at Livingstone's invitation to talk to leading members of the Left, including Tony Benn, and senior GLC members including Tony Banks and George Nicholson. This time, Thatcher was powerless to prevent the visit because the Sinn Féin president had just been elected as the new MP for West Belfast. Benn welcomed the 'dialogue', describing the government's policy as 'one of absolute bankruptcy'.[62]

Livingstone is convinced that by engaging with Sinn Féin, he stopped the bombers. 'You notice,' he says, 'once that dialogue started bombings in London stopped with one horrible exception.'[63] The exception cited by Livingstone was the bombing of Harrods on 17 December 1983 in which six people died. This was done by a rogue cell without the authorisation of IRA leaders. But Livingstone overlooks the bombing seven days previously at the Royal Artillery Barracks which killed three people. There was also the bombing of the Grand Hotel in Brighton on 12 October 1984 which killed five people, but that clearly does not count because it is outside London.

As for Gerry Adams and Martin McGuiness, Livingstone believes he was right to talk to them then: 'You are dealing with people who, in any other situation, would have been presidents or prime ministers of their country.' Even if they had blood on their hands? Livingstone responds, 'Almost everyone in Northern Irish politics does, directly or indirectly, and there was no point talking to people who didn't.'[64]

By May 1983, Livingstone was a deeply unpopular figure for the press, the public and many in his own party. But his stance on Ireland had earned him the approval of possibly the most important people in his political sphere – the far left General Management Committee of the Brent East Labour Party constituency where a bitter civil war had been waged partly on Livingstone's behalf for the previous three years.

Notes

1   *The Times*, 13.10.81
2   *Sun*, 13.10.81
3   *Evening Standard*, 13.10.81
4   See Chapter 8
5   *The Times*, letter from Ken Livingstone, 14.10.81
6   John Carvel, *Citizen Ken*, p98
7   *Daily Telegraph*, 14.10.81
8   *Daily Telegraph*, Leader, 14.10.81
9   Ken Livingstone, *If Voting Changed Anything, They'd Abolish It*, p172
10 Ibid., p173; Interview, Ken Livingstone, 25.10.07
11 *Daily Mail*, 23.11.81
12 Interview, former Labour MP, 16.2.08
13 *Independent*, 17.11.87

14 *Tribune*, 11.5.84
15 *Irish Times*, 11.12.87
16 Central Statistics Office Ireland (www.cso.ie/statistics/popnbyage2006.htm)
17 Northern Ireland Statistics and Research Agency, 2001 Census, (www.nis-ranew.nisra.gov.uk/census/start.html)
18 Past editions of the IMG's paper, 'Red Mole', 1970-1973
19 *Evening Standard*, 'Ken Target of terrorist plot,' by Keith Dovkants, 10.6.03
20 Michael Stone, *None Shall Divide Us*, John Blake Publishing, 2004, p248
21 *Irish Times*, 11.12.87
22 *London Labour Briefing*, 'Brent East and Ken Livingstone', p10, June 1985
23 Interviews, see Chapter 13
24 *The Times*, 'A look at the Borough of Brent', interview with Cllr Robert Lacey, Conservative Leader of Brent Council, 15.12.86
25 GLC Minutes, Council meeting proceedings, 21.10.81; Item 8 'Censure of the Leader of the Council', pp194-197
26 *The Times*, 2.10.07
27 *Time Out*, 'GLC free-for-all', by Roland Freeman, 23.10.81
28 F.W.S Craig, *British Parliamentary Election Results 1974-83*
29 Ken Livingstone, *If Voting Changed Anything, They'd Abolish It*, pp178
30 Ibid.
31 John Golding, *Hammer of the Left*, p245
32 Ibid., pp298-299
33 See Chapter 8
34 Interview, Ken Livingstone, 1.11.07
35 Thirtieth anniversary of Troops Out, statement by Gerry Adams, President of Sinn Féin, August 2004, on website: www.troopsoutmovement.com/sinnfein.htm
36 Ibid.
37 Interview, Danny Morrison, 19.7.07
38 Ibid.
39 Northern Ireland Elections, ARK: ORB Online Research Bank, Nicholas Whyte, www.ark.ac.uk/elections/
40 Danny Morrison speech to Sinn Féin Ard Fheis, 1.11.81
41 Interview, Danny Morrison, 19.7.07
42 *Daily Telegraph*, 7.12.82
43 *Evening Standard*, 7.12.82
44 Ibid.
45 Ibid.
46 *Daily Mail*, 8.12.82
47 Interview, Lord Soley, former MP for Hammersmith North, 29.10.07
48 Interview, Michael Foot, 15.7.07
49 Prime Minister's Questions, Hansard HC [33/972-78], 9.12.82
50 *Daily Telegraph*, 8.12.82
51 *Daily Telegraph*, 24.2.83
52 *Sunday Times*, 'A week in Ken Livingstone's long march…', 20.2.83
53 *Guardian*, 2.3.81
54 *Daily Telegraph*, 23.2.83
55 Ibid.

56 *Evening Standard*, 22.2.83
57 Ibid.
58 See Chapter 11
59 Interview, Danny Morrison, 19.7.07
60 *Daily Star*, 28.2.83
61 Interview, Danny Morrison, 19.7.07
62 Tony Benn, *The End of an Era, Diaries,1980–1990*, (see 26.7.83)
63 Interview, Ken Livingstone, 25.10.07
64 Interview, Ken Livingstone, 8.11.07

Chapter 13

'Your faithful servant Reg', 1980–1985

Reg Freeson died in October 2006 near Marlborough in Wiltshire at the age of 80. He was born in St Pancras and from the age of five, he was raised by rabbis in the Jewish Orphanage at West Norwood. The fate of his parents was a mystery to all who knew this intensely private man. 'I don't talk about that,' he would tell enquirers tersely.[1] However, it was known that both sets of grandparents were from either side of the Polish/Russian border and he considered himself by origin, a Polish Jew.[2] He left the orphanage at 15 and two years later enlisted in the RAF. He joined the Labour Party shortly after being demobbed in 1947.[3]

According to Freeson's widow, Charlotte Freeson, the Labour Party was his family. She says, 'Reg had that loyalty to the Labour Party which one has for one's family.'[4] But Freeson was to discover that loyalty was a one-way street when Ken Livingstone and his friends came for his seat and his job.

◆

In his *Guardian* obituary of Freeson, Andrew Roth wrote: 'The name of Reg Freeson ... has became so identified with his political "murder" by the ambitious Ken Livingstone in 1987 that his earlier record as one of the most successful "sensible left" Labour MPs and ministers has been almost forgotten.'[5]

Reg Freeson devoted most of his adult life to the north-west London borough of Brent. In 1952, he was first elected to Willesden Borough Council and became its leader in 1958. In 1964, he seized what was then the Willesden East constituency from the sitting Conservative MP Trevor Skeet and helped form the new majority intake for Harold Wilson's first government. In 1969, Wilson made him minister for housing and local government and in 1974, minister for housing and reconstruction. His constituency was renamed Brent East the same year. Beneath Freeson's prickly introspection was an old Labour left-winger, a slight intense man who threw a big heart into many good causes: a founder member of both the CND and the anti-fascist magazine *Searchlight* and a stalwart of Poale Zion, the organisation which became the Jewish Labour movement, but he remained a critic of Israel over its invasion of Lebanon in 1982. 'He was modest, shy, principled and honest,' wrote his friend John Lebor. 'If he lacked one characteristic of a politician, particularly perhaps in comparison with Ken Livingstone who deposed him, it was raw naked ambition.'[6]

A former hard left MP, who was once close to Ken Livingstone, says, 'If I had to choose a Labour MP to knife up, then Reg Freeson would not have been at the top of my list.'[7] But Freeson was at the top of Ken Livingstone's list, not because of his many personal qualities, not because he was not a diligent and compassionate MP, not because he was not wholeheartedly committed to his local community but because he was in the way. In the final analysis, Freeson's many achievements stood for nothing when he came up against a force of nature he could not understand. To this day, his wife is in the dark about the people who destroyed her husband's political career with such obsessive calculation.[8]

◆

For at least four years, Ken Livingstone seems to have been obsessed about being the MP for Brent East. He has cited his fondness for the area, including the Indian restaurants on the Kilburn High Road. 'It's an area I would like to represent,' he once said. 'There's an affinity there.'[9] The real reason for Livingstone's determination begged the question asked by Reg Freeson at the time and Charlotte Freeson to the present day: Who was really in control of the Brent East Labour Party?

In his book on Livingstone, John Carvel wondered aloud how anyone could have felt 'affinity' for the Brent East Labour Party and the tumult in which it operated.[10] The simple answer was that that was where his political friends were, and they were largely responsible for the strife.

Essentially, Livingstone's seizure of Brent East from Reg Freeson was largely down to his old friends, the Chartists of *Labour London Briefing* fame, or the Trotskyist Revolutionary Communist League, as they called themselves. By 1980, they held key positions in the Brent East Labour Party. The story about how they took power and took out Freeson reveals much about the Trots who operated in the 1980s for Ken Livingstone.

◆

In 1979, when Margaret Thatcher came to power, the London

Borough Council of Brent was ruled by a fairly traditional old Labour Party, then under the leadership of Freeson's old friend John Lebor, a left-wing lawyer and former communist. The borough was made up of three constituencies: the two Labour seats of Brent South and Brent East; and the Tory constituency of Brent North. The first clue that the Brent East party had been infiltrated by Trots came on 12 October 1979 in an article in the *Willesden and Brent Chronicle*, the main newspaper for the area. Henry Fried, a 26-year-old civil servant and the chairman of the Mapesbury ward Labour Party, said, 'Mapesbury ward is dominated by Trotskyite supporters of the Socialist Campaign for a Labour Victory, an extreme left-wing grouping set up last year which includes people formerly in the Workers Revolutionary Party.[11] The constituency as a whole is much the same. It also has supporters gaining highly influential positions within the party.'[12] The allegations brought a flurry of denials from senior local Labour activists but Fried was telling the truth. Of course, the SCLV was formed by Livingstone and Ted Knight by bringing together the Matgamna Trots and the Chartists; the WRP were not involved.[13]

Brent East was one of only five constituencies represented on the SCLV and in its first few years, *Briefing* carried more articles about either Brent East or the borough of Brent than any other. Most of the Brent East Chartists who were now taking key positions in the local Labour Party were teachers who had cut their teeth in one of the most famous industrial disputes since the war, the Grunwick strike of 1976–77 which took place in the constituency. Workers, fed up with bad working conditions walked out of the Grunwick film-processing laboratory. The manager, who had refused to recognise their union of choice, APEX, sacked them. The dispute soon became a great cause célèbre. The Post Office workers refused to deliver the films processed by the 'scab' workers and the mass pickets outside often turned nasty.[14] The Chartist teachers along with others on the left took part in the dispute.

The deselection of Reg Freeson and his replacement by Ken Livingstone turned out to be the ultimate act in a determined campaign by the Left to take control first of the Brent Labour Party and purge the moderates and right-wingers by replacing them as council candidates. That would also leave the Left in position to win control of Brent Council at the London borough elections in May 1982. Then, they could finish off Freeson. They managed to achieve all goals with cold-hearted efficiency.

◆

Brent Council and other local authorities were being targeted by Ken Livingstone and the Left as part of an overall campaign called Target '82. It was a similar strategy to the one used by Livingstone to take over the GLC: purge the right and centre and get candidates selected from the Left.[15]

Sixteen councils were being targeted, including Labour-controlled Hackney, Islington and Camden. Keith Veness, one of Livingstone's Chartist plotters, says: 'Target '82 was the umbrella thing. It was about getting a left majority on the Labour groups and then winning the council. Target '82 met at County Hall and we just thought it was a logical follow-on to winning the GLC. Ken used to come to the meetings. It was an open conspiracy.'[16] *Briefing* advertised Target '82 meetings, and articles openly discussed tactics and gave details of forthcoming selection meetings.[17] The purges often had a dramatic result. In Islington, the campaign persuaded 16 Labour councillors at risk of deselection to defect to the SDP/Alliance amid allegations that the remaining 27 'had been infiltrated by the left wing'.[18]

Graham Bash, a founder member of the Chartists back in 1970, was a member of the Brent East Labour Party between 1970 and 1974. In 1979, he returned to London after working in Leeds for five years. Although he moved into south Ilford, he kept close contact with his Chartist friends in Brent East.

'We were left-wing Labour Party members who saw our role as part of the struggle for power within the Labour movement, so we did take positions of power within the movement. There were parallel things going on. One was to replace the council with a real Labour council, a left Labour council whilst one was to replace Reg Freeson who was an old-fashioned centre right MP with someone who reflected the realities of the new movement. We wanted a left-wing council and we wanted a left-wing MP and we were right to do so. We were trying to use the democratic process.'[19]

◆

In interviews for this book, Chartist sources identified six prominent ex-Brent East Labour Party officials as their former associates, including many teachers.[20] Ken Livingstone also confirms that he knew them through the Chartists.[21] Alongside the Chartists there were other longstanding Livingstone associates including his former personal assistant at Camden Council.[22] Many of Livingstone's supporters lived in the same block of flats in the Mapesbury area, 'Red House' on Walm Lane.[23]

Ken Livingstone insists that his supporters made up only around 20 per cent of the constituency's General Management Committee[24] but he is being modest. Many of the senior constituency positions were taken by his supporters. Even if that was the case, then it was 20 per cent more than Reg Freeson or anybody else. These activists were excellent at creating a majority from a minority, through tireless activism and ferocious energy. 'You do look for someone you can work with and someone you can trust,' he says.[25]

◆

The left-wingers were helped substantially by the changes wrought by the Campaign for Labour Party Democracy and others in the Labour Party. The mandatory reselection of MPs gave local activists enormous influence. They could now sack their local MP and replace him or her with someone who thought like them. But this proved not to be power for every member of the Labour Party, but for the determined select few who organised to take key positions in the local constituencies and had the energy to attend meetings. The fact that 81 per cent of Labour constituencies voted for Tony Benn in 1981 shows how successful they were.[26]

The modus operandi of the Brent East Left was described in February 1981 in a controversial article in the *Willesden and Brent Chronicle*. Under the headline 'How Brent's Left War Machine goes into action', Bill Montgomery, the paper's political columnist, wrote: 'The organisation of the Labour Party is such that it is only too easy for fringe groups and extremists to move in. Like many trade unions, it has a hierarchical structure which means there are lots of committees and lots of meetings.

'Before the war, people were willing to go to meetings – they were a social event and possibly an entertainment as well. In these days of television some people simply won't turn out.

'As a result many meetings are badly attended and can easily be dominated by a handful of activists who vote themselves into positions of authority. Thus small and unrepresentative groups from the far left can easily move in.'[27]

Montgomery described the people taking over. 'Many of these new activists are young middle-class lefties, including more than a sprinkling of teachers,' he said. 'There is a noticeable lack of those "ordinary working people" of whom they speak often and long.'[28]

John Lebor, the leader of Brent Council and an articulate Labour moderate was at the top of the Left's hit list. To the Chartists in particular he represented the biggest obstacle to taking control of the Brent Labour Party and the local council as well as replacing Reg Freeson. 'I think they wanted me out of the way to get Reg,' says Lebor.[29]

One Labour Party insider told Montgomery: 'There is a constant and growing pressure from the Left for more extreme and expensive policies. Having failed to get their way through democratic debate the Left is now using its grip on the party organisation in a crude and dangerous way to remove some of the ablest and experienced councillors we have.' Montgomery predicted the destruction of the moderate and right-wing forces then nominally in command of the local Labour Party: 'The present council leadership, John Lebor and Co., will be dumped without ceremony.'[30]

◆

On 5 February 1981, the day before the article appeared, the Left launched a ferocious assault on the moderate and right wing as each of Brent's 21 Labour ward branches began to hold meetings to select candidates for the May 1982 council election. The Kensal Rise ward was normally attended by fewer than 10 people. But on 5 February there were around 50 people, mostly newcomers from the West Indian and Asian communities, all clutching their brand new party membership cards. Two left-wingers were voted on to the candidates' shortlist. Two moderates, including a former Labour leader of the council, Ivor Davies, were dumped.[31]

During the previous three months, the Left had helped build a formidable weapon called the Asian Labour Party Alliance, or ALPA, a new Brent organisation. Writing in *London Labour Briefing* in March 1981, Subhash Patel of ALPA boasted, 'The past three months alone have seen the recruitment of over 500 Asians into the Labour Party in Brent and it is the right wing who have the greatest cause to worry! This influx has coincided with the formation of a new national organisation, the Asian Labour Party Alliance...'[32]

During February and March 1981, the events of the Kensal Rise meeting would be repeated across the borough and particularly in Brent East. Moderates were dropped at meetings packed by newcomers who would vote en bloc for candidates fielded by the Left. The Brent Labour Party swiftly descended into all-out civil war, the precursor to its 'Barmy Brent' dark ages of *Private Eye* fame.

◆

The most farcical events happened in John Lebor's ward, St Raphael's in Brent South. During the course of 1981 and January 1982, Lebor was reselected as a candidate twice when the Left could not get out its forces and deselected three times when the Left got its act together. Lebor was first deselected on 2 April 1981 when the meeting was packed by 20 new Asian members. 'They sat as a block and voted as a block,' wrote Bill Montgomery. 'It was a cheat, a fraud and a fix. The meeting had been packed by people some of whom wouldn't know Mr Lebor if they saw him.'[33] He described it as 'another combined operation by Brent Indian Association [*sic*-ALPA] and the extreme left of the Labour Party.'

John Lebor says, 'Eventually what happened – to cut a story short – is that they managed to bring along some local people who could not speak English, who had no idea about what was going on, had never been to the Labour Party before, or indeed since.' So the non-English-speaking new members could select 'the right person', each candidate was identified by a sign with an animal on it including a monkey and elephant. All the arms went up as the right sign was held aloft. 'I can't remember which sign I was,' says Lebor.

When it was pointed out that the strange arrivals were not even in the party, an enemy of Lebor's wrote out a cheque to pay the dues of 12 new members. 'This was accepted quite disgracefully,' says Lebor, 'and the outcome was that I was not reselected... I suppose I could have taken the matter to the courts but I decided that I had had enough'.[34]

◆

The national Labour Party, distracted by similar sectarian battles in the unions, within the NEC and across the country, made several half-hearted attempts to solve Brent's problems but could not prevent the demise of John Lebor and other moderates. At least

12 identifiably far left candidates were selected.[35] John and Connie Wales, members of the Cricklewood Labour Party in Brent for 44 years, called on sensible comrades to come to the aid of the party. They wrote: 'It is with great difficulty that we feel able to calmly assess the savage destruction and harm the Trots and the Marxists have inflicted on Brent East.'[36] An estimated 500 moderate members resigned from the Labour Party in Brent which only served to strengthen the Left's grip.[37]

But a combination of the vicious infighting and the '82 'Falklands Factor' deprived the Left of outright control of Brent Council at the May 1982 elections. Thirty-three Labour councillors were elected as opposed to 30 Tories and three for the SDP/ Alliance. The Left hung on to Brent with the casting vote of the mayor, but not for long.

◆

Against this background, Reg Freeson had also been fighting for his political life. The Left's campaign against Freeson started with contempt and hostility before degenerating into ostracism, bullying and aggression in a campaign lasting for at least four years. Again, it was Bill Montgomery who was the first to publicly ask: 'Is Reg due for the chop?' Writing on 8 May 1981, the day after Livingstone grasped control of County Hall, the reporter asked, 'If you will kindly remove your hats and bow your heads we will pay a last tribute to your faithful servant Reg. Brent East has indeed been fortunate in having such a dedicated MP for over 20 years.'[38] Freeson's record 'counts for little with the revolutionaries in Brent East' where a 'determined campaign was under way to dump Mr Freeson in favour of a far left champion.' Freeson's chances were 'less than evens.' [39] He identified Livingstone as the odds-on favourite to replace him.

By July 1981, the plotting to remove Freeson was being openly discussed. 'The lefties are keen to have him dropped,' reported Montgomery who repeated his claim that Ken Livingstone was a favourite to replace Freeson.[40] In a short unpublished autobiography, Freeson described this time as an 'ugly period of conspiratorial, factional, manipulative and extremist politics, largely centred on County Hall; with abuse of party democracy and procedures, personal attacks and undermining my position as MP.'

He added that there was 'violence in the town hall, "loading" of meetings to remove targeted council candidates and an organised campaign, using unconstitutional and other improper methods to replace me with the leader of the Greater London Council.'[41]

'Reg never engaged in personalities, rare in politics,' wrote Lebor later. 'I never heard him denigrate anybody very sharply, with the understandable exception of Ken Livingstone, who he saw as a shallow, self-interested manipulator.'[42]

During this period, Freeson was also going through a traumatic separation from his first wife, who took their two daughters, Jenny and Ruth, with her. He also grew close to Charlotte, who became his second wife at this time.

◆

The increasingly bitter conflict between the activists holding sway in Brent East and Freeson spilled out into the public arena over the fight for the deputy leadership between Denis Healey and Tony Benn. In common with a sizeable section of the British electorate, Freeson considered Benn a 'major political and electoral liability'.[43] The Trots insisted that Freeson vote for Benn. Clearly many MPs elsewhere yielded under the threats of deselection, but Freeson defied the bullies publicly: 'The tendency to snarl, sneer, personal abuse and misrepresentation has become far too apparent in certain quarters of the party in recent times. There is nothing socialist about such conduct.'[44]

Freeson voted for Healey and further enraged the Trots later in the year by calling for a party inquiry into the Trotskyist Militant Tendency.[45] For four years, the Left in control of the General Management Committee of the Brent East constituency failed to invite Freeson to speak at any of its meetings.[46]

Charlotte Freeson remembers two sinister events which occurred during her husband's battle with the Left. In 1982, his briefcase was stolen from the members' cloakroom at the House of Commons. Freeson reported it to the parliamentary authorities, but it never reappeared. 'That must have been an insider job because nobody else could get into those rooms where it was stolen,' she says. 'It couldn't have been by a member of the public because there was the members' cloakroom where he had left it and that was where it was taken. It contained all his tax papers. It wasn't terribly exciting but what it contained wasn't useless in terms of doing your tax returns.'[47]

On a second occasion, a year later, the couple returned from a holiday to discover that someone had broken into their home at

159 Chevening Road in Queen's Park. Mrs Freeson adds, 'Nothing was taken in terms of valuables. Even some cash that was lying there was not taken but all the papers had been gone through – all of Reg's papers.' No evidence was found to link these acts with the infighting but the couple felt there had to be a connection.

In reality, it did not really matter what Freeson did. His cards had been marked by the Left even before Labour's decision in 1979 to bring in mandatory reselection for all MPs. Peter Firmin, the former Mapesbury ward secretary, and a non-Chartist, says, 'We on the Left thought he [Reg Freeson] was useless. In a way it came to a head a few years earlier with the Grunwick strike which was local, where basically Reg Freeson didn't give it the support we thought he should.'[48]

Factional infighting in Brent East forced the Left into an error. The *Socialist Organiser* Trots and their leader Sean Matgamna, who had little time for Ken Livingstone, challenged the Chartists' right for a free run at the parliamentary candidacy by fielding their own hopeful, Ms Gerry Byrne, at a meeting on 12 September 1982 at the Trades and Labour Hall in Willesden.[49] It had been agreed to hold a debate between both candidates at a previous meeting between the two groups in July 1982. In his circular to 60 members of the Left, Pete Firmin wrote: '...it was agreed that we have a united Left candidate if we are to stand a chance of defeating R. Freeson.'[50] Livingstone beat Byrne by 37 votes to 16. Naturally, the local MP was not invited to this Trot fest.

The *Chronicle* broke the story of the meeting later that week on 17 September 1982 with the headline 'RED KEN V. REG – SECRET BID TO DUMP BRENT MP.' Now at last, there was real evidence of the Left holding a caucus, an event which was bread and butter to Ken Livingstone but frowned upon by the Labour Party. By the time the story broke, an 'inquiry team' dispatched by the Labour Party's NEC had been investigating the 'irregularities' in the selection of council candidates. Leading this 'inquiry' was Eric Heffer, the hard left MP for Liverpool Walton. Getting Eric Heffer to head an inquiry into Trotskyist misconduct was a complete waste of time.

For the *Sunday Express*, the old working-class MP from Merseyside was 'the hind legs of the Benn-Heffer pantomime horse.'[51] To John Golding, the right-wing MP who sat alongside both men on the NEC, Benn and Heffer were the 'Don Quixote and Sancho

Panza of the Labour Party', inseparable and seemingly unstoppable during this key period.[52] Heffer was widely considered to
be 'well and truly under the thumb'[53] of the Trotskyist Militant
Tendency which was firmly in control of the local Labour Party
and Liverpool City Council. His commitment to rooting out the
Trots in Brent East was given away by his bluff remark to Lebor:
'Hello John, how are we going to stop the witch-hunting?'[54] Heffer, Benn and Livingstone would also oppose the 'witch-hunt'
against Militant launched by Foot later that year and continued
vigorously by his successor, Neil Kinnock.

Heffer's inquiry found that 'it was impossible to test the truth
of the allegations made'[55] and meekly suggested placing both
Brent South and Brent East Labour parties under the close super-
vision of Joyce Gould, one of the party's assistant general secretaries. But it seemed little could rescue Freeson from the clutches
of Livingstone's supporters.

Freeson once described the disgraceful conduct of his monthly
General Management Committee meetings of constituency activists: 'Delegates wander in and out of the meetings continuously...
there are snide and personal remarks about Party members, both
present and absent, local and national... generally there is an
acrimonious and oppressive atmosphere.'[56] Trotskyist newspapers including *Socialist Worker*, *Militant* and *Socialist Organiser*
were sold openly.

◆

From autumn 1982 onwards, as Livingstone became more visible
in Brent East, the political situation became increasingly fraught.
In September 1982, there were scuffles at a public meeting in
Willesden Green attended by both John Lebor and Livingstone
to discuss Israel's controversial invasion of Lebanon.[57] 'The meeting had an atmosphere, intimidation and incipient violence from
the very start,' wrote Morris Howard, who was in the audience.
'...the former leader of the council, John Lebor, was jostled in
his seat without even having said a word and then was threatened with violence in foul language by a member of the Labour
Party... all this in the name of Marx and Trotsky! How they must
turn in their graves.'[58]

Livingstone was also accused of currying favour with the
28,000 Irish families in Brent, 12 per cent of the population.[59]
In late 1982, Livingstone received a letter of complaint from

the Brent branch of the Irish in Britain Representation Group, IBRG, about an offensive cartoon by the cartoonist Raymond Jackson, known as Jak, published by the *Evening Standard* on 29 October 1982. It shows a man walking past a poster advertising a film called 'The Irish, The Ultimate In Psychopathic Horror', featuring 'the IRA, INLA, UDF, PFF [*sic* – possibly UFF], UDA, etc.' Until then, the only controversy created by Jak came with *Private Eye's* exposure of his dodgy agreement with a publicity agent.[60] Regularly in Jak's cartoons, there would be discreet references to high-street products including Bonjela teething gel and Supersoft Shampoo, clients of his friend, PR agent Tom Richards, who would pay him handsomely in return.[61] What is clear from Jak's output in its entirety was his hatred for terrorists rather than any contempt for Irish people.[62] There was no comment at the time on the little-known fact that Jak himself was half-Irish. Jak's son, Patrick Jackson, says, 'I always found it ironic that Mr Livingstone accused our father of racism without knowing that his mother, Mary Murphy, was Irish. You don't get more Irish than that.'[63]

The complainant on behalf of the IBRG was Pat Delaney, from Brent, who was a big fan of Livingstone. In his sentence on the 'evil trash' Jak cartoon, Delaney mentioned that he worked for the Labour Party in Brent, adding, 'I hope one day you will be in office in Brent. I am sure IBRG and Ken Livingstone work very well together.'[64] Ken Livingstone, in his capacity as chairman of the Ethnic Minorities Committee, agreed that the cartoon was 'atrocious'[65] and recommended that the GLC stop placing adverts in the *Evening Standard* 'until a published apology appears' on the grounds that the cartoon was 'likely to stir up racial hatred against the Irish community'.[66] The GLC voted for the ban on 23 November 1982.

The *Evening Standard* refused to apologise on the grounds that the cartoon was aimed not at the Irish but at specific violent paramilitary groups on both sides of the divide and that the GLC ban was an attack on press freedom. Up to 1985, the ban cost the *Evening Standard* approximately £2 million in lost advertising revenue.[67] At the Press Council hearing brought about by Livingstone, he complained the cartoon portrayed the Irish as subhuman killers. In its adjudication, the Press Council rejected Livingstone's complaints and described the GLC's ban as a 'blatant attempt by a local authority to use the power of its purse to influence the contents of a newspaper and coerce the editor'.[68]

◆

A row broke out in February 1983 when it was announced that the Ethnic Minorities Committee was to give £300,000 towards a new Brent Irish and Cultural Centre. Bob Lacey, the Conservative parliamentary candidate, accused Livingstone of politicking with public money: 'This is a crude political bribe, lacking subtlety or finesse. I have no doubt about it and I don't think the Irish or the residents of Queen's Park are fooled by it either.' This was rejected by a spokesman for the GLC Labour group who declared it was 'scandalous to pretend there was some covert political intention behind the grant', adding: 'To say that because one of these properties happens to be in Brent East is a political bribe is a ridiculous claim without substance.'[69] February 1983 also saw the GLC attempt to give £53,000 to Troops Out and Livingstone's trip to Northern Ireland.[70]

◆

By March 1983, it was clear Freeson was being overwhelmed. But two forces combined to grant him a temporary reprieve and deliver a serious blow to Livingstone's political ambitions. One was Margaret Thatcher, and the other was John Golding. Critically, there had been a backlash against the Left by the moderates and right wing at the Labour Party's annual autumn conference in Blackpool in 1982. The party approved electorally disastrous policies including unilateral nuclear disarmament and the closure of US airbases, but the vital annual elections for the NEC shifted the power away from the Left for the first time in three years. Golding and his fellow right-wingers used their slim advantage and the abstention of Michael Foot to purge the Left from their positions of power on crucial NEC committees. Benn and Heffer were sacked as chairman of the Home and Organisation Committees respectively.[71]

'What we had done that morning,' wrote Golding later, 'was to end the dominance of extreme left-wing socialists in the Labour Party and bring about the fall of the Benn-Heffer axis, which would never carry credibility again.'[72] This shift in the balance of power would have a long-term effect on the political fortunes of Ken Livingstone and in the short term keep him out of Parliament for another four years. Now, the Livingstone caucus of September 1982 became a big issue. In early March 1983, the *Chronicle*'s reporter John Clohesy revealed that Livingstone 'had not endeared himself to the party's national executive'.[73]

◆

As the prospects for an imminent general election increased, Livingstone's supporters in Brent East twice wrote to the NEC, on 20 and 24 April demanding permission to hold a reselection meeting. The constituency had obtained a legal opinion from the barrister, Lord Gifford QC, who said the party had a duty to hold a reselection meeting. On 27 April 1983, the NEC decided against reselection. At a meeting on the following day in the Anson primary school in Cricklewood, Brent East decided to defy the NEC and go ahead with reselection by 71 votes to four.

On Monday 9 May 1983, Margaret Thatcher called a general election for 9 June. Two days later, John Golding recorded the following events in his 'Diary of an MP' for the *Stoke Sentinel*: 'At the NEC, I move that Reg Freeson be the Labour candidate in Brent East and this is carried by 19 votes to 9! This will freeze Ken Livingstone, the leader of the GLC, out and so there is bound to be a spot of bother…' Shortly after the decision, Livingstone bumped into Margaret Hodge, the leader of Islington Council, and pointed to a piece of paper which showed that Neil Kinnock had been one of those who voted against him. 'Bastard,' Livingstone allegedly told Hodge. Later she wrote: 'He alleged that the reason Neil had voted against him was that he saw Ken as the only threat to his assuming the leadership of the Party after Foot. It's a mark of his self-delusion that he really believed it.'[74] Livingstone always vigorously denied the story related by Hodge at a time the Labour Party was trying to prevent him becoming mayor of London.

It was soon reported in the *Chronicle* that there were 'strong rumours within County Hall that Mr Livingstone and his supporters are planning to… stand against the officially selected Labour Party candidate', adding that he would face 'almost certain expulsion' if he did so. But eventually he accepted defeat.

◆

Reg Freeson would hang on as MP for Brent East for another four long years during which he would be treated with ill-disguised disdain by local activists and eventually forced to resign, allowing Livingstone to take his place. The Labour Party rules meant that the earliest possible date to reselect a parliamentary candidate was

18 months after the last general election, or 9 December 1984. The Brent East Labour Party set its first reselection hearing to replace Freeson with Ken Livingstone for 9 December 1984.

In his book, Brent Labour councillor Jim Moher asks the most pertinent question about Ken Livingstone and the Freeson affair, 'He [Livingstone] blamed the Chartist and *Socialist Organiser* factions and the Right for such behaviour, which he acknowledged, alienated a substantial body of opinion on the Left. But is it plausible that he didn't know what was going on, as his *Briefing* lieutenants were closely involved?'[75]

Ken Livingstone also rejects the *Guardian*'s claim that Freeson was the victim of a 'political murder'. Reaching out again for the insights of Mario Puzo, he says, 'There's that lovely bit in *Godfather Two*, where Hyman Roth knows Michael Corleone has authorised the murder of Moe Green, and he says to Michael, "Moe Green was like a son to me and when he died, I didn't complain; this is the life we've chosen." This is politics. There are mad people in it and there are unpleasant people in it. But it still remains a battle of ideas and Reg's ideas by that stage were not in keeping with the way the Labour Left was going.'[76] On 9 June 1983, it was also clear that the Labour Left was not in keeping with the way the British people were going.

Notes

1 Recounted by John Lebor in a speech in honour of Reg Freeson, 2007
2 *Independent*, obituary of Reg Freeson, by Tam Dalyell, 12.10.06
3 *Daily Telegraph*, obituary of Reg Freeson, 12.10.06
4 Interview, Charlotte Freeson, 4.9.07
5 *Guardian*, obituary of Reg Freeson, by Andrew Roth, 11.10.06
6 *Jewish Vanguard*, 'Reg Freeson, 1926-2006', Winter 2006, misdated Winter 2007
7 Interview, 2007
8 Interview, Charlotte Freeson, 4.9.07
9 John Carvel, *Citizen Ken*, p170
10 Ibid., p166
11 See Chapter 5
12 *Willesden and Brent Chronicle*, 'Trots ruling Brent says Labour man', 12.10.79, p1
13 See Chapter 5
14 Peter Hain, *Political strikes: The state and trade unionism in Britain*, pp117-119
15 See Chapter 5
16 Interview, Keith Veness, 24.8.04

17 *London Labour Briefing*, April 1982, pp1,36
18 *Guardian*, 9.9.81
19 Interview, Graham Bash, 7.9.07
20 Interviews, September/October 2007
21 Interview, Ken Livingstone, 1.11.07
22 John Carvel, *Citizen Ken*, p170
23 Jim Moher, *Stepping On White Corns, Race, Education and Politics: the Brent experience*, JGM Books, 2007, p211
24 Interview, Ken Livingstone, 1.11.07
25 Ibid.
26 Patrick Seyd, *The Rise and Fall of the Labour Left*, pp130,134; Labour Party Annual Conference Records 1981, p26
27 *Willesden and Brent Chronicle*, 'How Brent's Left War Machine goes into action', by Bill Montgomery, p4
28 Ibid.
29 Interview, John Lebor, 29.8.07
30 Ibid.
31 *Willesden and Brent Chronicle*, 13.2.81
32 *London Labour Briefing*, article by Subhash Patel, March 1981
33 *Willesden and Brent Chronicle*, 'How the left knifed John Lebor', by Bill Montgomery, p4, 17.4.81
34 Interview, John Lebor, 29.8.07
35 *Willesden and Brent Chronicle*, 29.1.82 and 5.2.82
36 *Willesden and Brent Chronicle*, 'This lunatic gang is destroying our party', letter from John and Connie Wales, p2, 14.8.81
37 Ibid.
38 *Willesden and Brent Chronicle*, p3, 8.5.81
39 Ibid.
40 *Willesden and Brent Chronicle*, p4, 10.7.81
41 Unpublished autobiography by Reg Freeson (29.6.95), courtesy of Charlotte Freeson
42 Speech by John Lebor in honour of Reg Freeson, 2007
43 *Willesden and Brent Chronicle*, 4.9.81
44 Ibid.
45 *Willesden and Brent Chronicle*, 25.12.81
46 *Willesden and Brent Chronicle*, 'Bill Montgomery's Notebook', p4, 18.3.83
47 Interview, Charlotte Freeson, 4.9.07
48 Interview, Pete Firmin, 30.7.07
49 John Carvel, *Citizen Ken*, pp172-173
50 Ibid.
51 John Golding, *Hammer of the Left*, (from 'Crossbencher', *Sunday Express*, July 1983), p26
52 Ibid., p83
53 Ibid., p28
54 Interview, John Lebor, 29.8.07
55 John Carvel, *Citizen Ken*, p173
56 Letter from Reg Freeson MP to Jim Mortimer, general secretary of the Labour Party, 27.10.82; Jim Moher, *Stepping on White Corns*, p212

57 *Willesden and Brent Chronicle*, 24.9.82, p4
58 *Willesden and Brent Chronicle*, letter by Morris Howard, 1.10.82, p2
59 1981 Census information, published in *Willesden and Brent Chronicle*, 22.10.82
60 *Private Eye*, Issue 498, 16.1.81, p20
61 Letters, Tom Richards, TJR Ltd, to Raymond Jackson, 'Jak', 21.2.80, London Metropolitan Archives, GLC xx/01/109
62 www.jakthecartoonist.com/terrorism.html
63 Email, Patrick Jackson to author, 22.2.08
64 Letter, Pat Delaney to Ken Livingstone, received on 3.11.82, London Metropolitan Archives, GLC xx/01/109
65 Letter, Ken Livingstone to Pat Delaney, 13.11.82, London Metropolitan Archives, GLC xx/01/109
66 Report of the GLC Ethnic Minorities Committee, GLC Agenda, p6, 23.11.82
67 Mark Hollingsworth, *The Press and Political Dissent: a question of censorship*, p92
68 Ibid., p93
69 *Willesden and Brent Chronicle*, 11.2.83, p2
70 See Chapter 12
71 John Golding, *Hammer of the Left*, p253-261
72 Ibid., p261
73 *Willesden and Brent Chronicle*, 11.3.83, p1
74 *Independent*, 18.10.99; *Mail on Sunday*, 10.10.99
75 Jim Moher, *Stepping on White Corns*, p213
76 Interview, Ken Livingstone, 1.11.07

Chapter 14

Abolition and resurrection,
June 1983–September 1984

The leaders of the Left gathered with their shredded standards at Chris Mullin's London flat on 12 June 1983 three days after the heaviest defeat suffered by the Labour Party since before the war.[1] Mullin, at that stage the editor of *Tribune*, took photographs of the event. Tony Benn is pictured there taking notes. Only 18 months previously, Benn was considered the most powerful force in the Labour movement and on the brink of seizing the Labour deputy leadership and role as heir apparent; now he was no longer an MP.

Margaret Thatcher summed it up in her memoirs 'The 1983 general election was the single most devastating defeat inflicted upon democratic socialism in Britain. After being defeated on a manifesto that was the most candid statement of socialist aims ever made in this country, the Left could never again credibly claim popular appeal for their programme of massive nationalisation, hugely increased public spending, greater trade union power and unilateral disarmament.'[2]

At 22,849 words, the Labour Party's 1983 manifesto, *The New Hope for Britain*, was long; to Gerald Kaufman, it had been the 'longest suicide note in history'. John Golding wrote: 'I was determined that the Left should get the blame for the certain defeat in the coming general election, as we on the right had been blamed in 1979.'[3]

Thatcher was right. The 1983 manifesto proved to be a shopping list of electorally inedible items drawn up by the Left. Despite all the opinion polls, the Left had convinced itself that what the people wanted was not less socialism but more. In the *Labour Herald* shortly before the election, Benn wrote: 'The campaign which Labour is fighting is very different from that which we fought in the 1979 election. Then the policy was dictated by the then prime minister. Now we have a policy which has been drafted and carried by successive TUC Congresses and Labour Party conferences.

'That is why we can genuinely say that the Labour movement has created the policy Labour is now fighting.' Benn was confident he could sell the policies because 'this time we are up against a cabinet of hard-faced men led by a hard-faced woman, proud to say that they want to go back to a Dickensian Britain.'[4]

The election results were shattering. Labour held 209 seats with just 27.6 per cent of the vote, just slightly above the 25.4 per cent polled by the combined forces of the Liberals and the SDP. The Tories won 397 seats with 42.4 per cent of the vote.[5] But the cloud had a silver lining. When Benn's defeat in Bristol East was declared, Golding said, 'We took it as a Labour gain,'[6] adding: 'The truth was however that many working-class British people knew that what he [Benn] was offering was, in fact, hell on earth. They would never vote Labour until he was removed. He was God's greatest gift to Thatcher and had to be stopped if the Labour Party was to survive.'[7]

More than anyone, Golding had overseen his removal. Before the election, Benn's safe Bristol South East seat had been abolished as a result of boundary changes. Golding had helped prevent Benn's selection for the new safe Labour seat of Bristol South. He had organised a campaign to get union members to affiliate to the new constituency and vote against Benn, forcing him to stand in the unsafe seat of Bristol East where he was beaten by 1,789 votes.[8] The self-styled 'Hammer of the Left' had done for both Livingstone, whom he often derided as 'Newtman',[9] and Benn.

So it was a depleted flock without a shepherd that gathered at Mullin's flat. To make matters worse, it was also the day that Michael Foot announced he would be standing down to spend more time among the works of Hazlitt, Swift and Bagehot. Out with the philosopher king; in with a hard-headed pragmatist to lead the party from the brink of oblivion.

◆

Neil Kinnock was the clear favourite but was despised or mistrusted by the bewildered smattering at Mullin's home for ratting on the Left, particularly by leading the critical abstentions among soft left MPs in 1981 which deprived Benn of victory. But who would lead the Left's challenge for the leadership? Tony Banks offered to resign his newly won parliamentary seat of Newham North West to give Benn a chance of returning to Parliament and hold aloft the tattered banner. He would not hear of it, but wrote:

'I have *never* [Benn's italics] known anyone make such a generous offer.'[10]

The Left decided to field Eric Heffer against Kinnock. To draw on Golding's analogy, Don Quixote handed his lance to Sancho Panza for another charge at the windmill. Heffer gained a derisory 6.3 per cent of the vote at the electoral college for the leadership; only Peter Shore was more humiliated with 3.1 per cent. Kinnock was all-conquering with 71.3 per cent.[11]

At his post-election wake, Chris Mullin also photographed another figure, a casually dressed man in his late thirties with a moustache. It was Ken Livingstone, looking absolutely crushed. He told the meeting that Kinnock was 'repellent' and suggested supporting Roy Hattersley for the leadership because he would 'at least have to accommodate the Left'.[12] Purely in terms of a successful parliamentary career, his open contempt for Kinnock would be a serious miscalculation in the years to come.

Like Benn, Livingstone was also part of the failed Left project to take over the Labour Party and forge a new socialist Britain. John Golding's decisive action to confirm Freeson for Brent East meant Livingstone could not be in Parliament for at least another four years. Other formidable, younger contenders for the future leadership of the party including Tony Blair and Gordon Brown entered Parliament in 1983. Livingstone would never make up for lost ground.

Clearly, Livingstone knew he had missed out on a major opportunity to lead the Left. Between Golding's decision to thwart Livingstone and the election, Mair Garside, the Labour GLC member for Woolwich East, remembers meeting Livingstone at a time he was bemoaning both his failure to secure Brent East and Benn's impending defeat in Bristol. 'All this trouble in Brent; it's such a shame,' he told Garside. 'Now I won't be there to lead the Left – to take the place of Tony Benn.'[13] Garside says, 'It was like he was weeping on my shoulder. He really seemed to have his heart set on leading the Left after Tony Benn.'[14]

Furthermore, Livingstone was the leader of a council which would be abolished during Mrs Thatcher's second term. Politically, he was tethered to a corpse. But Livingstone has been always at his best fighting against the odds and he managed to outmanoeuvre the government through one of the most brilliant political campaigns seen in post-war Britain. It did not come cheap but he succeeded in humiliating a powerful government machine and a seemingly omnipotent prime minister – not for the last time.

◆

In many ways and despite many provocations, the abolition of the GLC was an afterthought, a last-minute decision by Margaret Thatcher to spice up an otherwise unexciting manifesto. It would be a decision many in the Tory Party would soon come to regret. There had always been people wanting to abolish the GLC. As far back as 1974, at the height of the financial crisis, the *Evening Standard* columnist Simon Jenkins said the GLC should be disbanded. Few people bothered to vote in GLC elections and its services could theoretically be distributed either below to the boroughs or upwards to central government. 'There is simply no gap for the GLC to fill,' he wrote. 'There is no new political air for it to breathe and it is dying as a result.'[15]

Two years later, a former GLC alderman called Oliver Stutchbury led a small abolition campaign, which included the cricket writer Robin Marlar.[16] He blamed the GLC's failure to control rising wage costs, which accounted for 70 per cent of its budget, and said it was a 'heartbreaking' waste of money.[17] Sir Horace Cutler, the Tory who preceded Livingstone as leader, had tried to define the GLC's role by commissioning an inquiry into its functions. In 1978, the inquiry led by Sir Frank Marshall, a former leader of Leeds City Council, said the GLC should be a slimmed-down strategic body with fewer day-to-day responsibilities and fewer staff. As a result, the GLC sold off assets, transferred housing estates to the London boroughs and made thousands of staff redundant.[18] When the Marshall report was being debated by the GLC in March 1979, Livingstone called for abolition: 'I do not believe you need two tiers of local government and I very much regret that Horace Cutler has not been the ruthless Tory he likes to project and come forward with the biggest axe of all and axed the whole appalling show.'[19]

◆

In his first three years, Livingstone increased spending substantially, by 90 per cent compared with overall inflation in that period of 20 per cent. A big factor was the eventual modest reduction in fares. By mid 1984, fares were approximately a fifth lower than at the time of the 1981 election.[20] The government had tried to penalise high-spending councils by cutting its main grant, forcing them to increase the rates and lose votes. Within two years, the GLC claimed to have lost £600 million in grants from central government.[21] Livingstone raised the money through rate increases which were in any event added on to the bills of the London boroughs and passed on to ratepayers. The government's measures, enshrined in Heseltine's 1980 Local Government Finance Act, had failed to prevent municipal profligacy.

Before leaving the Department of the Environment in January 1983 to become defence secretary, Heseltine argued against more drastic measures to control high-spending councils which would only provoke unnecessary conflict. He argued that the easiest thing would be to simply abolish the high spenders: the GLC and the six deeply unpopular metropolitan authorities.[22]

Another decision taken by Heseltine as environment secretary proved critical. He had been saddled with investigating Thatcher's promise made in 1974 to replace the rates with something fairer. In December 1981, his department produced an equivocal discussion Green Paper which pushed a difficult ball into the long grass. The disastrous decision to replace the rates with the Poll Tax, or Community Charge would have to wait for Mrs Thatcher's third term. The six metropolitan goliaths of Greater Manchester, Merseyside, South Yorkshire, Tyne and Wear, West Midlands and West Yorkshire were already due for the chop. Thatcher put the GLC down for execution at the last moment as the manifesto was being finalised.[23]

◆

The first real clue that the vultures were swooping over County Hall came six months previously in late 1982, shortly after the furore over Livingstone's invitation to Sinn Féin. *Private Eye* reported remarks made by the prime minister's husband, Denis Thatcher, to two Tory politicians, John Bull and John Marshall at a Christmas fair in Finchley on 27 November 1982: 'That damn GLC should be abolished. Livingstone must be on his last legs.'[24]

Patrick Jenkin, a jolly avuncular barrister with bushy eyebrows and a virtually imperceptible bat squeak of menace, was appointed environment secretary to kill off the GLC. At the time he was industry secretary with hopes for promotion to the new cabinet post combining the Departments of Trade and Industry. After her election victory she rang Jenkin and said, 'Patrick, I want you to do Environment; you're so good at getting legislation through the House.'[25]

A little later, Jenkin summoned Illtyd Harrington, then the chairman of the GLC to tell him that Thatcher was in deadly earnest over her manifesto commitment to abolish the GLC. Over tea and biscuits from the Army and Navy store at the Department of the Environment, the environment secretary got to the point: 'She's going to get rid of you.'[26]

'It's nothing against you personally,' Jenkin told Harrington, 'we have got great respect for you.' Harrington says, 'I realised I was being handed the death certificate of the GLC.'[27]

Back at County Hall, Livingstone asked Harrington: 'What did they say to you?' 'We're fucked,' replied Harrington. 'We'll see about that,' said Livingstone, 'you're too defeatist.'[28] Ironically, as things turned out, GLC abolition would help damage Jenkin's political career and transform Livingstone's.

Patrick Jenkin says, 'The GLC had become, under Ken, a by-word for left-wing extremism and profligacy and the boroughs were increasingly up in arms at the precepts that were being demanded by the GLC.'[29] But Jenkin insists that although Livingstone's 'antics' helped make the arguments for abolition, it was not directed at him. 'It was not aimed primarily at Ken – not at all.

'You make policy on the merits of the case and the merits of the case were that we were getting rid of two-tier government in all the other areas in England and Wales. That was agreed by the cabinet and was going to go ahead, why shouldn't it apply to London?

'In addition, [when] there was the growing clamour by the boroughs and more specifically from the ratepayers in London at the huge sums they were being asked to fork out for this expensive monstrosity, you were presented with a very attractive political argument. Ken's excesses made the case for that easier than it might otherwise have been but I can say categorically, it was not the prime driver.'

This is what Jenkin said in 2007 but at the Conservative Party conference in 1983, he said: 'The GLC has become the South Bank of farce. No one has done more than Ken Livingstone to bring local government into contempt. He struts the world stage and invites the Provisional Sinn Féin [sic] into our city.'[30]

From the government's vantage point, getting rid of the GLC must have seemed like shooting rats in a barrel. The Labour Party had been crushed and was in disarray; after two years of crisis and controversy, Livingstone and his GLC had little popular support. A series of MORI polls for the *Evening Standard* in April 1983 demonstrated that 58 per cent of Londoners were dissatisfied with Livingstone and only 26 per cent satisfied. The Tories enjoyed a 10 per cent lead and would have romped home in any GLC election, but the GLC had had its last election.[31]

◆

In May 1983, the SDP GLC member Anne Sofer started a regular column about life at County Hall in *The Times*. More in sorrow than anger, she wrote: 'In the two years of the present administration the charade has been transformed from a genteel parlour game to a full blown pantomime.' Debates at the GLC were increasingly on issues about which the GLC had no control: defence, Northern Ireland, monetarism and the future of the Falkland Islands.[32] Groups that had recently gathered at County Hall included the Black Trade Unionist Solidarity Movement, Lawyers for Nuclear Disarmament and Women's Media Action Group. Underlining the GLC's increasing irrelevance, she added, 'Most of the services that affect the daily life of London's citizens – housing, policing, education and training, social services and rubbish collection and libraries are run by other authorities.'

The government bill to abolish the GLC, 'Streamlining the Cities', also emphasised how the GLC accounted for only 16 per cent of the total expenditure on services in its areas. The remaining 84 per cent was done by the boroughs and central government.[33] The legislation proposed doing away with the GLC by 1 April 1986. Some functions, including trading standards and building control, would go to the boroughs. Other powers would go to central government[34] or a jumble of quangos, *ad hoc* committees, 'special joint arrangements' and appointed boards.[35] Many parks and commons would go to the City of London Corporation. Assets including County Hall itself would go to a new unelected body called the London Residuary Body and sold off.

Although Thatcherite borough leaders like Shirley Porter in Westminster rejoiced, there was growing concern among the professionals who would have to deal with the mess. The chief executives of the 32 boroughs, most of which were Tory-controlled, told the government that its proposals would 'not meet the general principle that any reorganisation should be based on the principles of local government and accountability'.[36]

The proposals were shorn of any political vision. There was a good argument for getting rid of the six metropolitan authorities. No one in the cities of Leeds, Bradford or Wakefield was going to miss a folly like the West Yorkshire Metropolitan County, essentially a half-baked piece of regional government. However the bill would leave London the only capital in western Europe without its own directly-elected strategic body. Given a blank sheet of paper to establish governance for the capital and few statesmen would come up with the administrative dog's breakfast the government now proposed. 'My dear Philip,' Margaret Thatcher told the Tory MP for Beckenham, Philip Goodhart, on 21 March 1985, 'there is no such thing as a voice for London.'[37] But then, she would say the same thing about society two years later.[38]

◆

From the outset, Jenkin made a big strategic error. The next GLC elections were scheduled for May 1985, a year before the GLC could be abolished. The government was extremely anxious that the election could become a referendum on its proposals. So Jenkin planned to abolish the elections and for the last year of its life, hand the power of the GLC over to the leaders of the borough council. As most London boroughs were Conservative-controlled, that would mean transferring control of the GLC from elected Labour members to unelected Tories without giving the electors a say. Abolishing the 1985 elections also required legislation, and so Jenkin had drawn up the now notorious 1983 Local Government (interim Provisions bill). It was known as the Paving bill because it would abolish the elections and pave the way for abolition. It proved to be crazy paving on a path to a farce.

The government had started the work of dismembering the GLC after the election by removing its most important function: the control over the London Underground. Effectively, this would be the only renationalisation of a public asset by Margaret Thatcher. The Tube was taken from London Transport, a GLC subsidiary, and handed over to London Regional Transport, a government subsidiary. By April 1982, Tory MPs like John Greenway were urging the prime minister to remove the Tube after the recent doubling of both the fares and the rates 'through the mismanagement of London Transport by the GLC'. Citing the Fares Fair fiasco, Thatcher has seen 'much merit in the solution'.[39] The removal of the Tube from County Hall in 1984 would do much to erode the argument for a GLC.

◆

During the autumn of 1983, Livingstone toured the party conferences on a road show costing the GLC £845,000 to whip up opposition against abolition.[40] He got off to a bad start. Livingstone's first stop-off was Blackpool for the TUC annual conference where he heard Eric Hammond, the new general secretary-designate of the right-wing electricians' union, the EEPTU, launch an astonishing attack on the GLC: 'There may be enough terrorist groups, lesbians and other queer folk in inner-London Labour parties to support Mr Livingstone's antics, but there's little support in the ranks of ordinary trade unionists.'[41]

But there was something in the air; people were beginning to smell a rat, and for once it was not Livingstone. Other trade unionists queued up to shake his hand. Livingstone persuaded the SDP conference to oppose abolition, despite the fact, as he said later, that it was 'filled with people who left the Labour Party because of people like me'.[42] After his speech at a fringe meeting in Salford University, one young SDP member was heard to proclaim: 'They *can't* abolish him!'[43] David Rose, the *Time Out* writer accompanying Livingstone, observed, 'Red Ken has done it again; entering the lion's den ... and emerging not only unscathed but triumphant.'

Later, Livingstone travelled to Harrogate for the Liberal's annual conference where he worked the same magic. Rose recalled him 'surrounded constantly by adoring young Liberals' wearing "I'm Red Ken" badges'. For Rose, the road show played to Livingstone's greatest strengths: 'Supreme media ability and personal charisma with the rank and file – which can sometimes undermine his position.' Only in Blackpool for Labour's conference did he fail to charm, with Neil Kinnock 'repeatedly snubbing Livingstone's attempts to hold a conversation with him'.[44] After the Brent East affair, it seemed Livingstone had run out of options. At the age of 38, added Rose, with another four years to go to a general election, Ken Livingstone faced 'a severe problem with his career'.[45]

◆

Also on tour with the Red Ken road show was Tory GLC member and rock star biographer, George Tremlett. He liked Livingstone and thought he had broad interests. 'He was never a swivel-eyed Trot,' says Tremlett, who is dismissive of some of his former senior Tory colleagues who went along with abolition. He says, 'Margaret Thatcher made it perfectly clear that if people kept their heads down there would be honours spread out. But here were four or five of us who would not go along with Thatcher's feud.'[46]

To overcome public apathy about County Hall, the GLC would have to spend £11 million of public money on campaigning against abolition. County Hall ran a highly sophisticated operation with a three-pronged strategy: press, advertising and parliamentary lobbying. Handling the press and the media were Nita Clarke and her colleagues. Tony Wilson, a polished publicist, headed the campaigning and publicity team and brought in the advertising company Boase Massimi Pollitt, or BMP. Founded by Martin Boase, Gabe Massimi and Stanley Pollitt, BMP had become famous in 1974 for creating the small metal Martian characters that starred in the television commercials for the Smash potato mix, and later the Honey Monster who sold the Sugar Puffs breakfast cereal for the Quaker Oats company.[47] In the 1970s, the agency had formed close links with the Labour Party. At first Livingstone chaired the campaign strategy meetings but 'progress was unspectacular', according to *The Economist*.

The ad men and the Labour councillors often clashed. According to Livingstone later: 'Behaviour, dress and jargon often grated on both sides,' and there were some rather 'pyrotechnic rows'.[48] Livingstone despised ad men presentations of campaigns and preferred to be told the best line to run.[49] He wisely delegated the campaign's running to Wilson.[50]

◆

Harry Barlow joined the GLC campaign at the end of 1983 and would later play an important role in many of Livingstone's mayoral campaigns. 'No one had bothered to tell people what the GLC did,' says Barlow, 'and by then it was too late, so you had to go on the big issues of democracy and bureaucracy – telling people about what happens when Whitehall takes over rather than going on about people losing a particular service.'[51] The loss of democracy was enforced by the initial 'Say no to no say' campaign which helped make the cancellation of the elections such an obvious hostage to fortune. Initially Barlow had his doubts about the 'Say no' slogan. 'It didn't exactly trip off the tongue,' he says. 'But it did seem to work.'

Shirley Porter, the Thatcherite leader of Westminster City Council, was at the forefront in the fight to silence the campaign. She challenged the 'Say no to no say' campaign claiming it was politicking with public money. In January 1985, the High Court ruled the GLC could only inform, not persuade.[52] But the slogans were so fixed in people's minds that a slight mutation in the campaign's message kept Livingstone out of trouble and out in front.

The campaign team decision also gave people subliminal messages reinforcing the importance of the GLC. Barlow says, 'We did things like a branding survey so that just about everything the GLC owned or operated had a sticker on it or a badge: every lamp post, every traffic light and that sort of stuff; all the buildings and any vehicles because the GLC owned lots and lots of property.'[53] The stickers often said 'GLC – working *for* London', although after legal challenges about the use of public money for political propaganda it was changed to 'GLC – working *in* London.'[54]

◆

Barlow found Livingstone a 'breath of fresh air'. 'I never thought local government could ever be interesting. It's so boring but he could talk in a normal way and engage people. He did the words, and I ended up doing a lot of the pictures.' The advertising men always knew people either loved or loathed Livingstone; few were ambivalent. But, Livingstone gradually became the public face of the campaign.

Barlow says, 'What I like about Ken is that he's got a sense of humour and we tried to play that in the ads. It's almost a London-type cheekiness. Ken was basically the outward face of the GLC and he was a brand you could use and because the papers had given him such huge coverage, most of it of course negative, he was someone who was instantly recognisable.'

Later Livingstone's press officer Nita Clarke said the abolition campaign transformed Livingstone from being the *Sun*'s 'most odious man in Britain', 'the epitome of the fratricidal Labour left wing' to 'cuddly Ken, beloved of commentators and celebrities'. She added: 'Our strategy was clear – sell Ken as something different from your average politician, someone who couldn't possibly be a threat. Sell the GLC as the little guys against the Thatcherite steamroller.

'There was nothing – and I mean nothing – that Ken wouldn't do to get himself and the campaign on to the front pages.' She added, 'I'm not denying it was fun to do – but it was news management, nothing more and nothing less. The huge GLC media operation swung behind Ken and delivered the goods, and the storybook we created lives on.'[55]

◆

The GLC provided marvellous photo opportunities. When Eros was returned to his plinth in Piccadilly Circus after a clean-up, who better to lead the ceremony than Ken Livingstone and when better than Valentine's Day, 14 February 1984, two months before Parliament was due to debate Jenkin's Paving bill? Through the late winter and spring of 1984, the polls started moving dramatically in Livingstone's favour. By March 1984, the number of people dissatisfied with the GLC had fallen from 58 per cent to 42 per cent.[56] By the summer of 1984, opposition in London to abolition had reached 74 per cent.[57] By then £7 million had been spent on the campaign.[58]

Press and advertising performed essential roles but the real blow against the government was delivered by the third team – the parliamentary lobbyists. The team was led by a Tory. Until 1975, Roland Freeman had been the Tory GLC member for Finchley, and had subsequently joined David Owen's SDP. He also ran his own lobbying company and was able to use his old contacts to funnel material and sound bites, all paid for by the GLC, to Tory opponents of GLC abolition.[59] Another important figure in the political lobbying team was Reg Race, who had lost his seat as the hard left Bennite MP for Woodford Green. A hard-headed pragmatist, Race was appointed the third most senior officer at County Hall; for the last three years of the GLC's life, he oversaw the fight against abolition.[60]

To become law, there had to be three readings of the Paving bill in both Houses of Parliament. For the bill to be defeated, it would have to be voted down either at any of the six readings and two committee stages. On 29 March 1984, the day before the bill started its parliamentary journey, 20,000 public servants, including teachers, typists and dinner ladies, held a 24-hour strike in support of the GLC and a rally in central London.[61]

The first debate on the bill in the Commons was a dramatic affair. On 10 April 1984, Ted Heath, the former Tory prime minister, flew back to Britain from Nairobi to take part in the Commons debate scheduled for the following day.[62] He launched a vitriolic attack in which he told the government it was making a catastrophic mistake in cancelling the 1985 elections and handing power to the Tory borough leaders: 'There cannot be any justification for this. It immediately lays the Conservative Party open to the charge of the greatest gerrymandering in the past 150 years of British history.'[63]

There were knowing laughs from the Labour benches[64] when Heath said: 'The way the government had handled the issue had achieved the inconceivable – it had mobilized the weight of public opinion behind Mr Kenneth Livingstone. Who would have thought that possible two years ago? It was an achievement unknown in the annals of local government.'[65] The government emerged from the debate bloodied and battered. Its huge overall majority of 141 had allowed the bill to go forward to a second reading but 19 Tories including Heath and three other former cabinet ministers had defied the whips and voted against the bill; 20 others abstained.[66]

What was not known at the time, even by them, was that Heath and other senior Tories were reading speeches essentially written for them by Reg Race's team back at County Hall. Increasingly, behind the scenes, Livingstone's campaigning machine took over the parliamentary opposition particularly when the bill eventually reached the Lords.

Reg Race says: 'We took over the arguments and we literally took over the working operation of the opposition in the Lords from the rather flaccid operation which was there at the time. We were writing everything: we were writing briefing notes speeches and sound bites; we were writing amendments for the committees discussing the bill. We even took over the Labour whips operation in the House of Lords.'[67]

◆

In 1984, life peers, often individuals ennobled on merit, were in the minority. Remarkably for the late twentieth century, a legislative body for a Western European democracy was nominally controlled by a majority of hereditary peers who could not claim with conviction that they ought to be there. Many had the decency to absent themselves at critical votes, and the country was none the poorer for that. But on occasion, like cadavers in a Michael Jackson video they were often called upon to strut their stuff, and in the Thatcher period, in support of the Tory Party. But on the Paving bill, thanks to the Reg Race squad, it was Livingstone who called the tune.

The bill came before the Lords for its second reading on 11 June 1984. The GLC lobbyist Roland Freeman had built up a card index of the biographical details and political interests of every member of the House of Lords.[68] He deployed his two assistants, Damien Welfare and Ann Pettifor, to the House of Lords to 'butter up' the elderly members.[69] A Tory hereditary Baron, Charlie Teviot, gave up his job as a bus driver and was put on the campaign payroll.[70] He also played a vital role in persuading many Lords to oppose the government.[71]

Livingstone gave a glimpse of the GLC operation: 'Working with the opposition whips we contacted everyone and planned a fleet of cars to get them to and from the Lords. We hired rooms in the Lords in which food and drink would be continually available on the day so that none of them had any excuse to slip out of our sight. Every foible was pandered to and it eventually paid off.'[72] As a result, the government scraped home 237 votes in favour of abolition to 217 against – a majority of just 20. All eyes were on the third and final reading of the bill set for 28 June 1984.

◆

In the interim, there was a very odd incident involving a prostitute, a briefcase, a photocopier and Bill Bush, Livingstone's chief of staff. Chris Mitchell, the senior grants officer, tells an extraordinary story about a letter sent to Livingstone by a prostitute. Mitchell says, 'She wrote to Ken saying, "Some of my clients are government ministers and they come in here and they leave their briefcases with my maid. If I had a photocopier, my maid could photocopy everything and I could pass it on to you, Ken."'[73] Consequently, highly confidential information about abolition came into Livingstone's possession.

The truth was apparently more complicated. Livingstone did receive confidential government documents via a prostitute, including circulars written by Patrick Jenkin which copied in only a handful of senior civil servants and ministers. The documents had 'fallen out' of her client's briefcase while he was tied or handcuffed to the bed during a sado-masochistic bondage session. Through intermediaries, Livingstone offered to lend the prostitute a GLC photocopier. But she declined on the grounds that it 'would look out of place and might worry the clients'.[74]

Unusually for someone in her business, the prostitute got cold feet and the supply of documents dried up. In March 1984, while Livingstone was out of town campaigning against abolition, John McDonnell, Livingstone's deputy, leaked the documents to the *Guardian*'s John Carvel, including a letter revealing that the government planned to allow direct elections to the ILEA following GLC abolition in 1986. The leak was done on the advice of Bill Bush and Nita Clarke.[75] The story appeared in the *Guardian* on 13 March 1984.[76]

At 9.10, on the morning of 26 June 1984 and two days before the critical Lords' debate on the Paving bill, Bill Bush dropped his two-year-old son Thomas at a day nursery on the other side of the river from County Hall and was driving back towards Waterloo Bridge when his car was stopped by three Special Branch officers, one on a motorcycle and two in an unmarked car. He was arrested and locked up in a cell at Rochester Row police station for 15 minutes before questioning.

Since the Carvel story, the government had been quietly holding a leak inquiry. The arrest was condemned by Labour's environment spokesman Jack Straw as an absurd overreaction to an issue which had nothing to do with national security.[77] After two hours of questioning, a baffled Bush was shown the confidential cabinet minute at the heart of Carvel's story before being released unconditionally. Nothing more was heard of the matter. In the meantime, Livingstone ordered the destruction of all existing copies of the confidential material.[78]

On 28 June 1984, the Reg Race team again went into action. A fleet of around 30 cars was again laid on for the Lords. Not everyone took up the offer, including Joe Gormley, the Baron of Ashton-in-Makerfield and former leader of the National Union of Mineworkers. Race says, 'Joe was difficult over this because he didn't like Ken. We said to him, "Look, this is an issue about democracy; it's not about Ken." Eventually I instructed our team to send a car for him and it went down to his house in Surrey and he wouldn't get in the car to save London's democracy because of Ken!'[79]

The sporting calendar played a crucial role. It took a special kind of incompetence to hold the debate on the first day of both the Lord's Test Match and the Henley Royal Regatta, and when the Wimbledon tennis championships were in full swing. As a result, many of the government's potential supporters failed to appear and the bill was defeated by 191 votes to 143, a majority of 48.

◆

In little more than a year, Livingstone had gone from pariah whose future lay behind him to popular champion who had inflicted a serious defeat on a powerful government. His fortunes had been transformed by Margaret Thatcher. Patrick Jenkin says, 'Ted Heath's accusation was that I had turned Livingstone who was effectively a left-wing nut into a folk hero. And that's true. That was the effect of what we were doing. He played it very skilfully; he's a very skilful operator.'[80]

In May 2000, Patrick Jenkin bumped into Livingstone who had just been elected mayor of London for the first time and congratulated him on a 'very remarkable win'. 'Oh Patrick,' replied Livingstone. 'You made it all possible!'[81]

Notes

1   Tony Benn, *The End of an Era, Diaries 1980-1990*, (see 12.6.83)
2   Margaret Thatcher, *The Downing Street Years*, p339
3   John Golding, *Hammer of the Left*, p289
4   *Labour Herald*, 20.5.83, p1
5   Peter Joyce, *Guide to UK General Elections 1832-2001*, pp351-362
6   John Golding, *Hammer of the Left*, p310
7   Ibid., p366
8   Ibid., pp233-238
9   Ibid., pp273, 300
10 Tony Benn, *The End of an Era, Diaries 1980-1990*, (see 12.6.83)
11 Robert Harris, *The Making of Neil Kinnock*, p237
12 Tony Benn, *The End of an Era, Diaries 1980-1990*, (see 12.6.83)
13 Interview, Mair Garside, 17.8.07
14 Ibid.
15 *Evening Standard*, 'Scrap the GLC?', by Simon Jenkins, 16.7.74
16 *Time Out*, 11.2.77
17 *Evening Standard*, 'Why the GLC must go', by Oliver Stutchbury, 7.12.76
18 Tony Travers, 'GLC Leaders, 1965 to 1986', London School of Economics
19 Andrew Forrester, Stewart Lansley and Robin Pauley, *Beyond our Ken, A Guide to the Battle for London*, p103; *Daily Mail*, 15.2.84
20 Andrew Forrester, Stewart Lansley and Robin Pauley, *Beyond our Ken, A Guide to the Battle for London*, pp40-41

21 John Carvel, *Citizen Ken*, p122

22 Michael Crick, *Michael Heseltine, A Biography*, Penguin, 1997, pp215-216

23 Interview, Patrick Jenkin, Baron Jenkin of Roding, 2.10.07

24 *Private Eye*, Issue 547, 3.12.82, p8

25 Interview, Patrick Jenkin, Baron Jenkin of Roding, 2.10.07

26 Interview, Illtyd Harrington, 30.3.04; Andrew Hosken, *Nothing like a Dame, The Scandals of Shirley Porter*, p106

27 Interview, Illtyd Harrington, 4.7.07

28 Ibid.

29 Interview, Patrick Jenkin, Baron Jenkin of Roding, 2.10.07

30 *Daily Telegraph*, 12.10.83

31 *Evening Standard*, 5.4.83, p1; Andrew Forester, Stewart Lansley and Robin Pauley *Beyond our Ken, A Guide to the Battle for London*, p80

32 *The Times*, 'Ken Livingstone's pantomime cow', by Anne Sofer, 6.5.83

33 'Streamlining the cities', by the Department of the Environment, HMSO, Cmnd.9063, 7.10.83

34 Andrew Forrester, Stewart Lansley and Robin Pauley, *Beyond our Ken, A Guide to the Battle for London*, pp138-139

35 Tony Travers, Michael Hebbert and June Burnham, *The Government of London*, Joseph Rowntree Foundation, 1991, pp33-47

36 *Evening Standard*, 'Boroughs warn over the abolition of the GLC', statement by Association of London Chief Executives, 15.3.84

37 Kenneth Baker, *The Turbulent Years, My Life in Politics*, Faber and Faber, 1993, p103

38 *Woman's Own*, 31.10.87

39 Prime Minister's Questions, Source: Hansard HC [22/969-74], 29.4.82

40 *Time Out*, 20.10.83

41 *Guardian*, 9.9.83

42 Ken Livingstone, *If Voting Changed Anything, They'd Abolish It*, p264

43 *Time Out*, 20.10 .83

44 Ibid.

45 Ibid.

46 Interview, George Tremlett, 26.6.07

47 *Time Out*, Frontlines, 2.8.84

48 Ken Livingstone, *If Voting Changed Anything, They'd Abolish It*, p276

49 Interview, Harry Barlow, 20.11.07

50 *The Economist*, 'Ken and Queen turn the tide', 12.5.84

51 Interview, Harry Barlow, 20.11.07

52 Andrew Hosken, *Nothing Like a Dame, The Scandals of Shirley Porter*, p111

53 Ibid.

54 Ibid.

55 Ibid.

56 Andrew Forrester, Stewart Lansley and Robin Pauley, *Beyond our Ken, A Guide to the Battle for London*, p80

57 Ibid.

58 *Time Out*, Frontlines, 2.8.84

59 Note to Andrew Hosken from Reg Race, 20.9.07

60 Ken Livingstone, *If Voting Changed Anything, They'd Abolish It*, p278

61 *Daily Telegraph*, 30.3.84
62 *Guardian*, 10.4.07
63 *The Times*, 'Heath attacks bill as gerrymandering', 12.4.84
64 *Daily Telegraph*, 12.4.84
65 *The Times*, 'Heath attacks bill as gerrymandering', 12.4.84
66 *Daily Telegraph*, 12.4.84
67 Interview, Reg Race, 23.8.07
68 Andrew Forrester, Stewart Lansley and Robin Pauley, *Beyond our Ken, A Guide to the Battle for London*, p81
69 Note to Andrew Hosken from Reg Race, 20.9.07
70 Email from Reg Race to Andrew Hosken, 17.12.07
71 Interview, Reg Race, 23.8.07
72 Ken Livingstone, *If Voting Changed Anything, They'd Abolish It*, p279
73 Interview, Chris Mitchell, 12.9.07
74 Ken Livingstone, *If Voting Changed Anything, They'd Abolish It*, pp273-275
75 Ibid.
76 *Guardian*, 13.3.84 and 27.6.84
77 Ibid. and *Daily Telegraph*, 27.6.84
78 Ken Livingstone, *If Voting Changed Anything, They'd Abolish It*, p281
79 Interview, Reg Race, 23.8.07
80 Interview, Baron Jenkin of Roding, 2.10.07
81 Ibid.

Chapter 15

'Though cowards flinch', May 1984–November 1985

On 8 May 1984, the Queen, the Duke of Edinburgh and Ken Livingstone's mother boarded a GLC barge by County Hall and sailed off towards Woolwich Reach to open the newly built Thames Barrier. Ethel Livingstone had paid £100 for a new outfit, pale pink, and a hat with a feather. The Queen asked her to sit with her at the back of the boat. 'Are you warm enough, my dear?' asked the Duke of Edinburgh. She replied, 'I've got plenty on underneath!'[1]

Ethel Livingstone did not know that after the Monarch and the Duke, she was probably the most important person there. It was the height of the abolition campaign and nerves were jangling in corridors of power at both ends of Westminster Bridge. Livingstone's decision to reject an invitation to the Royal wedding in 1981 had not been forgotten at Buckingham Palace, nor had his black balloons in support of the hunger strikers. Trepidation filled hearts in Buckingham Palace as the opening of the Thames Barrier loomed large on the horizon and realisation dawned that the hosts would be Red Ken and friends. Any student of French or Russian history will tell you: Royals and revolutionaries don't mix. Sir Phillip Moore, the Queen's private secretary, wrote a discreet note to Maurice Stonefrost asking him to guarantee that there would be no 'untoward occurrence' at the opening.

Maurice Stonefrost had recently been promoted to the top job in the GLC, as director general. He succeeded Sir James Swaffield who had taken retirement, much to his and Ken Livingstone's relief. The two men did not like each other and could scarcely bear to be in the same room together.[2] As well as his experience and financial expertise, Stonefrost was clubbable and clever and dispensed advice in a kindly Bristol burr. He was not the type to tell Livingstone to behave himself but he knew that Livingstone's mum would be the best guarantor against anything 'untoward' happening. He wrote back to Moore asking the Palace to invite

Ethel Livingstone.[3] She would say later: 'I am a royalist,' and nod-
ding to her son, added, 'no matter what he thinks.'[4]

◆

The Palace was right to be concerned. The original idea from the
Left was to ask one of the Barrier builders to perform the opening
ceremony. Stonefrost says that the unions said, 'We're not having that. We want the Queen.' There had been an ugly row about
inviting the Queen to the opening at a group meeting of the GLC
Labour members. According to a report by a Labour observer,
Paula Watson, Livingstone had decided to invite the Queen
'apparently in the hope that this would imply royal support and
produce royal pressure to save the GLC.' 'The idea was ludicrous,'
snorted Watson in her report. 'Elizabeth Windsor is a shrewd,
grasping woman, determined to preserve the privileged position of
herself and her family.' Eight left-wingers wanted a debate on the
proposed £340,000 cost of the ceremony. Livingstone furiously
accused them of disloyalty, 'hypocrisy' and 'left-wing careerism'.
Without a trace of irony, Watson concluded: 'The opening of the
Thames Barrier should have been used to help mobilise working-
class support against Thatcherism and the Capitalist State.

'The sight of "the people's Ken" bowing to the living embodiment of a class society based on hereditary wealth and privilege
will not help raise consciousness or build workers' solidarity.'[5]
Livingstone did bow to the Queen. 'You fucking hypocrite,' whis-
pered Harrington. 'Did you have to bow that low?'[6]

Livingstone sported a 'GLC – Working for London' badge
but behaved impeccably. Many of the spittle-flecked Left were
kept out of sight at their own Barrier party laid on by Stonefrost.
Later, after the fireworks, Livingstone and his mother were walking together down the corridors at County Hall. He turned and
said, 'Wouldn't it have been nice if Dad had been with us?'[7] Ethel
Livingstone would die a little more than 12 years later in August
1997, aged 82.

◆

Livingstone was only prepared to go along with the Left to the
outer limits of his comfort zone, and no further. Time and again,
the Left, particularly the Trots, seemed to go out of their way to
land him in the mire with the courts or the government; time
and again, his nimble footwork kept him out of trouble. But in
March 1985, he had a catastrophic falling out with the Left which

changed the course of his political career. At one stroke, he shattered the careful alliances of Trots and others on the hard left, including Ted Knight and the Chartists, that he had built up over the previous 15 years.

The Lords' defeat on abolition proved to be a humiliation for Thatcher but not a complete disaster. To answer the Lords' concerns expressed by Ted Heath about democracy, the government suggested an amendment which would still cancel the 1985 elections but leave Ken Livingstone in charge right up to abolition on 1 April 1986 instead of transferring control to the Tory borough council leaders for the last year. The amended bill was passed by the Lords on 23 July 1984.[8]

At the same time, Jenkin gave himself the power of veto on any contract worth more than £100,000, partly in an attempt to prevent County Hall spending more millions on publicity. Livingstone had anticipated the move by paying all the campaigning bills for the next 18 months. By the deadline, at midnight on 24 July 1984, the GLC had issued more than £40 million worth of contracts. After that, it would deluge the Department of the Environment with 250 contracts a week while the expensive abolition campaign boomed away in the background; Jenkin was powerless to stop it.[9]

◆

In August 1984, Livingstone and three other Labour GLC members, his deputy John McDonnell, Lewis Herbert and Kenneth Little, resigned their seats to force by-elections and effectively a plebiscite on GLC abolition. But the Tories refused to play ball by fielding candidates in the by-elections. There was heavy rain on polling day, 21 September 1984; all four men were re-elected. The highest turnout, at 29.71 per cent, was recorded in Livingstone's Paddington seat. He was returned with a majority of 9,685. Mrs Thatcher mocked Livingstone: 'It was a very, very small turnout. It must have been a great disappointment for him.'[10] But the *Daily Telegraph* said it was a 'solid performance' by a 'major politician', adding: 'He is more astute than Mr Benn, better able to simulate likeableness while remaining quite outstandingly ruthless with anyone innocently getting in the way, something to which Mr Reg Freeson can testify.'[11]

Livingstone had become the official darling of the Left. In his 1984 book based on interviews with Livingstone, Tariq Ali, the author and former Trot, described Livingstone as 'the most gifted representative of the New Labour Left', adding: 'He speaks a different language from the careerist Labour politicians who end up in the House of Lords.' Livingstone was 'first and foremost a militant socialist'. Ali rejected allegations that Livingstone was 'an opportunist simply using the Left to climb up the ladder'.[12] Within months, Livingstone would be accused not only of using the Left but betraying it at a critical point in the struggle against Thatcher.

The great political issue of the day which threatened Thatcher was not the abolition of the GLC but the miners' strike which began in March 1984 and would convulse the country for the following 12 months. Also in March 1984, Parliament passed the Rates Act, one of the toughest laws ever introduced to curb council spending.

During her 11 years in power, Margaret Thatcher introduced roughly 50 Acts of Parliament, which were designed to restrain council spending in one way or another.[13] The 1984 Rates Act introduced the most draconian measure called 'rate capping' which gave the government the power essentially to set a council's budget and impose cuts directly from Whitehall. Earlier legislation had punished high spenders by withdrawing central government grants but the only people who suffered were local people and businesses, because councils like Lambeth and the GLC simply raised rates to maintain the growing budgets.

Rate capping was not just another Thatcher scheme to force restraint on local authorities; it fundamentally changed the balance of power between central and local government. To the Left, rate capping destroyed the freedom of a local community's political representatives to determine spending levels. Writing later, the former leader of Sheffield Council, David Blunkett, said, 'The government's aim was now clearly to challenge the political independence of local authorities.'[14] Many saw it as the end of local government itself.

On 24 July 1984, the same day the Lords passed the Paving bill, Jenkin announced a list of 19 councils which would be 'rate capped'. Only one Tory council, Portsmouth, would be capped; the rest were Labour-controlled. The list included the GLC and ILEA as well as the usual 'loony left' suspects like Lambeth, Hackney and Islington.[15]

The Left, and especially the Trots, saw a campaign against rate capping as part of the overall struggle alongside the miners to bring down Thatcher. Many on the left were convinced both fights could help create the conditions necessary for revolution. There were repeated attempts to couple the strike with the rate capping. Both struggles would end in ignominious failure.

◆

In June 1984, Livingstone invited striking miners to County Hall. 'For now,' said *Private Eye*, 'let's just report that once the staff bar had been drunk dry, hordes of striking pit-men went on the rampage in the main block, abusing and assaulting young female staff.

'No doubt the "Wimmins" Committee would be rightly out-raged at such behaviour, but not a bit of it – these louts were, after all, the personal guests of their beloved leader, Red Ken.'[16]

In a speech in late 1984 at the Royal Festival Hall, Ken Livingstone said, 'We have the chance to defeat this government, to break its will and to bring it down. That is the option before us. It involves total support for the miners, total resistance to everything this government seeks to do to local government.'[17] The *Labour Herald* supported calls by the National Union of Mineworkers for an all-out general strike, something which Gerry Healy had been urging for the past 40 years.[18]

The Left had fabulous illusions about what it could achieve by defying the government on rate capping. Ted Knight, the leader of Lambeth Council, was convinced that the government would fall if enough local authorities broke the law by refusing to set an annual budget. In the past, councils like the GLC had borrowed billions of pounds from banks and City institutions to build houses, roads and schools. Local government was considered a safe borrower because it had the power to raise revenue in rates.

'The view was taken that we should not set the rate,' says Knight. 'If councils did not do that they were not raising the money required: the services would stop and they wouldn't be able to repay the money on loan and the impact on the City of London would be tremendous. The arguments were that the councils would go into bankruptcy, frighten the money markets, the government wouldn't be able to contain the panic and as a consequence they would have to concede.'[19]

At first there were 34 would-be rebel councils, including the

GLC. They had been emboldened by the example of Liverpool City Council, then in the grip of the Militant Tendency. In the febrile climate created by the Tendency in Liverpool, the council had threatened to set an illegal budget.

Jenkin made a remarkable journey to the city to see some of the appalling housing conditions for himself, and on 9 July 1984 made further financial concessions worth approximately £20 million.[20] Militant touted the climbdown as a 'victory'.[21] The government was clearly concerned at the prospect of revolutionary troublemakers in charge of a city which had been wracked by serious riots three years previously and hit by rising unemployment. 'Liverpool was one of the things that really kept me awake at night,' says Jenkin. 'I had visions of streets packed with rioting crowds while I flew commissioners into the City Hall at Liverpool and landed them on the roof in helicopters and wondering how the hell I would ever get them out again!'[22]

Jenkin is dismissive of Ted Knight's strategy to bring down the government: 'There were arguments on this but it was always dismissed as pure fantasy. To use a crude phrase, they were building castles in the air. It never had any basis in reality because in fact the British people don't behave like that; elected councils don't behave like that.'

Commissioners were officials appointed by the government to run public bodies like councils in extreme situations. In 1979, as secretary of state for health and social security, Jenkin had appointed five commissioners to take over the running of the Lambeth, Southwark and Lewisham Health Authority which had been refusing to set legal budgets.[23]

As early as the autumn of 1984, Jenkin's junior minister Kenneth Baker was warning that defiance of rate capping could lead to the government having to appoint commissioners to take over Labour councils like the GLC. But cooler heads prevailed. At a meeting of ministers, Thatcher said, 'We don't need commissioners. No point in discussing them.'[24] Jenkin felt all along that the rebel councils lacked the backbone for a fight and never even made contingency plans to appoint commissioners in the event that the 34 rebels would refuse to set a rate.

◆

Jenkin remembers attending a two-hour meeting at the Department of the Environment with representatives of the

1. Family group, with bear. Ethel, Lin, Ken and Bob on holiday, 1955.
   (Courtesy Ken Livingstone)

2. Ken and Christine with Eddie Lopez, Lambeth, 1971.
   (Courtesy Eddie Lopez)

3.   Livingstone sings the 'Red Flag' with Lambeth comrades at Eddie Lopez's leaving party. 'Red Ted' Knight is on his immediate left, 1971. *(Courtesy Eddie Lopez)*

4.   Ken Livingstone at Philippa Fawcett, circa 1973. Christine Chapman, a year below. The couple divorced in 1982. *(Courtesy Angela Cook)*

5.   Sir Reg Goodwin, GLC Labour leader, and Jim Callaghan discuss mending bridges, but not with the left, circa 1976. *(Courtesy Peter Walker)*

6.   The people's palace under Livingstone. Now the 'London Marriott County Hall' thanks to Margaret Thatcher.

7. 'My partners and I are agreed that the nation cannot afford you.' Like the Tory press, the *Labour Herald* often lampooned Michael Foot as a frail old man, and Livingstone liked him! 4.6.82

8. The *Labour Herald* at the time of the Israeli invasion of Lebanon. For Livingstone, Israel was a 'creature of terror.' 1.10.82

9. Controversial cartoon by Jak. As a result, Livingstone imposed a three year ban on advertising in the *Standard* – costing the paper millions. **29.10.82** *(Courtesy Patrick Jackson and family)*

10. Livingstone insisted that the *Labour Herald* publish this cartoon. The Board of Deputies of British Jews found it offensive and complained to the Commission for Racial Equality. 25.6.82

11. On the road to nowhere. Livingstone contemplates the defeat of 1983. Frances Morrell doesn't look much happier. 12.6.83
Photo: Chris Mullin MP

12. The Left in flight. The Chris Mullin garden conference, 12.6.83. Tony Benn's back is the nearest to the camera. Livingstone is at the bottom, head in hands. *Photo: Chris Mullin MP*

13. Babies against the bomb! The group's meagre £800 grant in February 1983 helped give the press and the government the excuse to abolish the GLC, October 1983. *(Courtesy Tamar Swade)*

14. Red Ken speaks to the National Pensioners Convention, 1984. Left, NPC leader, Jack Jones.

15. Livingstone's brilliant campaign against GLC abolition. It caught the mood and a government on the hop, 1984. *(Courtesy Harry Barlow)*

16. The government's 1984 Lords' defeat gave Livingstone an extra year in power but GLC abolition went ahead on schedule. Tony Banks and Val Wise are either side of Livingstone, July 1984.

17. Turning the tide. Within 12 months, a new kind of political campaign turned indifference into active support for County Hall. It provided the bedrock of his mayoral campaign 16 years on, 1984. *(Courtesy Harry Barlow)*

18. John McDonnell as Dick Whittington's cat. GLC pantomime, Christmas 1984. *(Courtesy Harry Barlow)*

19. Neil Kinnock visits Paddington in support of Livingstone's
Paddington by-election protest over GLC abolition, September 1984.
Photo: Jonathan Rosenberg

20. Neil and Ken, again. A salamander keeps the peace, September 1984.
Photo: Jonathan Rosenberg

21. Livingstone opens the Camley Street Natural Park in the heart of deprived King's Cross. He supported the project and it still provides refuge for wildlife and people, 1985. *(Courtesy Harry Barlow)*

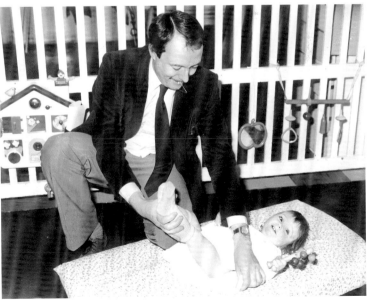

22. Not one of Ken's, but the nappy training would come in handy much later, 1985. *(Courtesy Harry Barlow)*

23. Ken with the reggae band UB40. Livingstone's important rapport with artists and celebrities began in the 1980s, circa 1985.

24. County Hall war room. Offices of the GLC anti-abolition campaign. The posters tell the story, and one that cost £12 million, 1985.
(Courtesy Harry Barlow)

25. Ken Livingstone supports his old mentor Eddie Lopez, who stood as Labour candidate for Slough in the 1987 general election. *(Courtesy Eddie Lopez)*

26. Livingstone on the campaign trail, April 2000. *Photo: Jonathan Rosenberg*

27. Livingstone takes his place at the cabinet table, but as mayor of London to discuss Crossrail. 7.3.07 *Photo: PA Photos*

28. Poor old Dobbo! Livingstone shakes Frank Dobson's hand, which seems reluctant to engage. 5.5.00 *Photo: Andrew Wiard/reportphotos.com*

29. Livingstone's purple bus, April/May 2000. *Photo: Jonathan Rosenberg*

30. Livingstone's 'glass testicle' under construction. On time and on budget. City Hall, circa 2001. *(Courtesy Harry Barlow)*

31. Self-styled 'General' Lee Jasper with Livingstone and Holocaust survivor Henry Guterman MBE. 3.2.04
Photo: Andrew Wiard/reportphotos.com

32. Livingstone breaks Bob Crowe's 11th commandment and the brothers look distinctly displeased. RMT picket line at Leytonstone Tube station. 30.6.04 *Photo: Andrew Wiard/reportphotos.com*

33. Livingstone and Sheikh Yusuf al-Qaradawi at City Hall, 7.7.04
     Photo: PA Photos

34. One year after the 7 July 2005 attacks. The mayor and George
     Psaradakis, the driver of the bombed number 30 bus in Tavistock
     Square, remember the 52 victims of the attacks. *Photo: PA Photos*

35. Livingstone's wax *doppelgänger* dons dubious hat to celebrate the mayor's forthcoming visit to China. 7.4.06 *Photo: PA Photos*

36. Re-elected as Labour's mayoral candidate in 2004. Livingstone is congratulated by Steve Norris, his two-time Tory opponent. Simon Hughes, the Liberal Democrat candidate, waits his turn. 11.6.06 *Photo: Andrew Wiard/reportphotos.com*

37. Climate change summit in New York. Bill Clinton singled out Livingstone's green initiatives for praise. Left, New York's Mayor Michael Bloomberg. 16.5.07 *Photo: PA Photos*

38. Livingstone and President Hugo Chávez at City Hall. 15.5.06
    Photo: Andrew Wiard/reportphotos.com

39. The mayor and the prime minister at the 2007 Labour Party conference. Never the warmest of relationships but they would need each other in 2008. 26.9.07 *PA Photos*

40. The people's Ken. Annual Gay Pride festival in Trafalgar Square. 3.7.04
Photo: Andrew Wiard/reportphotos.com

renegade councils. Livingstone, Ted Knight, Derek Hatton and others were there. But the only two men who talked were Jenkin and David Blunkett, the leader of Sheffield Council and future home secretary. But Jenkin sensed they were bluffing.

'I had got the impression all along that they were tilting at windmills,' says Jenkin. 'I had all the support from the parliamentary party on this that I could have wanted. Rate capping was seen as an essential protection for the domestic rate payer coupled with a demand that there must be a reform of the rates because this was a very unfair system of taxation.'[25]

The rate capping campaign was supposed to culminate in the first week of March 1985, 'Democracy Week', when the first councils would 'go illegal' together. The GLC would be central to the campaign. But Livingstone would play the leading role in killing it. He would be accused of betrayal and abandoning the hardliners to their fates. His closest political friends, including Ted Knight and the Chartists, and his deputy John McDonnell would later accuse Livingstone of chickening out – of laying down his friends for his political career.[26]

In reality, Livingstone had two main problems with refusing to set a rate, even if he had wanted to. The first was that the centre- and right-wing pragmatists in the GLC Labour group would never vote for surcharge and political oblivion; they could and indeed would defeat illegality simply by voting with the opposition. The other main problem for the GLC, if you can call it a problem, was that, after three years of big rate increases and high spending under Livingstone, it was literally awash with cash. When Reg Race was appointed to the number three position in the GLC, he could not believe the financial mismanagement and incompetence of many of the politicians at County Hall. Spending had almost doubled within two years but the machinery at County Hall could not spend all the extra money.

'The GLC was not actually implementing its policies and spending its money,' says Race. 'It had massively increased the rates and wasn't spending it. Speaking from memory, the underspend when I arrived was at least 60 per cent, if not more. In other words, if you look at it cold, the Labour group had agreed to put the rates up and had not gained the slightest difference because nobody was spending the money.'[27]

Partly responsible was Livingstone's abhorrence of borrowing and debt; everything had to be paid out of that year's revenue. Race continues: 'At one point he was against all forms of credit. You had to pay for everything, schools, hospitals and roads, out of revenue which if you look at it for more than two seconds is just barking mad. So we had a 99 per cent tax rise in any given year simply to accommodate this! It's just completely insane. I was just standing in the corridor completely open-mouthed thinking this guy's never heard of counter-cyclical economic policy or John Maynard Keynes.'[28]

'That was the great thing at the GLC: you had the money,' says Valerie Wise, chair of the Women's Committee, 'we did have enough money; we had no end of flipping money. We all went on spending sprees, for God's sake! All the time of the GLC, we had money – the whole five years.'[29]

♦

The real hardliner for defying the government at the GLC was John McDonnell, the finance chairman; he had also succeeded Illtyd Harrington as deputy leader. For McDonnell, the GLC's financial situation was immaterial; the government's attempt to destroy local government independence had to be defeated. In a note to Livingstone on 1 October 1984, McDonnell made clear his opposition to fudge the issue. He rejected two proposals which would allow the GLC, 'with a measure of financial juggling', to 'comply with the government and survive into next year without cuts'.

This, argued McDonnell, would mean: 'We would have submitted to rate capping and the government would have effective control over us.' To cling to office 'by means of creative accountancy' would be 'an act of betrayal'. He added: 'The effect of a defeated, acquiescent GLC on the morale of the Left in the long term is also an important consideration for me.'[30] Failure to set a budget in defiance of the government would have led to the members voting in favour of being surcharged by the district auditor and banned from office for five years. That would effectively have ended Ken Livingstone's political career.

Livingstone and McDonnell were the cornerstones of the Labour administration at County Hall and they had a lot of mutual affection and respect for each other. At the GLC Christmas pantomime that year, Livingstone had been Dick Whittington with McDonnell as his cat. But, at a critical stage in the rate capping battle, Livingstone would be fatally distracted by his obsession to replace Reg Freeson in Brent East. By law, the GLC had to decide its budget on 10 March 1985 and set its precept, in other words the amount of money it wanted the 32 boroughs to collect on its behalf. The boroughs could not set their budgets until they knew how much the GLC wanted them to raise. Once the GLC had 'gone illegal' and failed to set the budget, places like Lambeth and Greenwich were essentially protected by the GLC's illegality because they could claim legitimately that they were unable to comply with the law. For all the rhetoric, Ted Knight in Lambeth would be protected from the auditor if Livingstone 'went illegal' and totally exposed if he backed down.

On 5 November 1984, McDonnell urged the Labour group to confirm that it would not be setting a rate but he failed to get agreement. At least eight Labour members made it clear they would not vote for illegality.[31] Together with the opposition Tory and SDP members, the eight would comfortably defeat an attempted illegality. At that early stage, it must have been obvious that the GLC would buckle under and obey the law.

Livingstone was caught between the Left hardliners like McDonnell and Knight and the reality that the GLC was never going to vote for illegality; he was astride two horses which wanted nothing more than to gallop away from each other. While talking tough with the Left, he would always chip in with a caveat: 'Comrades will recall that *whenever* I spoke on rate capping... I pointed out that given our narrow majority of four, I did not expect that it would be easy to carry this policy...' He insisted that his warnings were 'always brushed aside'.[32]

Livingstone did not endorse McDonnell's defiant proposals at the group meeting but two days later at a rally, he came out publicly in favour of not fixing a rate and refusing to make cuts in jobs and services.[33] At this stage, John McDonnell was claiming that the government's rate cap for the GLC would result in cuts of between £50 million and £80 million.[34] The figure would more than double to £180 million.[35] In fact, far from being in the red by nearly £200 million, the GLC would soon find itself in the ludicrous and enviable position of being in the black by a potential £325 million, a difference of more than £500 million, and that was back in the days when half a billion pounds was a lot of money.

As McDonnell prepared for defiance and Livingstone talked

tough, *Private Eye* revealed in early February 1985 that the GLC was trying to resolve yet another huge underspend of £13 million before the end of the financial year: 'With one breath, Ken is exhorting all the other rate capping authorities to defy the law over setting a legal rate and imposing cuts, and with the next he is trying to "lose" £13 million in a hurry to disguise his inability to spend this year's budget.'[36]

◆

As far as Stonefrost was concerned, there were no real financial problems ahead for the last year of the GLC's life, as he made clear in his budget reports which were piled high on GLC trolleys and shunted around County Hall to committee rooms during January and February of 1985. 'They thought the government would set very antagonistic rate capping levels,' says one former senior GLC officer, 'but essentially Thatcher had been very clever.'[37]

To appear to the government as if the GLC were suffering, Stonefrost's budget included 'paper cuts', in other words, phoney or cosmetic cuts of between £50 million to £100 million.[38] Left intact, says Stonefrost, were all the things Livingstone wanted to achieve in the final year of the GLC's life. It appears that McDonnell was citing these so-called 'cuts' as his way of holding the line on defying rate capping.

Stonefrost says, 'Essentially if they passed a budget that included some "paper" cuts out of "paper" budget requests we would still have enough money in the kitty to do everything that they could reasonably get through in their process. Do it this way, I said, and we could do what we want.'[39]

The problem with the budget was that it gave comfort and discomfort in equal measure to both proponents of illegality and the pragmatists who thought it pointless and completely bonkers. The Left could claim the 'cuts' provided the excuse; the rest could say 'come off it', be grateful yet again for the government's largesse and abandon the less better off comrades in the frontline of the struggle to their fates. The positions of Livingstone and McDonnell ended up being both honourable and dishonourable. As a result, both emerged with little or much credit, depending on your point of view, although, it has to be said, McDonnell emerged with his reputation with the Left enhanced and Livingstone with fewer friends.

According to Valerie Wise, Ken Livingstone hated to be 'outlefted'.[40] Occasionally she saw him bridle at the suggestion that anyone could take a truer left position than him. Livingstone's dilemma was simple. He could either keep in with McDonnell and his Left comrades like the Chartists and Ted Knight and commit political suicide for nothing, or he could bite the bullet and support legality. By the end of February 1985, with the legal budget deadline for 10 March fast approaching, he was running out of time. It was clear that both choices would end in chaos and fiasco; either way it was going to be ugly, and it was.

♦

By the last week of February 1985, the Left was now claiming there would have to be 'cuts' of £140 million. Meanwhile, Livingstone was becoming increasingly rattled by rumours that some would-be rebel councils were bottling out. The idea was to go 'illegal together' by refusing to set a budget on or around 10 March 1985 but he had heard that both Camden and Lambeth were planning simply 'to defer' the decision. At their regular weekly *Labour Herald* meeting, he and Knight had an 'explosive row'. 'Trust me, Ken,' Knight said. 'We're all going illegal together. I promise you there's no backsliding. They can't fight us and the miners. We can bring Thatcher down and then all is possible.'[41]

In the end, the issue was brought to a head by Reg Race at the end of February 1985 after a comedy of errors. Race had become disillusioned with many on the Left at the GLC who he felt were incapable of 'running a whelk stall'; he also concluded that the real reason for the rate capping campaign was 'in conjunction with the miners to create a political crisis'.

On 20 December 1984,[42] Race and Peter Brayshaw, assistant director general, had produced a memo for John McDonnell stating that far from having to make cuts to the budget of £140 million, the GLC could actually afford to increase spending on top of its existing commitments by £25 million. According to Race, McDonnell was so desperate to keep the rate capping show on the road, he said: 'I hear what you say; shred the documents!'[43]

The rate capping fiasco happened in slow motion. Reg Race says he was not able to see Livingstone until late afternoon on Thursday, 28 February 1985, two months after McDonnell's daft shredding instruction. That is when ugly things started to happen. Livingstone later claimed to be 'horrified'.[44] But how on earth could he have been so surprised when everyone else knew what the position was, and Stonefrost's reports were being pushed about County Hall for anyone to see?

◆

At this stage, Reg Race was convinced that Livingstone was still hopelessly obsessed with replacing Reg Freeson in Brent East, a campaign which had been renewed with unabated determination in early 1985. All sides had taken up the cudgels. Livingstone's four-year battle to replace an obscure Labour MP in a humdrum part of north-west London collided with McDonnell's desire to bring down Thatcher. Reg Freeson, aged 59, who had been struggling against the Trots in Brent East for at least four long years, was still fighting.[45] He was finally forced out, blaming 'unacceptable and unconstitutional' conduct of local party officials; news of Freeson's resignation trickled out in early March 1985.[46]

Race says Livingstone's reaction to his deputy leader's alleged deceit was 'shock, astonishment and probably a lot of anger with McDonnell and that's where the budget crisis started'.[47] He adds, 'My great criticism of McDonnell is that even after he knew that the numbers didn't stack up and it wasn't necessary to make cuts and that nobody was going to lose their jobs, he continued to go around saying "It's going to be Armageddon."'[48]

Livingstone acted fast as the situation threatened to spiral out of control. He told Race to draw up a proper budget and spoke to McDonnell who 'begged' him to stop Race drawing up the budget. Livingstone refused and said, 'And if these figures are right we are going to look like the biggest fucking liars since Goebbels.'[49]

◆

Livingstone and McDonnell clashed two days later on Saturday, 2 March 1985 at the annual conference of the Greater London Labour Party. McDonnell was still sticking to illegality 'whatever the consequences'.[50] To make matters worse, some of the would-be rebels had resolved to change the wording of their budget resolution from outright defiance to 'it will be impossible for the authority to make a rate'. This could be read two ways: impossibility due to government-enforced cuts or impossibility because the GLC had failed to set a rate leaving the boroughs with no choice to postpone their own decisions and be protected under law.

On Sunday, 3 March 1985, as the wheels started coming off the rate capping campaign, the year-long miners' strike came to an end; the rate capping campaign would soon follow. Karl Marx once said that history repeats itself, first as a tragedy and then as a farce, but even he could not have expected that process to take place during the course of a weekend.

◆

Strangely, Democracy Day, the bringing together of the two great struggles, went ahead as planned on 6 March 1985, two days after the failure of both. Accompanied by the Barrow Colliery the miners marched on County Hall for the speeches in Jubilee Gardens. Norman Willis, TUC general secretary, ploughed through his speech in the face of boos and calls of 'scab' and 'traitor' from the assembled miners. In his speech, Livingstone gave every impression the GLC would defy the government: 'The government had warned that defiance would mean breaking the law. So be it! Because there is a higher law, which is our responsibility to the people who voted for us to defend jobs and services. We will not betray them simply because this government had moved the legal goalposts.'[51] Four days later, Ken Livingstone voted for a legal budget.

That week saw a public onslaught on Livingstone by McDonnell. In one LBC radio interview, Livingstone's deputy said, '...there is no doubt that he [Livingstone] has betrayed the whole campaign to save his political career.'[52]

Valerie Wise took the rows particularly badly and burst into tears during a meeting of her committee. 'I personally found it a very emotionally traumatic time because I was being torn in two by two people I had a lot of time for,' she says. 'I'm not in favour of martyrdom for the sake of martyrdom. We were expected to be martyrs when we had no justification for being martyrs. But it was never the same afterwards.'[53]

The budget meeting was a nasty overwrought affair with a menacing public gallery teeming with testy Trots and others demanding illegality. Of course, they were not the ones risking their homes or their political futures. At one point, the Tories threatened to abstain, forcing the Labour members to vote for an illegal budget or endure a humiliating public climbdown. Furious at the chaos, the Labour right-wingers walked out of the group and formed their own caucus.

Larry Whitty, general secretary of the Labour Party, arrived at County Hall and worked hard to prevent the right-wingers from voting for a Tory budget of deep cuts. He told everyone it would be folly to be surcharged and thrown out of office.[54] Audrey Wise, the former hard-left Labour MP and Valerie Wise's mother, tried to persuade the 10 left hardliners to support a legal budget which would allow for growth and only cosmetic cuts.[55] This was the budget that got Livingstone's vote. Later, he made much of the fact that this was the only time he voted to set a rate, but in the eyes of the Left, once was more than enough.

◆

His fellow *Labour Herald* editors, Matthew Warburton and Ted Knight, concluded: '. . . Ken in practice accepted the Tory government's right to dictate both the rate limit and the expenditure level, and therefore give credibility to their legislation.'[56] 'I think Ken Livingstone was scared,' says John Grigsby, then local government correspondent of the *Daily Telegraph*. 'There was a lot of pressure from Kinnock who had no time for these people. For him it was a disaster which could lose the next election.'[57]

True to form, the farce was finally concluded at 8 p.m. on 10 March 1985, four hours from the deadline, when the GLC voted by 60 votes to 25 to set a legal budget, some 6.5 per cent below the government's cap! Bryn Davies, one of the 'McDonnell Ten', had become fed up 'with being told what to do by the government'. 'It was very fraught,' he says. 'It was the heaviest pressure I've ever been under politically.' But Davies was relieved when a rate was set and illegality was avoided.

But John McDonnell was not relieved; he was furious and deployed GLC staff employed in the 20-strong 'abolition outreach team' not to preach against abolition but against those Labour GLC members who had voted for a budget. Livingstone sent Reg Race to re-impose discipline on the team. McDonnell also agreed to speak at a public meeting in Brent East at the end of April 1985, just before the final selection of a parliamentary candidate, as part of his attempt to prevent Livingstone being chosen.[58] Later, when the dust had settled, Maurice Stonefrost received a little note from McDonnell saying, 'Mea Culpa.'[59]

On 24 April 1985, Reg Race presented a paper on the finances which finally did for McDonnell: far from needing cuts of £140 million, the GLC had an extra £150 million to play with plus another £150 million if it liquidated its capital fund. Financially, County Hall had never had it so good. Five days later, with Livingstone's support, McDonnell was replaced as deputy leader by Mike Ward and as finance chairman by Alex McKay, both Livingstone supporters, by 21 votes to 13.[60] The following day, Livingstone himself survived a motion of no confidence, 37-37, thanks only to the casting vote of the outgoing GLC chairman, Illtyd Harrington.[61]

In February 1985, Neil Kinnock had tried to dissuade councils from defying the law or making similar futile gestures: 'Better a dented shield than no shield at all.'[62] Livingstone had survived – just – but at the risk of alienating the very people who had propelled him into office at County Hall and had cleared his path to Parliament.

Notes

1 *Woman,* interview with Ethel Livingstone, 2.11.85
2 Interview, Maurice Stonefrost, 21.11.07
3 Ibid.
4 *Woman,* interview with Ethel Livingstone, 23.11.85
5 *London Labour Briefing,* 'Royalty or Class loyalty?', report by Paula Watson, Westminster South Labour Party, June 1984, p18
6 Interview, Illtyd Harrington, 4.7.07
7 *Woman,* interview with Ethel Livingstone, 23.11.85
8 *Guardian,* 24.7.84
9 Ken Livingstone, *If Voting Changed Anything, They'd Abolish It,* pp286-287; Interview with Ken Livingstone, 1.11.07
10 *Daily Telegraph,* 22.9.84
11 *Daily Telegraph,* 'A vote for what?', 22.9.84
12 Tariq Ali, *Who's Afraid of Margaret Thatcher? Tariq Ali in conversation with Ken Livingstone,* Verso, 1984, pp35-36
13 Nigel Lawson, *The View from Number 11, Memoirs of a Tory Radical,* Corgi, 1993, p564
14 David Blunkett and Keith Jackson, *Democracy in Crisis: The Town Halls Respond,* The Hogarth Press, 1987, pp158-159
15 Ibid. and *Daily Express,* 25.7.84
16 *Private Eye,* 'London Calling', Issue 588, 29.6.84, p7
17 *Labour Herald,* 16.11.84
18 *Labour Herald,* 7.12.84
19 Interview, Ted Knight, 4.7.07
20 Kenneth Baker, *The Turbulent Years, My Life in Politics,* p105
21 Derek Hatton, *Inside Left, The Story So Far... ,* Bloomsbury, 1998, pp82-85; David Blunkett and Keith Jackson, *Democracy in Crisis,* pp156-158
22 Interview, Baron Jenkin of Roding, 2.10.07
23 Ibid.
24 Kenneth Baker, *The Turbulent Years, My Life in Politics,* p109
25 Ibid.
26 Author interviews

27 Interview, Reg Race, 23.8.07
28 Ibid.
29 Interview, Valerie Wise, 23.7.07
30 Note from John McDonnell to Ken Livingstone, 1.10.84, reproduced in *London Labour Briefing*, April 1985
31 *London Labour Briefing*, 'Enforce Socialist discipline on the GLC Labour Group', report by John McDonnell, December 1984, p6
32 'Rate capping and the GLC Budget debate', report by Ken Livingstone, March 1985, file no. GLC xx/01/270, London Metropolitan Archives
33 *London Labour Briefing*, 'Enforce Socialist discipline on the GLC Labour Group', report by John McDonnell, December 1984, p6
34 Ibid.
35 Ken Livingstone, *If Voting Changed Anything, They'd Abolish It*, pp316-317
36 *Private Eye*, Issue 604, 8.2.85, p10
37 Off-the-record interview, August 2007
38 Ken Livingstone, *If Voting Changed Anything, They'd Abolish It*, p316
39 Interview, Maurice Stonefrost, 21.11.07
40 Interview, Valerie Wise, 23.7.07
41 Ken Livingstone, *If Voting Changed Anything, They'd Abolish It*, p315
42 Ibid., p316
43 Interview, Reg Race, 23.8.07
44 Ken Livingstone, *If Voting Changed Anything, They'd Abolish It*, p316
45 Ibid., p9
46 *The Times* and *Daily Telegraph*, 9.3.85
47 Interview, Reg Race, 23.8.08
48 Ibid.
49 Ken Livingstone, *If Voting Changed Anything, They'd Abolish It*, p317
50 David Blunkett and Keith Jackson, *Democracy In Crisis,* pp174-175
51 *News Line*, 7.3.85, p2
52 Ken Livingstone, *If Voting Changed Anything, They'd Abolish It*, pp322-323
53 Interview, Valerie Wise, 23.7.07
54 Interview, Bryn Davies, 16.7.07
55 Interviews, Valerie Wise, 23.7.07; Ted Knight, 4.7.07
56 *London Labour Briefing*, 'Our Answer to Ken', by Ted Knight and Matthew Warburton, May 1985
57 Interview, John Grigsby, 13.7.07
58 Ken Livingstone, *If Voting Changed Anything, They'd Abolish It*, Ken Livingstone, pp328-335
59 Interview, Maurice Stonefrost, 21.11.07
60 *Daily Telegraph* and *Evening Standard*, 30.4.85
61 *Daily Telegraph*, 1.5.85
62 Michael Leapman, *Kinnock*, Unwin Hyman, 1987, pp88-89

Chapter 16

Twilight of the Tin Gods, May 1985–April 1986

The rate capping fiasco exposed the fault line running through Ken Livingstone's political career. Up until then, he defied the odds by standing astride it, somehow appeasing the wilder fantasies of the Trots and the hard left while simultaneously keeping the support of members on the centre and exercising power at County Hall. But he was forced to make a choice, the only rational one on offer. There were the screeches of betrayal, but many of the denunciations of Livingstone's actions took the form of shrugged shoulders and resigned expostulations of 'I told you so!' In *London Labour Briefing* it was acknowledged that some people felt they 'would never have trusted Ken in the first place' adding: 'He was never a revolutionary anyway. Is Arthur Scargill? ...we did not expect revolution from Ken. We did, however, expect him to show at least some degree of commitment on his own chosen level of struggle as was shown by Tony Benn and Arthur Scargill on theirs.'[1]

Livingstone's Chartist friends in Brent East were livid with Livingstone's 'betrayal' but were still sufficiently enamoured by him to support his candidature against Diane Abbott, who had been fielded by others on the Left still incredulous over events at County Hall.

The decision by leading Chartists and others on the left in Brent East to support Livingstone's successful candidacy is an oddity of the great rates fiasco. Such was the Left's fury over the 'betrayal' that the constituency party ended up putting forward a total of three candidates including Livingstone for the seat. But his powerful allies in Brent East were always going to carry the day. In the final ballot, he defeated Diane Abbott, the future MP for Hackney North and Stoke Newington, by 50 votes to 25 on 28 April 1985.

'For many comrades it was a matter of clearing up unfinished business,' wrote an important Brent East Labour Party official and Chartist supporter, Colin Adams, at the time. 'I have never considered him [Livingstone] to be, nor has he ever claimed to be, a revolutionary. His performance during the GLC budget-making was inexcusable and has damaged his reputation on the Left... not a bad thing, as hero worship is no good for anyone.'[2] But others remained bitter at Livingstone. Graham Durham, a former long-term hard left supporter, was emphatic. 'For most delegates, Livingstone's right-hand turn had gone too far...' he wrote. 'A political career had been put before Party policy on the most important issue in local government.'[3] The final destruction of the sitting MP Reg Freeson was Durham's one crumb of comfort: 'It is partly a tribute to the determination of Brent East Constituency Labour Party that Freeson has ended up a defeated and isolated figure.'[4] But some really serious communists still liked Livingstone, including the Soviet ambassador, Viktor Popov, who sent him a present on his fortieth birthday with the greetings: 'I wish you good health, happiness and success in all your endeavours.'[5]

As for Reg Freeson, deselected at 58, he rejected pressure by many, including fellow Labour MPs, to stand as an independent.[6] He became an urban regeneration consultant but he continued to work for the Labour Party in Brent – and nationally– until he died in October 2006. On his death, his son Jeremy received a note from Livingstone expressing his 'sincere condolences' and saying he would be 'sadly missed by the people of Brent'. Of course, by then Livingstone had successfully stood as an independent against Labour in the 2000 mayoral election. In a hand-written postscript, Livingstone said, 'I am particularly glad that he supported my readmission to the Labour Party three years ago when he could have said nothing.'[7] 'I detest the man,' says Freeson's widow, Charlotte, 'I am still angry at what he did to Reg. Everyone has their trigger and unfairness is mine. Reg would bottle things up but once it came all pouring out, the bitterness, not just at Livingstone but also the party.'[8]

◆

The first weekend of March 1985 was a defining moment for the Left. The collapse of the miners' strike and the rate capping campaign marked the final decisive defeat of Margaret Thatcher's 'enemies within'. In her second term, Thatcher had been determined to storm the Left's three main citadels: the trade unions, the Labour Party and local councils. Before 1983, she felt the revolutionary puppet masters had been content to hide behind their puppets such as Benn and Livingstone. After 1983, the Trots cast aside their broken dolls and went blinking for broke into the light. 'In the aftermath of defeat,' she wrote later, 'they were free from constraint and thirsting for battle on their own terms.'[9] But in March 1985, they were defeated and, although no one knew it then, they would not rise again. Many of the more ambitious left-wingers in the Labour Party read the runes and as jellyfish began a listless drift on the rightwards-flowing tide; some would even end up in New Labour governments. But after their few years in the spotlight, the leading Trots all ended up in the political graveyard, including Ted Knight, Derek Hatton and Militant Tendency, Gerry Healy and the Workers Revolutionary Party.

Hard-line councils including Hackney, Southwark and Islington held out until the end of May 1985 before collapsing and setting a rate,[10] but Knight and Hatton delayed fixing a legal budget for too long and paid a heavy price, financially and politically. In June 1985, the Lambeth district auditor issued Knight and 48 other Lambeth Labour councillors with surcharge certificates demanding they pay personally a total of £105,586 along with a ban from holding public office for five years. Knight was destroyed politically and now runs a successful language school opposite Brixton Tube station.

◆

Derek Hatton and the other Militants played into the hands not only of the Tories and the district auditor but also of the Labour leader Neil Kinnock who was determined to purge Militant, which he and many others considered a cancer within the party. On 27 September 1985, as part of his puerile Mexican stand-off with the government, Hatton sanctioned the use of taxis to deliver redundancy notices to the city council's 31,000 employees as a 'technical device' on legal advice. It was a crass miscalculation exploited by Kinnock in his landmark speech at the 1985 annual Labour Party conference in Bournemouth: 'You start with far-fetched resolutions. They are then pickled into a rigid dogma, a code, and you go through the years, sticking to that – outdated, misplaced, irrelevant to the real needs – and you end in the grotesque chaos of a Labour council, a *Labour* council, hiring taxis to scuttle around a city handing out redundancy notices to its own workers.'[11] Hatton shouted, 'Lies,' and Eric Heffer stormed out of the conference; witnessing the distress of Hatton's supporters Tony Benn almost wept.[12]

Hatton and 31 Liverpool councillors were surcharged a total of £106,000 and banned from office for five years, like Knight and the others. Later, he and seven of his comrades were expelled from the Labour Party. He too was finished politically; he has subsequently attempted a number of careers, including radio presenting and modelling suits, and even rejoined the party in May 2007. Of Livingstone, Hatton says, 'I think his principles are administrative rather than political principles. What you saw in the eighties was when the chips were really down, not only didn't he go over the cliff with us, he actually helped to push us over… He's not a visionary; he doesn't see the bigger picture and he's certainly not a political animal.'[13]

But in comparison to the demise of Gerry Healy, the exits of Hatton and Knight seem positively dignified. Alone of the Trotskyist press, there were no words of censure or even criticisms of Livingstone from Healy's fire-breathing *News Line,* to the intense irritation of Healy's WRP cadres. The fall of Healy also spelled the end of the WRP, the *News Line* and the *Labour Herald* – four for the price of one.

It was obvious that many members of the WRP felt that after the collapse of rate capping and the miners' strike that conditions – once again – were no longer favourable for revolution. Now, some of the group's leading members turned on Healy. In the summer of 1985, Healy's opponents planted bugs in his offices and intercepted his mail. At their instigation, Healy's secretary Aileen Jennings wrote a letter to the WRP political committee on 30 June 1985 naming 26 women cadres who had been forced to have sex with the 'great leader'.[14]

The Jennings note would eventually destroy Healy and the WRP. On 8 July 1985, in an attempt to cover up the scandal, the 71-year-old Healy was forced by some of his senior comrades to sign a short note promising not to rape any more young women: 'In accordance with our agreement dated 5.7.85 I unreservedly undertake to cease immediately my personel [*sic*] conduct with the youth, yours fraternally, G. Healy.'[15] Even now, the old grotesque tried to set terms for his agreement, insisting it should allow him full rein to abuse women of a certain age: 'It should say "under 25". As it is, it will ruin my lifestyle.' Sheila Torrance, one of Healy's cadres told him, 'Just get on and sign it.'[16]

The situation disintegrated rapidly as parents of Healy's sex-abuse victims began calling for a full inquiry. At the same time, the WRP's political fanatics began to link Healy's 'moral degeneracy' to his 'political degeneracy'. At a meeting of the WRP central committee in August 1985, there had been a row about the 'cover-up for Ken Livingstone' over the rates betrayal.[17] As the *News Line* put it later, 'Healy's sexual practices were and are inseparably linked to his philosophy and political theory which are permeated with subjective idealism...' The same degeneracy was also responsible for Healy's 'cover-up for the brutal execution of Iraqi communists in 1979-1980' and 'the renegacy [*sic*] of Ken Livingstone'.[18]

For anti-Healyites, Healy's failure to condemn Livingstone had long been a running sore until the break-up: 'These right-wing political positions, to the horror of most party members, culminated with the *News Line* refusing to condemn GLC leader Ken Livingstone when he abandoned the struggle against Tory rate capping.'[19]

In early October 1985, Healy decided to renege on his agreement to 'retire' by entering the WRP HQ in Clapham in a pathetic attempt to reassert his authority. His critics, who now included his once unquestioning lieutenants Mike Banda and Cliff Slaughter, moved against their leader by taking temporary control of the *News Line* and announcing on 23 October 1985: 'Healy abused the position of authority and respect which he enjoyed in the movement. He violated comrades' constitutional rights and established non-communist and bureaucratic relations inside the party.

'He abused his power for personal gratification. The central committee now have proof of this abuse. Healy has failed to answer the charges and the party does not know where he is.'[20] Following exposure by the WRP's own official paper, this tawdry Trotskyist bedroom farce would now be played out in public. 'The witch-hunt had been started by the witches themselves,' joked Paul Foot, member of the Socialist Workers Party and investigative journalist.[21]

For 48 critical hours, Healy had been allowed to occupy the Clapham headquarters and was able to spirit away incriminating documentation, but he left some tantalising fragments behind.

After re-asserting control of the HQ, the anti-Healyites found documentary evidence of Healy's secret funding from Libya, Iraq and other Middle Eastern countries. There were more bizarre 'financial manipulations' including the discovery of a secret purchase of a £15,000 BMW car and a fund of £20,000 in the dashboard, to finance a Healy rush to the continent in the event of a military putsch in Britain and the feared Thatcherite round-up of leading revolutionaries.[22] But, in common with the rest of humanity, Margaret Thatcher had never given much thought to Gerry Healy.

For more than six weeks, the *News Line* under the anti-Healy faction spewed out as much scorn as it could until the winding up of Astmoor Litho, the WRP's printers in Runcorn, on 10 December 1985. Somehow, a rather drab final edition limped on to the stands on 13 December 1985 and then appeared no more. Following the rate capping collapse, Livingstone resigned from the editorial board of the *Labour Herald* on the grounds that it had started to rubbish Neil Kinnock's leadership as it had, rather predictably, Michael Foot's.[23] Livingstone's place was taken by John McDonnell in May 1985.[24]

But the *Herald* died with the WRP. The edition of 25 October 1985 saw the last colour photo centre-page spread – a CND demo in Hyde Park. After an absence of nearly three weeks, the *Herald* reappeared for the last time on 4 December 1985 with a plea for funding: its death came only a week before that of the *News Line*. Apparently, none of the three editors could find any other printer to match the WRP's commercial rates. There can be no greater demonstration of the *Herald*'s dependence on Gerry Healy than that. Within a year, there were three WRPs, tiny grouplets each as irrelevant as the other.[25]

◆

Healy spent his last years in a house in West Road, Clapham, bought for him by Vanessa Redgrave, occasionally venturing forth to deliver 'incomprehensible lectures in his unique brand of pseudo-dialectical gibberish'.[26] At Healy's funeral in 1989 Ken Livingstone, by then MP for Brent told mourners: 'I haven't the slightest doubt that the upheavals in the Workers Revolutionary Party were not some accident or a clash of personalities.

'They were a sustained and deliberate decision by MI5 to smash that organisation because they feared it was becoming too pivotal in terms of domestic policies, linking too many international struggles both inside and outside the British Labour movement.'[27]

No evidence has emerged or is likely to emerge of an MI5 plot to bring down the WRP. The only bugs in Healy's office had been placed there by his own so-called comrades. Even the sensationalist ex-MI5 spy Peter Wright described the WRP and other similar groups as 'largely irrelevant'; the security services then were much more worried about KGB infiltration of the unions and civil service.[28] In interviews for this book, Ken Livingstone did not repeat his theory.

◆

On 2 September 1985, Patrick Jenkin was sacked by Margaret Thatcher who promoted Kenneth Baker, previously minister of state for local government to take his place. Jenkin agreed to make way for 'some fresh faces'.[29] Later, his 'scalp' would be claimed by both Hatton and Livingstone. But Jenkin had told Baker back in 1984 that he was thinking of stepping aside to 'move on and earn some money'.[30] In several ways, Jenkin, to be ennobled as Lord Jenkin of Roding, had the last laugh. In the final analysis, he had successfully passed laws that not only abolished the GLC and helped destroy the Labour Left, but gave the government the ultimate power to set the budgets of local councils.

Kenneth Baker, the environment secretary who would have to read the GLC's last rites claimed that during the summer of 1985, he was in regular contact with shadow environment ministers Jack Straw and Dr Jack Cunningham. 'As regards London,' Baker wrote later, 'Cunningham held Ken Livingstone and the other loony left leaders in utter contempt.' 'Let them twist in the wind,' Cunningham told Baker.[31]

◆

The last year of the GLC witnessed a lot of twisting and jiving and boogieing and rocking in Jubilee Gardens and makeshift stadia throughout London. The GLC hosted one of the hottest gigs in town. On 7 July 1985, a glorious sunny day, there was its 'Jobs for a Change' festival. An estimated 100,000 people attended for performances by artists including Billy Bragg. Bragg described the festival later as 'the ultimate great free day out on the GLC'. He thought to himself, 'This must be what socialism is: free gig, everyone singing, sun shining.'[32] An earlier GLC 'Jobs for a Change' festival had been marred by a gang of neo-Nazi brutes who clambered on to the stage in Jubilee Gardens, assaulted members of the Redskins and Hank Wangford's band before yelling *Sieg Heil* to the disgusted crowd.[33]

The GLC concerts also promoted campaigns such as 'London against Racism' as well as the miners' strike, both in 1984, and provided the inspiration for Red Wedge,[34] a collective of radical young musicians who would help communicate the Labour Party's message through their music at regular concerts. Artists including Billy Bragg and Paul Weller, of The Style Council and The Jam, met at the Labour HQ in Walworth Road for the inaugural meeting of Red Wedge.[35] The collective would play at the GLC's farewell show on 31 March 1986.[36]

Bragg often saw Livingstone at the concerts. 'Ken puts on a good gig,' says Bragg. 'To me, he always seemed to be much more representative of us; much more one of us than other politicians. There was always a political light touch about what he did; you never thought you had to follow a particular party line. We never had any qualms dealing with him because we didn't really see him as a politician.'[37]

The last year of the GLC was a difficult time for both politicians and staff at County Hall. In May 1985, three GLC members[38] resigned rather than experience the last doomed year: Livingstone supporters Andy Harris and Bryn Davies, and a Tory, Bernard Brooke-Partridge, who was disgusted about GLC abolition and left pronouncing Thatcher 'politically illiterate.'[39]

When the author John O'Farrell campaigned for Labour in the GLC North Battersea by-election in June 1985, he came across extreme apathy. 'GLC? I thought they'd abolished it,' was one reaction on the doorstep. The rest of the conversation went as follows: 'No they haven't yet. They've just confirmed they are going to abolish it.' 'So what's the point in voting for it then?'[40] For the 20,000 GLC staff, fear of unemployment stalked the corridors of County Hall as abolition approached. Many would be given jobs by the 32 borough councils, but not all. According to Livingstone, two members became so depressed they committed suicide.[41]

The embodiment of the bleak future for London's government came in the bustling form of Sir Godfrey 'Tag' Taylor, appointed by Kenneth Baker to chair the London Residuary Body, or LRB. At 59, Taylor was a businessman, the chairman of the Southern

Water Authority and a former Tory chairman of Sutton Borough Council in south London.[42] Not surprisingly, Livingstone saw his appointment as a provocation. 'Having taken away Londoners' right to vote in local elections,' he said, 'they have now appointed someone who couldn't have got elected anyway.'[43]

Taylor's job was to help wind down the GLC and dispose of its assets, following abolition. Taylor became an increasingly familiar figure at County Hall, an unwelcome storm crow. At first Livingstone refused to help the LRB team but relented after Taylor told him, 'Don't be so bloody silly Ken, I can demand your presence and you've damn well got to come.'[44] Tony Banks, chairman of the GLC for its last year, was the most awkward. Once, Banks spotted one of Taylor's team at a party hosted by the unions and told him to get out. 'Banks was just nasty,' says Taylor, 'but Ken was no problem really.'[45] Taylor was outraged by the failure of Livingstone and Co. to secure better terms for staff facing the sack. He adds, 'I think the most awful thing that old Ken Livingstone and so on did was that they didn't fight the government on getting decent redundancy terms for people; they just got statutory redundancy. He did not pursue it all.'[46] Taylor's team found some assets easier to sell off than others. Housing estates and the GLC's many seaside holiday homes were transferred to borough councils or housing associations with relative ease; the poor quality 'brown gravy' paintings of former GLC and LCC chairmen going back to 1888 were virtually worthless and were eventually given away to the City of London Corporation for safekeeping.[47]

At the end of July 1985, Maurice Stonefrost declared his own job as director general redundant and saw out the last eight months of the GLC as a consultant;[48] Reg Race took over the day-to-day running of County Hall. On 18 December 1985, Livingstone appeared in the star role of the last GLC pantomime, 'Robin Ratepayer and His Merry Persons'.[49] Livingstone had asked Neil Kinnock to take part: 'You'll see from the attached script that you've been written a key role – as the saviour of London.'[50] Kinnock was otherwise disposed. No one could save London now. As the curtain came down, there were just 104 days left before the end of the GLC.

Ken Livingstone's main priority now was to get as much money out of County Hall to mainly Labour-controlled London boroughs and voluntary organisations, and the government's main priority, with the help of friendly allies like Westminster City Council, was to prevent him doing it. 'My broad view was that you actually tried to get the money out [of County Hall],' remembers Ken Livingstone. 'In the end we got the money out of the building by giving it to housing associations and councils to spend on property.'[51]

There was concern about the continued existence of voluntary groups, many representing the kind of minority interests Livingstone had fought to promote. Crèches and even law centres would now have to fall on the tender mercies of hard right reactionary councils like the City of Westminster under Shirley Porter for future funding. Many would be swept away without a penny by a tidal wave of political spite.[52] The vindictiveness was not the reserve of the loony right in Westminster. According to one of his opposition spokesmen, Jack Straw, Kenneth Baker had brayed at a lunch in the City that he wished he could take down County Hall brick by brick; fortunately the building was protected by its listed building status.[53]

Porter, who would later claim notoriety as perhaps one of Britain's most corrupt politicians, would play a leading part in taking out court actions to prevent the GLC's largesse in the final days. On 11 February 1986, the *Daily Mail* claimed that the GLC planned to hand out grants totalling more than £96 million: 'RED KEN'S £96M BONANZA DAY FOR GAYS AND ACTIVISTS.'[54] On the following day, the press reported how the High Court had granted 16 London boroughs a temporary injunction to halt the payments.[55] Livingstone was on a train to Sheffield at the time with some drunken soccer yobs who called out, 'Here Ken! Give me £100 million and I'll be a lesbian!'[56] In March 1986, the higher Court of Appeal blocked the scaled-down payments of £76 million.[57] The court objected to so-called 'tombstone funding' in which the GLC was attempting to give voluntary groups several years funding in advance so they could survive beyond abolition.

Although the GLC still managed to transfer millions of pounds to voluntary groups and poor Labour boroughs, it was far more successful when it came to pumping a fortune into housing repairs. On 29 March 1986, the Saturday before abolition, it paid out two cheques worth a total of £78.5 million to a company called Satman Developments Ltd to carry out future repairs on old GLC housing. If County Hall had delayed by 48 hours, the money would have gone to Tag Taylor's LRB.[58]

◆

In the last few months before abolition, County Hall experienced widespread pilfering and plundering. An Italian marble fireplace disappeared as did a huge grand piano.[59] 'The task was to get as much money as possible out of County Hall,' says Keith Veness. 'We would get the typewriters and photocopiers and we were loading lorries at one o'clock in the morning; it kept the Left going for years after that… One night we took out 2,000 boxes of paper. It was like a flock of vultures had been through the place.'[60] But some dreams fell through the cracks. The GLC failed to transfer £11 million to the Roundhouse arts venue in Camden for its redevelopment; it would have to wait another two decades. George Nicholson, the GLC's vice chairman of planning, had an agreement on the last day to fund the setting up of a national jazz centre in Covent Garden with £2 million of GLC money. But the money had to go back because Nicholson had failed to get a contractor to sign the contract before abolition.[61]

At lunchtime on the last day of the GLC's existence, 31 March 1985, draughtsmen at County Hall made a dummy of Thatcher and hung it out of a window. 'One of the young lads brought in some clothes and a Thatcher mask,' remembers one of the draughtsmen, Al Haroon, 'but the porters cut it down. We never thought abolition was going to happen. But it did and it was very sad. For many of us, County Hall was like a second home.'[62]

◆

Livingstone commemorated the passing of the GLC with a free concert at the Festival Hall on the South Bank. It was a three-stage gig and the acts included the ubiquitous Billy Bragg, Eddie Grant and the Latin Quarter. The day clearly got to Ken Livingstone, according to John Grigsby of the *Daily Telegraph*. 'That was the only time I saw him getting pissed,' says Grigsby. 'It was very emotional.'[63]

Before the midnight fireworks and above the din and cries of 'Maggie Out!', Ken Livingstone, wreathed in tears, told the huge crowd, 'You're the reason she's [Thatcher] abolishing the GLC because you care enough to come… we showed there is an alternative to Thatcher and it's all of you!'[64] He said ominously, 'We'll spend the rest of our lives trying to do it again,'[65] adding, 'I do not believe – I am sure I speak for my colleagues on all sides – nothing else that happens to us in our lives will be as rewarding and fulfilling as the years that we have spent in this building.'[66]

As midnight approached, Livingstone joined others on the stage to sing the 'Red Flag'. Then Elgar's 'Nimrod' soared above County Hall, and the candles around the orchestra went out one by one. As the last candle was extinguished, plunging everyone into darkness, Maurice Stonefrost, County Hall's last director general, asked his daughter Hilary: 'Take that candle because I don't really want to be a thief.' Stonefrost kept the candle in a box and would present it to Livingstone 14 years later when he became the first directly-elected mayor of London.[67]

Of course there were the fireworks. 'Then, on the stroke of midnight,' wrote John O'Farrell later, 'workers from the London Residuary Body moved in and started stripping everything down, signs, placards, banners – anything with a GLC logo on it – while the crowd looked on and booed.'[68]

The farewell bash had cost £250,000, but that was nothing compared to the GLC's vast expenditure. In the five years of Livingstone's administration, the GLC had spent £8.87 billion, an increase of 170 per cent compared with a 29 per cent increase in prices over the same period.[69] It also paid out £119 million to 15 Labour-controlled London boroughs, of which £76.89 million was transferred in the last year.[70]

In five years, gay and lesbian organisations received £5 million, peace groups £1.5 million, women's centres and play groups a total of £29 million and police monitoring groups some £6 million. Ethnic minority groups in Livingstone's newly adopted borough of Brent received £2 million. Astonishingly, Livingstone spent £50 million on advertising and publicity during his rule, a lot of it fighting abolition.[71]

But the achievements of Livingstone's GLC are much harder to quantify although the myth that it was some sort of 1980s municipal Camelot began to take root long before Maurice Stonefrost's candle went out. It did not lead the Labour Party out of the darkness and point it towards a popular new socialism. Until Thatcher announced abolition in 1983, Livingstone was deeply unpopular and the GLC was seen as a huge electoral liability to the Labour Party.

Only once, in 1970, an existing political administration was returned to power at County Hall; for the rest of the time, political control switched every four years. During its short troubled existence, the GLC was never loved because its duties were never constant or they were replicated by central government or the boroughs. Livingstone's definition of what the GLC should be, would be just as much hated by the Tories and others as Labour had despised the bleak Thatcherite vision of his predecessor, Sir Horace Cutler. During Livingstone's five years, the GLC had lurched from one crisis to another, without respite, and much of that was due to the actions and words of the leader.

◆

The biggest GLC function was transport and that was removed two years before abolition. By 1986, the fact is that Labour had long tired of gestures such as Fares Fair and the proposed abolition of the GLC. 'We do not want glorious historic defeats,' Neil Kinnock said in July 1985, 'there have been too many of those.'[72] The *Guardian* had a point when it concluded that 'County Hall politics were frequently bedevilled by ideological posturing, hypocrisy and the caucus mentality rather than tolerance and a problem-solving approach', and that Livingstone had showed 'how much could be done by spending a lot of money on good PR.'[73] But the paper was harsh to observe that the GLC 'made a lot of noise' about its approach to women, ethnic minorities and the police without accomplishing a great deal.[74]

Livingstone's achievement in focusing attention on these crucial but overlooked issues would endure. As on so many issues, including Ireland and homosexuality, he was ahead of his time but in politics, as he learned repeatedly to his cost, timing is everything.

Notes

1 *London Labour Briefing*, Briefing National Supplement, p3, June 1985
2 *London Labour Briefing*, 'Why Brent East made the right choice', by Colin Adams, June 1985, p12
3 Ibid., 'Personalities or politics?', by Graham Durham, p11
4 Ibid.
5 Letter, Viktor Popov to Ken Livingstone, 17.6.85, file no. GLC xx/01/27, London Metropolitan Archives
6 Unpublished autobiographical account, by Reg Freeson, 29.6.95
7 Letter, Ken Livingstone to Jeremy Freeson, 12.10.06
8 Interview, Charlotte Freeson, 4.9.07

9 Margaret Thatcher, *The Downing Street Years*, p339
10 Kenneth Baker, *The Turbulent Years, My Life in Politics*, p107; Author interviews
11 Michael Leapman, *Kinnock*, p102
12 Tony Benn, *The End of an Era, Diaries 1980-1990*, (see 1.10.85)
13 Interview, Derek Hatton, 20.7.07
14 *News Line*, 30.10.85, p1
15 *News Line*, 31.10.85, p1
16 *News Line*, 6.1.85, p1
17 Bob Pitt, *The Rise and Fall of Gerry Healy*, Chapter 11
18 *News Line*, 30.10.85, p1
19 *News Line*, 'Down with Healyism', 13.11.85, pp6-7
20 *News Line*, 23.10.85, p1
21 *Socialist Worker*, 9.11.85, p4
22 *News Line*, 30.10.85, p1
23 Letter of resignation, Ken Livingstone to Matthew Warburton, Elksett Ltd, 20.5.85, file no. GLC/xx/01/29, London Metropolitan Archives
24 *Labour Herald*, 17.5.85, p2
25 Bob Pitt, *The Rise and Fall of Gerry Healy*, Chapter 12
26 Ibid.
27 Vanessa Redgrave, *An Autobiography*, Arrow Books, 1992, p288
28 Peter Wright, *Spycatcher, The Candid Autobiography of a Senior Intelligence Officer*, Viking, 1987, p361
29 Resignation letter, Patrick Jenkin to Margaret Thatcher, 2.9.82, Thatcher Archive
30 Kenneth Baker, *The Turbulent Years, My Life in Politics*, p98
31 Ibid., p108
32 Billy Bragg and Andrew Collins, *Still Suitable for Miners*, Virgin Books, 2007, p166; Interview, Billy Bragg, 31.10.07
33 Ibid., p131
34 Ibid., p146
35 Ibid., pp167-168
36 Ibid., p182
37 Interview, Billy Bragg, 31.10.07
38 GLC Agenda, item 5, report by director general of the council, 25.6.85, p8
39 Interview, Bernard Brooke-Partridge, 28.6.07
40 John O'Farrell, *Things Can Only Get Better*, p99
41 Interview, Ken Livingstone, 1.11.07
42 Interview, Sir Godfrey 'Tag' Taylor, 22.7.07; *Guardian*, 20.5.85
43 *Guardian*, 20.5.85
44 Interview, Sir Godfrey 'Tag' Taylor, 22.7.07
45 Ibid.
46 Ibid.
47 Ibid.
48 *The Times*, 1.8.07
49 *Evening Standard*, 12.12.85
50 Letter, Ken Livingstone to Neil Kinnock, 28.11.85, file no. GLC XX/01/29, London Metropolitan Archives

51 Interview, Ken Livingstone, 1.11.07
52 Andrew Hosken, *Nothing Like a Dame, The Scandals of Shirley Porter*, pp111-113
53 *The Times*, 'Quality plus jollity', article by Jack Straw, 27.11.85
54 *Daily Mail*, 11.2.86
55 *Evening Standard*, 'Freeze on £96 million GLC giveaway', 12.2.86
56 Interview, Ken Livingstone, 1.11.07
57 *Evening Standard*, 'The GLC Giveaway', 17.3.86
58 *Independent*, 'Law report', 12.12.86
59 Author interviews
60 Interview, Keith Veness, 24.8.07
61 Interview, George Nicholson, 17.8.07
62 Interview, Al Haroon, 27.7.07
63 Interview, John Grigsby, 13.7.07
64 BBC TV News, 31.3.86
65 Billy Bragg and Andrew Collins, *Still Suitable for Miners,* p182
66 Wes Whitehouse, *GLC – The Inside Story*, p174
67 Interview, Maurice Stonefrost, 21.11.07
68 John O'Farrell, *Things Can Only Get Better*, p105
69 GLC Agenda, 27.3.86; *Daily Telegraph*, 27.3.86
70 GLC Agenda, 27.3.86
71 Ibid.
72 Michael Leapman, *Kinnock*, p92
73 *Guardian*, Editorial, 29.3.86
74 Ibid.

Chapter 17

Views without a room, April 1986–October 1989

Sir Tag Taylor received a phone call from Ken Livingstone a few days after abolition. 'I'm in a bit of a mess,' Livingstone said, 'I've got no equipment here. I haven't got a typewriter; I haven't even got a decent desk.' Taylor gave Livingstone the name of the woman at the London Residuary Body who dealt with such minor matters and told him to sort a price out with her.[1] Overnight, Ken Livingstone went from being the billion-pounds-a-year boss of County Hall with enormous powers of patronage, a team of secretaries and an office half the size of a football pitch to being that most worthless of things – an unemployed former councillor. At least he was the prospective parliamentary candidate for Brent East, which is more than could be said for the ousted incumbent, Reg Freeson. At the age of 41, the same age as Neil Kinnock, Ken Livingstone enjoyed a gap year. No one knew then that Margaret Thatcher would call an early general election for June 1987, but it was likely that she would, given the improving economy.

Immediately after abolition, Livingstone had helped his Labour friends in Paddington with their attempts to seize the Tory flagship council of Westminster in the May 1986 London borough elections. Labour's campaign in the city's marginal wards very nearly toppled the complacent leadership of Shirley Porter. 'I just move on,' says Livingstone. 'I do not sit around thinking that it's been a terrible setback. I thought, the GLC has been abolished. Right, let's go and get even with Lady Porter.'[2]

Otherwise, Livingstone made some money through journalism. 'I liked getting my life back,' he says about abolition. 'It wasn't unpleasant at all.'[3] Robert Maxwell, the kleptomaniac press baron, asked him to write a weekly column for his ultimately doomed attempt to challenge the *Evening Standard*'s dominance, the *London Daily News*. He also wrote his autobiography for HarperCollins, published in 1987, which netted him a rumoured advance of £60,000.[4] He even stood in as a holiday relief for the BBC Radio 2 disc jockey Jimmy Young,[5] reinforcing his rapidly growing celebrity portfolio, as well as being a judge for the 1987 Whitbread literary prize.[6] But appearances of success were deceptive. 'On the day after the GLC was abolished,' says Livingstone, 'I worked out that the only things I had in the world were my clothes, my record collection, my books and the fridge. Everything else belonged to my partner [Kate Allen] and so people assume I must be pretty rich after all these years in public life and I'm struggling to pay the bloody mortgage!'[7]

Livingstone suggested he would like to sink into 'well-deserved obscurity' after abolition but he was joking. In a radio interview, he also made clear his ambition. 'I want power,' he said. 'I want to change Britain and I'm not ashamed to say it. Anyone who wants to achieve change would grab at the leadership.' He thought he would have to wait for a decade for his chance. He insisted he had no desire to oust Neil Kinnock.[8]

◆

At Labour's conference in Blackpool, Livingstone considered trying to replace Sam McCluskie, the seamen's union leader, as party treasurer in the NEC elections but withdrew his challenge.[9] However he would be on the NEC for the first time within a year. Livingstone still harboured ambitions to lead the Labour Party, but told the Radio 4 psychiatrist Anthony Clare: '...most probably like Churchill my party is never going to turn to me until they are absolutely on the floor and they have nothing left. And even if they did, the Americans would probably bump me off. I'm not certain America is ready to have someone like me running Britain.'[10] But privately, he was still intensely ambitious, telling Tony Benn over lunch in November 1985 that he expected to be pushed to the 'forefront' by the new intake of MPs. Benn didn't think MPs 'would turn immediately to him to take over' if Labour lost the next election. Benn's analysis was spot on. Neil Kinnock was not Andrew McIntosh.[11]

Three big obstacles stood in the way of Livingstone's advance to Number 10. His past was against him. Swathes of the Left may have eulogised Livingstone but many Labour MPs either blamed him for costing them votes or resented his high profile. More importantly, the Labour Party was undergoing a dramatic transformation, plainly visible at the 1986 Blackpool conference. Delegates confirmed the expulsion of the leaders of Militant Tendency and Eric Heffer was voted off the NEC. 'The Red

Flag' was still sung at the end but with less gusto than in previous years. The party's new director of communications was Peter Mandelson, later high priest of New Labour. It was Mandelson who handed the symbol of Labour's rebirth in the form of red roses to Neil and Glenys Kinnock which they cast to the jubilant congregation.[12] The red rose had literally replaced the red flag as Labour's new symbol. Denis Skinner, the hard left MP for Bolsover, would scoff to the tune of 'The Red Flag': 'The people's rose in shades of pink gets up your nose and makes a stink.'[13] The continued fall of the Labour Left would not be enhanced by the next two general election defeats of 1987 and 1992, but inexorably hastened by it.

◆

Ken Livingstone's own tactics in dealing not only with his colleagues in the Parliamentary Labour Party but the leadership were also a political disaster for him in the long term. They may have enhanced his reputation for honesty and plain talking, but they proved hopeless in building the alliances and foundations necessary for a successful parliamentary career let alone a successful leadership bid. Livingstone never lacked the important qualities of charm and affability, but in Parliament, this political loner struck many observers as a fish out of water.

Before the 1987 election, Ken Livingstone and Reg Race were enjoying a meal in the Red Fort Indian restaurant in Soho. Race, Labour MP for Wood Green between 1979 and 1983, gave Livingstone some advice on how to behave in Parliament: 'You've got to be very careful with the Parliamentary Labour Party [PLP], because people will not like you referring to the GLC and being told how to do things or your experiences there. They will resent it and they will attack you for it.' Later Race heard from contacts that Livingstone mentioned the GLC in one of his first addresses to the PLP.[14]

In fact, Livingstone started to alienate the PLP before the 1987 election. Writing in the London *Daily News* in February 1987, Livingstone said: 'Many MPs never see the London that exists beyond the wine bars and brothels of Westminster.'[15] The remarks hit a raw nerve and dominated a 20-minute debate in the Labour whips' office. One whip demanded that Livingstone be barred from standing in the election. Derek Forster, the chief whip, decided to register 'the widespread concern of colleagues' with Neil Kinnock.[16] Though not yet a member, Livingstone had broken the code of silence operating in Parliament about MPs' nocturnal activities outside the Chamber.

Margaret Thatcher called the general election for 11 June 1987 – her last and Livingstone's first. Livingstone found himself defending the hard-won majority of 4,834 in Brent East bequeathed him by Reg Freeson against Harriet Crawley, the attractive 39-year-old pregnant and unmarried Tory candidate. Crawley proved to be a formidable opponent for Livingstone; she described him as a 'charming snake' and observed that his oft-quoted comment that everyone was fundamentally homosexual was 'evidence of a desperate man'.[17] She was such an effective performer on the doorstep that she was told by one old voter: 'You must be the one who's having Ken Livingstone's baby.'[18] Some polls gave Livingstone a 19 per cent lead over Crawley but she very nearly pulled off an extraordinary victory.[19] On a disastrous night for Labour, Livingstone's majority was slashed by more than half to 1,653; he polled 42.6 per cent of the vote. Thatcher's third successive election victory had given her an overall Commons majority of 102, down 42 on 1983. But the swing to Labour from the Tories had been a feeble 1.7 per cent.[20]

There was much press anticipation about how Livingstone would fare in the House of Commons. He was considered to be one of the stars of the new intake. 'The ordinariness of Ken Livingstone, however, is beyond question,' wrote Stephen Pile in the *Sunday Times*. 'If you saw him train-spotting at King's Cross with a mac and a box of egg sandwiches you would not be the slightest bit surprised. He is the most unlikely media star.' Observing Livingstone give a speech to a gay and lesbian legislation conference in Camden, Pile compared Livingstone to 'a great actor', adding: 'We are never shown Ken giving a speech on television, so it is a surprise to find what an outstanding speaker he is. His speech was a humane and uncontroversial call for justice to which nobody could possibly object.'[21]

◆

Shortly after the election, he told a London conference on 'sexual politics' that he had no idea how much he would dislike being in Parliament until he attended his first meeting with fellow MPs in the Commons. He likened it to going back to the days of

King Alfred; the atmosphere was 'absolutely tribal' and the male members of the PLP 'grunted and growled.'[22]

Livingstone initially struck many people in the Commons as a lost soul. David Hencke, the *Guardian*'s investigative Whitehall correspondent and former Tulse Hill pupil, remembers, 'He looked as if he wasn't cutting it really. He looked almost like a little lost boy, almost overcome by the oppressiveness. Parliament was still then very class conscious, particularly under Thatcher.

'Parliament was the sort of place that when you saw a woman you assumed she was a secretary because there were so few women MPs. Ken Livingstone, given his major reputation at the GLC, just seemed to be cut down to size, ignored and not given any permanent role. I suspect that the Labour whips at the time didn't want him to progress at all; he really was quite a lonely figure.'[23] A few months after his election, Craig Brown, *The Times*' acutely observant parliamentary sketch writer, described Livingstone in the Commons: 'Mr Livingstone usually skulks, sheafs [*sic*] of correspondence in hand, in a lonely position somewhere around the middle of the Labour benches.'[24] Livingstone would later admit: 'I've never felt at home at Westminster. I avoid lobby correspondents, I avoid all those lunches, all that endless chat. I miss County Hall. But politics is my religion. It's my moral framework. I believe a socialist society is inherently the best thing, and that's like an act of faith.'[25]

Chris Mullin, the newly elected MP for Sunderland South, considered Livingstone 'an exceptionally talented man' and 'that rare phenomenon – a Labour politician who was more popular than his party'. But even he thought Livingstone's behaviour in Parliament odd and counterproductive: 'The thing about Ken in our first term of office between '87 and '92, and I put this to him at the time, was that he never made the slightest effort to build a base in the Parliamentary Labour Party.

'I was quite surprised about that because people like him, Tony Banks and me, who were known before we got into Parliament, were regarded as bogey men by most Labour MPs. So we couldn't expect to be carried shoulder high to the tea rooms when we had been elected! But in the cases of Banks and myself we made an effort to get on with people and show them we weren't quite as we had been painted in the newspapers.'[26]

Livingstone replied to Mullin using Tony Banks as an example:

'Well, look at Banksy; he's done all the right things since he got in here and how many votes did he get in the shadow cabinet elections? About 49 or something. In my case, I might get five more, but what's the point?'[27] By July 1987, Tony Benn observed the PLP's 'bitter hostility' directed at Livingstone and a few other troublemakers.[28]

The Labour whips' revenge on Livingstone was to deny him an office in Parliament or even a desk with a telephone for a long time. He spent his first 322 days as an MP 'drifting around like a medieval ghost'. His patience finally snapped on 28 April 1988 when he held a press conference to complain about his treatment.[29] In a further humiliation, he was forced to write to Margaret Thatcher asking her to intervene with government whips on his behalf.[30] The *Financial Times* observed: 'His cold relationship with the Labour leadership and his well-publicised remarks about the anti-social behaviour of some out-of-town MPs were not best calculated to attract support in his hour of need.'[31] He told the 41 journalists who crowded into a committee room for the announcement that henceforth he would be working from home until appropriate office accommodation could be found.[32] No one held their breath.

Harry Barnes, the newly elected left-wing MP for Derbyshire North East, found himself in a similar predicament and regularly shared cramped corridors and office space with Livingstone. 'We all had problems finding rooms in the Commons,' says Barnes, 'and we were amongst the last two. We all found it very awkward.'[33] At one point, the two men had adjoining desks tucked away in the dark recesses of the cloisters in Parliament before being shunted to a tiny windowless room elsewhere, and then finally deposited in a pleasant little room with a window off Committee Corridor South.

'I was always keen to share with Ken, not just because I liked him,' says Barnes, 'but because when he first came to the Commons he didn't involve himself too much in the Commons and he was not liable to be around as much. I thought if I shared a room with him, I would virtually occupy it. I think he found it difficult becoming a backbencher after being prominent at the GLC.'[34]

Ken Livingstone demonstrated his contempt for parliamentary traditions immediately, with his maiden speech. There was a convention in the House of Commons that parliamentary debuts should be anodyne.[35] But Livingstone's could not have been more explosive or designed to shock and offend. Naturally, it was about Northern Ireland.

◆

On 7 July 1987, Livingstone made a series of serious allegations about an Army intelligence officer, Captain Robert Nairac, who had been tortured and murdered by the Provisional IRA back in May 1977[36]. He accused Nairac of being behind a cross-border assassination of a senior IRA terrorist, John Francis Green, and complicit in one of the most appalling massacres of the Troubles – the murder of three members of the Miami Showband.[37]

On 31 July 1975, the band had been stopped by a bogus military checkpoint. It was manned by paramilitaries from the notorious Ulster Volunteer Force, who tried to plant a bomb in the band's minibus. The device went off accidentally killing two of the bombers. The rest of the gang, including at least two British army soldiers serving with the Ulster Defence Regiment, then shot three band members in cold blood. Livingstone widened his Commons attack to include MI5 which he claimed had orchestrated murders in Northern Ireland to wreck a ceasefire agreed between the then Labour government and the Provisional IRA. He also implicated Airey Neave, the MP, shadow Northern Ireland secretary and close Thatcher confidant murdered by the Irish National Liberation Army shortly before the 1979 general election. Livingstone said that 'reasonable people' would not be able to avoid the conclusion that Airey Neave, who had close contacts with the security services, would have kept his friend Margaret Thatcher informed 'in some degree' about MI5's activities.

There was a row with angry intercessions from two Tory MPs, Tim Yeo, and Ian Gow, who would be murdered by the IRA less than three years later. Thatcher described Livingstone's remarks as 'utterly contemptible' and called on Kinnock to repudiate them.[38] An embarrassed Kinnock replied that Livingstone's comments were 'probably unfair'; Craig Brown from *The Times* said that was 'rather like a doctor saying a patient was probably alive'. Brown continued: 'Mr Ken Livingstone, somewhat red-faced, began to beam. They were talking about him! In the first few weeks of this Parliament, he has looked curiously small and lonely, even nondescript. But now that the world is calling him despicable and nasty, things are back to normal and he is happy once more.'[39] The speech also cost him a lucrative financial sideline. Livingstone returned home to find a handwritten note from Robert Maxwell. 'I'm not prepared to have someone like you writing in my paper,' he said.[40]

Livingstone's main source for his allegations was Captain Fred Holroyd, who had served with the Special Military Intelligence Unit (MI6) in Northern Ireland. After leaving the Army in 1976, Holroyd alleged that British security services had colluded with Loyalist paramilitaries to assassinate key targets. Holroyd also told Livingstone that the same gun 'used by Captain Nairac' in the cross-border shooting of John Francis Green was also used to murder the Miami Showband Three.[41] Similar allegations would be made by Colin Wallace, a former employee of the intelligence services. In April 2003, Sir John Stevens, then commissioner of the Metropolitan Police, concluded in the third of his special inquiries into the 'dirty war' in Northern Ireland that some members of the British security services had colluded with the loyalist Ulster Defence Association during the 1970s and 1980s over the Loyalist murders of republican targets, including the solicitor, Pat Finucane.[42] As yet, no definitive evidence has emerged to link Nairac with the Miami Showband murders; in February 1979, Nairac had been posthumously awarded the George Cross for gallantry, the civilian equivalent of the Victoria Cross.

♦

Livingstone's views on Northern Ireland caused further disgust in the wake of the IRA bombing of the Poppy Day commemoration in Enniskillen on Remembrance Sunday, 8 November 1987 in which 11 people died and 60 were injured. There was a ferocious backlash against Sinn Féin and Ken Livingstone for having supported them for so long. But on 16 November 1987, only eight days following the massacre, he upped the stakes. 'I do not think anybody seriously believes the IRA will not eventually get their own way,' he said. 'As with all other colonial situations we have been in eventually Britain will go.'[43]

It would be almost two decades before Livingstone learned how close he may have come to being murdered for his views on Ireland. In November 2006, in an interview with Keith Dovkants of the *Evening Standard*, the infamous loyalist murderer and hit man, Michael Stone, revealed how the paramilitary wing of the Ulster Defence Association had ordered him to assassinate Livingstone.[44] Dressed as a jogger, Stone claimed he stalked Livingstone for two days and resolved to shoot him in the head as he came out of a Tube station. Stone said: 'There was no sign of any security at all. He was on his own, with a kind of attaché case slung over his shoulder. I thought that's how I would do it. I'd clip him on the steps of the Tube.' Stone claimed that his UDA terror godfathers got cold feet three days before the planned murder because the operation had been compromised by an informer.

But there is confusion about when or even if these events took place. Stone was arrested and later jailed for the three murders he committed during his attack on a funeral at the Catholic Milltown Cemetery in west Belfast on 16 March 1988. So the aborted Livingstone hit would have had to have taken place before then. But on closer inspection, irreconcilable inconsistencies creep into Stone's story. In fact, he first told the tale in his autobiography published in 2003. In that account, he claimed the front door to Livingstone's modest home in Brent opened outwards, 'an indication that there was extra security'.[45] But Livingstone insists that he did not move into this house until May 1989.[46] Stone also says Livingstone was a Labour MP, so the planned assassination would have to have taken place between the June 1987 general election and the Milltown massacre nine months later.

There is also the possibility that Stone has fabricated the whole story or he heard about a later plot after May 1989. He is currently back in jail after breaking the terms of his release under the Good Friday Agreement for a botched attempt to murder Martin McGuiness and Gerry Adams at Stormont Castle in November 2006. Livingstone says he was warned several times by Special Branch during the 1980s to take extra care of his security.[47] During his first Parliament, Livingstone returned repeatedly to Northern Ireland issues, particularly to the rumours on collusion between loyalist paramilitaries and the security services. In October 1988, it was even suggested that Livingstone would fall the wrong side of a government ban on broadcasting interviews with paramilitaries and their supporters.[48]

Chris Mullin was puzzled at Livingstone's obsession with the Wallace and Holroyd allegations. He says: 'I have no criticisms of the cause but to make it your main thing? We had major local government legislation going through Parliament at the time and

Ken knew more about local government than anybody. He could have made a major impact on that and impressed a lot of people but he made no effort whatsoever. That's the great mystery to me.'[49]

Most Labour MPs were in one of three caucuses: the Solidarity group for right-wingers, the Tribune group organised round the Labour weekly *Tribune* and the hard left Socialist Campaign Group. Livingstone joined the last two but was particularly active within the Socialist Campaign Group whose father figure was Tony Benn. After losing his seat in the 1983 election, Benn had briefly occupied the position of the Left's 'king o'er the water' before re-entering Parliament as the MP for Chesterfield following a by-election in March 1984. The Socialist Campaign Group had formed in 1982 following a split in the Tribune group over the 1981 Benn deputy leadership challenge and the purge of Militant, which some on the soft left supported and the hard left had condemned as a 'witch-hunt.'

◆

During the '87 campaign, the Tories often alleged, surely tongue-in-cheek, that Livingstone would soon do to Kinnock what he had done to Andrew McIntosh. It was 'always a Conservative fantasy', wrote Robin Oakley, then political editor of *The Times*, adding: 'But it now becomes laughable: Livingstone is a lonely, isolated figure.'[50] But within three months, on 28 September 1987, Ken Livingstone sat at Labour's top table as a member of the NEC. 'Anyone who regards Mario Puzo's *The Godfather* as a guide to political life is unlikely ever to be far from power,' observed Peter Riddell of the *Financial Times*.[51]

During his local government career, Livingstone was habitually disloyal to all his Labour leaders: David Stimpson in Lambeth, Roy Shaw in Camden, Sir Reg Goodwin and Andrew McIntosh. But this pales beside what he had to say about *national* Labour leaders: Harold Wilson and James Callaghan betrayed the Labour Party; Michael Foot sold out over the Falklands War and countless other issues; as shadow chancellor, John Smith helped lose the 1992 election with his tax raising manifesto; Tony Blair was the 'most right-wing leader in Labour's history'[52] and furthermore he should have fired his chancellor, Gordon Brown, for alleged 'incompetence' over the 1998 budget.[53]

But the 'repellent'[54] Neil Kinnock occupied pole position in the pantheon of Livingstone hate figures. At an NEC meeting, Livingstone told Kinnock to his face that the party would never win with him in charge, which drew calls of 'Shame!' from David Blunkett.[55] 'We all knew we weren't going to win with Kinnock,' says Livingstone. 'My assumption was that he would grow in stature and become formidable and perhaps go on to be a very good prime minister. There was no way of anticipating that at that point he just wouldn't grow in stature.'[56]

The Left still represented a significant bloc but its influence declined during this Parliament as the Labour Party began to review the unpopular policies which had cost it the two previous general elections. Labour was still encumbered by the vote-losing Left baggage of the early 1980s, such as unilateral nuclear disarmament.

Labour's commitment to de-commissioning Britain's current Polaris submarine deterrent and cancelling the Trident replacement system had provided the Tories with one of its biggest weapons during the 1987 election campaign.[57] But other policies for dealing with taxation, trade union reform and the economy, on which the Tories had a formidable lead, had also cost Labour dear.

◆

Livingstone's election to the NEC was thanks to the continued dominance of the hard left in the constituencies, and help from a small band of committed supporters – as explained in the next chapter. Critically, his candidature for the NEC was supported by the Socialist Campaign Group of MPs and secured by 200 constituencies, giving him a total of 385,000 votes.[58] But, despite Livingstone's surprise victory, the elections were good for Kinnock, giving him a rough majority on the NEC of 20 to six.[59] Livingstone was put on the NEC by the Left to do its bidding and to fight Kinnock's party and policy modernisation. 'He is our prisoner, and he knows it,' a leading member of the Campaign Group told *The Times*. 'Any major deviation and he will be off next year.'[60]

Livingstone did not disappoint. He would remain on the NEC for two years and fight Kinnock's changes all the way. Speaking at a *Tribune* rally two days after his election, Livingstone warned that 'any attempt to abandon our non-nuclear defence policy would lead to a civil war inside the party which would render it unelectable in 1991.'[61]

Over the next few years, Kinnock initiated seven policy reviews and introduced reforms to the organisation of the Labour Party itself.[62] It would be the first comprehensive policy review for Labour since 1955.[63] Both reviews and reforms would have the effect of finally breaking the power of the Left not only in the constituencies but also on the National Executive Committee and in the PLP. Ken Livingstone would be in the vanguard of the Left's fightback, which would be decisively defeated.

Kinnock's first policy review paper, 'Statement of Democratic Socialist Aims and Values', was produced in early 1988. Drafted by Kinnock's deputy Roy Hattersley, the document strongly indicated an acceptance that many of Mrs Thatcher's reforms were irreversible and that the market economy should be regarded as innocent until proven guilty. The operation of the market 'where properly regulated, is a generally satisfactory means of determining provision and consumption'.[64]

For Benn, Livingstone and their 46 colleagues in the Socialist Campaign Group, this was heresy and a provocation. On 23 March 1988, Benn and Eric Heffer challenged Kinnock and Hattersley for the party's leadership and deputy leadership.[65] By this stage, the two were yesterday's men; it was a case of Don Quixote and Sancho Panza ride again. At the time, Livingstone approached the shadow chancellor, John Smith, and urged him to stand against Kinnock for the leadership. It was widely known within the PLP that Smith and Kinnock did not get on.[66] 'I said to him he had to run,' says Livingstone. 'I told him all the Left will switch to you when Benn gets knocked out. We're never going to win with Kinnock.' Smith replied emphatically, 'I can't do that.'[67] Both the Labour leadership and most of the press saw the challenge as a futile and melodramatic gesture which would do the party only harm. In the event, it was a damp squib which highlighted the impotence of the Left and affirmed Kinnock's authority.

On 25 May 1988, a historic meeting of the NEC debated the seven policy statements from the review groups established by Kinnock. Livingstone derided as 'pure Wilson' the first paper 'The Productive and Competitive Economy'[68] which advocated an overhaul of Labour's economic policies and included a proposal rejecting the renationalisation of industries privatised by the Tories.[69] Other papers sounded ominous to Benn and Livingstone, particularly 'Britain and the World', presented by foreign affairs spokesman, Gerald Kaufman. The document accepted the Common Market and left open the thorny question of nuclear disarmament. Livingstone wanted the repeal of Section 2 of the European Communities Act restoring full sovereignty over legislation to the British government. He also demanded an amendment agreeing to the mutual dissolution of NATO and the Warsaw Pact.

According to Benn, Kinnock said, 'Repeal of Section 2 equals withdrawal [from the Common Market]. The electorate rejected that in 1983 and it would wreck the economy if we withdrew.' Both of Livingstone's amendments were defeated and Kinnock carried the day on all fronts. The draft economic proposals presented by John Smith, which placed the reduction of inflation before the reduction of unemployment as Labour's first priority, were also carried by 20 votes to three with Livingstone abstaining.[70]

'To cut a long story short,' observed Benn, 'this is the Thatcherism of the Labour Party. We have moved into the penumbra of her policy area and our main argument is that we will administer it better than she will.'[71] Although defeated then, Livingstone remains bullish about his opposition to Kinnock: 'It wasn't going to win us the election, and it didn't win us the election. Who was right?'[72] At the party conference in Blackpool on 2 October 1988, Benn and Heffer were heavily defeated in the leadership battle. Kinnock polled 89 per cent of the vote. By then, the press had long lost interest in the fight. 'When the result came, it was appalling,' Benn said.[73]

On 8 May 1989, the NEC met at the start of a two-day session to discuss the policy review. It culminated on 9 May with the acceptance, in the teeth of opposition from Benn, Livingstone and Dennis Skinner, of the paper setting out the new policies, 'Meet the Challenge, Make the Change'. Ten years almost to the day of Thatcher's first election victory, hard-won Left shibboleths like renationalisation and unilateral disarmament were abandoned. 'The NEC *has* abandoned socialist principles and any idea of transforming society,' wrote Benn. The decision finally confirmed his belief that the party had accepted the principles 'not only of capitalism but Thatcherism'.[74] 'We intend to fight throughout this summer to save the party we love and all believe in,' said Livingstone.[75] But soon he was fighting to save his own political career.

In September 1989, he faced two serious threats. Many of the Chartists had long dispersed from Brent East and the constituency party now had a noisy contingent of right-wingers intent on deselecting Livingstone, partly because of his opposition to the policy review. At the time, Roy Hattersley was asked whether Kinnock, given the opportunity, would push Livingstone off the cliffs at Beachy Head. 'I don't think so,' replied Hattersley. 'In fact, he'd dive in to save him. But he'd deselect him if he could.'[76] Livingstone fended off the attempt to replace him with either a former Labour MP, Michael Barnes, or Mary Turner, a local school dinner lady, by polling 60 per cent of the 218 votes cast at a local reselection meeting on 27 September 1989.[77]

He was not so lucky with the NEC elections a few days later at the party conference in Brighton. On 2 October 1989, Livingstone was voted off the NEC;[78] he lost his place to John Prescott, the transport spokesman. A change in the party rules transferred the voting power from the small number of often hard left activists controlling local constituency parties to individual party members – One Man One Vote, or OMOV. More than half the constituencies adopted OMOV and it was predicted that others on the Left, even Tony Benn, could one day face the same fate if the rest followed suit. More than 100 constituencies that had voted for Livingstone in 1988 had abandoned him a year later.[79] It was the day Ken Livingstone's dreams of leading his party died. 'The moment I was kicked off Labour's NEC in '89 all my plotting to be prime minister died,' says Livingstone. 'That's when I started to get all this media work – when they thought I was harmless.'[80]

Livingstone would make two forlorn attempts at the party leadership over the next five years, but essentially he entered the 1990s no longer the darling of the Left but as a curious new hybrid, the politico-celebrity.

Notes

1   Interview, Sir Godfrey 'Tag' Taylor, 22.7.07
2   Interview, Ken Livingstone, 1.11.07
3   Ibid.
4   Reuters News, 9.9.87; Author interviews
5   *Sunday Times*, 2.11.86
6   *The Times*, 14.1.87

7   Interview, Ken Livingstone, 1.11.07
8   LBC Radio interview, 30.3.86; *Daily Telegraph*, 31.3.86
9   *The Times*, 22.10.86
10 *In the Psychiatrist's Chair*, presented by Anthony Clare, 28.8.88
11 Tony Benn, *The End of an Era, Diaries 1980-1990*, p428
12 Michael Leapman, *Kinnock*, pp1-2
13 Ibid., pp2-3
14 Interview, Reg Race, 23.8.07
15 *London Daily News*, 18.2.87; *The Times*, 19.2.87
16 *The Times*, 19.2.87
17 *The Times*, 3.6.87
18 *Observer*, 5.4.92
19 *Financial Times*, Harris Research poll for ITV's *Weekend World*, 8.6.07
20 Peter Joyce, *Guide to UK General Elections 1832-2001*, pp363-375
21 *Sunday Times*, 'Ken and Edwina – political superstars', 31.5.07
22 *Sunday Times*, 21.6.87
23 Interview, David Hencke, 29.10.07
24 *The Times*, 9.12.87
25 *Guardian,* 14.11.98
26 Interview, Chris Mullin, 3.10.07
27 Ibid.
28 Tony Benn, *The End of an Era, Diaries 1980-1990*, p515
29 *Financial Times*, 29.4.88
30 Ibid.
31 Ibid.
32 *Sunday Times*, 1.5.88
33 Interview, Harry Barnes, 16.7.07
34 Ibid.
35 *The Times*, 9.7.87
36 Toby Harnden, *Bandit Country*, pp302-303
37 Hansard Parliamentary Debates, volume 118, 7.7.87
38 *Financial Times*, 10.7.87
39 *The Times*, 10.7.87
40 Interview, Ken Livingstone, 1.11.07
41 Ken Livingstone's maiden speech, published in Hansard Parliamentary Debates, volume 118, 7.7.87; See also Fred Holroyd, *War Without Honour – The True Story of Military Intelligence in Northern Ireland*, Medium, 1989
42 Stevens Inquiry 3, 17.4.03
43 *The Times*, 17.11.87
44 *Evening Standard,* 'My plot to murder Ken Livingstone, by former hit man', by Keith Dovkants, 1.11.06
45 Michael Stone, *None Shall Divide Us*, pp248-249
46 Interview, Ken Livingstone, 28.12.07
47 Ibid.
48 *Broadcast*, 28.10.88
49 Interview, Chris Mullin, 3.10.07
50 *The Times*, 10.7.87
51 *Financial Times*, 30.9.87

52 *The Times*, 22.7.94
53 *People*, 15.3.98
54 See Chapter 14
55 Interview, Ken Livingstone, 25.10.07
56 Ibid.
57 Peter Joyce, *Guide to UK General Elections, 1832-2001*, pp370-371
58 *Financial Times*, 29.7.87
59 Ibid.
60 *The Times*, 30.9.87
61 *Financial Times*, 1.10.87
62 Ibid., pp378-379; Author interviews
63 Raymond Plant, Matt Beech and Kevin Hickson, *The Struggle for Labour's Soul, Understanding Labour's Political Thought Since 1945*, Routledge, 2004, pp80-8
64 'Statement of Democratic Socialist Aims and Values', 1988, p10
65 *Guardian*, 23.3.8
66 Mark Stuart, *John Smith, A Life,* (citing Philip Gould's diary), Politico's, 2005, p207,
67 Interview, Ken Livingstone, 25.10.87
68 Tony Benn, *The End of an Era, Diaries 1980-1990*, (see 25.5.88)
69 *Financial Times*, 10.7.88
70 Mark Stuart, *John Smith, A Life*, p166
71 Tony Benn, *The End of an Era, Diaries 1980-1990*, (see 25.5.88)
72 Interview, Ken Livingstone, 1.11.07
73 Tony Benn, *The End of an Era, Diaries 1980-1990*, (see 2.10.88)
74 Ibid., (9.5.89)
75 Reuters News, 9.5.89
76 *The Times*, 28.9.89
77 *Independent*, 28.9.89
78 *Financial Times*, 3.10.89
79 *The Times*, 3.10.89
80 Interview, Ken Livingstone, 1.11.07

Chapter 18

Ken and the rise of Socialist Action, 1985–1994

In October 2007, the *Evening Standard* published a list of the 25 most influential people running London.[1] Livingstone headed the list which contained the names of 13 other individuals who worked directly or indirectly for the mayor. Four of the people on the list were Livingstone's closest mayoral advisors; they have also been members of a tiny Trotskyist party which has worked closely and discreetly with Ken Livingstone for more than 20 years.

Socialist Action is an organisation so discreet and secretive that it does not even admit its own existence and its members will not confirm they have ever belonged to the group. When I interviewed Ken Livingstone about Socialist Action for this book, he pressed me for evidence at first, before acknowledging its existence and the importance of the role played by those who had been associated with it.

It has a website and it has a printing press and those who have been associated with it have enjoyed great influence over London. By my calculation, at least five of the mayor's advisors are or have been members of Socialist Action, and there are several others who do work for the mayor or organisations with which he is associated. They include: Simon Fletcher, the mayor's chief of staff; John Ross, director of economics and business for the Greater London Authority (GLA); Redmond O'Neill, GLA director of public affairs and transport; Mark Watts, GLA climate change advisor; and Jude Woodward, senior policy advisor. Others have included Atma Singh, the former advisor on Muslim issues and Professor Alan Freeman, who became prominent in the Unison branch at City Hall, and also runs the Venezuelan Information Centre – a propaganda organisation of which Ken Livingstone is president.

The concentration of power by Socialist Action is the more astonishing when according to Ken Livingstone, it has probably had no more than 120 members in the last decade.[2] On the face of it, Livingstone appears to have drawn much of his political talent from a comparatively small political gene pool. Livingstone's close association with Socialist Action is an integral part of his story. Under his patronage, the group has become probably the most successful and influential revolutionary Marxist organisation in Britain. Socialist Action has long been Livingstone's guiding light, his foot soldiers, his mentors, and his political family. It is clear that from 1985, Socialist Action set out to make itself indispensable to Ken Livingstone and to seek control, or 'hegemony' over the forces and groups making up the Labour Left. It has proved phenomenally successful.

Socialist Action has made remarkable attempts to cover its tracks and even disappear altogether as an organisation, as part of the deep entryist policy adopted in the mid 1980s to protect members from any potential Militant-style purge. In part it has derived its power over the years from its secrecy and its deniability. As far back as 1983, the group resolved to disappear from public consciousness, or as one internal document put it at the time, to bring about 'the dissolution of the public face'.[3] Leading members of Socialist Action are unquestionably talented and highly able but they blundered in thinking they could make their organisation invisible because they have left a paper trail a mile wide.

◆

In their early years, members of Socialist Action churned out hundreds of agendas, documents and other discussion papers which I have been able to obtain. They tell the remarkable story of how the group absorbed itself into the Labour Left and became a major force within it; as well the efforts it made to disappear from view as an organisation. Socialist Action made a concerted attempt to cultivate Ken Livingstone back in 1985 in the wake of the failed rate capping campaign. John Ross, the leader of the group, interviewed Livingstone for its relatively new paper, also called *Socialist Action*. Livingstone had already heard about Ross as the author of a small book called *Thatcher and Friends* which predicted the terminal decline of the Tory Party.[4] 'I recognised this was someone with formidable intellect,' says Livingstone. 'After the rate capping fiasco, when most of the rest of the hard left were boycotting me, he turned up and did an interview and we started talking about economics and I realised this was somebody who could give me the grasp on economic policy which I didn't have. So when I became an MP I retained him to actually do that.'[5]

John Ross's influence grew from that moment; he became Livingstone's most important advisor from 1985 onwards. After Livingstone, he is the most influential personality in the mayor's office. The rates farce stripped Livingstone of most of his Left contacts and friends. Ross supplied Livingstone not only with the support and network he needed to continue but also the education necessary to tackle the Labour leadership on the vital battleground of economic policy. For 20 years, Ken Livingstone has really been a double act; John Ross and Socialist Action have been the silent partners.

Ross worked as a lecturer at Enfield Polytechnic and once he fought the Newham North East parliamentary seat as the candidate for the International Marxist Group, the forerunner to Socialist Action.[6] By the time Ross met Livingstone, he had emerged triumphant from an internecine struggle within the International Marxist Group, or IMG, one of Britain's main Trotskyist parties. During 1982, the IMG split over strategy: how to bring about that elusive revolution. That split led to the creation of Socialist Action.

The IMG was built fundamentally out of the student movements of the late 1960s and helped organise some of the biggest protests against the Vietnam War in London.[7] During the 1970s, its revolutionary strategy was focused on industry and the unions, which made sense during this period of economic instability and intense industrial unrest. Members, often highly educated, were encouraged to get blue collar jobs to play a role in encouraging the workers to turn towards revolution, 'The Turn'.

An internal IMG note in 1982 reiterated, '...it is vital that we are rooted among the industrial workers, going through joint experiences with them and drawing common lessons. Any other perspective will only alienate us from the forces who will be key in building a revolutionary party and expose us to class pressures.'[8] Jobs were often advertised internally: 'London Transport are taking on bus drivers at Stamford Hill; contact Wood Green Job Centre'; or 'Jobs available in small chemical factory in Hounslow; we have a comrade who is a convenor.'[9]

But the IMG had always been hopelessly confused about its approach to the Labour Party: to enter or not to enter. 'We hopped into the Labour Party around 1975,' wrote one member John Marston, in his exasperated letter of resignation of

December 1982, 'and then out again in 1977 for the joys of regroupment and Socialist Unity. Any pretence of a strategic perspective vanished.'[10]

In late 1982, the IMG split over whether or not to join the Benn crusade within the Labour Party, or the 'Bennite Current'. A paper presented to the IMG's conference in December 1982 stated: 'It is clear that, at the leadership level, fundamental differences are emerging as to the nature of the party we are trying to build and how to build it. A gulf is developing between those who, basing themselves on the positions of the 1981 conference, wish to build an independent combat party rooted in the industrial working class, and those who are moving towards the idea of an ideological tendency operating in the Labour Party as left critics of the Benn current.'[11]

John Ross was at the forefront of the internal struggle to ditch the industrial strategy and get all IMG members to join the Labour Party en masse and then seek to control the Left bloc within it. Supporting Ross was another key figure in Livingstone's political career, Redmond O'Neill. At the December 1982 conference, Ross carried the day and over the next few months IMG members joined the Labour Party. A minority who disagreed with the policy of 'deep entryism' split away and formed its own party, the International Group which became a political irrelevance. Despite becoming Labour members, the Ross majority still remained organised as a separate political organisation. They decided to rebrand themselves as the Socialist League, and to establish a newspaper called *Socialist Action*. Like Militant, the group became known by the name of their paper rather than as the Socialist League.

'The next steps towards a revolutionary party comprise a fight for a class struggle within the Bennite current,' said one discussion paper at the time. 'For this a new newspaper is necessary – one that is seen as the voice of revolutionary socialists within the Labour Party and which can thereby give political expressions to the mass struggles of workers and youth who in the next period will seek overall political answers within the Labour Party. '...Socialist Action will fight for leadership within the Bennite current.'[12]

The Socialist League/Socialist Action met for the first time as a central committee at the Intensive English School in Star

Street near Marble Arch for the start of a two-day conference on Saturday, 22 January 1983. The official launch of *Socialist Action* took place the following morning[13] and it first appeared on 16 March. The group's old paper, *Socialist Challenge*, ceased to exist.[14]

The group's overall revolutionary objective did not change, only the strategy to bring it about, as an internal document in January 1983 made clear: '... Socialist Action believes that it will be impossible to make the transition to socialism without incurring the armed resistance of the ruling class and thereby the necessity for violent self-defence by the working class.'[15]

◆

From the outset, Ken Livingstone was clearly an important force within the 'Bennite current' for Socialist Action. John Ross and comrades identified two Bennite wings: the Labour Co-ordinating Committee, a left-wing coalition within the Labour Party comprising Chartists from *Briefing*, and the Campaign for Labour Party Democracy, CLPD.

Socialist Action identified the second wing 'crystallising around forces such as the Campaign Group of MPs, Livingstone, the left of Labour Campaign for Nuclear Disarmament (LCND)... and the constituency left...'[16] Its slogans were now: 'Deeper into the Labour Party!', 'Deeper into the trade unions!', 'For a new newspaper!',[17] 'Defend socialist policies!', 'Stop the witch-hunt!', 'Remove the right-wing Labour leaders!'[18]

Socialist Action threw itself into the general election of 1983: 'Throughout we want to forge a fighting alliance of forces by linking up with the trade union left wing and to struggle for the inclusion of Labour's socialist policies in the manifesto, for Labour to give a fighting lead against the Tories and against the witch-hunt [Kinnock's purge of Militant.]'[19]

Coming just six months after the launch of Socialist Action, the 1983 election defeat was a shattering blow. 'The Bennite left has been outmanoeuvred and disarmed,' pronounced one internal post-election Socialist Action discussion paper. 'As a result the Bennite left has suffered serious defeats in the election: the defeat of Benn, the failure to select Livingstone, and the loss of other left MPs.'[20]

Led by John Golding, the NEC now stepped up its purge of the Militant Tendency. This sent a tremor through the Labour left, particularly among those entryist Trotskyist groups like Socialist Action. The hard left, including Benn and Livingstone, supported Labour Against the Witch-hunt, or LAW, established in October 1982,[21] but it certainly did not provide enough of a security blanket for Socialist Action.

Like Militant Tendency, Socialist Action was a party within a party, something explicitly forbidden under Labour Party rules. Like Militant Tendency, it was organised around a newspaper and like the Tendency, it had assets which clearly identified it as an organisation in its own right. Socialist Action had a bookshop in Islington at 328 Upper Street called the Other Bookshop, as well as that absolute requirement of any self-respecting revolutionary group, a printing press, Lithoprint Ltd, based not far from the bookshop at 26-28 Shacklewell Lane in Stoke Newington. Socialist Action still owns Lithoprint and its members are the company's directors. As a *Socialist Action* paper made clear in 1985: 'Lithoprint is a company totally under the control of the organisation.'[22]

In September 1983, Socialist Action took the decision to disappear from public view. This meant closing down the Other Bookshop and taking extreme security measures to guarantee invisibility and deniability. Two months after the decision, Socialist Action's leadership drew up a document entitled 'The dissolution of the public face'. It said: 'This is a historical fact – namely that the public face dissolved itself. This requires no public announcement but all bodies of the [Trotskyist] world movement must be informed and act accordingly.'[23] Some members disagreed with the decision; one wrote: 'The September meeting took a momentous decision. It voted 23 for and one against to formally dissolve our public organisation. The decision was taken on the basis of a false prognosis: that following the Labour Party conference there will be an immediate witch-hunt of our supporters within the mass organisation.'[24]

Although the purge stopped at Militant, no one at Socialist Action was taking any chances. The paranoia was evident in a Socialist Action document marked 'top secret', and called 'Practical implementation of the new security measures in the centre'.[25]

The note warned that Socialist Action had to be on its guard against any unexpected visits from the media, and that 'any undesirable material should be kept out of sight'. 'In addition, the print shop must be just a print shop and the bookshop just a bookshop,' it added. There had to be checks on anyone entering both buildings. 'This is important,' continued the note cryptically, 'because these areas have outside visitors, although some of the most sensitive visitors at present (i.e. GLC) come UPSTAIRS frequently.'[26]

One big problem was the post office box number used by Socialist Action. It was the same box number as for the bookshop, the newspaper and its youth wing, later called Youth Action: P.O. Box 50, London N1 2XP. 'We cannot continue with sending everything out with the same box number,' according to the security document. 'Moreover, the box number is in the name of an organisation.'

Comrades were instructed to consider security even when writing memos and other documents: 'It is possible to write them so they appear to those not in the know that they do not necessarily originate from an organisation – i.e. writing in the third person, using more of a commentary style etc… If documents are written with security in mind, there should not be so many problems.'[27]

It also meant being extra careful about what was thrown out: 'We have a real problem in that we have <u>no idea</u> what happens to our rubbish when it is taken away by the bin persons… The only solution is to make the rubbish safe <u>before</u> it is taken away which means we have to get a shredder.'[28] A new cleaning rota was instituted; leading figures in Socialist Action, including John Ross and Redmond O'Neill, took it in turns to clean HQ.[29] Leading members now started using pseudonyms: Redmond O'Neill was 'Lark', Jude Woodward was 'Lee', while another member, Anne Kane, was 'Swift'.[30] Atma Singh, who was 'Chan' says, 'The reason was secrecy so as not to let people outside know who was doing what.'[31]

After the closure of the bookshop, members met in rooms above pubs in the local Hackney/Islington area, namely, the Cedar Room pub in Islington, the Cock Tavern in Mare Street, the Lucas Arms in Grays Inn Road and Taylor's in Shacklewell Lane near the print shop. The witch-hunters did not come for Socialist Action, but secrecy and security became second nature to the group over the next quarter of a century.

During the mid to late 1980s, the group did successfully

ingratiate itself with the Labour Left. For a fee, Socialist Action also put its printing press at the disposal of many left-wing groups, including the CLPD and the Socialist Campaign Group for MPs.[32] At one stage, Socialist Action was losing an average of £762 a week and the press was vital for earning extra income.[33] It experienced money anxieties throughout the 1980s.

Trotskyist parties always inflate their membership numbers along with their sense of self-importance but by the mid 1980s, it is clear that about 500 people belonged to Socialist Action. This is made obvious in an internal document which stressed the impor- tance of selling 4,000 copies of Socialist Action a week: 'This means an average of eight per comrade.'[34] Later, Socialist Action members would be encouraged to give 10 per cent of their pay to the party.[35] Its members acquired a reputation for being intel- ligent, hard-working and even subservient to powerful left-wing figures, which meant they were often despised by other voices on the far left. Gerry Healy's News Line was one: 'This is how they [Socialist Action] see themselves: the chosen few, the brains trust, the intellectual elite, the bright people with all the smart answers who are just waiting for the poor old working class to catch up.'[36]

Certainly, Socialist Action considered Ken Livingstone to be influential and clearly took time to cultivate him. In a rather convoluted reference to Livingstone's importance, one paper from John Ross showed that 'an intelligent reformism of the Livingstone type can incorporate elements of support for the oppressed. Socialist Action of course welcomes such support. But it does not represent intelligent reformism as the answer to Kinnock.'[37]

Livingstone remembers being paid a visit by John Ross shortly after his falling out with the Chartists and the others on the far left over rate capping. 'He was the first in to say this was a tempo- rary setback,' remembers Livingstone. Ross grew in importance, particularly after Livingstone became an MP. He had always felt vulnerable dealing with balance sheets, finance and economics,[38] as Reg Race had observed at the GLC.[39] With a first-class eco- nomics degree from Oxford, Ross proved to be a valuable teacher for Livingstone, who says: 'When I became an MP I employed John Ross to teach me economics, basically to be my economics advisor, and he'd turn up three times a week and we'd go through what was happening in the British economy and the world economy. He'd explain the theories behind it. This went on for two years. And after about 18 months to two years we were asked to do a debate at a fringe meeting about the way forward and we went through it and I knew I was on top of the brief.'[40]

♦

By 1985, according to Atma Singh, a former long-term member of Socialist Action, Livingstone was possibly the most important figure on the Left; the group considered both Arthur Scargill and Tony Benn to be spent forces. 'They supported Ken Livingstone to make him as powerful as possible,' says Singh. 'Socialist Action understood that what they were after was some political power. If they couldn't see a way of getting political power, they just wanted to be the most powerful; the term they used was [to achieve] "hegemony over the Left". So they wanted to be the main group to dictate what was going on in the Left.'[41]

Socialist Action became increasingly powerful on the left of the Labour Party. Members of the group were elected to important positions in key left-wing bodies and campaigns, including CLPD, Labour CND and various student bodies, including its own, Youth Action. Socialist Action stood for many of the same issues as Livingstone: equality regardless of race, gender and class; troops out of Ireland; unilateral disarmament. It was for the miners and the Greenham Common Women, Fidel Castro and so on, and against Kinnock and his witch-hunt and pretty well everything else for which he stood. Atma Singh says that Socialist Action was 'instrumental' in getting Livingstone elected on to the NEC in 1987 and 1988.[42]

But some felt the group was becoming too aggressive and divisive. In 1987, a member of another Trotskyist group Socialist Viewpoint wrote to complain of Socialist Action's sectarianism in relation to yet another left grouping, the Labour Left Committee: 'Since S.A. have been participating, they have sought to be deeply involved in various joint projects. But they have also lied and taken over one project for themselves which makes their motives in participating in other projects very suspect.' Socialist Action thought other far left groups 'are to blame for setbacks and defeats and should be smashed'.[43]

The group and its links to Ken Livingstone first came to attention over its bitter sectarian battles for control of the anti-racist movement. From the mid 1980s, Socialist Action had long supported a campaign for black sections within the Labour Party. At the forefront of the campaign was the journalist and left-wing black activist, Marc Wadsworth, who worked closely with John Ross to secure support for black sections from the Socialist Campaign Group of MPs. Ross promised to use his influence with the Campaign Group. 'If the Campaign Group did not support black sections,' wrote John Ross to Wadsworth in March 1986, 'this would lead to a problem between Socialist Action and the Campaign Group, not between Socialist Action and the black section. Support for the black section is a bedrock of politics.'[44] The Campaign Group did support Wadsworth[45] and despite Kinnock's initial reluctance,[46] black sections under the umbrella of the Black Socialist Society were eventually recognised by the Labour Party in October 1990.[47]

In 1991, Marc Wadsworth set up the Anti-Racist Alliance, or ARA, an organisation which would be predominantly led by black people in the struggle against neo-Nazis and racism. The organisation acquired offices in Red Lion Square in Clerkenwell and soon secured the support of powerful trade unions like the Transport and General Workers Union.[48] Wadsworth approached John Ross for Socialist Action's support for the new campaign. Wadsworth says: 'I went way back with Socialist Action. Socialist Action not only supported the principle of self-organisation for black people's campaigns but they also appeared at the time to support that much thornier issue of black leadership. We had white allies but we did it ourselves. Socialist Action appeared to us to be very good on principles very dear to our heart.'

Ross suggested appointing Ken Livingstone, as co-chairman of the ARA, a titular position only, leaving the bulk of the work with co-chair Leela Ramdeen. Eventually, approximately seven Socialist Action members were put on the executive committee, including some who later became Livingstone's mayoral advisors.

The establishment of the ARA acted as a 'provocation' for Socialist Action's main rivals on the Trotskyist far left, the Socialist Workers Party, or SWP, which then decided to resurrect its own dormant anti-racism organisation, the Anti-Nazi League or ANL. These two anti-racism organisations and the causes they espoused now became proxy warriors for two Trotskyist organisations – the SWP and Socialist Action – fighting to control this important campaign. Ken Livingstone went to extraordinary lengths to help join Socialist Action in its sectarian scraps with its main rival.

The SWP/SA race war rapidly forced itself on the attention of the Socialist Campaign Group of hard left Labour MPs who had always strived to make links with their fellow travellers on the Left outside the PLP and were often perplexed by their uncomradely feuds. Tony Benn's diaries make it clear that the spat was already an issue in early 1992. On 15 January 1992, Benn wrote that there had been a 'flaming row between those who support the Anti-Nazi League in its recreated form' and the Anti-Racist Alliance 'supported by Ken Livingstone and the Black Sections' adding: 'It is absolutely absurd that there should be these arguments between anti-racist organisations. It is left-wing politics at its most ludicrous.'[49]

At the annual general meeting of the Campaign Group a fortnight later, another row broke out between Bernie Grant, the black MP for Tottenham who supported the ANL, and Ken Livingstone when Wadsworth attempted to distribute an ARA leaflet. Grant tried to prevent distribution, at which point Livingstone stood up to leave saying, 'I am leaving if this behaviour continues... This is how Kinnock behaves. We have always been allowed to distribute literature.' Benn observed the 'boiling hatred' between the two groups, describing it as 'so crazy'.[50] It perhaps was not that crazy when you realise the increasing importance that Trots placed on anti-racism politics. During the early 1980s, black people had been predominant among those rioting in Brixton, Toxteth and Bristol. Here was a large group of people possibly in need of leadership who really understood oppression and injustice.

The ARA highlighted what it claimed to be a rapid increase in the number of racially motivated attacks in Britain, from 4,383 in 1988 to 7,780 three years later.[51] But within two years the ARA would be destroyed in a nasty internal battle over campaigning strategy between Ken Livingstone and Socialist Action on one side and Marc Wadsworth and his supporters on the other. The trigger was the most infamous racial murder since the war.

The murder of Stephen Lawrence, an 18-year-old black student, by a gang of white racists on 22 April 1993 was a shocking and seminal event. He was stabbed to death in an unprovoked attack near a bus stop in Well Hall Road near Shooter's Hill in south-east London. It later led to an inquiry by the judge Sir William Macpherson who strongly criticised the failure of detectives to bring the killers to justice and condemned 'institutionalised racism' within the Metropolitan Police.[52]

Marc Wadsworth, as national secretary of the ARA, contacted Stephen's parents, Doreen and Neville Lawrence, and played a significant role in bringing the tragedy to public attention. According to one BBC commentator later: Wadsworth was 'determined to present the Stephen Lawrence case differently, and to break through the indifference of the tabloid press towards black victims of racism'. Wadsworth highlighted the fact that Lawrence wanted to be an architect and that he had been law-abiding, diligent and respectful. 'We were saying to white society: "Stephen Lawrence was like you."'[53] Few people thought it a coincidence that the bookshop-cum-headquarters of the far right British National Party were in Welling, not far from where Lawrence died.

Wadsworth says he came under increased pressure from the Socialist Action contingent to use the Lawrence couple more aggressively in the ARA campaigns: 'They wanted complete control and the problem was how they were going to move that campaign along. Their primary aim was their sectarian battle with the SWP. They wanted to use the Lawrence campaign to trump the Anti-Nazi League.'[54] He says he told Socialist Action: 'We've got to have a much more softly-softly approach to this couple. They're not a pushover; not that I would want them to be. I'm black myself and a parent. You can't just use them as pawns.'

Racial tensions increased during 1993 and culminated on 17 September 1993 in the shock victory of the British National Party in a by-election for Millwall, a seat on Tower Hamlets Council in east London. The flash point came in October 1993 when the ANL and the ARA held rival protests on the same day. Wadsworth's 'crime' was to organise a peaceful anti-racist demo of 3,500 people for 16 October 1993 in central London after police consultation while 12 miles away up to 15,000 people attended a violent ANL demo at the BNP's bookshop. To make matters worse, Doreen Lawrence attended part of the ANL protest.[55]

It is clear that the Lawrence parents were becoming increasingly confused about being caught in the crossfire between the two groups. They had come to realise that the ANL was a 'front for the Socialist Workers Party'. Writing later, Doreen Lawrence said, '...the various groups that had taken an interest in Stephen's death were tearing each other apart and were in danger of destroying our campaign which we wanted to keep focused and dignified.'[56] In the end, Doreen and Neville Lawrence wrote to both the ANL and ARA to demand that they 'stop using Stephen's name'.[57]

Wadsworth claims that Ken Livingstone and Socialist Action now colluded to get rid of him because he would not do what they wanted. 'Socialist Action thought they could impose decisions on me including how we focused on the Stephen Lawrence campaign,' says Wadsworth. 'When I refused to go along with that they said, OK we're going to get rid of you.' Through late 1993 and early 1994, the ARA deteriorated rapidly.

A former Socialist Action member of the ARA insists Wadsworth's strategy was wrong, both in terms of the Lawrence campaign and towards the BNP by-election victory in the East End: 'The correct response was to have a demo in the East End and Marc didn't want to do that so he was increasingly separating himself out from the most important issues that were going on in racism in order to pursue his own things.'[58]

On 17 March 1994, Livingstone chaired a meeting of the ARA executive.[59] During the four-hour 'rowdy meeting' in a House of Commons office, Wadsworth threw a punch at Livingstone. He says: 'It was at one of these crazy meetings where he was making these rulings and telling me to shut up that I launched at him. I didn't actually hit him. I hit his hand. I was going to hit him. This had gone on for months and he treated me like a boy sitting next to him.'[60] At another meeting, on 30 March 1994, Livingstone and the Socialist Action contingent failed by only one vote to persuade the executive to dismiss Wadsworth on grounds of professional misconduct.[61]

The infighting continued for another six months as Livingstone and Socialist Action attempted to wrest control from Wadsworth. On 23 September 1994, the Anti-Racist Alliance issued the following statement: 'Ken Livingstone, supported by a faction called Socialist Action and a handful of unprincipled and unrepresentative members of the executive committee, has been waging a relentless campaign to sack the national secretary. This behaviour is undemocratic and has led to unnecessary divisions in the ARA which the chair has made even worse by his repeated attacks on national office staff.'[62]

'When they come for you they are incessant and they are like pit bulls,' Wadsworth says of Socialist Action. 'It's just incessant obsessive politicking.'

On 30 September 1994, Livingstone went to the High Court to determine voting rights for the delegates to the ARA's forth-coming annual meeting and an out-of-court settlement was reached. At the meeting on 15 October 1994, both Livingstone and Wadsworth stepped down; Wadsworth gave way to Kumar Murshid, a future Livingstone mayoral advisor on race but not a member of Socialist Action. Murshid walked away from the job after turning up at the ARA offices to find that Wadsworth had changed the locks.

The ARA collapsed rapidly after unions including the Trans-port and General Workers Union withdrew support. By February 1995, the National Assembly Against Racism, or NAAR, had been established largely by Socialist Action members, namely Red-mond O'Neill, Jude Woodward and Anne Kane.[63] Former mem-ber Atma Singh says that Socialist Action was so used to splits and sectarianism that 'breaking one organisation and creating a new one is nothing dramatic for them'.[64] Lee Jasper, who became Livingstone's senior mayoral policy advisor on equalities, was its first secretary. He had also been one of the few non Socialist Action opponents of Wadsworth on the ARA.

Today, the NAAR is one of Britain's biggest anti-racism groups with several subsidiary organisations, all supported strongly by Mayor Livingstone. Members of Socialist Action would continue to work closely with Livingstone throughout the 1990s. But they would come into their own when Livingstone became the first directly-elected mayor of London.

Notes

1   *Evening Standard*, 5.10.07
2   Ibid.
3   Internal Socialist Action paper, UW file no. mss.128.212
4   John Ross, *Thatcher and Friends, The Anatomy of the Tory Party*, Pluto Press, 1983
5   Interview, Ken Livingstone, 28.12.07
6   *Guardian*, 2.10.00

7   Resignation letter, John Marston, file no. mss128.212, 9.12.82, University of Warwick (UW); Interview, Keith Veness, 5.10.07
8   Document, 'The IMG is in crisis', 1982, UW file no. mss.128.229
9   Document, 'Jobs, jobs, jobs', UW file no. mss128.229, 11.11.82
10 Resignation letter, John Marston, 9.12.82, file no. mss128.212
11 Document, December 1982 conference, UW file no. mss128.229
12 Document, Socialist League/Socialist Action central committee, UW file no. mss128.129
13 Agenda, Socialist League, launch of Socialist Action, 22/23.1.83, UW file no.mss128.129
14 Letter from Phil Hearse, Socialist Challenge, February 1983, UW file no. mss.128.212
15 Document, by 'Roberts' for January 1983 plenum central committee, appendix 2, 16.1.83, UW file no. mss128.212
16 Document, central committee, 14.3.83, UW file no. mss128.212
17 Document, Socialist Action, 1982, UW file no. mss128.229
18 Document, Socialist Action, 2.11.82, UW file no. mss128.229
19 Ibid.
20 Document, Socialist Action central committee mailing, 'The Leadership battle in the Labour Party,' p5, 1983, UW file no.mss128.212
21 Michael Crick, *Militant*, pp190-191
22 Document, information bulletin, 'For members and sympathisers only', July 1985, UW file no. mss128.230
23 Document, 'The dissolution of the public face,' by 'Roberts', 17.11.83, UW file no. mss128.212
24 Document, internal Socialist Action memo, 11.11.83, UW file no. mss128.212
25 Document, 'Practical implementation of the new security measures in the centre,' 1983-1984, UW file no. mss128.247
26 Ibid.
27 Ibid.
28 Ibid.
29 Document, 'The new cleaning rota, The office', 2.1.84, UW file no. mss128.247
30 Interview, Atma Singh, 29.1.08
31 Ibid.
32 Author interviews
33 Document, central committee report, 6/7.11.82, UW file no. mss128.229
34 Document, central committee report, 22.1.83, UW file no. mss128.212
35 Interview, Atma Singh, 27.1.08
36 *News Line*, 24.11.84, p8
37 Document, central committee report, circa October 1986
38 Interview, Ken Livingstone, 25.10.07
39 Interview, Reg Race, 23.8.07; See Chapter 15
40 Interview, Ken Livingstone, 25.10.07
41 Interview, Atma Singh, 27.1.08
42 Ibid.
43 Letter to all participating organisations in the LLC, from Jenny Fisher, Socialist Viewpoint

44 Letter, John Ross to Marc Wadsworth, 15.3.86
45 *Sunday Times*, 8.3.87
46 *The Times*, 14.4.07
47 *The Voice*, 9.10.90
48 Interview, Marc Wadsworth, 1.10.07
49 Tony Benn, *Free at Last, Diaries 1991–2001*, Arrow Books, 2003, (see 15.1.92)
50 Ibid., (see 29.1.92)
51 *Guardian*, 20.2.93
52 Stephen Lawrence Inquiry, by Sir William Macpherson of Cluny, February 1999
53 BBC News Online, article by Nick Higham, 19.2.99 (http://news.bbc.co.uk/1/hi/special_report/1999/02/99/stephen_lawrence/282378.stm)
54 Interview, Marc Wadsworth, 1.10.07
55 *Sunday Times*, 24.10.93
56 Doreen Lawrence, *And Still I Rise, Seeking Justice for Stephen*, Faber and Faber, 2006, p117
57 Ibid.
58 Off-the-record briefing, December 2007
59 *Evening Standard*, 31.3.94
60 Interview, Marc Wadsworth, 1.10.07
61 *Evening Standard*, 31.3.94
62 *Guardian*, 24.9.94
63 Interview, Marc Wadsworth, 19.1.08
64 Interview, Atma Singh, 27.1.08

Chapter 19

The life and times of Ernold Same, 1990–1998

There was no disguising Neil Kinnock's joy at Livingstone's ejection from the NEC on 3 October 1989. One aide said the Labour leader was 'doing cartwheels' in his office.[1] When Kinnock did appear, it was to jauntily observe: 'I would not have voted for him and Ken knows that.'[2] Coming on the same day that Labour abandoned its policy on unilateral nuclear disarmament, Gerald Kaufman, the party's foreign affairs spokesman, described Livingstone's demise as 'the cherry on the ice cream sundae'.[3] According to 'left-wing allies' Livingstone planned to stand for the leadership if Labour lost the next election.[4] His plans lay in ruins but that would not prevent him in the years ahead from making two hapless attempts at the Labour leadership.

Livingstone would have to endure another decade of Parliament before his triumphant return to the centre stage as London's first directly-elected mayor in 2000. During those years, Livingstone witnessed the fall of Margaret Thatcher, the defeat of Neil Kinnock in the election of 1992, Britain's disastrous forced withdrawal from the Exchange Rate Mechanism on 'Black Wednesday', 16 September 1992, the death of John Smith less than two years later and the coming of New Labour under Tony Blair as the party moved further to the right leaving him, Tony Benn and the others beached on the hard left, either ignored, or worse, patronised with bemused affection or weary resignation. 'He really hasn't done very well in Parliament,' observed the *Evening Standard* of Livingstone in 1991. 'He makes the wrong speech at the wrong time on the wrong subject'[5]

For an ambitious politician like Livingstone who loves wielding power and running things, it was an intensely frustrating period, but he kept himself busy during his wilderness years. In 1989, he published a book setting out his thoughts and hopes for a new decade, *Livingstone's Labour, A Programme for the Nineties.* John Ross received special thanks from Livingstone for assembling both the economic database used in the book and much of the material dealing with international relations.[6] Help also came from his old Chartist friend, the anthropologist Chris Knight, who allowed access to his work on early civilisations, and Neil Grant, the chairman of the Brent East Labour Party, who carried out detailed research on the allegations of Colin Wallace and Fred Holroyd.

Dedicated to his partner Kate Allen, *Livingstone's Labour* runs to almost 300 pages and it would be an injustice to attempt a detailed summary in a few paragraphs here. The book reiterated his views on Ireland, Parliament, the USA, the economy and the way ahead for Labour, concluding with calls for a greater redistribution of wealth and the 'breaking up of the great, unaccountable concentrations of power both here and internationally... We must entwine democracy and socialism so they become inseparable. In doing this we will change the nature and potential of both in ways that we can only just begin to glimpse. Once such a process starts it will be irreversible. Without such a process I doubt it will be possible for humankind to survive on this planet for much more than another lifetime.'[7]

HarperCollins was the original publisher but pulled out. Livingstone claimed this was 'on the grounds that it was offensive to Rupert Murdoch'.[8] Unwin Hyman stepped in to rescue the project. But two years later, to many people's astonishment, Livingstone was hired by Murdoch to write a column for the *Sun* newspaper which had once described him as 'the most odious man in Britain'.[9] Following the rancorous Wapping printers' dispute between January 1986 and February 1987, Neil Kinnock and other Labour Party politicians had boycotted journalists from Murdoch's News International stable of newspapers including the *Sun*. Four years later, by the time he employed Livingstone, Murdoch remained a left hate figure.

First published on 3 October 1991, Livingstone's *Sun* column was a cause for angst among left-wingers in his Brent East constituency, including Pete Firmin. 'People weren't happy about him writing in the *Sun*; it didn't go down that well,' says Firmin. He adds: 'Ken isn't very good at working with critical friends – not very good at all. Ken prefers sycophants. There were quite a lot of us who were quite prepared to give Ken as much support as we could when we agreed with him and when we didn't, we would say so.'[10]

The *Sun* provided Livingstone with important extra income which helped to fund his developing interest in economics under the guidance of John Ross. In 1989, when taking out a mortgage for the home he shared with Kate Allen in Ivy Road in Cricklewood, he factored in the money he would need to buy Ross a computer which he could use to analyse economic data. Only Livingstone could have taken money from Murdoch and used it to help fund leading members of a discreet Trotskyist faction! Livingstone paid £25,000, an astronomical sum for a computer in 2008 let alone in the late 1980s. He says, 'At the time, when we bought it, the guy selling it said, "I don't know of any other computer of this size in private hands in Britain."'[11]

◆

In October 1987, Ross[12] had also introduced Livingstone to Redmond O'Neill, another key figure in Socialist Action,[13] who was very involved in Irish politics. Gradually, Livingstone came into contact with more of Ross's and Redmond's associates. In 1992, Livingstone met Simon Fletcher,[14] then 24, who was going out with a reporter on the local *Willesden and Brent Chronicle*.[15] Fletcher was also a close associate of Redmond O'Neill and one of his supporters on the ill-fated Anti-Racist Alliance; he had also worked as a researcher for Tony Benn in 1991. That made Fletcher a 'Teabag,' as Benn would describe his researchers, or a member of The Eminent Association of Benn Archive Graduates.[16] Fletcher would later serve as Livingstone's chief of staff for eight years – to all keen observers and for all intents and purposes, the mayor's deputy, his closest confidant, his shadow and his best friend.[17] He also became involved with Socialist Action.

Livingstone says, 'When I entered Parliament, the objective was to become prime minister and I set out to work with John Ross on economic policy, getting on the NEC and fighting Kinnock's policy review, building links with the trade unions, and the people I assembled and started to work with, had I become party leader, would have come into government.'[18]

Another constant fixture in Livingstone's political life was Maureen Charleson, who became his secretary in 1987 when he entered Parliament for the first time. On hiring Charleson, he told her, 'You'll never do another job interview.'[19] Twenty years later, she is still Livingstone's secretary and the Socialist Action triumvirate of Ross, O'Neill and Fletcher are still his closest aides.

◆

In March 1990, armed with their big new computer, Livingstone and Ross launched the *Socialist Economic Bulletin*, priced at £5.[20] According to Livingstone, the goal was nothing less than to make the Labour Party 'literate in economics for the first time in its history'.[21] After all, no aspiring Labour leader could afford to be ignorant of economics. To some, Livingstone seemed to talk of nothing but economics. 'He is obsessed with economics,' wrote Lynn Barber. 'In fact he talked so much about it that I eventually wailed, "This is terribly boring – can't you talk about gay rights or Ireland or something?"'[22]

According to the *Guardian's* coverage of the *Bulletin's* launch: 'Mr Livingstone believes Labour will win the next election, but to prevent a rerun of the debacles of the 1960s and 1970s he needs to do more than merely keep its head below the parapet.' Livingstone stressed that a new Labour government 'should take advantage of the end of the Cold War to reduce defence spending to the average European level, thereby releasing £9 billion for public investment such as training and education.'[23] The *Bulletin*, which would run for the next nine and a half years, was primarily funded by Livingstone and printed by the Socialist Action presses at Lithoprint in Hackney. Livingstone's financial support also proved important for Socialist Action during the 1990s. He had provided not only John Ross with the computer necessary for their joint economic project in educating the Labour Party but also work for the printers in Shacklewell Lane. 'Socialist Action makes itself indispensable,' says a former close associate of Livingstone and Ross. 'They got money because Ken used to put thousands into *Economic Bulletin* – it was printed by Lithoprint. He must have put in tens of thousands of pounds.'[24]

In the period until the general election in April 1992, Livingstone primarily made the news with his opposition to the Desert Storm operation against Iraq in January 1991, one of 55 Labour MPs to defy Kinnock and oppose the war.[25] He also refused to pay the Poll Tax on principle. He made several appearances at magistrates' court for failing to pay a bill of £470.[26] In July 1991, the Militant MP for Liverpool Broadgreen, Terry Fields, was sentenced to 60 days in jail by Bootle magistrates for failing to pay his bill of £373. Two weeks later, Livingstone and three other hard left MPs visited Fields in his small tiled cell in Walton prison to show solidarity. Within two months, Fields was expelled by the Labour Party, which felt that 'lawmakers cannot be lawbreakers'.[27] Livingstone received threatening letters from bailiffs John Crilley and Son and eventually paid up, as he said he would, once the Tories had agreed to scrap the tax.[28]

◆

On Thursday, 9 April 1992, Labour suffered a traumatic defeat at the polls; John Major had won by a slim overall majority of 21. Five days later, Kinnock and his deputy Roy Hattersley announced their intention to resign. John Smith was the obvious heir apparent.[29] Ken Livingstone announced his intention to stand as leader. Tony Benn spoke to Livingstone at the weekend after the defeat. 'I think he's going to stand for leadership,' wrote Benn, 'but I don't think he can get the votes.'[30] Benn was right. Livingstone failed even to get the support of most of the Socialist Campaign MPs but he did get the backing of the *Sun* which realised he did not have a hope of winning.

Livingstone announced his candidature on Thursday, 16 April 1992[31] and demanded a rethink of Smith's economic policies, making it clear at a press conference that he blamed the shadow chancellor for the election defeat. Smith's well-publicised attempts at 'cuddling up to the system over endless prawn cocktails' in meals with business leaders had failed,[32] He added, 'We lost this election because we promised to make anyone earning over £21,000 pay more tax.'[33] But few people thought Livingstone would get the necessary 20 per cent of the PLP or 55 of the 271 MPs he needed in order to go before the leadership electoral college scheduled for 18 July 1992. Five days later, on 21 April 1992, Bernie Grant, the black 48-year-old MP for Tottenham, announced he would be standing as deputy leader alongside Livingstone on an agenda of unilateral disarmament, defence cuts and currency devaluation to take Labour back to its socialist roots.[34] Grant was a controversial and colourful cricket-loving doyen of the Left who campaigned against racism and police harassment of ethnic minorities.

But the election split the Socialist Campaign Group, now reduced to a rump of around 34 hard left MPs. At the group's meeting on 27 April 1992, Audrey Wise, the MP for Preston and mother of former GLC Women's Committee chair Valerie Wise, announced she would be switching her support from Livingstone to another candidate – Ann Clwyd. Another MP, Alan Simpson, said, 'We should not put up a candidate unless we've nominated [Dennis] Skinner or Benn.' Yet another, Alice Mahon, said no left candidate should be fielded. According to Tony Benn, Bernie Grant 'absolutely blew his top' and started swearing, at which point two women MPs walked out.[35]

The following day witnessed the humiliation of Livingstone's and Grant's hopes. Grant got 15 votes and Livingstone a meagre 13, including his own and that of Bernie Grant.[36] This compared to the 162 secured by John Smith, and the 63 for Bryan Gould. Smith went on to secure an overwhelming victory over Gould with 90.9 per cent of the electoral college votes. Margaret Beckett won the deputy leadership with 56.8 per cent.[37]

Harry Cohen, one of those MPs who voted for Livingstone, believes many of his colleagues mistrusted the former GLC leader or resented his apparent self-sufficiency: 'I think he was a bit of a loner and that led to him being badly misjudged, because a lot of MPs are loners. So what? Gordon Brown's a loner!' Cohen found Livingstone's well-resourced economics machine with the computer and the *Socialist Economic Bulletin* 'remarkable'. 'As an MP, you get a bit of an allowance but it wouldn't be enough for that,' says Cohen. 'I just thought there was some support [for Livingstone] out there. I thought maybe there were groups out there who wanted to put out an alternative economic view.'[38] Cohen had not heard about Socialist Action's support of Livingstone.

◆

Livingstone's new-found economics knowledge gave him the confidence to speak out on the biggest issue of the day: the Exchange Rate Mechanism, or ERM. During 1991, he made repeated calls for sterling to be devalued within the ERM so there could be a cut in Britain's high interest rates, then hovering around 10 per cent.[39] John Smith and his new shadow chancellor Gordon Brown had both been enthusiastic supporters of ERM entry as the necessary precursor to the introduction of the Euro, as well as ratification of the controversial Maastricht Treaty which laid the foundations for economic and monetary union.

But Livingstone proved to be right. Sterling was pegged to the

Deutschmark but ultimately, this could only be sustained by high interest rates. Throughout the summer of 1992, Brown had taken a hard public line that Britain should not devalue or engage in agreed realignment as demanded by Livingstone.[40] Realising that the pound was vastly overvalued, the currency speculators struck on Black Wednesday by borrowing sterling and then selling it for Deutschmarks. They hoped to force the British government to devalue sterling so they could then repay their debt with devalued pounds and pocket the difference. The government tried to tempt speculators away from this course of action by raising interest rates from 10 to 12 per cent and then again during the day to a ruinous 15 per cent, before finally conceding defeat and leaving the ERM. Interest rates went down to 12 per cent. It was a disaster for John Major's government from which it never recovered; the Bank of England lost hundreds of millions of pounds. The Tories' poll rating dropped from 43 per cent to 29 per cent in the following weeks.[41] Livingstone continued to argue against rejoining the ERM, stating the case for 20 per cent devaluation and a further two per cent cut in interest rates.[42]

'I must say,' observed Tony Benn in December 1992, 'Ken is very active. He has a column in the *Sun*, which he uses to finance his *Economic Bulletin* and his trips to America for the presidential election and he has been to Russia twice this year. He is involved in the Anti-Racist Alliance and he is building up a movement on Europe, on socialism and on race.'[43]

Livingstone's interest in Russia was also fuelled by John Ross who had gone to work in Moscow in the summer of 1992 to advise trade unions.[44] Ross would spend the next eight years in Russia before answering Livingstone's call for help in his first mayoral election as an independent.[45] Both men managed to maintain their partnership, despite the distance. Livingstone says: 'With the Internet and email and all that, he was doing all my questions to John Major and my articles on the economy.'[46] Ross's contacts on Moscow later paid huge dividends when it came to winning the Olympic Games for London in 2005.[47]

◆

On 12 May 1994, John Smith suffered his second massive heart attack and died. Despite his views on Smith's economic policies, Livingstone had liked Smith. The Labour leader had made attempts to soothe the feelings of the declining left after the bruising years of Kinnock's rule. Larry Whitty, former general secretary of the Labour Party told Smith's biographer Mark Stuart: 'I remember John saying, "I've got to get away from this business of treating people like outcasts." John even had a good word to say about Ken Livingstone.'[48]

Again, Livingstone threw his hat into the ring for the leadership but if anything, this second bid was even more of a fiasco than the first. During May and June 1994, Livingstone flipped and flopped from one position to another to the exasperation of his Socialist Campaign Group colleagues. According to Benn on 15 June 1994, 'He announced that he was going to be a candidate before the Campaign Group met, then later he said he was going to vote for [Margaret] Beckett; then he announced that he was a candidate and Jeremy Corbyn [MP for Islington North] was his running mate without telling Jeremy Corbyn, then today he withdrew on the grounds that he couldn't get any nominations.'[49] Livingstone's old GLC comrade Tony Banks thought only Skinner and Benn could get the support of the group's 34 members. 'Ken has completely blown it and it's pointless now,' he said.[50]

Tony Blair quickly emerged as the clear favourite and was duly elected leader on 21 July 1994 with 57 per cent of the vote. John Prescott was chosen as his deputy. Ken Livingstone told the press he thought Blair would be 'the most right-wing leader' in Labour's history.[51] It was the opening salvo in Livingstone's eight-year war on the New Labour project.

There was a slight backlash at the 1994 conference in Blackpool when Livingstone narrowly missed getting back on to the party's ruling NEC. In fact he polled more votes than one victor, the Hackney North and Stoke Newington MP, Diane Abbot, but had to cede his seat to her under Labour Party rules as the woman who gained the second biggest poll in the elections. Dennis Skinner was the second left-winger to be elected, winning back the seat he lost the previous year.[52] At the conference, Blair's spin meister Peter Mandelson, the MP for Hartlepool, denounced left-wingers like Arthur Scargill and Livingstone as 'the enemy' for undermining the new leader's attempts to modernise the party. Livingstone responded: 'There must be something really tragic that happened to him in his childhood, but I am so used to his views I am prepared to forgive him his bitter little asides and I hope he will get better soon.'[53]

◆

During the first months of 1995, Livingstone fought a losing battle against Blair's attempts to rewrite one of the Labour Party's great socialist totems, Clause Four, promising to secure for workers 'the common ownership of the means of production, distribution and exchange'. New Labour considered the Clause Four pledge to nationalise industry an embarrassment and plotted to replace it with something more appealing to the middle class. But the bare text of Clause Four mattered much less than the symbolism.

However, Livingstone and other left-wingers considered the suggested rewording with its woolly assurances of a 'common endeavour' and placing wealth, power and opportunity 'in the hands of many' a betrayal of Labour's socialist ideals. On 29 April 1995, a special Labour Party conference voted to abandon the old Clause Four by 65 per cent to 35 per cent. Writing in the *Sunday Times*, Andrew Grice, the paper's chief political correspondent closely observed the three members of the party's unholy trinity: Tony Benn sat 'sullen and silent'; Arthur Scargill was 'hissed and slow hand-clapped; Livingstone 'avoided the delegates' by sitting with the media. 'Yesterday,' added Grice, 'the loony left became the lonely left.' When the Clause Four decision was ratified by the 1995 conference in Brighton, Benn said, 'The Left has been obliterated with the abandonment of Clause Four.'[54] Within four months of the conference, Scargill announced his resignation from the party to establish the Socialist Labour Party.[55] Not very much has been heard of either since. The Socialist Campaign Group became sidelined and ignored; eventually, the soft left Tribune group withered on the vine completely.[56]

Ken Livingstone's career as a celebrity seemed to grow in direct proportion to his increasing political irrelevancy and largely because of it. Advertisers had long since earmarked Livingstone's potential and in 1989 the firm D'Arcy Masius Benton and Bowles hired him on behalf of the National Dairy Council to help sell cheese.[57] Livingstone promoted Red Leicester while Ted Heath agreed to push Blue Cheshire.[58] Later in 1989, Saatchi and Saatchi hired Livingstone and Edwina Currie, sacked as a junior minister the previous year for making indiscreet comments about salmonella in eggs, for a new advertisement for the miners' strike victors – British Coal. The two politicians' initial frosty greeting was softened by a combination of a traditional coal fire and a rendition of the song 'Strangers in the Night'.[59]

Livingstone says the celebrity-endorsement aspect came more to the fore as he ceased to be a political force: '... [from] the moment I was kicked off Labour's NEC in 1989, so all my plotting towards being prime minister died, I ceased to be a threat and then the media work started to come in. They started to use me only once they thought I was harmless. The *Sun* wouldn't have given me a regular column until they thought I was harmless. So there was this period of really intense media oppression right through the 1980s on poor old me. Then right the way through the 1990s, it was decided that I was just this colourful local character – so [it was a case of] "stick him on this" and "stick him on that".'[60]

The media maintained his profile, boosted his popularity and even absorbed him more into popular culture. This process had been started back in his GLC days by the satirists of *Private Eye* and the TV programme *Spitting Image*, where his dummy's voice was provided by the comic Harry Enfield,[61] but he had always been given a hint of Leninspart menace. Now, Livingstone gained yet another persona – 'cuddly Ken', friend of gossip columnists, TV producers and colour supplements. It would prove essential when he came to fight the first mayoral election as an independent against the New Labour machine in 2000. 'In those long years between gainful employment,' says Livingstone, 'that was the only thing that keeps you in the public eye. If people can see you and see you're human, it helps.'[62] With seven appearances in total so far, Livingstone became one of the most regular faces on the popular BBC television news quiz *Have I Got News For You?* He was also hired to write food columns for *Esquire* and then the *Evening Standard* magazine. It helped supplement his girth as well as his income.

In early 1990, the BBC's *Comic Strip Presents* series did a spoof Hollywood makeover of Livingstone's County Hall: *GLC: The Carnage Continues*. The comic actor Robbie Coltrane played the silver screen tough guy Charles Bronson as Livingstone with Leslie Phillips of *Carry On* fame as a strikingly credible Sir Horace Cutler.[63] In 1995, Damon Albarn, lead singer of the Britpop band Blur, asked Livingstone to narrate in a monotonous drone his song, 'Ernold Same', about a lonely man living out a life of work and tedium in the rat race:

> *On his way to the same place*
> *With the same name*
> *To do the same thing*
> *Again and again and again*
> *Poor old Ernold Same*

Livingstone has performed the song live twice with Blur with a relish and enthusiasm which would have made his mother proud.

◆

A company called Localaction Ltd was established by Livingstone to receive his outside earnings. In late 1994, it was reported that by combining both his cheques for media work and advertising and his MP's salary of £31,687, he was earning £7,000 a year more than the prime minister.[64] During the course of the 1992/1993 financial year, Livingstone earned more than £53,500 on top of his MP's pay.[65] He was exploiting a legal loophole which allowed him to avoid paying a higher rate of income tax on some of his earnings. The money was paid into Localaction and then out again to Livingstone not as a taxable salary, but as a 'loan'. Money spent on 'allowable expenses' was also deducted and a corporation tax of 25 per cent instead of the higher rate of 40 per cent was paid on the remainder. 'I just do what the accountant says,' Livingstone said at the time. 'It's all perfectly legal.' So it was. But later Livingstone would blunder by failing to declare some of his outside earnings; that failure, based on a genuine misunderstanding of parliamentary rules, would be used six years later in a series of Labour Party smears to prevent him becoming mayor.

◆

During the 1990s, Livingstone's image changed. Out went the shiny cheap slacks and safari jackets. He was now more tastefully attired, thanks to professional advice. In 1992, style consultant Diane Miller revealed Livingstone as one of her clients. 'He looks less like a salesman now,' she said tactfully.[66] In September 1995, he shaved off his trademark moustache. Peter Mandelson, who had recently done the same, waspishly remarked that it was 'a good career move'.[67]

Livingstone lived quietly at his house in Cricklewood with Kate Allen, his partner since 1980. Like Livingstone, she was intensely private about her personal life and has always refused to discuss her 20-year relationship with him. After the GLC, she worked for the Refugee Council where she headed the evacuation programmes for Bosnia (1995) and Kosovo (1999), two nasty Balkan conflicts where Livingstone demanded military intervention on humanitarian grounds. In 1998/99, she was seconded to the Home Office to work on the 1999 Immigration and Asylum Act. By the time of her split with Livingstone in 2001, she was the UK director of Amnesty International.

Despite their privacy, Livingstone provided a reliable supply of titbits about his home life, particularly his garden's pond life, to diary columns and features editors. There were not too many people who remained ignorant of Livingstone's slimy menagerie of a salamander, seven Manchurian toads and an Australian tree frog.[68] People read with fascination about what his edible French frogs got up to in the pond he built for them.[69] When developers endangered 30,000 rare great crested newts by threatening to fill in the disused Orton brick pits situated in John Major's Huntingdon constituency, Livingstone supported a campaign to save them. Writing in the *Independent*, he said: 'This is a tragedy. To sit on the edge of a pond and watch the gentle courtship of the great crested newt is still one of the most wonderful moments for any nature watcher… The thought that one day children will no longer be able to watch this beautiful display leaves me feeling very sad and depressed.'[70] It was always a great source of pride to Livingstone to be made a vice president of the London Zoological Society in 1996/97.

◆

By early 1996, it was becoming clear that Labour was likely to win the next general election; the stench of putrefaction emanating from the Tory benches was overpowering. The 'back to basics' sleaze scandals which began in earnest in early 1994 showed few signs of abating, and at one stage, a despairing Norman Tebbit grabbed the ex-GLC leader by the lapels and said, 'When are you going to get rid of this government?'[71] Livingstone had named one of his toads Norman, after Tebbit, because he 'only comes out at night and is very poisonous'.[72] But in reality the two were unlikely parliamentary friends.[73]

During the gathering dusk of the Tories' hegemony, Livingstone continued to antagonise the New Labour leadership. In May 1996, he called on Blair to fire Alastair Campbell after a High Court judge had criticised the spin doctor during the course of a libel trial. 'I would expect Tony Blair to dismiss Mr Campbell without delay,' declared Livingstone. 'He [Blair] is surrounding himself with inward-looking characters, who manipulate access to the leader. Campbell has to go.'[74] Writing in the *News of the World* in September 1996, Livingstone warned about the growing power of the spin doctors: 'We need to think back to the recent past and remember the attempt by the Militant Tendency to take over the Labour Party by infiltrating it from below.

'This new model army of Oxbridge-educated spotty spin doctors are in many ways doing just the same thing, except they are planning to take over the Labour Party from above.'[75] He mirrored the warnings by Clare Short about 'the people who live in the dark'.[76] He described this 'army' as the 'Millbank Tendency' and his concern about their activities would be confirmed when it turned on him.

In December 1996, he rubbished a new code of conduct for Labour MPs, widely seen as a Blair device to bring recalcitrants to heel, describing it as 'unbelievably crass'.[77] In the month leading up to the 1997 election, he repeatedly attacked Blair and his entourage, at one point claiming that through his reforms of the Labour Party, Blair was concentrating all the power in his own hands.[78] Bizarrely, just before the election, Livingstone displayed an unlikely talent for sycophancy, telling the press: 'I believe that Tony Blair will turn out to be our best prime minister since Clement Attlee. His reforms are here to stay. He has replaced sterile division within the party with genuine consultation and debate.'[79] But he still continued to warn of the threat posed by the sinister 'Millbank Tendency'.

As for Blair at this time, he had long held a low opinion of Livingstone dating back to Labour troubles in the early 1980s, despite his support for Fares Fair.[80] In early 1983, Blair had travelled to County Durham to help out in the by-election on 28 March in Darlington, a seat bordering his own constituency, Sedgefield. He said later, 'I remember canvassing in the Darlington by-election and getting the antics of the London Labour Party thrown in my face.' In a pointed reference to Livingstone, whom he was then desperately trying to prevent from becoming mayor, Blair described the London party as 'a byword for extremism and gesture rainbow politics'[81]; it was alleged later that the Labour leader was 'fascinated' by Livingstone.[82]

Fascinated perhaps, but by the time of his huge landslide victory on 1 May 1997, there is little evidence that Blair needed to be concerned about Livingstone. The MP for Brent East had long been thought of as a shot bolt. Shortly before the election, along with the actor Charles Dance, Livingstone's head was removed and placed in cold storage while his body was recycled.[83] Of course, it was only his wax likeness but many considered Madame Tussaud's as the final arbiter of who was in or out and few could disagree with its dispatch of Livingstone. The museum was wise to keep the head in storage; it would soon be needed again.

Notes

1   *Sunday Times*, 8.10.89
2   *The Times*, 3.10.89
3   *Sunday Times*, 8.10.89
4   Ibid.
5   *Evening Standard*, 22.7.91
6   Ken Livingstone, *Livingstone's Labour, A Programme for the Nineties*, Unwin Hyman, 1989, pviii
7   Ibid., pp295-296
8   Ibid.
9   See Chapter 12
10 Interview, Pete Firmin, 30.7.07
11 Interview, Ken Livingstone, 28.12.07
12 Ibid., 1.11.07
13 See Chapter 18
14 Interview, Ken Livingstone, 8.11.07
15 Ibid.
16 Tony Benn, *Free at Last, Diaries 1991-200,1* (see 11.4.91)
17 Off-the-record interviews, 2007/08
18 Interview, Ken Livingstone, 28.12.07
19 Ibid.
20 *Guardian*, 17.3.90
21 Ibid.
22 *Independent on Sunday,* the Lynn Barber interview, 21.6.92
23 Ibid.
24 Author interview, October 2007
25 *The Times*, 16.1.91
26 *Guardian*, 11.1.91; *The Times*, 13.3.91
27 BBC News Online, (http://news.bbc.co.uk/onthisday/hi/dates/stories/july/11/newsid_2500000/2500365.stm)
28 *Evening Standard*, 21.4.93
29 Mark Stuart, *John Smith, A Life*, pp224-227
30 Tony Benn, *Free at Last, Diaries 1991–2001,* (see 12.4.92)
31 Agence France Presse, 16.4.92

32 Reuters, 16.4.92
33 Mark Stuart, *John Smith, A Life*, p207; *Independent*, 16.4.92
34 Reuters, 21.4.92
35 Tony Benn, *Free at Last, Diaries 1991–2001*, (see 27.4.92)
36 *Guardian*, full election results, 30.4.92
37 Mark Stuart, *John Smith, A Life*, p236
38 Interview, Harry Cohen, 19.11.07
39 Reuters News, 8.3.91; *Financial Times*, 25.7.91
40 Mark Stuart, *John Smith, A Life*, pp255-259
41 Gallup, October, 1992
42 *Guardian*, 19.9.92
43 Tony Benn, *Free at Last, Diaries 1991–2001*, (see 2.12.92)
44 Ibid., referring to Tony Benn's discussion with John Ross on 14.7.92
45 Interview Ken Livingstone, 8.11.07
46 Ibid.
47 Ibid.
48 Mark Stuart, *John Smith, A Life*, p245
49 Tony Benn, *Free at Last, Diaries 1991–2001*, (see 15.6.94)
50 Ibid.
51 *Guardian*, 7.6.94
52 *Independent*, 4.10.94
53 *Independent*, 6.10.94
54 Tony Benn, *Diaries, Free at Last, Diaries 1991–2001*
55 *Observer*, 14.1.96
56 Interview, Ken Livingstone, 28.12.07
57 *Marketing*, 9.3.89
58 *Campaign*, 10.3.89
59 *Guardian*, 27.7.89
60 Interview, Ken Livingstone, 1.11.07
61 *Independent*, 9.11.99
62 Ibid.
63 *Daily Mail*, 'GLC: Carnage continues', 17.2.90, (first broadcast 15.2.90 and partially available on YouTube)
64 *Observer*, 11.12.94
65 Ibid., and Companies House returns
66 *Financial Times*, 15.6.92
67 *Times*, 8.9.95
68 *Daily Mail*, 24.4.90
69 *Evening Standard*, 12.5.93
70 *Independent*, 15.7.95
71 Interview, Ken Livingstone, 1.11.07
72 *Sun*, 27.11.99
73 Interview, Ken Livingstone, 28.12.07
74 *Sunday Times*, 5.5.96
75 *News of the World*, 29.9.96
76 *New Statesman*, 8.8.96
77 *Independent*, 5.12.96
78 *Sunday Times*, 12.1.97

79 *Observer*, 6.4.97
80 See Chapter 9
81 John Rentoul, *Tony Blair, Prime Minister*, (citing *Observer* interview with Blair carried on 21.11.99)
82 James Naughtie, *The Rivals: The Intimate Story of a Political Marriage*, Fourth Estate, 2002
83 *Independent*, 30.12.96

Chapter 20

Smear we go again! May 1997–November 1999

If Margaret Thatcher rescued Ken Livingstone by deciding to abolish the Greater London Council, then it is equally true to say that Tony Blair performed the same role more than a decade later by deciding to establish a new metropolitan system of government for London. Both prime ministers used all the power at their disposal to crush Livingstone and both prime ministers lived to rue the day.

By the time of Blair's victory, London had been muddling by without its own capital-wide government for 11 years. In its place, a quangocracy had grown up – bodies of indeterminate powers and responsibilities. In 1993, it was estimated that there were no fewer than 272 'appointed' bodies in London devouring roughly £6 billion of taxpayers' money a year.[1] Even where common sense dictated there should be a body with London-wide powers, such as strategic planning, up would pop some fudge in the form of an appointed body, in this case the London Planning Advisory Committee, or LPAC, which had no statutory power to plan anything and whose advice could be simply ignored, and regularly was.

Through boneheaded intransigence, the Conservatives still insisted London was unique among the capitals of western Europe in not needing its own government, despite all the evidence to the contrary. 'There is no such thing as a voice for London.'[2] Thatcher's words to her backbenchers during the GLC abolition saga had long become a petulant mantra for a group of Tory politicians who were then more intent on tearing each other apart like wild beasts on Europe and other issues than admitting they had made a mistake in getting rid of metropolitan government for London. Instead of a voice, the capital was given a discordant frogs' chorus with conductors in the form of unelected civil servants at the Government Office of London, or GOL.[3] What had been sold to the public as devolvement of power down to the more accountable 32 boroughs had in fact been a blatant centralisation of power by the government. In 1992, alongside GOL and its 300 staff, the government set up a cabinet subcommittee for London chaired by the secretary of state for the environment.[4] Nowhere was this bankruptcy of political vision more obvious than at County Hall itself which went from beating heart of London democracy to white elephant faster than you can say 'Millennium Dome'.

◆

By 1995, County Hall was a rotting husk providing only poign-ant images for newspaper feature writers. 'Peer through one of its 3,000 windows and the scene is one of dust and decay,' wrote Paul Valley in the *Independent*. 'Deep holes, long abandoned, have been dug through the floors of those of its 1,200 rooms that are visible from the riverside. Its 12 miles of corridor serve no purpose other than to exercise the dogs of its security guards. Empty papers blow around the courtyards…'[5] Given the choice of ill-deserved absolution by selling the building to the London School of Economics rather than the Japanese Shirayama hotel chain, the Major government surprised no one by opting for the latter. Central London gained yet another luxury hotel while one of the country's finest universities remained in cramped accom-modation in Aldwych. 'I have nothing against the Japanese,' observed animal lover and former GLC chairman Tony Banks, 'except when they buy County Hall and kill whales.'[6]

By the time of its abolition, the GLC was providing very few direct services to the populace. The government had effectively renationalised the Tube and Horace Cutler had transferred much of the GLC's housing stock to the London boroughs in the late 1970s. 'A degree of mythology grew up around the now absent Greater London Council,' wrote Professor Tony Travers later. 'Its abolition was blamed for a variety of urban ills.'[7] Various academic reports highlighted the growing malaise in London, a capital city which was slowly de-populating and getting grubbier by the day. A report by the academics Keith Boyfield and Professor William Letwin, 'A Minister for London: A Capital Concept', was com-missioned by Shirley Porter, the leader of Westminster Council, to promote her own doomed bid to get into government.

Published in April 1990, the report highlighted an education system in decline, increased burglary and vagrancy: 'Living and working in London is increasingly painful, tending towards the brutish.'[8] After abolition, the roads and council houses were still repaired, and the Tube still clattered along and through a decaying infrastructure. What was missing was a real voice for the capital. London businessmen attempted to fill the vacuum by establishing the London First organisation in 1994 for the promotion and improvement of London,[9] and began campaigning for a world-class transport system and a fortification of the capital's skills base. But, as well-intentioned as they were, no one had voted for the City types on the board of London First. Nothing could make up for the obvious 'democratic deficit' in the decision-making affecting the lives of more than seven million Londoners.

Many people overlook the Tories' key blunder in getting rid of the GLC; it effectively wiped the slate clean for any other political party wanting to establish a new body in its own image and on its own terms. During the 1980s, Labour's standing in the polls had been badly affected by the antics of the 'loony left' at County Hall and in places such as Lambeth and Liverpool. Despite that, Labour had recovered enough of its composure to include in the 1992 manifesto a pledge to create a new Greater London Authority.

◆

In 1996, a number of public figures from the former environment secretary Michael Heseltine to Tony Banks were proposing the idea of directly-elected mayors for some cities, including London. Simon Jenkins, the influential journalist and author, was also a strong advocate of the idea. In 1995, he chaired a group called the Commission for Local Democracy which reported: 'The post would be highly visible and thus highly accountable. Local decisions would be more readily identifiable with one person than with the notion of a party group.'[10] Jenkins claimed later his intervention was decisive in persuading Blair. 'I saw Blair for about an hour and he got out a bottle of whisky and said, "Persuade me,"' Jenkins recounted later.[11] Despite the opposition of his shadow environment secretary, Frank Dobson,[12] the proposal for a directly-elected mayor and a Greater London Authority made its way into the 1997 election manifesto; there would be a London Assembly of 25 members whose task would be to hold the mayor to account. Shortly after the general election, on 3 July 1997, the government announced there would be a referendum the following year on Thursday, 7 May 1998 to give Londoners the chance to say whether or not they wanted the proposed new system of government.

It would take nearly three years after the announcement to establish the new system thanks to the need for a referendum and the time required to draft the legislation and get it passed by Parliament. What should have been a celebration of democracy turned into a tawdry period of political chicanery and breathtaking farce with a bit of gerrymandering thrown in for good measure. Much of this was down to the 'Millbank Tendency', then at the height of their power, ensconced like magicians' apprentices at Labour Party HQ in Millbank Tower, armed with the full paraphernalia of spin doctors and media toadies willing to do their bidding. This formidable war machine, its tank tracks still fresh with the gore of hundreds of former Tory MPs, was turned on Ken Livingstone with all its fury only to end up rather like the daft pop star with the Mercedes Benz,[13] running over itself.

◆

After the election, Blair enjoyed a long honeymoon and almost completely unfettered power. It was a halcyon time when many people still thought the Millennium Dome was a great idea and John Prescott could name a crab after Peter Mandelson and everyone would laugh, and the new Lord Chancellor Derry Irvine could refurbish his offices with wallpaper, a mere snip at £350 a roll. But there were troubles on the not-too-distant horizon.

When the government announced plans for its London referendum, the name of Ken Livingstone began to rumble uneasily like mild indigestion in the gut of many astute Labour hacks. Who else? What if? Caustically, senior figures in the party said Blair should have had a firm idea who he wanted to be mayor before creating the role.[14] However, most of those who made this point either wanted the job for themselves or a friend.

Initially, Livingstone made it clear that he opposed the idea of a mayor for London and suggested that people should be given the option of voting for a London Assembly and Greater London Authority *without* a mayor. In November 1997, he said: 'Tony [Blair] is saying that Londoners cannot be trusted. I find that overwhelmingly embarrassing and absolutely barmy.'[15] But by the spring of 1998 he had changed his mind; after all, as he often says, consistency in politics is vastly overrated. But what made him change his mind?

♦

Before the election, Livingstone was clearly hankering after a job with real power as a member of the government. Margaret Hodge, the former left-wing leader of Islington Council and future Blairite minister, urged him to go and see Blair. 'I'm sure he'll give you a job,' she said. 'I never thought they'd get away with being so right-wing,' says Livingstone. 'I thought they'd be more radical.' Six weeks before the election, Livingstone went to see Blair and told him straight: 'Look, I would like a job in the government.'[16] 'I can't promise anything,' replied Blair. 'But I'd like to bring you in and if I can I will.'[17] 'I would have taken whatever they offered me, of course,' says Livingstone, 'and would have tried to make it work.'

Ken Livingstone's hopes were boosted when at the 1997 party conference in Brighton he replaced Peter Mandelson on the NEC on 29 September 1997 to almost universal joy. For Tony Benn, it was 'marvellous!'[18] Blair asked to see Livingstone within a fortnight of the NEC elections. 'How do you think it's going?' asked Blair. 'Very much worse than I expected,' replied Livingstone. With brutal candour Livingstone set out what he considered the mistakes of Blair's first tentative six months including granting the Bank of England independence to set interest rates. 'I told him what I thought of it,' remembers Livingstone. 'I said, "You're doing that wrong and this wrong." When you get the chance to spend half an hour with the prime minister, you want to try and push him in the right direction.'

It was a fraught meeting; Blair, usually unfailingly courteous, made it clear he did not accept Livingstone's criticisms. Following the encounter, Livingstone returned to his office where Redmond O'Neill, Simon Fletcher and his ever faithful secretary Maureen Charleson were waiting. 'The bugger's going to offer me a job,' said Livingstone. 'I'll have to take it; you can't refuse a job.' But actually, Livingstone had blown it. He says: 'It didn't occur to me that simply because I'd been very direct with him that he would feel grumpy about that and not offer me a job.'[19]

The episode demonstrates again the contradictions at the heart of Livingstone's political career: an oppositionist who loved to wield power. Few very of the former are allowed to achieve the latter. 'I like running things,' says Livingstone. 'I would rather have been part of his government pushing it in the right direction than sitting on the backbenches denouncing it. I like to do things.' Even some of Blair's cabinet ministers attempted to persuade Blair of Livingstone's qualities: there were attempts by Mo Mowlam, appointed Northern Ireland secretary after the election, to give Livingstone a job in government. After her appointment, she said Livingstone mediated between her and Sinn Féin president, Gerry Adams, at that critical time. She even lobbied Blair to make Livingstone a minister in Northern Ireland.[20]

Shunned once again, Livingstone reverted to opposition. On 10 December 1997, Livingstone joined a wide-scale revolt against Blair's cut in benefits to Britain's fastest growing army of welfare state dependants, single mothers. 'I think it became a macho thing for New Labour,' says Livingstone. 'They had to demonstrate they could be brutal with the poorest and most vulnerable in society.' Others thought the same. A total of 47 Labour MPs defied the whips. Malcolm Chisholm, a Scottish Office minister and four parliamentary private secretaries either resigned or were sacked for opposing the cuts.[21] As events turned out, it is questionable whether Livingstone would have survived more than a few weeks in the government without severe compromise.

◆

In March 1998, two days before the Budget, Livingstone launched an attack on Gordon Brown, accusing him of swallowing 'an awful lot of Thatcherite nonsense' and claiming that the chancellor was 'backward-looking and not orthodox'. 'The chance of getting re-elected to a second term is at stake,' he said in a TV interview. 'We wasted the first 10 months. The pound has gone up, our exporters are finding it difficult and people are being laid off work.'[22]

More significantly, Livingstone attacked Brown's plans to update the crumbling Tube network by raising the necessary £1.5 billion via the highly complex and controversial 'public-private partnership' initiative, PPP or P3: the private sector would modernise the infrastructure system in return for long leases to control the system of track, signalling and stations. PPP critics including Livingstone claimed the initiative meant privatisation by the back door and that it would prove exorbitantly expensive to the public purse over time. Livingstone got personal with Brown: 'Londoners are going to be very upset that they're going to pay through the nose in terms of higher fares and service cuts, perhaps for the next 20 years, because a Scottish chancellor is refusing to allow Londoners to have the same level of public spending he expects as a right for his own constituents in Dunfermline East.'[23] It was widely seen as Livingstone's opening salvo in his campaign to be mayor.[24] By that time, it was clear Tony Blair would do everything in his power to stop him.

Lance Price, the former BBC political correspondent then working as a senior Number 10 spin doctor, says : 'In those years, Tony Blair wasn't confident that New Labour had embedded itself sufficiently and that the party wasn't going to go back to its old ways and he was constantly obsessed with the danger of the Labour Party going back to its bad old ways, as he saw it, and he thought that having Livingstone there as a sort of rallying point for the Left and people who weren't happy with New Labour would undermine his leadership and his efforts to transform the party, to change the party to something different.'[25]

Blair made no secret of his fear of Livingstone during the next two years. In late 1999, he said: 'My problem with him is that while I was growing up in the Labour Party and he and Arthur Scargill and Tony Benn were in control of the Labour Party they almost knocked it over the edge of the cliff into extinction. It became unelectable. If that is the politics he still represents then, yes, I am going to have to go out and fight for the Labour Party I believe in.'[26]

But Livingstone would not fight the coming battle to be mayor alone. He would be accompanied by his stalwarts from Socialist Action, according to Atma Singh, a former member of the group and an ex-Livingstone advisor. The group had helped Livingstone in his fight to get back on to the NEC. 'After that,' says Singh, 'I would say that the relationship was so close that 98 per cent of the tactics were dictated by Socialist Action.'[27] At that stage in early 1998, it was becoming obvious that senior government figures were hoping to impose their own candidate, the black television presenter Trevor Phillips.

Phillips had been appointed as chairman for 'Yes for London', a supposedly politically independent campaign aimed at getting public support for London's proposed new government in the referendum scheduled for May 1998. There were raised eyebrows at the appointment. Phillips was considered to be a signed-up member of New Labour and to bear the stigmata of the 'Millbank

Tendency'; after all, Peter Mandelson had been the best man at his wedding.

The day-to-day running of the campaign would be down to its sole paid employee, a seasoned campaigner called Jonathan Rosenberg. On the basis of its supposed political neutrality, the campaign was gifted £20,000 from the Rowntree Foundation. Rosenberg kept a diary of the campaign and he soon concluded that the 'Yes for London' was really 'Yes for Trevor'.

On 19 January 1998, after his appointment, Rosenberg was forced to shield Phillips from a canny and persistent BBC reporter: 'Jo Coburn of [BBC] Newsroom South East tried to interview Trevor so that she could expose the campaign as a front for Trevor and the Labour Party.'[28] But on 13 February 1998, Rosenberg's naivety was shattered during a distressing meeting at 10 Downing Street with Pat McFadden, a future MP and government minister, who was then an advisor dealing with London government policy. McFadden, a wiry red-haired Scot said something to the effect of: 'Well you are going to make sure Trevor gets plenty of exposure.' Rosenberg said he was not prepared to run a front campaign for anyone and it was critical 'to involve the publicly perceived candidates such as Livingstone and [Jeffrey] Archer'. Under the Millbank hegemony, such niceties were evidence of eccentricity and political unsoundness.

Rosenberg recounted McFadden's fury: 'He did not like this and said that Livingstone was not a candidate. I said he was. He did not like this and went into a tirade against him.' Rosenberg retorted that he had spoken to Livingstone only the previous day: 'He [Livingstone] had said that barring his being prevented by some device he would be standing. McFadden did not like this… [I] told him that senior media people could see clearly that there was a plot to stop Ken and they did not take kindly to it at all.'[29]

Later that day, Rosenberg visited the bumptious Archer at his penthouse on the Albert Embankment. 'He immediately fired off with the campaign being a front for Trevor and the Labour Party,' recorded Rosenberg, who assured him it was not. 'I told the people who run the country they will not get away with it,' he added. But within 10 days, Rosenberg was being ostracised: 'They've cut me out of everything… They've carried out the instruction from Number 10 that I am not to be trusted.'[30] As the campaign continued, Rosenberg's estimation of Phillips sank. 'It was pretty obvious it was all to promote Trevor,' says Rosenberg. 'It wasn't a well kept secret.'[31]

♦

On 2 April 1998, the campaign was launched on a boat called the *Silver Barracuda* at Butler's Wharf near Tower Bridge. It was best remembered for the relentless pursuit of Jeffrey Archer around the boat by Michael Crick, the political correspondent of BBC *Newsnight* and the author of the highly acclaimed book, *Stranger Than Fiction*, which exposed the peer's dubious past. At one point, Rosenberg hid Archer in the galley before attempting to divert Crick. 'You shouldn't go for Archer,' Rosenberg said. 'You should go and ask Trevor Phillips whether the "Yes Campaign" is a front for his candidature and the Labour Party.' In the meantime, Archer made his escape through a door at the back of the boat.[32] The augurs for the millionaire writer were not good.

Rosenberg did his best to counter public apathy for the referendum by touring London in a double-decker bus complete with dancers and loudspeakers pumping music. On 7 May 1998, the day of the referendum, Rosenberg took the bus along Kilburn High Road and into Livingstone's Brent East constituency. 'I was pleased to be giving Ken's area a good rocking,' he said. Two years later, Rosenberg would be running a similar campaign for Livingstone's first mayoral campaign as an independent candidate.[33] The referendum was a qualified success. There was a 'yes vote' in each of the 32 boroughs – an average of 72 per cent. But the turnout had been a poor 34 per cent of the electorate. The government judged the result an overwhelming endorsement and pressed on with drawing up the legislation needed to establish the new system by 4 May 2000.

The legislative timetable meant there would be a long drawn-out battle between Ken Livingstone and the Millbank Tendency in the two years after the referendum and before the first election for mayor. In that time, the legislation would be drawn up and incorporated into the Greater London Act, at 476 pages, the longest Act of Parliament passed since the Government of India Act of 1935 which granted greater freedom to the provinces and the people of India, and helped pave the way to independence.[34]

At the end of 1999 and the beginning of 2000, the political parties would have to choose their candidates for the poll on 4 May 2000. Ironically, Livingstone and Archer, the favourite candidates for both main political parties were considered dangerous electoral liabilities by the leaders, Blair and William Hague.

As for Trevor Phillips, his biggest problem was not that he was seen as a New Labour placeman by the public, but that he was hardly seen as anything at all. Whatever the hopes and dreams of his Millbank mentors, Phillips' relatively low profile was always going to rule him out of contention. During the next two years, the names of possible candidates included the Virgin boss Richard Branson, Tony Banks, Glenda Jackson and possibly, most astonishing of all, the popular television actress Joanna Lumley. It was anyone but Ken.

Livingstone held a press conference on 25 March 1998 announcing his intention to stand as mayor. Dressed in the trademark GLC safari suit dug out from the back of the wardrobe for old times' sake, Livingstone said: 'If you have an all-powerful mayor, you open up the prospect of someone going raving mad and abusing those powers. It is far better to have someone like myself, who will exercise restraint, than someone else – like a well-known author.' Journalists detected a widespread nostalgia for Livingstone's nasal drawl and the populist policies of the GLC. [35] How was the government going to stop him?

The New Labour smear campaign against Livingstone began in earnest in late 1998 and would then continue in bursts with renewed ferocity over the following 18 months. Leading the charge would be 'the People who live in the Dark'. We know this because some of them have left the Dark and written books and others have written about their encounters with the Dark. On 11 November 1998, Oona King, the young Labour MP for Bethnal Green and Bow, was summoned to the presence of Alastair Campbell, the prime minister's official spokesman. Also there was Sally Morgan, who headed Blair's political office. The prime minister was in a neighbouring office reading some papers. Campbell asked King to write an article about Ken Livingstone 'saying he can't be trusted'. 'As you know,' continued Campbell according to King, 'he's trying to undermine the Labour Party and we have to ensure he doesn't succeed.'[36] King disagreed and said she thought Livingstone was going to win. 'Bollocks!' Morgan reportedly said before allegedly slamming the desk with her fist. King refused to help, and said that probably meant the end of her political career.

'It's not the end of your political career, Oona,' replied Campbell, 'just the next five years.'[37]

But others were not so discerning. Paul Boateng, GLC Police Committee chairman under Livingstone, was minister of state at the Home Office in February 1999 when he wrote an article in the *Evening Standard* attacking Livingstone: 'He could work out the angle on any political position and run with it on air to the maximum effect. He has not lost these skills. There has been no evidence, however, in his intervening years in Parliament of his acquiring a taste for detail and the nuts and bolts of public administration.'[38]

◆

In June 1999, Livingstone received a phone call from Trevor Phillips inviting him out to an Italian restaurant in Covent Garden. Livingstone described the meeting as very friendly. He told Phillips he was still desperate to get into the government and hoped one day to be brought into the cabinet. He asked Phillips to run as his deputy and said he would hand over to him after four years. Livingstone told him: 'I only want to do this for one term and set it up... I'll get it up and running and show you the ropes.' Livingstone says Phillips agreed.[39]

Phillips not only changed his mind the following day but publicly implied Livingstone's offer was racist: 'All of us who come from minority communities get rather used to and fed up of, any time we emerge on the public scene, people treating us as apprentices, you know.'[40] Livingstone managed to deflect what was by any standards a disgraceful slur with humour, hoping that Trevor would soon be 'feeling better' and adding: 'This reminds me of the old Masai warrior saying, "The mighty elephant does not mind that the gnat bites his bum".' But he did mind. The relationship between the two men would deteriorate over the following years and they would become bitter enemies, particularly on the issue of race. In 2008, Livingstone would be accused of leading a surreptitious and ultimately failed campaign to prevent Phillips' appointment as head of the new Commission for Equalities and Human Rights.[41] In the short term, Phillips soon conceded he had no chance of becoming mayor and dropped out. He would later run as Frank Dobson's deputy, making that two of the worst judgement calls in recent electoral history. [42]

According to former Number 10 spin doctor, Lance Price,

Blair's biggest problem was how to field a credible candidate against Livingstone for the party's nomination. During the early autumn of 1999, Blair and his team had tried to convince Mo Mowlam, the popular and gutsy Northern Ireland secretary, to stand. 'But Mo swung this way and that for God knows how long,' remembers Lance Price, 'she couldn't make up her mind what she wanted to do, which was a characteristic of her.'[43]

As Mowlam prevaricated, Frank Dobson, the health secretary, came under increasing pressure from Tony Blair to stand. Nick Raynsford, the government minister for London, was responsible for drawing up the necessary legislation for the new mayor and GLA. He remembers Dobson's reluctance: 'Frank was secretary of state for health; he wanted to stay there. He didn't want to do the London job.' Raynsford thought if Dobson was not going to stand, then he would.[44] Assured by Dobson, Raynsford called Blair and got what he thought was his support. But within two weeks, he would be betrayed by both Dobson and Blair. Raynsford's reputation was for decency and competence, not charisma. Clearly Number 10 decided he was not the man to beat Livingstone.

'Frank was leant on and changed his mind and didn't come back to me,' says Raynsford, 'so that's where I feel let down really.'[45] But Raynsford generously agreed to throw all his support behind Dobson and even run his campaign for him. But if Raynsford felt he had been humiliated, it was nothing compared to what awaited Frank Dobson. Dobson 'resigned' as health secretary to stand as mayor, necessitating a cabinet reshuffle: Mo Mowlam was moved to the cabinet office and Alan Milburn got Dobson's chair at the Department of Health.

Lance Price's diary is one of the most revealing insider accounts so far of how Blair's spin machine tried to stop Livingstone's selection as candidate and how Blair himself was convinced that Livingstone would bottle out of running as an independent if denied the Labour candidacy. It was apparent early on that Frank Dobson would never beat Livingstone. On 29 October 1999, Price wrote: 'TB [Tony Blair] thinks that if he [Ken Livingstone] has to win, it would be better as an independent. What we can't allow is to have an independent Old Labour power base set up in London around Ken.'[46] On 14 November 1999, Price reported: 'The hope is still that Frank can beat him [Livingstone] but nobody is at all confident... If Ken wins we can box him in with a very New

Labour manifesto… The mayor was always envisaged to be a very powerful post with its own mandate. So in all probability Ken has outfoxed us.'[47]

◆

Blair had one trick left up his sleeve which actually worked only to backfire catastrophically. Instead of One Member One Vote for the London Labour Party, which would be much more representative and would guarantee Livingstone's selection, he decided an electoral college would choose the candidate but one rigged to ensure a Dobson victory: a third of the votes each would go to London's 60,000[48] party members, the trade unions and London Labour MPs and MEPs. The MPs and MEPs were mostly obedient and would support Dobson as would enough of Blair's supporters in the unions. 'Tony Blair was assured that this would block Livingstone,' reported the *Sunday Times*.[49] Through his blatant gerrymandering, the prime minister had effectively sabotaged any credibility Dobson might have won if he had been left to his own devices. Privately, Dobson was furious at the sheer dishonesty of the so-called electoral college.[50]

No one denies now that it was a complete political fix. Lance Price says: 'It was his [Tony Blair's] obsession with how he thought the Labour Party had gone wrong in the past and how his government wasn't going to make the same mistakes that led him to some pretty extreme positions within the party. In this case he was actually using some very Old Labour techniques to stop an Old Labour figure from getting a position of authority within the party.'[51]

◆

By the middle of November, 1999, the Labour Party selection panel met to shortlist the candidates for mayor. Despite knowing that his man could not possibly lose, there was a deepening foreboding in the breast of Dobson's campaign manager, Nick Raynsford. 'The party was obsessed with mechanisms to ensure that Frank Dobson got the nomination,' remembers Nick Raynsford. 'But these were almost all mistakes because every time a new device was wheeled out like the electoral college it looked like Margaret McDonagh [Labour general secretary] contriving to get the outcome. The party was uncomfortable and Frank was uncomfortable with all of that. I knew it was going to be a disaster from very early on. And it just got worse and worse and worse.'[52]

Notes

1 Tony Travers, *The Politics of London, Governing an Ungovernable City*, Palgrave Macmillan, 2004, p36
2 Kenneth Baker, *The Turbulent Years, My Life in Politics*, p103; See Chapter 14
3 Tony Travers, *The Politics of London, Governing an Ungovernable City*, p337-38
4 Ibid.
5 *Independent*, 6.4.95
6 *Independent on Sunday*, 24.4.94
7 Tony Travers, *The Politics of London, Governing an Ungovernable City*, p35
8 Andrew Hosken, *Nothing Like a Dame, The Scandals of Shirley Porter*, p285
9 Tony Travers, *The Politics of London, Governing an Ungovernable City*, pp35-39
10 Ben Pimlott and Nirmala Rao, *Governing London*, OUP, 2002, p57; CLD report, p22
11 Mark D'Arcy and Rory MacLean, *Nightmare! The Race to Become London's Mayor*, Politico's, 2000, p8
12 Ibid., p12
13 BBC News Online, Brian Harvey accident, 31.5.05 (http://news.bbc.co.uk/1/hi/entertainment/music/4597607.stm)
14 Interview, Baron Soley, former MP for Ealing, Acton and Shepherd's Bush, 29.10.07
15 Mark D'Arcy and Rory MacLean, *Nightmare! The Race to Become London's Mayor*, pp9-10
16 Interview, Ken Livingstone, 1.11.07
17 Ibid.
18 Tony Benn, *Free at Last, Diaries 1991-2001*, (see 29.9.97)
19 Interview, Ken Livingstone, 1.11.07
20 *Mail on Sunday*, 17.9.00
21 John Rentoul, *Tony Blair, Prime Minister*, p377
22 *People*, 15.3.98; GMTV interview on 16.3.98
23 *The Times*, Leading article, 21.3.98
24 Ibid.
25 Interview, Lance Price, 11.1.08
26 *Guardian*, 19.11.99
27 Interview, Atma Singh, 27.1.08
28 Jonathan Rosenberg, unpublished diary, 19.1.98
29 Ibid., 13.2.98
30 Ibid., 23.2.98
31 Interview, Jonathan Rosenberg, 29.9.07
32 Jonathan Rosenberg, unpublished diary, 2.4.98
33 Ibid., 7.5.98
34 Greater London Authority Act, 1999, Stationery Office Ltd
35 *Financial Times*, 26.3.98
36 Oona King, *House Music, The Oona King Diaries*, Bloomsbury, 2007, pp113-115

37 Ibid.
38 Ibid.; *Evening Standard*, 'Why "good old Ken" should stay part of London's history', by Paul Boateng, 15.2.98
39 Interview, Ken Livingstone, 8.11.07
40 BBC News Online, 'Phillips accuses Livingstone of racism', 16.6.99
41 *Dispatches*, Channel Four, 21.1.08
42 *Sun*, 15.10.99
43 Ibid.
44 Interview, Nick Raynsford MP, 20.12.07
45 Ibid.
46 Lance Price, *The Spin Doctor's Diary*, Hodder and Stoughton, 2006, p155
47 Ibid., p159 (14.11.99)
48 *Mail on Sunday*, 17.10.99
49 *Sunday Times*, 17.10.99
50 *Guardian*, 24.1.00
51 Interview, Lance Price, 11.1.99
52 Interview, Nick Raynsford, 20.12.07

Chapter 21

London's ours, again! October 1999–May 2000

The political comedy now being acted out in the fag end of the last millennium would ensure there would be plenty of humiliation to go around for everyone, except Ken Livingstone. Mostly it would be heaped on Labour politicians like Frank Dobson and Tony Blair, as well as the Millbank Tendency. But ironically the Tory peer Jeffrey Archer was the first to come a cropper. The Conservative Party's decision to choose Jeffrey Archer as its candidate struck most sensible observers at the time as mad and reckless. He had a long and proven track record for getting himself and those around him into trouble. Even William Hague would admit it was the dumbest thing he ever allowed as leader of the Tory Party.[1] If Archer was anything he was an accident waiting to happen, and accidents waiting to happen, often happen. Television producer Ted Francis, an old friend, had stepped forward to admit that Archer had asked him to provide a false alibi for a libel trial.[2] Hague sacked Archer on 19 November 1999 two days before the *News of the World* broke the story.[3] In February 2000, he was expelled by the Tory Party and on 19 July 2001, he was sentenced to four years in jail for perjury and perverting the course of justice. He was replaced as Conservative candidate by the amiable former minister and MP Steven Norris.

Before Archer's fall, Norris had famously remarked that he would never support the peer as mayoral candidate 'dead or alive'[4] and afterwards was heard to remark that he was not prepared to take lessons 'from a party that had picked Archer'.[5] Livingstone and Archer had got on well, perhaps both recognising in the other the risk-taking political maverick. It was also a demonstration of Livingstone's ability to get on with people across the political spectrum. Livingstone thought the prison sentence meted out to Archer absurd and excessive and was one of the few people to offer him words of support after his fall.[6] 'Ken has always been decent and fair to me,' Archer told his aide, Stephan Shakespeare.[7]

As for Blair's placeman, only those with hearts of stone could fail to have sympathy for Frank Dobson and not wince at the ridicule and embarrassment he was forced to endure, mainly at the hands of his so-called supporters. The MP for Holborn and St Pancras was known and respected for his integrity, and his wit. Alan Clark, the former Tory minister and MP, used to swap jokes with Dobson: 'His are *so* filthy they're unusable, even at a Rugger Club dinner.'[8]

Over the next few months, Dobson would suffer innumerable humiliations which even now are painful to recount. At every stage in the proceedings, Dobson behaved with as much decency and honesty as the poisonous prevailing mood allowed. Having forced him out of the government to run against Livingstone, Blair and his spin doctors would try to sack Dobson as candidate, casually sabotage his candidacy by constantly briefing against him and once demanded that he shave off his beard. Such was the growing public disgust and ennui at the antics of 'the People who live in the Dark', that only the unexpected death of all the other mayoral candidates and their likely replacements would have ensured a Dobson victory in 2000.

Dobson, or 'Dobbo', as he was known, did try to rein in the Millbank Tendency. On a tour of Millbank on 7 November 1999, he told the whey-faced pimple squeezers of the Tendency: 'Just keep your stupid noses out.' But that proved about as useful as admonishing a shoal of piranha. Within 24 hours, 'senior party sources' were telling the press: 'One minute Frank is claiming he has the backing of the entire cabinet. Now he's trying to convince the public that he doesn't enjoy the support of party bigwigs. It's a toothless attempt to bite the hand that's feeding him.'[9]

The 'hand' had, rather unhelpfully as it turned out, fed Dobson the lists of all the Labour Party members in London, giving him an enormous advantage over Livingstone who was denied them; it also exposed him as a stooge when the story, as it was bound to, came to light. In fact, Livingstone was among the 60,000 party members to receive a mailshot on 25 October 1999 in an envelope embossed in green with 'House of Commons' from Frank Dobson: 'Dear Mr Livingstone, I'm writing to ask you to vote for me as mayor of London.'[10] Livingstone complained that it showed how completely biased the party was towards one candidate even before the selection process had been conducted. Glenda Jackson, the Hampstead MP who also fostered mayoral ambitions, felt the same.[11] It was hard to see how they would have concluded otherwise.

Speaking later on BBC Radio 4's *Today* programme on 1 November 1999, Elizabeth France, the data protection registrar, said no one had the right to use information for electoral purposes and indicated that Labour officials might have breached the Data Protection Act if they had not been licensed to distribute members' details.[12] France held an inquiry and reported after the mayoral election in June 2000 that there would be no prosecutions.[13]

It emerged later that a senior official in Millbank Tower had sanctioned the release of the computer disks bearing details of the entire London Labour Party membership to the Dobson campaign. Although Dobson called for all candidates to be given the lists, the damage was done: his stooge status was confirmed. In any event, a haughty Labour Party spokesman dismissed Dobson's demand as 'impractical'.[14] The affair was predictably called 'Dobbogate' by lazy hacks who had long become accustomed to adding the suffix 'gate' to any supposed scandal, great or small.

Lance Price, who spent a lot of time with Dobson during this period, says, 'Frank Dobson was a decent bloke. Why the hell he ever agreed to do it I don't know. He was massively frustrated. He's a sort of funny character on the whole and has a lot of integrity and having decided to do it, he was determined to see it through.'[15]

◆

Soon, well-sourced reports of arguments between Milbank and Number 10 over 'Stop Ken' strategies began to surface. The chief protagonists were Margaret McDonagh, the party's general secretary based with the Millbank Tendency, and Sally Morgan, head of Blair's political office. Morgan was apparently arguing for Livingstone to be banned from entering the selection process altogether; McDonagh thought that would be a disaster which would alienate thousands of Labour members.[16]

Ken Livingstone's first hurdle was the party's selection panel which met on 18 November 2000 to decide on a shortlist of candidates.[17] Livingstone was the one figure who was playing it straight. He made it clear to the press and to the selection panel when it met that he would not support the government's PPP plans for the Tube, although he knew it would count against him when the party came to pick its mayoral candidate. Clive Soley, then chairman of the Parliamentary Labour Party, chaired the selection panel. 'The problem [for us] was that Ken wanted to do his own thing,' says Soley. 'In a sense, he wanted to be an independent but he [also] wanted the backing of the party. The difficulty, particularly for me, was that I had been laying down the law to all candidates that if they were going to be a candidate for the Labour Party they had to fight on the manifesto and they could only get it changed by the normal party processes.'[18]

Soley already had reservations about Ken. 'My position on Ken is that he's a very able and very intelligent guy,' says Soley. 'But he is also somebody who doesn't play as a team member. He's one of these individualists in politics who can come up with some very good and very bright and useful ideas and he can also screw things up big time. He's like one of these figures like [Enoch] Powell or [Winston] Churchill or Tony Benn: they're always playing on the outside and unless something big comes their way, like the Second World War for Churchill, they tend to end up losing, as Powell and Benn did.'[19]

It was clear that for Livingstone, the mayoralty now represented his big chance to get back to the centre stage of politics; a last-ditch bid to prevent his political career ending in failure. Critically, for a sensitive man like Livingstone, his feelings were also hurt. Livingstone says, 'I think what was damaging for them was everything that was wrong with the New Labour machine which had this terrible reputation for being ruthless and efficient but it was unbelievably incompetent at times. Whenever the issue of the mayoralty was reported there would always be a paragraph or two about Ken Livingstone threatening to stand and there would always be a line from sources in Number 10 saying, "It's just not going to happen; he's not going to be allowed to stand."

'This went on for about 18 months and I don't think they were ever aware of just how offensive this is to anyone reading it. It was everything that was arrogant and unacceptable about that initial phase of the Labour government.'[20]

According to Blair's official spokesman, Alastair Campbell, Blair was still determined to prevent Livingstone making it on to the shortlist but was dissuaded not only by Soley's reluctance but Dobson's determination to allow Livingstone to stand against him. Dobson had made it clear to Blair he would pull out if Livingstone was blocked. Campbell was furious that Livingstone's attempt to be shortlisted was the main story on the news on the day of the Queen's Speech on 17 November 1999: 'Ken fucking Livingstone was leading the news.'[21]

After submitting Livingstone to a four-hour grilling on 18 November 1999, during which he rowed with the Lilliputian government minister Ian McCartney over the manifesto, Soley's panel put Livingstone on the shortlist, possibly in the knowledge that the rigged electoral college to be held early in 2000 would never let him get the candidacy in any event. The others on the shortlist included Glenda Jackson and of course, good old 'Dobbo', who more than anyone had insisted on Livingstone's inclusion. By this time, it is transparently obvious that Dobson had had a gutful of the mad woman's breakfast that passed for the prime minister's London mayoral strategy, and would have been only too delighted to jump ship if Blair had insisted on vetoing Livingstone's addition to the shortlist. But he had been forced out of the government to run as the candidate; to stand down after all that would be too much to ask of anyone.[22]

By then the paranoia was such that when the news broke the day after the shortlist announcement that Blair's wife, Cherie Booth, was about to have their fourth baby, one of the prime minister's advisors, Philip Gould, actually thought the announcement was timed to divert media attention from Ken Livingstone's short-term victory. According to Campbell, Gould seemed to think the baby announcement was 'a planned piece of news management to deal with Ken'. Campbell was able to disabuse him.[23]

The final choice of Labour's mayoral candidate would not be announced until 20 February 2000, just two months before the election itself. It would be a nasty time when the smears on all sides were ratcheted to new heights. Tony Blair was first into the fray on the day Livingstone made it on to the shortlist. 'My worry about Ken Livingstone – I am just being open about it – is that the extremism he stood for in the 1980s, he hasn't left behind,' Blair said in press interviews. 'In the eighties when he was in charge of the Labour Party in London we were a byword for extremism, we were seen as anti-law and order, we were hopeless on business, we were unelectable as a political party. I never want to go back to those days.'[24] He repeatedly warned that Livingstone would be 'a disaster for London'.

In early December 1999, Ken Livingstone's alleged first big smear about Frank Dobson began to do the rounds in the press. Livingstone was accused of putting it about that Dobson was 'clinically depressed'. Dobson went on the counter offensive: 'I know Ken has been going round for a month or so now saying to journalists that I am clinically depressed and at last he's got some clods to publish it.'[25]

At the time Livingstone denied accusing his opponent of being depressed, but there was truth in the Dobson charge. According to the columnist and author, Andrew Rawnsley, Livingstone put this rumour about on at least two occasions: once in a conversation with the journalist John Lloyd; and on a second occasion in the same terms during an off-the-record briefing with writers and editors from the *Guardian*.[26] The 'story' was also confirmed in an off-the-record briefing for this book by a source close to Livingstone, who was present at the *Guardian* lunch. 'He didn't say it as an anti-Frank thing,' insists the source. 'What he meant was "I'm genuinely worried about Frank; he's been asked to say and do things he's not happy with. He's been placed in an impossible position by the Millbank machine and he's looking like he's clinically depressed", or something.'[27] Well meant or not, it was a clumsy and insensitive remark.

Dobson continued to flounder. At Christmas 1999, *The Times* claimed that children were mistaking him for Father Christmas.[28] Dobson criticised all the great and the good who complained about having to queue outside the Dome for a long time on New Year's Eve due to an organisational cock-up. 'Frank Dobson's campaign in London seems as good as finished,' reported Lance Price on 10 January 2000. 'He'd made no progress at all, his relaunch last week flopped and he got slammed for sneering at "toffee-nosed people" having to queue for the Dome. So Ken looks set for an easy win.'[29]

♦

The panic about Livingstone really broke out in late January, a month before the final selection and three months before the election itself. On 20 January 2000, Alastair Campbell tried to persuade Dobson to pull out of the race following a bad poll in the *Daily Mirror* which was campaigning for Mo Mowlam to be the candidate. As ever, Mowlam was prevaricating on the grounds that Blair was now so unpopular even she might not be able to 'pull it off'.[30]

The spin doctors made a concerted effort to force Dobson's withdrawal the following day on 21 January 2000. Mowlam was now 'up for it' but it was obvious that Dobson had suffered enough without being pushed out when someone better came along. According to Lance Price, Anji Hunter, Blair's close friend and his director of government relations, said, 'It was essential that we avoid the huge damage that Ken winning would do to TB [Tony Blair] and that Frank could have whatever he wanted if he agreed – the Lords, an ambassadorship, whatever.' Blair told Frank Dobson and his wife Janet frankly that Mowlam could win but that Frank could not. Price added: 'Frank and Janet, however, said that Frank had been humiliated enough already and this was too much to ask.'[31] By 25 January 2000, Blair was in a 'real state'[32] over Dobson's stubbornness. The following day both Blair and Campbell made a concerted joint effort to persuade Dobson to pull out. Again he refused.[33] There would be no dodging the rendezvous with disaster.

Writing in the *Observer*, Andrew Rawnsley observed that not so long ago, Livingstone had been 'a witty but powerless heckler of the New Labour juggernaut, a 50-something had-been from the Jurassic eighties beached in the Blairite era.' His miraculous comeback was all thanks to one man: 'Tony Blair has played unlikely Christ to Livingstone's even more unexpected Lazarus.'[34]

◆

In late January 2000, there was another concerted attempt by Millbank to smear Livingstone with a very old story, but one that landed him in trouble with Elizabeth Filkin, the parliamentary standards commissioner. In December 1994,[35] the *Observer*'s Michael Gillard had broken the story about Localaction Ltd, the company used by Livingstone to shield some of his outside earnings from the highest rate of tax. In May 1996, Gillard again returned to the story, claiming that Livingstone risked possible prosecution and a fine for failing to file Localaction's accounts at Companies House for the previous two years.[36]

There was a brief flurry of interest in the story, particularly from the *Evening Standard*,[37] but it soon died away when everyone realised that Livingstone had done nothing legally wrong,

aside from a tardy submission of accounts which was soon recti-
fied. Following a long journalistic tradition, someone picked up
the story nearly four years later, polished it up a bit and spun it to
the *Sunday Times* for another outing. Thank goodness for short
memories! It was precisely the same story Gillard had run five
years previously. The only new line was a comment from a 'source
close to Frank Dobson's campaign': 'He [Ken Livingstone] has
called for higher income tax to be paid by those earning higher
or middle incomes, when he prefers to pay a lower rate. He also
wants London to have a higher rate of corporation tax, yet he
sets his company up outside the capital. It is one law for Ken and
another for the rest of us.'[38]

But some bright spark realised that Livingstone had failed to
publicly declare the bulk of his extra parliamentary earnings as
required: a lax oversight. Between June 1998 and January 2000,
Livingstone had earned an extra £220, 992, of which he should
have declared £158,999. The rules at the time stipulated that regular outside income had to be declared, but one-off payments did
not have to be. Livingstone says he was genuinely confused as to
what was and was not a one-off payment. The £158,999 was attrib-
utable to regular commitments, including his *Evening Standard*
restaurant column.

A complaint about Localaction Ltd and Livingstone's failure to register the payments was made to Elizabeth Filkin, then
the parliamentary standards commissioner; it was a transparent Labour smear. The complaint came in a typed letter sent on
19 December 1999 and signed by one John Christopher Jones, a
man in his late twenties who lived in a flat above a post office in
the Leicestershire town of Shepshed.[39] But Jones, a research fellow at Loughborough University, told anyone who would listen
that he knew nothing about the matter and even called Filkin's
clerk to deny any involvement in the affair. He told reporters outside his flat: 'Somebody must have used my name and address
without my knowledge – I didn't write any letter and I have no
connection with politics or with Ken Livingstone.'

The mystery was finally solved by an admission from a 31-year-
old lawyer and Labour activist that he had written the letter and
got his reluctant friend John Jones to sign it. The man behind
the complaint was Rob Smeath, the treasurer, no less, of Trevor
Phillips' campaign before it went belly up. Phillips was now

Dobson's running mate for the deputy mayoralty. Smeath had also been the election agent for Jeremy Fraser, who had taken over from Nick Raynsford as Dobson's campaign manager.[40] Really competent smearers are never identified; this was the worst of all worlds, a smear which rebounded on the smearers themselves. 'Like the coprophagous beetle,' observed Andrew Rawnsley of Livingstone in the *Observer*, 'the more crap that is thrown in his direction, the stronger he becomes.'[41]

'We knew that it was organised from someone of the Millbank Tendency,' Livingstone said at the time.[42] He was convinced Blair was behind the 'dirty negative campaigning' and accused him of being stuck in the 'politics of the Cold War'; Blair described Livingstone as 'a fool' whose time at the GLC coincided with Labour's 'lowest ebb' in the capital.[43]

'Girlfriends I hadn't seen for years were ringing up saying that they had had the press turning up on their doorsteps,' says Livingstone of the ceaseless smears pouring out of Millbank. But there were also more sinister happenings. Livingstone says attempts were made to break into his NatWest bank account. Someone would ring up claiming to be from a 'credit company' and ask for details about the account. A bank official called Jerry Mount was appointed Livingstone's personal bank manager. Livingstone says: 'He had a code word so that nobody could enter my bank account or my partner's [Kate Allen] without going through him to access them.'[44]

The crunch came with the rigged electoral college to decide who would run as Labour's candidate for mayor. Voting took place on 16 February 2000; the result would be announced four days later. But at around 5.30 p.m. that day, a source within Millbank rang Livingstone with the result.[45] Even then, Dobson just scraped through with 51.26 per cent of the total; Livingstone, 48.473 per cent.[46]

As expected, the third of the electoral college consisting almost entirely of Blair supporters made all the difference. The ballot of GLA candidates, MPs and MEPs, with each possessing the equivalent of 450 votes, was always going to be decisive, and so it proved: Dobson, 64; Livingstone, 9. Glenda Jackson's only vote, her own, went to Livingstone on second preference. But even this was not enough to clinch it for Dobson. That was left to the third of the electoral college decided by the votes of the trade unions and affiliated societies. Here, the rigging was even more obvious. Livingstone took 74 per cent, a huge chunk of the individual votes cast in the ballot, but decisively as it turned out, the leaders of the engineering union, the AEEU, ignored the wishes of their members and cast a bloc vote for Dobson.[47] The South London Co-op also used a bloc vote in his favour and together with the AEEU, handed Dobson eight per cent of the electoral college. He won by just 3.053 per cent. It made all the difference. The prime minister had stolen it, fair and square.

On Friday, 18 February 2000, Livingstone received an invitation via his former election agent Anne Harradine to take tea with Blair the following day at Chequers in Buckinghamshire to discuss the mayoral election result due to be announced on Sunday, 20 February. Livingstone was accompanied not only by his right-hand man Simon Fletcher, but also his nephew and niece, Matthew and Charlotte.[48]

The group arrived at Chequers the following morning. Both Blair and Livingstone were attired in open-necked shirts, jeans and trainers, but it was not a relaxed meeting. 'It was bizarre,' says Livingstone. 'I knew that Frank had won by three per cent and I genuinely believe he [Blair] didn't know.' Fletcher also thought Blair did not know the result but was trying to discover Livingstone's intentions if he lost. Livingstone replied, 'I'm not going to do anything to make it less bloody for you.'[49] Blair was perfectly polite as the two discussed the financing of the Tube and Dobson's chances of winning. On the last subject, Livingstone said unequivocally 'no way'. The meeting lasted 50 minutes and ended inconclusively. But it is surely inconceivable that Blair would not have known the results of the ballot about which he had obsessed for so long.

Later that day, Livingstone moved to pre-empt the vote by telling the press: 'I don't think you can defend the interest of democracy if you have won under those circumstances. I don't think you can win the mayoral election with a tainted candidate.' He urged Dobson to stand aside and warned the prime minister he would run as an independent if he did not.[50] But, Livingstone would not announce his decision to run as an independent for another 16 days.

Livingstone had long contemplated running as an independent. At the September 1999 Labour Party conference in

Bournemouth, Valerie Wise remembers him telling her he would stand as an independent if denied the candidacy.[51] But publicly he had repeatedly ruled out running as an independent. As recently as 28 January 2000, Livingstone said on BBC Radio 4's *Any Questions?*, 'It's an option I rule out 100 per cent. I very much want to run London. I also want to continue having a say in the way the Labour Party develops because that is very important – I've given my entire life to the Labour Party and I'm not going to walk away from it.'[52] He knew that would mean expulsion from the Labour Party but he had been left few options by Blair other than to rot away in obscurity on the backbenches.

Inside Number 10, there was still panic and prevarication. 'Ken is playing games…' Lance Price recorded in his diary on 21 February 2000.[53] '…If he runs, will we try to push Frank aside and let Mo in?' On 23 February 2000, Price reported that Blair was still unsure whether Livingstone had decided. In the meantime, the prime minister wrote a note to Dobson telling him to distance himself from Number 10 and wear an open-necked shirt, as well as offering him advice about his campaign. Price added: 'We tell the puppet to insist there is no way he's going to be our puppet!'[54]

◆

Livingstone took the final decision after a meeting with close associates in the cafe at the Royal Festival Hall on Saturday afternoon, 4 March 2000. Also present were Simon Fletcher and Neale Coleman, a friend from Livingstone's days in the Paddington Labour Party,[55] who had organised the meeting. Jonathan Rosenberg, another Paddington Labour member who had run the 'Yes for London' campaign, was also there. Rosenberg says, 'There's no doubt that the rigging of the election wound up ordinary Labour voters who took the view that they should have the right to vote for Ken Livingstone.' At the meeting Rosenberg urged Livingstone to stand and offered to run a bus campaign for him as a way of him getting his message to a lot of the electorate in the absence of a party machine.[56]

The following day, Livingstone rang Charles Reiss, the political editor of the *Evening Standard,* and told him he had decided to stand. He wrote an article setting out his reasons and sent it over to Reiss. The paper would splash the story on Monday, 6 March 2000. No one expected Livingstone to lose. A recent poll had put his support at a staggering 51 per cent, nearly 30 points ahead of Dobson, languishing on 22 per cent; Norris was nowhere on 13 per cent.[57]

In his *Evening Standard* article, Livingstone said: 'I have been forced to choose between the party I love and upholding the democratic rights of Londoners. I have concluded that defence of the principle of London's right to govern itself requires that I stand as an independent candidate for London mayor on 4 May.'[58] Shortly after hearing the news, Alastair Campbell rightly observed, 'There was a sense running through it that we had really fucked up.'[59]

Tony Banks was among the first to criticise Livingstone. Writing in the *Independent*, Banks admitted he had voted against Livingstone in the ballot. 'Judging by recent events, loyalty is no longer part of Ken's political baggage,' said Banks, adding: 'This is not David versus Goliath; it is ego versus party and for Ken, ego is in the driving seat.'[60] At one point Chris Mullin told Blair, 'It doesn't matter what you do. Ken is going to win under all circumstances. Remember you heard it here first.' Blair replied, 'You are not the first to tell me that.'[61]

What followed was not so much a campaign but a carnival for Livingstone and a ritualised humiliation for Dobson during which the former health secretary became the butt of every joke and almost a political leper for Labour's spin doctors. Blair had ended up in the absurd situation of having two Labour MPs as front-runners and wanting neither of them to be his mayoral candidate. It was a rerun of the recent devolution fiasco in Wales where the new Welsh Assembly had forced the resignation of Alun Michael, Blair's unpopular choice as first secretary, on 9 February 2000 and replaced him with Rhodri Morgan, the people's choice all along.

As usual, despite appearances, Livingstone was not fighting Millbank and Number 10 alone; he was getting support from his coterie of loyalists, including the contingent from Socialist Action. In January 2000, the *Guardian* named the two Socialist Action activists vigorously helping Livingstone as John Ross and Redmond O'Neill. Simon Fletcher, who was lodging with Livingstone at his home in Ivy Road, also played an important role in the campaign. When Ross received the call from Livingstone for help in running his campaign, he left his Moscow flat immediately in the clothes he was standing in and flew to London to be by Livingstone's side for the campaign. Later, a removals company collected the rest of his belongings and sent them to Ross in London.[62]

When asked at the time about his links to Socialist Action, Livingstone responded: 'The truth is that I am prepared to work for people when there is political agreement.' He denied being the 'tool' of Socialist Action. Neil Kinnock said of Livingstone's supporters: 'If you are relying on people to do your footslogging who are from the ultra left, they do have a certain temperament. Politics is their whole life, they've got no hinterland, they are obsessive and really the siege troops came from that element... despite, frequently, their intellectual intelligence, they're the daftest sods, so they must be easy to manipulate.'[63]

Jonathan Rosenberg, as anticipated, ran the purple bus campaign, complete with a band and dancers. The campaign team of Neale Coleman, Fletcher, Ross and O'Neill set up headquarters in the West End offices of advertising consultant, Harry Barlow, who had cut his teeth on various campaigns at the GLC.[64] For Livingstone, Barlow was a dream advertising man. 'What Ken didn't know at the time,' says Barlow, 'was that there was a brothel operating next door. There'd be all these journalists camped outside and then these blokes would turn up, see all these cameras and then suddenly turn away.'[65] Laid-back, clever and completely without side, Barlow understood Livingstone and how bored and infuriated he was by slick whiteboard presentations and all the trimmings. Barlow's method was to show him a poster and get his approval or not. Barlow was always an important figure in Livingstone's firmament.

Barlow advised Livingstone to hire the advertising agency, Euro RSCG Wnek Gosper, to run the campaign. But the candidate rejected suggestions of a negative campaign against Dobson. 'Ken always makes it difficult for us, of course,' adds Barlow. 'We obviously wanted to do a knocking campaign but Ken always insists that you must be positive. He won't let you have a go at the candidate – he thinks it's counterproductive. We had some lovely [knocking] ads but he wouldn't let us run them.'[66] Labour expelled Livingstone but wisely decided not to punish anyone who supported him. As things turned out, that might have resulted in the expulsion of most of the party's London membership.

The celebrity world also provided a rich harvest. All those

years in the parliamentary doldrums had not been for nothing. The GLC gigs with Billy Bragg and Red Wedge, the columns, the cheese ads, the guest appearances on *Have I Got News For You?*, and even good old Ernold Same, all came up trumps. Among the celebs to leap aboard the bandwagon were: Jo Brand, the comedian, the DJ Norman Cook, aka Fatboy Slim, the film director Ken Loach and the pop bands: Pink Floyd, the Chemical Brothers and of course, Blur. At the *New Musical Express* Premier Music Awards in March 2000, Blur's lead singer Damon Albarn wished Livingstone 'good luck' in two of his three acceptance speeches.[67] Damien Hirst and Tracey Emin were among 50 modern artists to donate works for an auction to raise funds for Livingstone. Neil Pearson, the TV actor, was Livingstone's unofficial fundraiser. The multi-millionaire broadcaster and redhead Chris Evans agreed to donate £100,000 towards the campaign.[68] When Dobson joked that his mother told him to 'keep clear of redheads',[69] Evans immediately doubled his donation to £200,000, nearly half the £420,000 Livingstone needed.[70]

◆

Nothing seemed to affect Livingstone's standing, not the petulant negativity of Labour's election campaign or the pathetic smears or the 60-second apology forced from him by the parliamentary standards commissioner over Localaction on 20 March 2000.[71] No one cared about anything much other than teaching Blair and his hated spin doctors a lesson they would never forget.

Dobson's campaign was so bad he was forced to beg the prime minister 'to spell out very clearly his support for me'.[72] The final straw for 'poor old Dobbo' as he was now universally known came when the prime minister's polling advisor Phillip Gould suggested he shave off his beard to attract women and younger voters. 'I told them to get stuffed,' Dobson told a TV interviewer, 'because, quite frankly, I'm not in the image business – with me, what you see is what you get.'[73]

◆

All bad things have to come to an end and finally, on 4 May 2000 after more than two years of slapstick and slander, people in London went to the polls to pick their first directly-elected mayor. On the following morning, the candidates gathered for the result at the Queen Elizabeth the Second Conference Centre. The first results were: Livingstone, 667,887; Steve Norris, 464,434; Dobson,

223,884; Susan Kramer, Liberal Democrats, 203,452. Dobson was a very poor third.

Their second preference votes were distributed. This left Livingstone overwhelmingly the winner with 776,427 and Norris with 564,137. At 12.20 p.m. on 5 May 2000, a tearful Livingstone ascended the podium and began his speech: 'As I was saying before I was rudely interrupted 14 years ago...' There were cheers. On All Fools' Day in 1986, they had sung Vera Lynn's 'We'll Meet Again' as the London Residuary Body heavies cleared the building. But no one had really believed it.

Notes

1   *Have I Got News For You?*, BBC TV, 2.5.03
2   Michael Crick, *Stranger Than Fiction*, Fourth Estate, 2000, pp298-301
3   *Sunday Mirror*, 21.11.99
4   *Guardian*, 15.9.99
5   Mark D'Arcy and Rory McLean, *Nightmare! The Race to Become London's Mayor*, p111
6   Interview, Ken Livingstone, 3.1.08
7   *Sun*, 'The 12 days that shook his life', diary by Stephan Shakespeare, 29.11.99
8   Alan Clark, *Diaries*, Phoenix, 1994, pp195-196
9   *Sun*, 8.11.99
10 *Independent*, regular column by Ken Livingstone, 27.10.99
11 *Daily Mail*, 2.11.99
12 *Independent*, 2.11.99
13 Mark D'Arcy and Rory McLean, *Nightmare! The Race to Become London's Mayor*, pp143-144
14 *Daily Mail*, 2.11.99
15 Interview, Lance Price, 11.1.08
16 Off-the-record interviews, 2007; *Mail on Sunday*, 7.11.99
17 *Guardian*, 19.11.99
18 Interview, Baron Soley, former MP for Ealing, Acton and Shepherd's Bush, 29.10.07
19 Ibid.
20 Interview, Ken Livingstone, 8.11.07
21 Alastair Campbell, *The Blair Years*, Hutchinson, 2007, p428
22 Ibid., pp428-429
23 Ibid., pp429-430
24 *Guardian*, 21.11.99
25 *Daily Mail*, 7.12.99
26 Andrew Rawnsley, *Servants of the People, The Inside Story of New Labour*, Penguin, 2001, pp356-357
27 Off-the-record briefing, 10.12.07
28 *Times*, 23.12.99

29 Lance Price, *The Spin Doctor's Diary, Inside Number 10 with New Labour*, p184

30 Alastair Campbell, *The Blair Years*, p440

31 Lance Price, *The Spin Doctor's Diary, Inside Number 10 with New Labour*, pp186-188

32 Alastair Campbell, *The Blair Years*, p440

33 Ibid., pp440-441 (26.1.00)

34 *Observer*, 30.1.00

35 *Observer*, 11.12.94

36 *Observer*, 5.5.96

37 *Evening Standard*, 13.5.96

38 *Sunday Times*, 23.1.00

39 *Guardian*, 16.3.00

40 *Independent* and *Express*, 18.3.00

41 *Observer*, 12.3.00

42 *Independent*, 18.1.00

43 BBC News Online, 20.11.99

44 Interview, Ken Livingstone, 8.11.07

45 Andrew Rawnsley, *Servants of the People, The Inside Story of New Labour*, pp360-361

46 Mark D'Arcy and Rory MacLean, *Nightmare! The Race to Become London's Mayor*, pp179-180

47 *Evening Standard*, 16.3.00

48 Mark D'Arcy and Rory MacLean *Nightmare! The Race to become London's Mayor*, p176,

49 Interview, Ken Livingstone, 8.11.07

50 Ibid.

51 Interview, Valerie Wise, 23.7.07

52 Mark D'Arcy and Rory MacLean, *Nightmare! The Race to Become London's Mayor*, p200

53 Lance Price, *The Spin Doctor's Diary, Inside Number 10 with New Labour*, p197

54 Ibid., p198

55 See Chapter 6

56 Interview, Jonathan Rosenberg, 29.9.07

57 *Evening Standard*, ICM Poll, 22.2.00

58 *Evening Standard*, 6.3.00

59 Alastair Campbell. *The Blair Years*, p443

60 *Independent*, comment by Tony Banks MP, 6.3.00

61 Interview, Chris Mullin MP, 23.1.08

62 Off-the-record briefing, 10.12.07

63 *Guardian*, 19.1.00

64 See Chapter 14

65 Ibid.

66 Ibid.

67 *Guardian*, 10.3.00

68 *Evening Standard*, 4.4.00

69 *Daily Mirror*, 21.3.00

70 *Evening Standard*, 21.3.00
71 Mark D'Arcy and Rory MacLean, *Nightmare! The Race to Become London's Mayor*, pp212-215
72 *Independent*, 13.3.00
73 GMTV, *The Sunday Programme*, 12.3.00

Chapter 22

The coming of the Kenocracy,
May 2000–January 2003

Ken Livingstone and his aides were escorted through an excited crush of reporters and cameramen to a waiting police car which ferried them, lights flashing, to Romney House in Marsham Street at the heart of Westminster – the new mayor's temporary headquarters. There, a 'transitional team' of civil servants waited anxiously not to hand over the keys to the city, but three-ring binders of documents detailing the powers and responsibilities of a directly-elected mayor of London. In the months before the elections, Livingstone had held discreet meetings with Bob Chilton, a civil servant who headed the Greater London Authority transitional team. Chilton, known for his calm efficiency, had set up the necessary bureaucracy for the mayor and the new Greater London Authority, GLA, to start operating from day one.[1] 'To the general horror of the transitional team,' says Livingstone, 'I suddenly arrived with an ugly and dishevelled group of lefties!'[2] Following a press conference, Livingstone and his entourage then went to his home in Ivy Road for a celebratory meal. A little later, Maurice Stonefrost, the last director general of the GLC, presented Livingstone with the candle he had appropriated from the orchestra at the abolition party in 1986.[3]

'The turnout was so low,' observed Lance Price on the day of the declaration, 'that Ken cannot claim to have a massive mandate... Frank looks pretty forlorn and really no one knows what he will do.'[4] After all first and second preference votes were accumulated, Livingstone had polled 58 per cent of the vote to Norris's 42 per cent. But the turnout was a derisory 32.58 per cent. Price had a point. Centuries of inexorable central state control would not be washed away so quickly. There had been a depressing public indifference to the election.

In his victory speech, Livingstone had talked of Margaret Thatcher's rude 'interruption' of his rule over London but in reality leading the GLC and being mayor were envisaged as starkly different roles. As leader of the GLC, Livingstone was first among equals as a member and his decisions had to be ratified, or rubber-stamped, by committees and council meetings, often in public. The GLC also provided services directly to the people of London. But the mayor's role was more shadowy and more strategic. His office would not directly run any services but oversee the subordinate new bodies which would. For the first time in its 171-year history, the Metropolitan Police became directly accountable to the people of London. The 23 members of the new Metropolitan Police Authority, 12 appointed by Livingstone, would establish the policing priorities of the Met and monitor its performance. The Met demonstrated both the power of the new post and its limits.

The mayor would set the Met's budget but could neither hire nor fire the Met's commissioner; that power still rested with the home secretary.[5] As with other functions, including planning and the Tube, the mayor could go so far and no further. The state would retain the whip hand in some critical areas. But Livingstone now enjoyed executive powers: like a feudal monarch he could take decisions and issue orders over a wide field of activity without needing anyone's approval.

The fire service also became his responsibility through the London Fire and Emergency Planning Authority. Other main bodies included: Transport for London, TfL, with responsibility for the Tube, buses and black cabs and the London Development Agency to promote London's economy. The body with the responsibility for scrutinising the mayor was the Assembly for the Greater London Authority. The Assembly's first chairman was none other than Trevor Phillips, who was Dobson's failed running mate for the deputy mayor's job. At the first meeting of the GLA on 3 July 2000, Phillips said: 'We know that the mayor is not above taking a risk or two. The Assembly's formal role is that of scrutineer. It is our job to ensure that the mayor and his team act in the interests of Londoners and not against them. I can assure you, Ken, that is genuinely meant... We remain servants of London. This is a democracy, not a Kenocracy. If you decide to use your position to advance policies that are not in the interests of Londoners, or if you choose to use the platform for other political ends, we will, I promise, kick your ass [sic].'[6]

Livingstone appeared irritated; he and Phillips really did not like each other, but he might have allowed himself a smile. On closer inspection of his most important appointments in his first few weeks, those in the know would have to conclude that the Kenocracy had already been established. It would still be running London almost eight years later. When asked about Phillips' remarks now, Livingstone laughs. He says, 'Wasn't he wrong? That's exactly what it is! And it would be a "Borisocracy" [under Boris Johnson, Conservative mayoral candidate, 2008] or a "Brianocracy" [under Brian Paddick, Liberal Democrat candidate, 2008] if they win.

'That's what it was set up to be. Blair created the system he would have liked for himself. When I said it to him, he laughed.'[7] As for the London Assembly, its only power was to veto the mayor's annual budget; most members of the public would not know their Assembly member if they ran them down in the street and increasingly Livingstone came to see many of its members as idle and useless.[8] To City Hall watchers in the press, some Assembly members seemed scarcely able to find their own 'asses' with both hands let alone kick Livingstone's.

In spite of all the media hoo-ha over the mayoral election, the initial few years of Livingstone's first administration proved to be the dampest of squibs for the press. Ken Livingstone may have just secured the largest and most direct mandate of any politician in British history, but there was not all that much he could do with it at the beginning. The first year seemed to be taken up with news of obscure people being hired to important new posts. And so it was.

Above all else, Livingstone's appointments were testimony to his hobby of collecting people he can trust and sticking to them; that included his Socialist Action friends. The 1999 Greater London Act allowed him to pick 12 principal advisors, including two political aides. In reality, he had known and worked with nearly all his initial appointees. Important appointments at this stage included Neale Coleman, approachable, down-to-earth and widely considered to be one of Livingstone's most able and trustworthy aides. An influential figure in the Paddington Labour Party, he had helped engineer Livingstone's selection for the GLC candidacy in 1981.[9] Coleman had played a critical role in exposing the gerrymandering and corruption of Westminster Council where he had been a member and Labour housing spokesman.[10] His knowledge of housing in particular was unsurpassed.

A number of GLC old hands got jobs. Mike Ward, who set up the Greater London Enterprise Board (GLEB), was appointed chief executive of the LDA. Livingstone had clearly patched up his relationship with John McDonnell, MP for Hayes and Harlington,[11] whom he appointed as an advisor on local government. Others included two old GLC stalwarts and Fares Fair warriors, Dave Wetzel and Paul Moore, who were both appointed to the board of TfL: Wetzel as vice chairman. Livingstone had known Moore, an ex-Chartist, since his Lambeth days where they had both been active in the Schools Action Union.[12] There were raised eyebrows at Wetzel's hiring. As GLC transport chairman, he had not only tried to create an insurrection over Fares Fair on the number 12 bus[13] but appeared five months later inexplicably dressed in a gorilla costume before the bemused magistrates on the South West London bench for refusing to pay the correct fare. 'We would regard his appointment as a failure by the mayor to take transport seriously,' sniffed a Tory spokesman at the time.[14]

After the GLC Wetzel ran an antiques shop at Mevagissey in Cornwall before moving back to west London to open a Chinese restaurant in Brentford with his daughter and son-in-law. In the summer of 1999, Livingstone reviewed the restaurant for the *Evening Standard* magazine and said to Wetzel, 'Do you want to piss around washing dishes here for the next four years or do you want to help me change London? I might have to stand as an independent. Would you still support me? You can risk your membership of the Labour Party.' Wetzel replied, 'Well you can sod that with this prime minister!' He immediately joined the Livingstone campaign.[15]

The importance of another hiring was largely overlooked. Maureen Charleson left her job working for the MP for Brent East to become the mayor's private secretary. Competent, discreet and warm, Charleson was always one of Livingstone's most valued assets. Livingstone's future partner Emma Beal, who had managed his restaurant column at the *Evening Standard* magazine, would become his office manager. Livingstone's old Socialist Action cadres formed by far the most significant bloc. They had also proved important during the campaign. As in 1981, Livingstone had taken control of London with the help of a tiny and obscure revolutionary group. His initial core of advisors included John Ross, Redmond O'Neill, Jude Woodward,

Atma Singh and his two former parliamentary researchers Simon Fletcher and Mark Watts. Others would follow as would those non-members who had worked closely with them in the past, including Lee Jasper and Kumar Murshid. Livingstone describes Socialist Action as the 'only really serious people on the hard left I ever dealt with'. He adds: 'That was the only organisation on the Left that had a coherent strategy of how we moved towards a socialist society from where you are at the present time; the others are all basically living in a fantasy world where they relive the October Revolution and have their wet dreams about the collapse of society and the vanguardist leadership arriving.

'Whereas when you're dealing with John and Redmond and Jude you are talking about people who are saying "How do we put together a coalition with either group to create the Anti Racist Alliance or around CND and others opposed to the Iraq War?" They're always focused on what is achievable in the current time. Whether or not they might be embarrassed – but I see them as the best left reformists I've ever met, although they might sue you if you write that!'[16]

Asked in December 2007 if Socialist Action still operated as a separate organisation, Livingstone responds: 'I have no idea nor have I asked and nor am I terribly interested. I spent so much of my life with small left groups, most of which when I look back on it was a total waste of time. I can't believe anyone who works for me has time to do anything else.' An insight into the relationship between Ken Livingstone and Socialist Action is provided by Pete Willsman, a member of Labour's NEC and a senior figure in the Campaign for Labour Party Democracy, or CLPD. Willsman says there are several Socialist Action members in senior positions within the CLPD which often uses the Socialist Action printing press in Hackney to print leaflets.

Willsman says, 'Ken's the boss. Ken wouldn't employ one member of Socialist Action if they didn't do exactly what he told them. The reason he employs them is the reason why I work with them in CLPD because they work incredibly hard. They're worth about 30 people – each one of them. If I want CLPD to be effective and I've got a couple of members of Socialist Action working away, I only have to say I want a leaflet and it's produced in 24 hours. They're fantastic. They never question anything. I never have to chase any of them up'[17]

According to Willsman, Socialist Action no longer regards Ross as the leader. The organisation has several leaders but effectively, although he is obviously not a member, Willsman considers Livingstone to be the top dog. 'Ken would be their leader,' adds Willsman. 'They would do whatever Ken says. If John Ross was to go against Ken, they would follow Ken. But John Ross would never go against Ken.[18] Ken pretty much understands Trots. He probably used them a while ago. They used to work hard and they were very loyal and he's carried on thinking they're a good bunch of workers. Socialist Action aren't nutcases; they're decent ordinary people.'

Keith Veness jokes, 'Socialist Action has about 30 members and about 25 of them work for Ken!'[19] He says the organisation essentially disappeared altogether in 1991. Its newspaper stopped appearing in 2001 and the only physical manifestation is its printing press. There is a Socialist Action website which is poorly maintained.[20]

Considered a founding father of Socialist Action, John Ross was possibly the most influential.[21] Fond of dominating the conversation, he once told reporters he knew Livingstone's thinking on most issues. One of the reporters present says, 'Ross told us that for 98 per cent of the time he speaks for Ken, he speaks with Ken's authority or he'll know exactly what his view will be on something. On one per cent of the time, he thinks he'd better just check; and on the other one per cent of the time, he just doesn't know.'[22]

Ross is also a regular presence around City Hall and can be spotted, stocky and with prominent eyes, haunting the edges of Livingstone's press conferences. He also acts as the mayor's main spokesman in TV and radio interviews. The adjectives used about Ross invariably include the following: highly intelligent, amiable, obsessive, dishevelled. Certainly, few would describe his office at City Hall as tidy. Ross can be difficult when crossed. 'He can get terribly het up,' says the reporter, 'I've see him explode on a couple of occasions.'[23] But he is also helpful, providing briefings for journalists and will occasionally have a drink with them.[24] During a speech in his revolutionary past, Ross once famously said, 'This is the only peaceful road to socialism. The ruling class must know that they will be killed if they do not allow a takeover by the workers. If we aren't armed there will be a bloodbath.'[25]

In 2000, Ross was more likely to put capitalist scum up against a wall, pass them a glass of claret and talk about economic fiscal policy than liquidate them in the name of the proletariat. Aged 53 in 2000, Ross loves opera and, it is strongly rumoured, has an encyclopaedic knowledge of famous tenors.[26] His value to Livingstone cannot be overstated. Livingstone would credit Ross with making crucial interventions that helped bring the 2012 Olympics to London and government agreement in October 2007 to build the Paddington to Liverpool Street Crossrail project.[27]

As expected Ross became Livingstone's main economic advisor. In the early months and years, his main role was to present olive branches to an initially wary City of London Corporation and build links with the business and property world. He also consulted widely with business organisations, including the London Chamber of Commerce, for suggestions on who to appoint as board members of the LDA.[28]

Simon Fletcher, who became his chief of staff, is the closest to Livingstone and at the age of 32 in 2000, the youngest of his key advisors. Fletcher once lodged with Livingstone at his house in Brent and would later invite him to be his best man.[29] He grew up in the Oxfordshire town of Banbury and his father was an executive for the Rover car company. He attended the City of London Polytechnic and was later a councillor on Camden Council, where he was known for his left-wing views.[30] One of Livingstone's advisors described Fletcher as probably Livingstone's closest friend.[31] Fletcher, personable, discreet and clever, would chair the daily meeting of the mayor's advisors in Livingstone's absence.[32] Fletcher's mild manner masked a fierce loyalty to Livingstone and a tough streak. 'I don't sneeze without the mayor's permission,' he once told the London Assembly.[33] At City Hall, his office was always the closest to Livingstone's. Conservative members considered him to be the de facto deputy mayor.[34]

Redmond O'Neill also became a power at City Hall, a short jump-jockey-like figure, energetic, not to say kinetic. 'There's more of an edge with Redmond,' says a former senior political journalist at the *Evening Standard*, 'he's the sort of mystery figure; the propaganda overlord. When you see a senior press officer looking miserable, we reckon they've just had their arse kicked by either Redmond or Simon or possibly both of them.'[35] Known for his abrupt emails, he is widely considered to be impressive and efficient. Luke Blair, a former mayoral press officer, says, 'You won't find very much written about Redmond; it's one of the fascinations journalists have about him.'[36] Aged 46 in 2000, O'Neill apparently became involved with revolutionary politics while at Sussex University between 1973 and 1979 and was introduced to Livingstone by Ross in October 1987.[37] O'Neill had also worked as an advisor to Livingstone,[38] and is known for his love of all things Irish and for his links to the Irish republican movement.[39] Initially, O'Neill was Livingstone's policy advisor on transport. Atma Singh, another member of Socialist Action, was appointed as Livingstone's advisor on Asian affairs.

Lee Jasper, aged 41, was made senior policy advisor on race relations and policing. Of mixed race, Jasper was considered one of London's most powerful black men and chaired many important bodies for the black communities including Operation Black Vote and the National Black Alliance. He was also involved in the battle against Marc Wadsworth which destroyed the Anti-Racist Alliance, and became the national secretary of the National Assembly Against Racism established by members of Socialist Action with Livingstone's support. Kumar Murshid was another involved in the Wadsworth feud. He became advisor on regeneration.[40] They also helped during the election.

Livingstone would rule London for the next eight years side by side with this tiny core of people, of whom scarcely anyone had heard. They were all bound by affection as much as loyalty and discretion. 'These aren't just my closest political advisors,' says Livingstone, 'we've all been around so long they're also mostly my best friends.'[41]

◆

The political repercussions of running as an independent were immediately obvious; there was ill-disguised hostility from the new Labour members of the London Assembly, who held nine of the 25 seats. At one point, they declined to enter Romney House and John Biggs, the new Assembly member for the City and East, even refused to shake Livingstone's hand.[42] Livingstone needed to appoint Labour members to senior positions on the official bodies under his control. The party's initial petulance was brought to an end by Tony Blair who at least had the good grace to call Livingstone on the Saturday following the poll to offer his congratulations. Among the Labour Assembly members to get jobs was Lord (Toby) Harris of Haringey as chairman of the Met Police Authority, and Nicky Gavron who became deputy mayor.

Following the intense media interest in the election, the first two years proved a barren wasteland for news. Despite the work done by the transitional team, Livingstone and his team had essentially to establish the new system of London governance from scratch and feel their way along. There was derision in some quarters when the Livingstone cabinet met for the first time on 20 June 2000. 'Coffee without caffeine is still coffee,' sniffed one observer, Simon Carr, in the *Independent*, 'but politics without power is just public relations. Ken Livingstone's new London cabinet met round its oval table for the first time yesterday but it doesn't have any power just now. After Ken is officially installed in the office of London Mayor on 3 July it still won't have any power. And it never will.'[43]

But Livingstone swiftly got into his stride. Dave Wetzel went to see the mayor shortly after the election and asked him how he was getting on. 'It's wonderful, 'replied Livingstone. 'If somebody comes through that door and they've got a bright idea, you can say "Go ahead and do it". You don't have to take it to the Labour Party and the Labour group and the Council Committee and the full council – it just gets done. It's so much better.' Then Livingstone added, 'But I wouldn't trust anybody else with these powers.'[44]

Hugh Muir of the *Evening Standard* covered the first phase of the new government system of London. But soon the media realised there was not much going on. Livingstone says, 'I remember telling people there's going to be nothing happening for the first two years. We have to create a machine because nothing exists. We have to appoint people and draw up strategies.'[45] For those first difficult years the cry would often go up: Where's the mayor? Simon Jenkins, who had helped persuade Blair to create the post, was among those leading the charge.[46] The first two and a half years would be dominated by Livingstone's continuing war with New Labour. This time he was the mayor, not MP for Brent East or possible mayoral candidate and the battleground was not Clause Four or single parent benefits but the government's PPP proposals for the London Underground. As in 1981, Livingstone's first big battle in the courts would be the Tube, and as in 1981, he would lose.

Years of under-investment, particularly under the Thatcher governments, had left the Tube in a dreadful state. But without it London would grind to a halt. Three million passengers were using the Tube and embarking and disembarking at its 275 Tube stations each day. It was run by a 16,000-strong labour force.[47] Livingstone had made his opposition to PPP consistently clear during his battles with the Millbank Tendency in the run-up to the election. The mayor through TfL may run the Tube but the government still had the whip hand when it came to deciding how to pay for its renewal.

The government had signed up to PPP as it had to the previous government's spending plans. The overriding objective of the first Labour government was to ensure there was a second. For Tony Blair and Gordon Brown, that meant sticking to John Major's budget strategy. The battle started unpleasantly and got worse before ending up in the courts. It started on 19 July 2000, when Livingstone received an unpleasant fax telling him that his new TfL body would have to fork out £104 million for an unpaid bill from the building of the Jubilee line. He suspected the fell influence of Gordon Brown and the Treasury. Livingstone complained that he had been 'stitched up' while John Prescott spluttered indignation over the mayor's ingratitude. After all, was he not getting an increase of 20 per cent in funding for the Underground? 'Doesn't this just show that you can't trust Ken?' snarled a 'political ally' of the deputy prime minister.[48]

Livingstone now conducted a hunt for the best person he could find to fill the crucial role of transport commissioner, who would head TfL and lead the battle against PPP. Initially, Anthony Mayer, a career civil servant who did the job on an acting basis thought the job was his, 'unless Jesus turns up', Livingstone assured him. A few months later, Mayer received a call from Livingstone: 'Sorry, Jesus just turned up.'[49] Bob Kiley was certainly not the Messiah nor could he claim later to be much of a saint, but he quickly became one of the best known and most controversial people working for Livingstone. At 65, Kiley had a fascinating career behind him. Born in Minnesota in the north mid-western region of the US, Kiley attended the University of Notre Dame and eventually joined the Central Intelligence Agency. He worked for the CIA for 14 years, becoming manager of intelligence operations and the executive assistant to the agency's director, Richard Helms. In 1972, he left to become deputy mayor of Boston. In 1974, Kiley suffered an appalling tragedy when his wife Patricia and two small children, David and Christopher, were killed in a car accident.[50] He remarried the following year and went on to have two further children. In 1979, he was appointed to run and revive the seriously ailing New York public transport system as head of the city's Metropolitan Transportation Authority. Kiley poured $16 billion into revitalising the MTA's subways, railroads and buses. By 2000, he was acknowledged as one of the world's foremost experts on transit systems. He was also the chief executive officer of the Massachusetts Bay Transportation Authority in charge of public transport systems there.

There were raised eyebrows at Kiley's salary. At £2 million performance-related pay over four years, it dwarfed Livingstone's own mayoral salary of £87,000. But Livingstone always believed that to attract the right people, you had to pay a lot of money; anything else would be a false economy.[51] Peter Hendy, appointed as the director of buses in 2000 and Kiley's eventual successor, says, 'Kiley was an inspired choice. He understood the mayoral system and the way that it worked. I think Kiley was much more used to talking to Ken about what he should be doing as mayor, what he could achieve as mayor and the political freedom he had as mayor. He used to encourage Ken to be bold and radical and not settle for crap from government.'[52]

Kiley shook up the new Transport for London which had initially inherited senior managers from the predecessor organisation, London Regional Transport, established by the Tories in 1984 to take the Tube away from Livingstone's GLC. Kiley started to bring over associates he knew in the US, including Jay Walder, a Harvard professor, as director of finance and planning.[53] He would often tell his managers: 'This place works for the mayor; it's not working for itself. It works for me; I work for the mayor. What he fucking says, we do.'[54]

Ken Livingstone displayed both ruthlessness and contempt towards the transport managers he had inherited. In November 2000, said he had 'a hit list as long as your arm'. In January 2001, he claimed that more than 100 senior managers had 'lost the will to govern... the key top layer of management has given up. They

know they're on the way out.' Derek Smith, the managing director of the London Underground accused the mayor of having a
'disruptive and unsettling affect on morale within the company'.
But Livingstone seemed oblivious. In April 2001, he labelled the
managers as 'dullards' and 'knuckleheads'.[55]

Of mind-boggling complexity, the Public Private Partnership
contracts were seen by the government as the only way of funding the necessary improvements to the Underground and abid-
ing by the previous government's spending plans. In essence, it
meant separating the Underground's operator – Livingstone
and TfL – from the infrastructure of tracks, stations and signalling. TfL would run the trains and manage the staff; three private
consortia would be given lucrative government contracts to run
and renovate the Underground itself for 30 years. Far from being
self-funded as the government initially claimed, it transpired
that the PPP would require a huge £1 billion annual subsidy to
work. According to the transport writer Christian Wolmar, this
was more than the management of London Underground had
sought during the 1990s to modernise the whole network under
a 10-year plan.[56] Both Kiley and Livingstone thought PPP was a
bad idea. The three consortia would have three or four Tube lines
each. They were convinced PPP essentially equalled privatisation
and worse, by fragmenting the service, it was potentially dangerous. Livingstone argued that PPP breached his legal duty to
run a safe and efficient Tube network.[57] Both he and Kiley would
point to the October 2000 train crash at Hatfield in Hertfordshire
in which four people died. This exposed the shortcomings of
the national railway's infrastructure company, Railtrack, which
maintained the rails separately from the train companies. It was a
very similar system to that being proposed by the government for
the Tube.

Peter Hendy adds, 'Kiley had modernised the MTA in New
York; he did understand very clearly the necessity of keeping
the track and the signals with the operation. He fundamentally
believed in his heart that the PPP was wrong, so he was an absolutely ideal character to fight it.'[58] Both Kiley and Livingstone
suggested financing the work with capital raised through a bond
issue, essentially a form of loan.

Livingstone's stand on safety was backed by the Tube workers'
unions, the RMT and ASLF. During the winter and early spring

of 2001, either one or the other brought London to a standstill with a series of strikes each lasting at least 24 hours in protest over PPP. Livingstone saluted the strikers who had taken industrial action 'not to increase pay, not to improve their conditions but to improve the safety of Londoners'. He even joined picket lines in support.[59] 'Mayor Livingstone's support for a Tube strike looks like a return to "Red Ken",' said Professor Tony Travers, London government expert at the London School of Economics. 'But his behaviour reflects ruthless political calculations which could go badly wrong for him.' He described it as 'perhaps the best glimpse London has yet had of Red Ken circa 1981'.[60]

In 2001 and 2002, both Kiley and Livingstone went to court to try and defeat PPP. Livingstone spent £4 million in legal and court costs but PPP had become a mantra; it was never going to be abandoned because it was driven by the Treasury which felt that this was the right and only way to finance the work that needed to be done. The government spent £500 million on consultants to create the contracts.[61] In January 2003, the contracts were signed and the Tube network passed into private hands.[62] Although Ken Livingstone always claimed his court battle squeezed another £200 million from the government, all his fight against the government managed to achieve was a delay in the start of the PPP. According to some London local government experts this drove the government to give the consortia extra guarantees that only made them more inefficient.[63] But Livingstone and Kiley would be proved dramatically right about the flaws in PPP more than four years later when one of the main consortia, Metronet, responsible for the upkeep of nine Tube lines, collapsed. In July 2007, Metronet went into administration due to cost overruns after getting its sums wrong and falling into financial crisis.[64]

Essentially, Livingstone's court battle proved to be a depressing and expensive struggle which showed – in stark definition – the limits to the mayor's powers. The government was more prepared to hand the capital's public transport system over to private companies than a new system of governance for London which it had just created. The primary phase was a frustrating period, battling with the government, baited by journalists wondering if anything was happening at all and establishing a new system. It did not even seem that the new mayor could even prevent people feeding pigeons in Trafalgar Square.

♦

Livingstone had been determined to end the pigeons' long dom-
ination of the square. He thought the birds spread disease and
reportedly referred to them as 'flying rats'.[65] In August 2000, he
suggested that seed-sellers could sell a special feed which would,
in effect, slowly kill their business. 'Either we cancel that con-
cession – or the feed contains a contraceptive,' he said.[66] But
Livingstone decided to get tough. He made repeated attempts
to force the square's resident seed-seller, Bernard Rayner, out of
business.[67] On 2 October 2000, officials from the Greater London
Authority made a swoop and turfed him off the square. He told
journalists: 'They said if I didn't move they could seize my trailer
and van, fine me £1,000, arrest me and make my life hell. They
were all well over six feet tall.' He was evicted in early October but
quickly returned to ply his trade and for months there seemed to
be no getting rid of him.[68] Livingstone's former comrade, Tony
Banks, could not stomach any potential cruelty to animals and
immediately weighed in to do what he could to save the pigeons
of Trafalgar Square.[69] 'They don't shit on their friends,' snapped
Banks. 'That's something Ken Livingstone ought to learn.'[70] In
early 2001, Livingstone launched an airborne offensive: the hawk.
A falconer called David van Vynck deployed his 14 hawks in
Trafalgar Square. But it seems with limited success. The pigeons
would retreat to the steps of the National Gallery, which was out
of Livingstone's jurisdiction, but eventually, even the steps would
fall under his sway in July 2006.[71]

♦

On 23 July 2002, the Queen and the Duke of Edinburgh opened
City Hall, the 10-story glass orb nestling between Tower Bridge
and HMS *Belfast* on the south bank of the Thames. Predictably
there were some teething problems with the lifts but, the ceremony went smoothly. Prince Philip fulfilled expectations by
putting his foot in it. On the ninth floor, he had been invited by
Assembly chairman Trevor Phillips to admire the wonderful view
over the river to the Tower of London and the City opposite. 'It's
terrible,' he said. 'Look at all these buildings.' It was assumed that
the Duke had been looking backwards across the urban landscape
of south London.[72]

For the Queen in her Golden Jubilee Year, opening City Hall
was continuing a tradition: her grandfather, King George V, had

opened County Hall in 1922. In a short speech, the Queen hoped the new HQ of the mayor and Greater London Authority would 'provide an exciting forum for Londoners as your debates ebb and flow'.[73]

The design of City Hall and choice of architect, Foster and Partners, were decisions taken by Nick Raynsford, the minister for London, who also created the institutions which would occupy the new building.[74] As expected of the quietly competent Raynsford, City Hall was delivered on budget, at £65 million, and on time – in direct contrast to the extraordinary ineptitude surrounding the building of the £430 million Scottish Parliament in Holyrood.[75] Many think this striking building resembles a monstrous shiny wood louse; Livingstone always likens it to a 'glass testicle' but quickly came to love the building as much as County Hall. As yet, the mayor still had to make his mark with the public but at least he had a City Hall to call his own.

Notes

1   Tony Travers, *The Politics of London, Governing an Ungovernable City*, pp82-83
2   Interview, Ken Livingstone, 8.11.07
3   Interview, Maurice Stonefrost, 21.11.07; See Chapter 14; Wes Whitehouse, *GLC – The Inside Story*, p242
4   Lance Price, *The Spin Doctor's Diary, Inside Number 10 with New Labour*, p216
5   Gary Mason, *The Official History of the Metropolitan Police, 175 years of policing London*, Carlton Books, 2004, pp152-153
6   *Evening Standard*, 3.7.00; Ben Pimlott and Nirmala Rao, *Governing London*, OUP, 2002, p98
7   Interview, Ken Livingstone, 28.12.07
8   Mayoral press conferences, 22.1.08 and Mayor's questioning by London Assembly, 13.6.07
9   See Chapter 6
10 Andrew Hosken, *Nothing Like a Dame, The Scandals of Shirley Porter*, p166
11 See Chapters 15 and 16
12 See Chapter 2
13 See Chapter 9
14 *Evening Standard*, 14.6.00
15 Interview, Dave Wetzel, 5.11.07
16 Interview, Ken Livingstone, 28.1.07
17 Interview, Pete Willsman, 29.9.07
18 Ibid.
19 Interview, Keith Veness, 17.9.07
20 www.socialistaction.org.uk

21 See Chapter 18
22 Off-the-record interview, 15.1.08
23 Ibid.
24 Interview, Simon Harris, ITN, 18.1.08
25 *Evening Standard*, 23.7.02
26 Ibid.
27 *Railway Gazette International*, 17.1.08
28 Tony Travers, *The Politics of London, Governing an Ungovernable City*, p89
29 Tony Benn, *More Time for Politics, Diaries 2001–2007*, Hutchinson, 2007, (see 15.10.06)
30 Interview, Camden councillor, 6.7.07
31 Off-the-record interview, 31.10.07
32 Tony Travers, *The Politics of London, Governing an Ungovernable city*, p88
33 London Assembly, minutes, oral questions to Simon Fletcher, 12.6.02
34 Ibid.
35 Author interview, November 2007
36 Interview, Luke Blair, 3.10.07
37 Interview, Ken Livingstone, 1.11.07
38 *Evening Standard*, 2.10.00
39 *Evening Standard*, by Keith Dovkants, 23.1.02
40 *Guardian*, 2.10.00; See Chapter 18
41 Interview, Ken Livingstone, 8.11.07
42 Interview, Ken Livingstone, 8.11.07
43 *Independent*, 21.6.00
44 Ibid.
45 Interview, Ken Livingstone, 8.11.07
46 *Evening Standard*, 'Don't dig up roads, get cars off them', by Simon Jenkins, 15.11.01
47 *Financial Times*, 9.10.00
48 *Evening Standard*, 20.7.00
49 Off-the-record briefing, 8.1.08
50 *Evening Standard*, profile of Bob Kiley, by David Cohen, 28.3.07
51 Off-the-record briefing by aide, 1.8.07
52 Interview, Peter Hendy, 13.12.07
53 TfL press release on retirement, CV, 22.11.06
54 Interview, Peter Hendy, 13.12.07
55 Ben Pimlott and Nirmala Rao, *Governing London*, p121; *Evening Standard*, 8.1.01; *Times*, 6.4.01
56 Christian Wolmar, *The Subterranean Railway, How the London Underground Was Built and How It Changed the City Forever*, p310
57 BBC News Online, 6.7.01
58 Interview, Peter Hendy, 13.12.07
59 Ben Pimlott and Nirmala Rao, *Governing London*, p120
60 *Evening Standard*, 'Suddenly Ken isn't quite so cuddly', 10.1.01
61 Christian Wolmar, *The Subterranean Railway, How the London Underground Was Built and How It Changed the City Forever*, p310
62 Tony Travers, *The Politics of London, Governing an Ungovernable city*, pp66-67

63 Ibid., p192
64 BBC News Online, 'Metronet calls in administrators', 18.7.07
65 *Evening Standard*, 25.1.01
66 *Evening Standard*, 2.10.00
67 *Financial Times*, 18.1.01
68 *Daily Mirror*, 3.10.00
69 *Evening Standard*, 25.1.01
70 *Independent on Sunday*, 28.1.01
71 Tony Benn, *More Time for Politics, 2001–2007*, (see 13.7.06)
72 *Evening Standard*, 23.7.02
73 Text of Queen's speech, the British Monarchy, (www.royal.gov.uk)
74 Interview, Nick Raynsford, 20.12.07
75 Holyrood inquiry, by Lord Fraser of Carmyllie QC, September 2004, (www.holyroodinquiry.org)

Chapter 23

Private lives and public risks, July 2002–March 2003

On 30 May 2002, the *Evening Standard* broke the news that Ken Livingstone was to become a father for the first time at the age when many men were becoming grandfathers. All newspapers commented on Ken Livingstone's reluctance to talk about the news. The *Guardian* observed how the mayor was 'keeping mum over press reports that he is to be a first-time dad'.[1] There were no comments either from the expectant mum Emma Beal, Livingstone's new partner. In a statement, the mayor's office said, 'We do not comment on the mayor's private life at all.'[2]

Simon Harris, the political correspondent of ITN *London Tonight*, says: 'It was a big story but he was very reluctant to talk about it. When the story broke I was door-stepping him at some event [at which] he was speaking in Pimlico and he wouldn't say anything about it; we had to rely on information from his press office that he was thrilled and happy about it. He has always maintained his silence about his family and by and large it works.

'His line on this is that it puts them [the children] in the public domain. And that he's opening up his private life and for pictures to be taken of the children when they're in the park. He says that if he never brings his family into his work and public life, then he can argue they're entitled to a private life.'[3] The couple's son Thomas was born on 14 December 2002 and again there was intense press interest and comment about Livingstone becoming a dad for the first time. Again, both Livingstone and Emma Beal maintained their silence. Their daughter, Mia, was born on 20 March 2004.

But in fact, Ken Livingstone is a father of five children. By the time he was elected mayor of London in 2000, he was already the father of three children: a boy by one mother; and two girls by another. All of these children are under the age of 18.

During the seven interviews for this book, Ken Livingstone repeatedly told me he did not wish to discuss aspects of his private life and he was emphatic that he was not prepared to discuss or even confirm the issue of his three additional children. During an interview with me on the subject of press intrusion, he said, 'This is not an inaccessible administration and I'm not an inaccessible politician but I expect that my private life is not in the public domain and I'm rude to any journalist who turns up either at home or who follows me around.' There have been rare occasions when he has appeared in public with his children. He was pictured hand in hand on stage with Mia at the huge celebration of the Muslim Eid in Trafalgar Square in October 2007 but on another occasion, he refused to allow a newspaper photographer who was chasing him down the street to take a photo of his son Thomas.[4]

Subsequently, it was made clear to me by a close associate of the mayor that Ken Livingstone is and has always been deeply concerned about the press intrusion the release of this information might cause and the effect it might have on those involved. But it is obviously a significant biographical fact even if Livingstone has declined to elaborate; it would be misleading not to mention it.

It is simply not the case, as the general public widely believe, that he had his first child at the age of 57 and nor therefore can it be true, as some interviewees have asserted to me, that Ken Livingstone's personality and way of operating as a politician had fundamentally changed since the birth of Thomas in 2002. Perhaps occasionally more tired, understandably; but a transformed man?

To be fair to Livingstone, not only has he been consistent in his refusal to talk about his private life, but even his entry in *Who's Who* contains no personal information; it is just a summary of his political career even down to the committee chairmanships of his time in local government.

Most of the City Hall journalists interviewed for the book have heard rumours that Livingstone had children besides Thomas and Mia. Rumours of his first son initially surfaced in July 1999 during Labour's smear campaign. The source for the story was identified by the *Sunday Times* as someone 'with connections high up in the Labour party and close to Downing Street'.[5] Livingstone made his fury clear at the time but declined to comment. But the paper was clear: 'The allegation is being used in an effort to stop him becoming the party's candidate for mayor of London.' As 'smears' go, it is a peculiarly old-fashioned one.

On the basis of information from several sources interviewed for the book, it is important to say that Ken Livingstone is fully involved with the lives of all his children and their upbringing. I have also been told that the mothers involved are satisfied with the arrangements which have been established for the care and maintenance of their children.

The news of Emma Beal's pregnancy emerged in late May 2002, almost certainly as a result of a party in Tufnell Park, north London 12 days earlier. The party presented Livingstone not only with political and personal problems but shone an unwelcome light into his private life. In summary, an employee of the *Evening Standard* had fallen involuntarily from a wall during a party in north London. The question was, did he fall or was he pushed?

Robin Hedges, the 35-year-old man who fell to earth, was no ordinary partygoer; he was also the best friend of Livingstone's partner Emma Beal and through her got to know Livingstone well. The party destroyed the friendship of Beal and Hedges. What might have been resolved with a simple apology instead blew up into a damaging political row.

The party, held on the night of 18 May 2002, was at the home of Beal's sister Kate, in Tufnell Park Road. Ken Livingstone first met Emma Beal while working as a restaurant critic for the *Evening Standard* magazine; he wrote a weekly column between 1996 and 2000.[6] She was the office manager and worked with Steve Fletcher, who happened to be Robin Hedges' partner. Livingstone, Fletcher and Beal would sometimes go to the restaurants as a group. Later Livingstone and Beal would meet at Hedges' flat in Hargrave Road, London.[7] On 5 November 2001, the mayor's office announced that Livingstone, then 55, had split from his live-in partner of 18 years, Kate Allen, who was 45. The statement was terse and brief: 'Ken and Kate remain good friends. Neither will make any further comment now or in the future.'[8] Allen, then UK director of Amnesty International, was an equally private person. The *Guardian* observed: 'They shared a deep political ideology but Ms Allen did not share his passion for media attention. She maintained a low profile during the relationship, shunning the role of dutiful political consort.

'Mr Livingstone, who took pride in the fact that he knew of only two press photographs showing the couple together, once said: "She couldn't be seen as an appendage of me."'[9] Livingstone stayed at their home in Ivy Road while Allen appears to have kept the house they bought in Brighton. Beal seems to have moved in to Livingstone's home, and by the time of the May 2002 party, she had been pregnant with the couple's first child for three and a half months.

Hedges and Beal were like brother and sister and they holidayed together at least six or seven times.[10] But in the months before the party, Hedges' relationship with Livingstone became increasingly strained. On one occasion, Livingstone returned to his house to find his partner outside in the garden as Hedges smoked a cigarette. Livingstone was convinced Beal had been smoking as well and became angry and verbally abusive before throwing him out of the house.[11] Hedges thought Livingstone was overly possessive of Beal and did not like her seeing old friends; for his part Livingstone thought Hedges resented his relationship with Beal.[12]

The party in Tufnell Park was for Kate Beal, who was celebrating her fortieth birthday. Their other sister Sarah was also present as was Mike Furniss, a former boyfriend of Emma Beal. The party started with a good atmosphere. At around 10.30, Livingstone went to Kate Beal's bedroom for a lie down. Hedges was adamant that Livingstone was sleeping off a lot of drink;[13] but the mayor said he had drunk only three glasses of red wine. To this day, he remains emphatic that he was sober and that he does not get drunk at parties.[14] There are a small number of facts which remain undisputed: Livingstone and Beal did have a row because he thought she had been risking their unborn baby by smoking; Hedges tried to intervene because he thought it had turned nasty; a little later Hedges fell from a wall lining the steps leading up to the house and into a dangerous stairwell, and the emergency services were called. But there were contradictory versions of what happened and a subsequent inquiry was unable to find any concrete evidence of misconduct by Livingstone.[15]

In a statement to the London Assembly in June 2002, Livingstone claimed that Hedges had wrestled him to the ground outside in the street during the row to protect Beal who then disappeared back into the house. The mayor then followed her up the steps to the front door and rang the bell. He heard someone say that someone had fallen off the wall. Livingstone said: 'I did not push him, nobody pushed him. It was an accident. This is exactly the sort of thing that can happen to anybody.'[16]

Hedges denied leaping on Livingstone but conceded he became concerned at Livingstone's conduct during the row and that he did try to prevent the mayor getting back into the house. Later, Hedges wrote an account for the *Evening Standard*: 'He was pushing her, lashing out. I tried to stop him. I remember thinking: this man is completely out of control. All I could think of doing was shouting for help. To this day I don't believe he meant to push me right over the wall, or cause me serious injury.'[17] During a brief tussle on the steps, Hedges went over the wall and fell 10 feet and one inch[18] down the stairwell and suffered bruising to his ribs and side.

Later in the casualty department at the nearby Whittington Hospital, as he drifted in and out of consciousness, Hedges asked people who had accompanied him from the party what had happened. He was furious and concluded he had been pushed by Livingstone; he was also in serious pain.[19] The usually mild-mannered Hedges was incandescent with fury and told Emma Beal several times what he thought of Livingstone.

The situation became hazardous politically for Livingstone when his old enemies at the *Evening Standard* ran an unhelpful version of events on 31 May 2002 just a day after it had broken the news of the impending birth. Hedges freaked out when journalists started turning up at his flat and even more so when he got a call from Emma Beal who was clearly distressed and asked him to agree to a statement City Hall wanted to issue about the party. He heard a voice in the background and recognised one of Livingstone's senior aides. Hedges later claimed: 'She was hysterical, crying. She said they had to "keep Ken out of it". She said she wanted a statement from me for "damage limitation to both sides". There is no way in the world she would use a phrase like that but at that stage I still felt extremely protective towards her. I wanted to help her; I didn't want her to suffer. So I agreed they could put out a statement from me saying the fall had been an accident. I told Emma that I knew it was not the truth and she knew it was not the truth. But, if it helped her, then she could have it.'[20] Hedges, who at one point considered pressing charges, regretted it soon afterwards. He said that he would have accepted an apology from Ken Livingstone but it never came. Ken Livingstone does not do apologies – he clearly sees it as a sign of weakness, rather than strength.

The Liberal Democrats on the London Assembly referred the matter to the Standards Board for England, a new quango set up by the government to investigate allegations of misconduct against local politicians, and with the power to suspend them from office for up to five years. Livingstone considered the *Evening Standard*'s coverage of the incident, which included four front page leads, 'disgraceful' and on 25 June 2002, actually travelled to Tufnell Park to measure the drop to disprove the paper's claim that it had been as much as 15 feet.[21] The Standards Board cleared Livingstone of any breaches of the code of conduct for politicians it was set up to maintain.[22] When Hedges received a copy of the report of the inquiry on 23 July 2003, he wrote that he felt 'cold fury', but he was on the record as stating it had been an 'accident'. In the circumstances, the Board could scarcely conclude otherwise.

◆

But unquestionably the greatest risk Livingstone took during the period was the political decision for which he will probably be best remembered. On 17 February 2003, Livingstone introduced the congestion charge to central London. It has never stopped being controversial since its introduction and would provide a key battleground for the following two mayoral elections. The idea of road pricing to hold back the relentless rising tide of congestion in London was nothing new, and it had always been a political hot potato. In the early 1970s, Edward Heath lost his temper while stuck in a traffic jam in Whitehall and decided to shout at the Tory leader of the GLC, then Sir Desmond Plummer. Plummer, now Lord Plummer of Marylebone, whose name adorns the Blackwall Tunnel, was taking a shower at the time in a Tokyo hotel when the call came through. Plummer was blunt with Heath, telling him, 'I asked you for the powers to deal with this problem and you wouldn't give them to me and now you're asking why I haven't done it.'[23]

Plummer was convinced that traffic was damaging London's economy and he was frustrated at the government's myopia when it came to granting County Hall potentially vote-losing powers to deal with the problem effectively. In February 1968, he introduced London's first bus lanes in Park Lane and on the Vauxhall Bridge and toyed with the idea of a monorail along Oxford Street.[24] Denied the power by Heath to introduce road charging, Plummer fell in love with the wretched Motorway Box which ultimately resulted in only two successful schemes: the road to his own self-destruction at the GLC elections in 1973 and Ken Livingstone's own path to power eight years later.

Plummer's successor as GLC leader, Sir Reg Goodwin, jettisoned the 'Box' but preferred to put up fares instead of rates while staving off bankruptcy during the devastating OPEC oil crisis.[25] Goodwin's successor, Sir Horace Cutler, the GLC's last Tory leader (1977–81), had also examined road pricing for London but concluded that charging private motorists to enter central London was never going to prove popular and that there was no evidence that it was workable.[26]

In 1981, Livingstone's strategy had clearly been to get people out of their cars and into Tubes and buses by cutting fares. The evidence provided by Fares Fair suggested that it was working but the judges and the London Borough of Bromley decided otherwise. Faced with the failure to invest in public transport, people had no incentive to leave their cars in the garage. Undeniably, in terms of a real transport policy for London, the 1980s and 1990s were the years the locusts had eaten.

When Edward Heath was complaining about the traffic, the average speed of a journey through London was 12mph; by the time Livingstone was first elected mayor nearly 30 years later, it was 9.5mph and getting slower by the year.[27] Something dramatic had to be done. Livingstone was always convinced that building roads was not the answer: 'Even if we had built those motorway boxes, the congestion would be exactly the same in London today because people fill whatever capacity you supply.'[28]

◆

The congestion charge had been Livingstone's most prominent and most radical manifesto commitment. Ken Livingstone hated the motor car. He had failed his driving test in 1966 while working at Chester Beatty and never retook it, at first because he could not afford to, and later because he thought it unnecessary.[29] At the GLC, he had dispensed with the leader's official car and made use of County Hall's 11 chauffeur-driven cars as infrequently as possible.[30] He also introduced the wheel clamp – the so-called Denver Boot. On becoming mayor, he made it clear to his officials that there were to be no company cars.[31] He has always taken the Tube to work. To him the congestion charge was the jewel in the crown;

to others it was a potential millstone which could sink his political career. For the Labour government and even all his closest advisors, the charge had the stench of death, a pungent scent of a Poll Tax on wheels. Livingstone would carry out his manifesto pledge in the teeth of fierce opposition from businesses, resident groups, the powerful roads lobby and those around him.

Livingstone's plan was to charge motorists £5 a day during the working week for driving into an area of central London covering roughly eight square miles within the Inner Ring Road, with Park Lane as the western boundary and Commercial Street and Tower Bridge in the east. It was obviously a new tax, and furthermore, a tax on motorists who were already paying through the nose for their tax disc, parking permits and fuel. Potentially, it was political suicide.

For Livingstone, the congestion charge was essential. If he did not introduce it in his first four-year term, then what was the point of him? Many were already asking the question. It was difficult to see at that stage the relevance of a directly-elected mayor for the capital, especially when Simon Jenkins was signing off his articles with: 'Where is the mayor?' If Livingstone did try it, the charge could fail and destroy him. After all, few other important cities had ever risked a new tax simply for driving a car into the centre.[32] The Labour Party would never readmit Livingstone if the congestion charge failed which explains why it would not sanction his readmission until after it had proved not to have been a disaster.

Livingstone had to decide what kind of scheme to introduce. Before the mayoral election, Livingstone and John Ross had travelled to the capital's business district governed by the City of London Corporation to reassure the business world of their good intentions. Despite their left-wing credentials, they would not seek to abolish the ancient City of London and the Lord Mayor's parade.

Michael Synder, then deputy chairman of the Corporation's Policy and Resources Committee, told Livingstone, 'Look, if you're serious about this congestion charge, look at our "Ring of Steel" camera system.'[33] In 1994, after two IRA bombings at the Baltic Exchange in 1992 and Bishopsgate a year later, the Corporation had set up a security and surveillance system which automatically photographed front seat occupants of all vehicles entering the City of London and computer-checked if a vehicle was stolen or suspicious.

A similar scheme was proposed in 2000 when a group of transport experts called Road Charging Options for London or ROCOL were commissioned by the government to look at road pricing. It concluded that of all the possible schemes, 'a charging system based on vehicle registration numbers with a £5 daily charge and enforced by cameras could have a significant impact on traffic conditions in central London.' ROCOL described this option as both 'feasible and enforceable.'[34]

TfL agreed it was the best system and the only one that could 'become operational during the mayor's first term of office'.[35] For Livingstone, time was crucial; politically, it had to be introduced before the next mayoral election in 2004. There was to be no pilot before implementation, essentially because this would have delayed congestion charging beyond the first term.

Shortly before the scheme started, *The Times* reported, 'He has introduced it quickly because he wants it to have time to settle down and to be seen to be working before he seeks re-election in 2004. But he knows that by rushing it in he is taking a huge risk; if it falters he could be doomed... he said recently that he would be finished as mayor if congestion charging fails. He could well be doomed anyway.'[36]

Over a period of nearly two years, beginning before the election, Livingstone's advisors had tried to talk him out of it. Before the election, they had presented Livingstone with a paper setting out reasons why the charge should be dropped from the manifesto. 'They all thought it was going to be a disaster,' says Ken Livingstone. 'There had been a governmental report talking about the great difficulty of it all and so they all clearly had a meeting before to plan how they were going to talk me out of it, for my own good!'[37] Livingstone took the advisor's paper and dropped it into the bin and said, 'Now let's talk about how we're going to do it.' There then followed 'a short furious row' but clearly his advisors' concerns remained.[38]

There were serious attempts to prevent Livingstone going ahead with the scheme both internally and externally. Although Livingstone was nominally independent, the Labour Party was clearly terrified about the potential political damage caused by one of its MPs, albeit one without the Labour whip. Determined attempts were exerted on the mayor to abandon his key policy. In late 2001, it was rumoured that the government was considering using its reserve powers to prevent the introduction of the charge. It was strongly suggested that the government would contemplate a climbdown over the PPP, if Livingstone abandoned his plans. In particular, John Spellar, the transport minister was said to regard the charge as 'as an electoral liability for Labour, and would be very happy if it was ditched.' According to the *Independent*'s respected transport editor, Keith Harper, in December 2001, Spellar had apparently already said that 'ministers could use special powers to block Mr Livingstone's scheme'.

But Harper's article caused serious palpitations at City Hall due to one pointed paragraph towards the end: 'His [Livingstone's] advisors also believe that his plans to introduce the scheme by February 2003, less than 15 months away, is far too optimistic. They say that the technical equipment needed to underpin the charging scheme is unlikely to be ready.'[39] This proved to be a bombshell within City Hall, where Livingstone's close-knit circle of advisors was known for their loyalty and discretion – bordering on secrecy. The timing of the story was also bad coming on the day Livingstone was passing the point of no return by signing the contract with Capita,[40] the firm which had been given the job of setting up the system.

The internal opposition to the scheme came particularly from the important Socialist Action contingent of the mayor's advisors. Atma Singh, who became an advisor on Asian affairs for the mayor, finally left Socialist Action in 1994 but continued to pay his £20 a month dues to the group. At a meeting of Socialist Action in September/October 2000, Singh made handwritten notes as members discussed the role of 'SA shaping the mayor's agenda'. Also discussed was the proposed congestion charge, which was described as a 'regressive tax'.[41]

Bob Kiley, the transport commissioner, was convinced powerful forces at City Hall were trying to derail the scheme. Kiley and senior figures at TfL, like Dave Wetzel, were fully committed to the charge. There was now a threat of a huge rift between City Hall and people at Transport for London HQ. As a senior TfL press officer, Luke Blair worked closely with the commissioner. He says, 'I remember Bob being sort of very concerned that people were briefing against the project and briefing against him and there were a couple of pretty pointed stories saying there had been a showdown between Bob and Ken's advisors about this, et cetera. To be honest, you rarely do get to the bottom of how these stories get out.'[42]

Again his closest advisors made a last-ditch attempt to dissuade Livingstone from going ahead. 'It was their unanimous advice not to proceed,' says Livingstone. 'Politically, they thought it would crush my support. But Kiley and the TfL people wanted to proceed, so the transport officials believed it could be done and they were confident. That was actually the most demoralising point, because these aren't just my closest political advisors. They've been around so long that they're also my best friends and I knew that none of them agreed with me and that if I called it wrong they'd all be out of a job. But once I made the decision, they all shut up and got on with it.'[43]

One of Livingstone's advisors who tried to prevent him introducing the charge says, 'Ken was genuinely upset because his closest friends were against him on something. We didn't necessarily think it was going to be a disaster but people had been raising all these issues about rat-running [on the periphery of the zone to prevent paying]. If you looked at it, it was a tax. When has a politician ever imposed new taxes and been thanked for it?'[44]

Luke Blair says, 'There were plenty of people around that project who were terribly nervous and flapping about, but not Ken. One of the key things I realised was that a project like this needs a strong political champion. You need a Ken. There were moments in the project when unquestionably everyone was doubting it: things had gone wobbly; the contractors [Capita] were not performing, some of the cameras weren't working. All sorts of things were going wrong. The Driver and Vehicle Licensing Agency database was a typical problem; we were always worried about it. All the way through, we got this message – look, Ken wants this to happen, just bloody fix it and get on with it – and people did. But there are very few politicians who are so over-committed to such risky projects in that way.'[45]

◆

The key figures behind congestion charging included Derek Turner, TfL's director of street management, who handled the day-to-day running of the project. Redmond O'Neill was charged by Livingstone to oversee Turner. Also important was Jay Walder,

Kiley's number two, who had had experience of the world's first real road-pricing scheme in Singapore in 1975.[46]

To negotiate the contract with Capita, Kiley brought in Richard Granger, a partner for the Deloitte consultants and a diminutive but tough character. Luke Blair says, 'Richard massively beat up Capita and screwed them down on the contractual deal. I remember someone at TfL saying, "Well Granger's just won his fee several times over".'

◆

In the summer of 2002, Livingstone's traffic management came under criticism from some quarters after traffic lights were rephased in favour of pedestrians to bring them into line with safety procedures elsewhere. But others thought there were more cynical reasons behind it. In June 2002, the *Independent* reported: 'Motoring groups claim that Mr Livingstone has approved changes to traffic light timings that have created chaos. More lights are now on red for longer so pedestrians have more time to cross. Critics allege that the mayor will change the lights back once his congestion charging scheme is introduced to make it appear successful.'[47] Livingstone lost his temper with his press officers for their failure to refute a story he insisted was wrong.

Few were predicting success for the charge. The *Observer* stated: 'Two years into his mayoralty, Livingstone is popularly seen as a let-down. As the scheme has grown, so has the need for it to be a triumph. It has ridden roughshod over planning norms. The *Observer* has learnt that Livingstone signed contracts with software firm Capita to implement the scheme in December 2001, two months before the completion of a public consultation on the plan. He then ignored the results of that consultation, which showed a majority against the plan. He refused to hold a public inquiry and went to court to defeat those who tried to force it.'[48]

The public consultation carried out between July and September 2001[49] had revealed a lot of hostility to congestion charging. The scheme was modified as a result but nothing was going to prevent its introduction on Monday, 17 February 2003, during the school half-term break, when traffic levels were always reduced by about 14 per cent.[50]

◆

In the week beginning 8 July 2002, Westminster City Council, which had thrown lawyers at Livingstone during his GLC days, tried to get the scheme rescinded. Westminster argued that Livingstone's order was 'fatally flawed' and claimed that the mayor breached European Union requirements by not conducting a formal environmental impact assessment, and the Human Rights Act by not doing more to protect residents. Livingstone's legal footwork had been sound and he won the case; he had learned a lot since Fares Fair.[51]

Luke Blair thought Livingstone was remarkable under pressure: 'He always seemed to have very much the same demeanour – the same temperament. One rarely seemed to see him flaring up and that's a huge asset if you're anyone in a position of influence or power to have this even temperament. Even when he's laying into someone pretty viciously he seems to do it in that same flat nasal way. In its way, it's terribly powerful. More powerful than someone who keeps getting red in the face like John Prescott.'[52]

But with less than a month to go, congestion charging was already proving to be a massive vote loser. In January 2003, a survey by the RAC showed three quarters of drivers were either deeply opposed to the scheme or sceptical about its chances of success. A lot more than just Livingstone's political future was at stake. Professor David Begg, chairman of the government's Commission for Integrated Transport, warned that failure in London would mean congestion charging as a solution to traffic chaos would be scrapped for a generation. Others warned it would mean Britain becoming the most congested country in Europe.[53] A few days before its introduction, some in the Labour government were rubbing their hands with glee at the prospect of Livingstone's imminent fall. Mark Mardell, then a BBC political correspondent, remembered being told by one smiling senior minister clearly ignorant about the way the scheme would operate: 'There'll be people crashing into the barriers because they don't know they are there, and huge jams because drivers are turning round rather than paying and it'll all end up with complete gridlock.'[54] Before day one of the scheme, Livingstone deliberately played up the possibilities of failure. 'It's going to be a bloody day,' he would tell any journalist who would listen to him as the launch loomed. But on the day itself, it would prove an astounding success.[55]

◆

Livingstone planned to be at City Hall as the congestion charge started at 7 a.m. on 17 February 2003. As he opened his front door, Livingstone was greeted by the lights of more than 20 TV cameras. 'The room was illuminated,' remembers Livingstone. 'It was like something out of *Close Encounters [of the Third Kind]*. And then they all followed me down the road. Most of the media had worked on the assumption that it was going to be a catastrophic failure – his career's going to end today and we're going to film every balls-achingly gut-wrenching moment of it.'[56]

Neale Coleman, one of Livingstone's key policy advisors, says, 'I remember coming in to work [City Hall] on the day it came in and it was eerie because there had been so much scare stuff in the press about how it was going to lead to the Apocalypse and I looked at Tower Bridge and literally for five minutes – no car! We thought Oh God, what's happened here?'[57] At one stage, Livingstone worried that he might have 'overdone it'.[58] On the first day, 190,000 cars entered the zone compared to the usual 250,000 – a reduction of 25 per cent.[59] Livingstone described the first day as the 'best day in traffic flow we've had in living memory'.[60]

In a fact, in a way, he had overdone it. For those first few years 70,000 fewer cars entered central London each day instead of the 35,000 cars projected. As a result, the contractors Capita looked to be heading for a possible £65 million loss. The five-year £230 million contract[61] was hastily redrawn to allow the company to operate the scheme profitably.[62]

Peter Hendy, then director of buses, says, 'The congestion charge has changed the city permanently… it may be a clunky system, but it works and it's reduced traffic. It the best bus priority measure I've ever seen in my life. Overnight the bus reliability improved in central London dramatically and it's remained improved.'[63] The congestion charge has its detractors and many have questioned its long-term success. But according to TfL's most recent report in 2007, the level of traffic was consistently 16 per cent lower than in the pre-charge days of 2002.[64] There are approximately 60,000 fewer cars entering central London each day, although during 2007 and into 2008, as Thames Water dug up roads across London to replace 1,000 miles of rotting Victorian mains, it certainly did not seem like it.[65] The charge was allowed for in legislation and is the only tax – along with the low emission zone fee for polluting lorries – the mayor would be allowed to levy directly. It has also proved a big money spinner. In its first three and a half years, the charge generated revenues of £677.4 million, with a surplus over running costs of £189.7 million, which has been ploughed back into London's public transport.[66]

'He was right and we were wrong,' says one of the advisors who tried to prevent Livingstone going ahead with the charge. 'Of course the trouble after that was that it became more difficult to tell him he was wrong on something!'[67] For Ken Livingstone, it was another gamble against the odds which had come off. He was showing no sign of running out of luck. At last he had properly arrived as mayor of London. Now surely, the Labour Party would have him back.

Notes

1   *Guardian* Unlimited, 30.5.02
2   BBC News Online, 30.5.02
3   Interview, Simon Harris, ITN *London Tonight*, 18.1.08
4   Interview, Ken Livingstone, 3.1.08
5   *Sunday Times*, 'Labour smears Livingstone in "secret son" story', 11.7.99
6   *Guardian* Unlimited, 11.2.05
7   Interview, source 1, November 2007
8   *Guardian*, 6.11.01
9   Ibid.
10 Interview, source 2, November 2007
11 Interview, source 1, November 2007
12 Interview, source 2, January 2008
13 Documentary source B, 13.6.02; Documentary source A, 4.11.02; Documentary source C, 3.6.03
14 Interview, Ken Livingstone, 3.1.08
15 Inquiry summary, Standards Board for England, Case SBE3384.02, June 2003
16 Statement to the London Assembly, by Ken Livingstone, 26.6.02
17 *Evening Standard*, article by Robin Hedges, 24.7.03
18 *Today* programme, BBC Radio 4, evidence of Dr Martin McCall, Imperial College, London, 28.6.02
19 Documentary source A, 4.11.02
20 *Evening Standard*, article by Robin Hedges, 24.7.03
21 Statement to the London Assembly by Ken Livingstone, 26.6.02
22 Standards Board for England Report, July 2003, case no. SBE384.02
23 Desmond Plummer, GLC Leader 1967–73, in conversation with Professor George Jones and Ken Livingstone, City Hall, 31.5.07
24 Wes Whitehouse, *GLC – The Inside Story*, p69
25 See Chapter 4
26 Ibid., p103
27 Ken Livingstone in conversation with Lord Plummer, City Hall, 31.5.07

28 Ibid.
29 Interview, Ken Livingstone, 28.12.07
30 *Daily Mail*, 12.8.81
31 Interview, Peter Hendy, 13.12.07
32 Commission for Integrated Transport, 31.3.04
33 Interview, Ken Livingstone, 8.11.07
34 The Greater London (Central Zone) Congestion Charging Order 2001, Report to the Mayor of London, TfL, February 2001
35 Ibid.
36 *The Times*, 7.1.03
37 Ibid., 8.11.07
38 Ibid., 8.11.07
39 *Independent*, 'Ministers consider trade-off over Tube', by Keith Harper, 10.12.01
40 *Observer*, 13.10.02
41 Handwritten note, Atma Singh, 2000
42 Interview, Luke Blair, 3.10.07
43 Interview, Ken Livingstone, 8.11.07
44 Interview, August 2007
45 Interview, Luke Blair, 3.10.07
46 Commission for Integrated Transport, 31.3.04
47 *Independent*, 22.6.02
48 *Observer*, 13.10.02
49 www.tfl.gov.uk
50 BBC News Online, 'Congestion charge cuts traffic levels', 18.2.03
51 *Scotsman*, 1.8.02
52 Interview, Luke Blair, 3.10.07
53 *Observer*, 19.1.03
54 BBC News Online, 'Thorny issue of congestion charges', by Mark Mardell, 11.2.03
55 Interview, Luke Blair, 3.10.07
56 Interview Ken Livingstone, 8.11.07
57 Interview, Neale Coleman, 1.8.07
58 Interview, Ken Livingstone, 8.11.07
59 Mayor's press conference, City Hall, 18.2.03
60 Ibid.
61 *Computer Weekly*, 21.2.03
62 Interview, Ken Livingstone, 8.11.07
63 Interview, Peter Hendy, 13.12.07
64 Impacts Monitoring, Fifth Annual Report, TfL, June 2007
65 Thames Water, (www.thameswater.co.uk)
66 BBC News Online, 'Where has the money gone?' 21.11.06
67 Author interview, August 2007

Chapter 24

Seb and Co., March 2003–July 2005

On 2 July 2003, Ken Livingstone turned up in Trafalgar Square for its formal re-opening. The mayor had not only led the pigeon purge but also the transformation of one of London's iconic landmarks. Traffic was removed from the north side of the square and after an 18-month construction project, it had been transformed from a seedy traffic island to an important public space with a cafe, public lavatories and lifts for the disabled.[1] It was also another blow against the hated motor car and another success story for the mayor. The transformation of Trafalgar Square seemed to symbolise a resurgent London and the arrival of Mayor Livingstone as a power in the land.

As for Livingstone himself, he was apparently a picture of confidence and contentment. In the 1980s, he would be at Trafalgar Square in his safari suit and slacks delivering rabble-rousing speeches against Thatcherism. Now, here he was, attired in a £895 deep purple Ozwald Boateng suit standing on a stone staircase literally strewn with rose petals and celebrating with his favourite architectural advisor, Lord Foster, over a glass of wine.[2] To Keith Dovkants, the *Evening Standard*'s feature writer, Livingstone was Emperor Ken, right down to the imperial purple, on the cusp of taking control of the London Underground and with the congestion charge acknowledged as a success. '…as Ken speaks there is indeed an imperial quality in his bearing,' observed Dovkants, adding, 'This is the charismatic figure, a modern political legend, who trumpets his successes unashamedly. And rightly so, perhaps.'[3] After years of decline, police numbers had been increased by Livingstone up to 28,602, a rise of 3,000 or more than 10 per cent; there had been a dramatic transformation of the bus fleet which was now carrying the highest number of passengers since the days of the Beatles.[4]

There was also an extra bounce in Livingstone's step for another reason, which had to remain secret for a while longer. Livingstone's days as an independent mayor were drawing to an end. He was on his way back into the Labour Party. Sally Morgan, who had headed Tony Blair's political office and once tried to 'encourage' Oona King to write an anti-Ken piece for the papers,[5] arranged a discreet meeting at City Hall with Livingstone and bluntly asked, 'Will you come back and be the candidate? Tony wants you to come back.' Livingstone just answered, 'Yes.' Livingstone says, 'It then took six months to finesse all the people who hated me.'[6]

There had been early indications that Blair, ever the pragmatist, was contemplating allowing Livingstone to rejoin before the five-year expulsion period was up. Wisely, the party had decided against expelling those members, particularly the dozen who signed Livingstone's nomination papers.[7] It is abundantly clear from the press coverage following the election that Livingstone was desperate to get back into the Labour Party. In June 2002, he applied to join the Labour Party, only two years after his expulsion. Deputy Prime Minister John Prescott reacted contemptuously, claiming Livingstone was dishonest: 'I just don't believe this man in whatever he says.'[8] On 23 July 2002, the day the Queen officially opened City Hall,[9] the National Executive Committee, rejected Livingstone's application by a narrow majority of 17 to 13.[10] But a little later that summer, Blair agreed to see Livingstone. He remembers: 'There was a secret meeting where I was hustled into the cabinet office and told not to sign the entry register and hustled out again so it could all be denied.

'I saw Blair and we had a very friendly discussion but it was quite obvious that they were really worried [about] how the congestion charge was going to go.'[11] By July 2003, it was clear that the congestion charge was not going to be a vote loser; people seemed more concerned about the missing weapons of mass destruction following the Iraq War and the government's propaganda leading up to it.

There was a minor problem to be overcome: Labour had already selected a mayoral candidate, Livingstone's Labour deputy, Nicky Gavron, who though decent and approachable, was not highly regarded as a political operator. The more formidable Tony Banks had also stood for nomination but was beaten into second place by Gavron.[12] It struck many seasoned City Hall watchers as an odd decision. It seems Labour was wisely keeping its options open. Simon Harris from ITN *London Tonight* was at the 2002 Labour Party conference in Blackpool, and saw both Banks and Gavron perform at the hustings. 'Nicky was dreadful,' says Harris. 'Clearly, Tony Banks was a star performer. There was no way Nicky could have won [the 2004 mayoral election]; she would have come a poor fourth.'[13]

Nyta Mann, the political correspondent for BBC News Online, observed at the time of Gavron's victory: 'Many of the activists in the London Labour Party and its affiliated trade unions who backed her made no secret of the fact they were doing so purely to maximise Mr Livingstone's chances of being re-elected.'[14] In fact, behind the scenes, Gavron was a willing participant in the plot and would play a key role in engineering Livingstone's return to the Labour Party. In an act of generosity rare in politics, she went to see Tony Blair in November 2003 and offered to step aside to allow Livingstone to stand as the candidate. 'It was a big risk for me,' she says. 'I didn't tell Ken I was seeing Tony Blair and it wasn't a foregone conclusion that he would get back in. There was still a lot of opposition in the cabinet to his return and I got a lot of grief from women when I eventually stepped aside.'[15] After working alongside Livingstone for two years, Gavron had formed a high opinion of his abilities. In May 2002, she ruffled a few feathers with an article in the party's house magazine, *Tribune*: 'Far from being the "loony left" demagogue of popular demon-ology, Ken has increasingly shown good sense and steadiness of purpose. One cannot fail to be impressed by his encyclopaedic knowledge and understanding of London.'[16]

Livingstone's old enemy Neil Kinnock, then vice president of the European Commission, opposed Livingstone's readmittance and said so publicly and loudly as it looked increasing likely. He told BBC Radio 4's the *Today* programme: 'I am fundamen-tally and irretrievably against it. Ken Livingstone has only ever belonged to one party – the Ken Livingstone party. There is no possibility, whatever his immediate future, of the Labour Party being able to rely upon sufficient loyalty and commitment to its aims and obligations.'[17] But this time, after months of Blair's cajoling, the NEC formally readmitted Livingstone to the party on 6 January 2004[18] and within a month he had replaced Nicky Gavron as the mayoral candidate for 2004[19]; Gavron agreed to run as his deputy. It is unlikely that Tony Banks would have been quite so accommodating.

Once again, Livingstone's Conservative opponent would be the flamboyant former transport minister, Steve Norris. At the start of his administration, Livingstone had embraced the 'big tent' concept of politics and given Norris a seat on the TfL board. But by November 2001, they clashed on the congestion charge and Norris's own transport-related business interests. On 22 November 2001, Livingstone took great pleasure in sacking Norris. Norris took his dismissal in his stride, telling journalists that Livingstone had become 'fixated' on the idea of him being the Tories' mayoral candidate in 2004, adding, 'When he appointed me, Ken said he wanted a broad church, but he has found it impossible to live with.'[20]

♦

In 2004, Livingstone campaigned on his record, something which had become increasingly rare in British politics: the congestion charge, 5,000 more police officers, free bus travel for children aged under 11 and a thousand extras buses.[21] A main plank of Steven Norris's campaign was the abolition of the congestion charge. It proved not to be a vote winner and Livingstone was returned as Labour's mayor at the elections on 10 June 2004 by a large majority over Norris: 55.4 per cent of the vote, including first and second preference votes, to Norris's 44.6 per cent.[22]

In January 2008, a programme by Channel Four's *Dispatches* alleged that three of Livingstone's senior aides had breached electoral guidelines by helping on his campaign despite holding politically restricted posts which forbade them doing so while at work.[23] Part of the documentary evidence used to support this allegation was an email in May 2004 from Livingstone's campaign team to his former advisor, Atma Singh, containing details about which aide had been asked to write an article in the press on Livingstone's behalf.[24] Livingstone strenuously denied these allegations and insisted his advisors had helped out with fundraising and other aspects of the campaign in their own time.[25]

To all intents and purposes, Livingstone continued walking and talking as an independent. His occasional gaffe would be greeted by the Labour Party with a collective shrug of the shoulders and the general public would be referred to his outspoken and controversial past. On allowing Livingstone back into the party, Blair had reportedly told him, 'I am running foreign policy', but the mayor ignored him, as he had on so many issues.

In April 2004, two months before the election, Livingstone told the *Guardian*: 'I just long for the day I wake up and find that the Saudi royal family are swinging from lamp posts and they've got a proper government that represents the people of Saudi Arabia.'[26] Steve Norris responded, 'With the threat of a terrorist attack on London in the air, this kind of Livingstone rant is downright dangerous. This is exactly the kind of incitement that could have very serious consequences for our country – and the mayor does not give a damn. The trouble is that he is in danger of making London a laughing stock.'[27]

Livingstone also upset large sections of the Left in late June 2004 by urging members of the RMT union to cross picket lines of the threatened Underground strikes over pay because the latest offer was 'extremely generous'.[28] For Bob Crowe, the RMT's hard-left general secretary, the eleventh commandment was 'thou shalt not cross picket lines.'[29] He too resigned as a TfL board member in disgust, adding, 'This kind of crude knee-jerk union bashing has brought condemnation from all corners of the Labour movement.'[30]

◆

During Livingstone's first term, the positions of both the mayor and his advisors grew more powerful at the cost of other bodies which had been established to scrutinise them, including the relatively toothless London Assembly which they treated with increasing and often justifiable contempt. At first, a so-called 'advisory cabinet' of outside advisors and Labour MPs including Diane Abbott and John McDonnell would meet in the mayor's office. But it lacked any real authority and attendance fell away during 2001 and 2002 and it withered on the vine. Increasingly, his own team of advisors coagulated into the real power at City Hall.[31]

The advisors' power was enhanced by Livingstone in the spring of 2002. Six of his most important aides received promotions and bigger salaries. Each of the six, including Ross, O'Neill, Fletcher and Coleman were given the title of executive director to cover the areas of public affairs, media relations, economic and business policy, environmental services, equalities integration and housing.[32] The mayor came in for fierce criticism and allegations of cronyism from both Labour and Tory Assembly members who tried and failed to prevent the appointments. Lord Harris, leader of the Labour group, accused Livingstone of 'hoarding cronies', adding, 'These arrangements mean that existing staff will be bypassed... It looks as though the posts are tailor-made for people already operating in the mayor's advice corridor.'[33] Eric Ollerenshaw, the deputy leader of the Tories, said, 'He has suddenly set up a secret cabinet of officers whose jobs are dependent upon him being re-elected. He has basically set up his re-election campaign at great cost.'[34] He would later concede that being an executive mayor was similar to someone running a personal fiefdom, adding, 'That's exactly what Tony Blair – and I was opposed to the idea at the beginning – set out to create.'[35]

The mayor and his men often appeared impatient with much of the bureaucracy of the Greater London Authority. He refused to allow 'some Sir Humphrey culture' to prevent the execution of his executive powers. He would say, 'My officials are there to make sure that the decisions I make are carried out by an often reluctant or lazy bureaucracy.'[36]

Occasionally, there have been allegations of bullying against some of Livingstone's senior staff. This first came to public attention in April 2002 when the Liberal Democrat chairwoman of the Assembly, Baroness Hamwee, received an anonymous email which said that 'some of the mayor's advisors have demonstrated an abysmal grasp of even basic management techniques, frequently bullying and threatening officers to obtain results.'[37] A subsequent Assembly inquiry came to nothing but the rumours persisted. Atma Singh became estranged increasingly from the administration and eventually stepped down as a mayoral advisor in July 2007. He claims there was a culture of intimidation and bullying at City Hall, and that as a result, 'dozens' of staff had been forced out over the years after signing so-called 'compromise agreements' which usually come with a sum of money and an undertaking of confidentiality over the reasons for departure.[38] But a reliable senior source at the Greater London Authority says that since 2000, approximately eight staff had left as a result of compromise agreements and none as a result of bullying. 'There is undoubtedly a hothouse environment here,' says the source who wished to remain anonymous, 'but bullying is not tolerated and it is certainly not the issue Singh makes it out to be.'[39]

The face City Hall would present to the media was tough and no-nonsense. Defended by a corps of roughly 18 press officers, errant reporters are swiftly dealt with. Joy Johnson, the mayor's director of media and marketing, would deal aggressively[40] with Livingstone's enemies in the media, particularly the hated *Evening Standard*. Johnson first bumped into Livingstone in the Holborn Labour Party where they had both been members and later, in her role as an ITN TV producer, had filmed him putting a few desultory items in plastic bags in the last hours of the GLC. Warm-hearted but tough, she is fiercely loyal to Livingstone and very protective of him. Livingstone has only been known to shout three times in seven years at Johnson, once for not crushing the allegedly untrue story about him deliberately manipulating the traffic lights to make the congestion charge look more successful.[41] Her press officers drive journalists[42] to distraction by referring virtually every request for comment or information, however mundane or seemingly innocuous, up the City Hall food chain to be mulled over by Livingstone's senior staff. Johnson's semi-serious motto is 'Even the most mundane question will be twisted; trust no one!'[43] Rebuttals come hard and fast. During one media onslaught, no fewer than nine of the 14 headlines on the mayor's website carried savage refutations of media falsehoods.[44]

'When Joy Johnson's away,' says Tory Assembly member Brian Coleman, 'things fall apart.'[45] Over the years, Simon Harris of ITN *London Tonight* has received furious texts and emails from Johnson about his reports. 'It goes with the territory,' says Harris, 'Joy sometimes will get very angry with the coverage and frankly I don't know why they waste their time because it's water off a duck's back to a journalist to have people complaining about you.'[46]

◆

Ken Livingstone is considered a formidable operator at City Hall where he expects loyalty and commitment from his closest political advisors who he says often work up to 70 hours a week.[47] He does not like paper and strives to create that mythical beast – the paperless office. Often, minutes are not kept of meetings and he says he never sends emails.[48] Livingstone always says he loves running things and to his senior staff, he is the consummate technocrat who gets across the minutiae and has no fear of taking decisions and delegating responsibility. The days when he was too obsessed with Brent East to get his head around the budget are apparently a distant memory.[49] None of his aides can compete with Livingstone on his intimate knowledge of London. His Labour deputy Nicky Gavron was impressed at the outset by Livingstone's managerial skills, telling *Tribune* at the time he was still outside the party that she was 'struck by how at ease he is with taking the myriad of executive decisions which are shaping the authority.'[50]

Neale Coleman, the mayor's director of business planning and regeneration, says Livingstone insists on mastering detail before taking a decision. 'He reads voraciously,' says Coleman, 'he reads papers and reports. You can put a 60-page report in front of him, something you wouldn't dream of giving to a politician, and he will read it. He enjoys it and he immerses himself in paperwork and the details of issues.'[51] Some envious Labour MPs still refer to Livingstone as 'the people's Ken',[52] and although he can scarcely be described as 'cuddly', Livingstone has retained the common touch. A former City Hall press officer says, 'Ken was always fantastic to deal with. I must have been on the Tube with him a couple of dozen times and I never had a negative experience. He really knows how to interact with people.'[53]

◆

Like the congestion charge, Livingstone's role in winning London the 2012 Olympic Games is often cited as another great success story of the way he and his advisors get things done, come what may. It was certainly a battle no one expected London to win and unquestionably Livingstone played a decisive role. The 2012 Olympics promised to boost tourism and London's reputation as a world city, as well as promising to regenerate a significant area of east London, but financially, say the critics, the price may be too high and certainly substantially higher than people were originally led to believe.

In the way history often repeats itself in Livingstone's story, a bid by London to host the Olympics featured in his time at the GLC in the late 1970s. The Tory leader, Sir Horace Cutler, a sports fanatic who introduced the London Marathon, was keen to win London the 1988 Olympic Games. In 1979, Cutler favoured the Royal Victoria Dock in the East End as the Olympic site. It was soon to be abandoned by cargo handlers and the Games could have also helped solve the problem of chronic inner city decay and dereliction, a major concern of Cutler.[54]

But the Thatcher government was extremely sceptical, and with good reason.[55] A feasibility study commissioned by the GLC set out the big risks involved with the project: the economy and the extension to the Jubilee line. The consultants, Peat, Marwick and Mitchell estimated the cost as £750.1 million[56] but in June 1979, inflation was running at 10 per cent. If it continued at that rate, prices would be double by the time the Games were opened in 1988.[57] Also, the productivity rate of the average British builder was among the lowest in Europe and there were bound to be cost overruns as a result.[58] Managers of the London Underground, still under GLC control, were emphatic that there could be no Olympics in Docklands until the Jubilee line was extended far enough east by 1988, and that looked unlikely.[59] In February 1980, Ken Livingstone spoke out against the project describing it as a 'gimmick' and 'one of Sir Horace's megalomaniac ideas'.[60]

At the start, London's chances of winning the 2012 Games looked bleak at best. In October 2001, Britain's reputation as the provider of sporting venues took a serious knock when the government was forced to withdraw London's offer to stage the 2005 World Athletics Championships at a new purpose-built stadium at Picketts Lock in Hertfordshire. This followed a report by a businessman, Patrick Carter, raising serious concerns about costs and infrastructure.[61] The government was also embroiled in a fiasco over the building of the new Wembley Stadium,[62] as well as licking its wounds over the jinxed Millennium Dome.

Late in 2000, Livingstone was visited by Craig Reedie, chairman of the British Olympic Association and asked to support a bid for London. At that stage, there were rumours that the BOA favoured Wembley as a possible site. According to the mayor's principal advisor on regeneration, Neale Coleman, Livingstone said, 'Yes but I have two or three fundamental conditions. It's got to be in east London and the most important thing is regeneration and legacy. If you do that, we'll support you.'[63]

◆

While the government timidly contemplated going for the 2012 Olympics, Livingstone threw his wholehearted support behind the London bid. On 1 November 2002, he invited the luminaries of the British Olympic Association, BOA, to City Hall and announced to the press, 'An Olympic bid has my total support and I know I speak for my successors in the 10 years to come.

This opportunity will not come around again during the lifetime of anyone here. It would be madness not to go for it.'[64]

Carrying the Olympic torch around Whitehall was Tessa Jowell, the culture secretary. Her cabinet colleagues demonstrated mainly 'ambivalence' towards the bid. At a meeting on 15 January 2003, the chancellor Gordon Brown told Jowell there would be no Treasury money for either the bid, estimated to cost £30 million, or the project itself.[65] The project seemed dead in the water. In her desperation, she contacted the then renegade independent mayor of London and set up a meeting for the following day.

Mike Lee, who would later become director of communications and public affairs for the 2012 Olympics, gives an occasionally misinterpreted account of the meeting on 16 January 2003. According to Lee, Jowell knew that 'without the financial backing of Livingstone, it was all over'. During the hour-long meeting at Jowell's offices in Cockspur Street overlooking Trafalgar Square, it became clear 'that the mayor was prepared to do whatever was needed to get the bid off the ground'.[66]

Lee adds, 'Livingstone and Jowell carved out a financial deal, which would cover the £2.4 billion public price tag of the Olympics if the bid was won.'[67] This was based on a study carried out at Jowell's behest by an experienced civil servant called Robert Raine. Raine, who worked in the cabinet office, had gained experience reviewing projects from Picketts Lock to the 2002 Manchester Commonwealth Games. He concluded that an earlier report by the consultants Arup had underestimated the costs by £800 million[68] and that the actual price tag would be the £2.4 billion discussed by Livingstone and Jowell.[69] Raine's own estimate would prove to be woefully inadequate. As of late November 2007, Livingstone was estimating the total cost of the Olympics to be roughly £8.3 billion.[70]

Even before the meeting, few people in government put much faith in the early cost estimates. In November 2002, Richard Caborn, the sports minister, warned that the Olympics were in a league of their own 'when it comes to financing', and that overspending was almost inevitable. His own estimate was £4 billion, again half the eventual possible cost.[71] During the two years of the bidding process, from July 2003 when the first shortlist of nine cities was announced to the declaration of the winner in July 2005, the costs kept changing – for the worst. Such was the sensitivity of the subject that meetings of consultants, mayoral advisors and civil servants to discuss the costs of 'Project Raven' were held behind closed doors. In September 2004, the consultants KPMG were warning of a possible £1 billion deficit in the Games' proposed financing. VAT alone would take up £1 billion. As for security costs, those looked likely to be £750 million to £1 billion,[72] and could eventually be a great deal higher, depending on the international situation in 2012.[73]

Ken Livingstone insists that there was no chance of knowing the exact costs in the early days: 'To know what the Olympics actually cost you need to spend £200 million in architectural, quantity surveying and accountancy fees to put that level of detail together. It's not justified when you've got a one in five chance of winning. The world would have gone mad if we'd spent £200 million on a bid and lost.'[74] The agreed site was the lower Lee Valley in east London, a vast wasteland of untapped potential covering roughly 200 hectares between Hackney Marshes and the River Thames.[75] Like Horace Cutler before him, Livingstone wanted to win the Olympics to help regenerate a run-down and polluted part of London. 'Why did I bid for the Olympics?' Livingstone says, 'So the government would be forced to spend billions of pounds on remediating the lower Lee Valley.'[76]

Despite the commitment by the government and the mayor to the bid, few took London's 2012 campaign that seriously. The city to beat was Paris. 'We all assumed Paris was going to get it,' remembers Simon Harris of ITN, 'I very quickly took an interest from a purely selfish point of view: I thought I could make the Olympic story my brief as the political correspondent rather than it going to a sports correspondent because there was a potential for foreign travel!'[77]

The government's backing would be crucial to the success of the bid. On 15 May 2003, Tessa Jowell managed to convince the cabinet to support the Games. Above all, it was the commitment and energy of Tony Blair that made the difference with the vain old men in control of the Olympics movement. Later Blair said, 'I am not going to pretend there wasn't a real debate in the government. There was. But in the end, we all decided to go for it and John Prescott was critical in swinging everyone behind that decision.'[78]

The first big hurdle was 15 July 2003, the deadline by which the nine competing cities had to submit their submission bids. One month before that date, London's Olympics operation was shaken up by the arrival of a American businesswoman to chair the bid. Barbara Cassani was a tough Bostonian who did not suffer fools gladly or otherwise. She had been a management consultant with Coopers and Lybrand before working with airlines. She set up British Airways' budget airline Go! with just £25 million start-up money and by the time it was sold four years later in a management buyout, its value had risen to £374 million. There was some surprise at the choice of an American to breathe new life into the bid but Livingstone, with his fair share of Americans at TfL, had no qualms.[79] Cassani worked wonders to make London a credible contender but soon after her appointment, stories started to circulate that she would be sacked long before the final decision was taken by the International Olympic Committee, or IOC, in July 2005.[80] One of the most important early decisions taken by Cassani was to appoint Sebastian Coe as vice chairman. A two-time Olympic gold medal runner, Coe possessed the necessary personal qualities, experience and sporting contacts needed to help make the bid a success. He would also soon replace Cassani.

◆

On 18 May 2004, the IOC announced that London had made it on to the shortlist along with Paris, Madrid, Moscow and New York. Out went Havana, Singapore, Leipzig and Istanbul. Although, there was cause for celebration, London still looked a poor bet. The IOC report stated: '...rail public transport is often obsolete and considerable investments must be made to upgrade the existing system in terms of capacity and safety. Urban expressways and main arterial road facilities lack the capacity to provide reasonable travel times and speeds.'[81] London has also performed poorly by the IOC's own marking system, on issues such as government support and public opinion, coming behind places like Havana and Rio which were ultimately rejected. Overall, it was a poor third behind Paris, which was first and Madrid second.[82] With more than a year to go, London appeared to have too much ground to make up and too little time.

Critically, Cassani now resigned to make way for Coe who was revered by many key figures in the Olympics movement. Cassani had been appointed for her expertise in starting new businesses from scratch. At first, she started with nothing more than a chair and an empty office. Within a year, the London 2012 operation had a staff of 80 blue-chip corporate partners and a master plan setting out the proposed Olympic complex.[83] But everyone agreed that she was not the type to hover around the bars of five star hotels chatting up elderly officials of the International Olympic Committee.

Livingstone and Coe visited Athens for the August 2004 Olympiad and spent much of the time schmoozing IOC figures. Livingstone was now convinced London could win.[84] Tony Blair, Coe and Livingstone spent time charming and cajoling members of the IOC evaluation commission when they arrived on 16 February 2005 for a three-day visit.[85] A critical objective by the London 2012 team was to persuade the IOC officials to overcome their concerns about transport. They were taken down the tunnel for the rail link being built between the site of the Games and the Eurostar terminus at King's Cross. Livingstone formed part of the London 2012 team that flew out to Singapore for the final announcement of the IOC. Paris was still out in front but there was everything to play for. At the time no one knew, but behind the scenes a deal had been struck with the Russians.

Russia and France had long been historic allies. French had been spoken at the court of the czars for centuries and Moscow was expected to give its three critical votes to Paris once its own bid had been defeated, as was widely anticipated. Here again Livingstone proved important. The mayors of Moscow, Paris, London and Berlin have regular meetings to discuss issues of common interest. Livingstone got on particularly well with his Moscow counterpart, the urbane Yury Luzhkov.[86] The relationship was key in winning Moscow's support for the Games.

Tapping the sources he had gathered during his eight years in Moscow, John Ross played a substantial role in lobbying key people there, including the Russian IOC officials. It was abundantly clear that Luzhkov carried immense influence with the Russian IOC officials. Before Singapore, Livingstone had also helped brief Tony Blair on what to say to the Russian president, Vladimir Putin, when they met for talks. Putin told Blair, 'I understand we're voting for London.'[87]

◆

On 5 July 2005, on the day before the final IOC decision in

Singapore, Livingstone and Luzhkov met. 'This was a very critical discussion,' remembers Neale Coleman who was present. 'The Russian IOC delegates didn't just do what Luzhkov told them but obviously they listened carefully to what he said.'[88]

On 6 July 2005, Livingstone and the rest of the London 2012 team gathered at the Raffles conference centre at the Stamford Hotel in Singapore for the final decision. As expected, Moscow went out in the first round. In the second round, Madrid received 32 votes followed by London with 27 and Paris with 25. New York, with 16 votes, was eliminated. In the penultimate round, London got 39 votes, Paris 33 and Madrid 31. The Spanish capital was eliminated. It was later alleged by a senior IOC official, Alex Gilady, that Madrid was knocked out because of a mistake by one of his colleagues who accidentally voted for Paris instead of Madrid[89] and that Madrid would have beaten London in the run-off. There was also controversy regarding the failure of the Greek IOC member to vote.[90] But whatever the reason, Madrid was eliminated.

At 7.49 p.m. in Singapore, Jacques Rogge, the IOC president, announced the winner of the third and final round: London, by 54 votes to 50 for Paris. The three Russian votes had made all the difference. 'Although Tony Blair played a huge role in winning the Olympics for Britain,' says Nick Raynsford, the former minister of London, 'I don't think we would have won if we hadn't had a mayor committed to them.'[91] On 6 July 2005, it was time to celebrate, but not for long.

Notes

1   Mayor of London and Greater London Authority, (www.london.gov.uk)
2   *Evening Standard*, 'Emperor Ken', by Keith Dovkants, 14.7.03
3   Ibid.
4   Ibid.; Factsheet, 'London Buses', Transport for London, 2007
5   See Chapter 20
6   Interview, Ken Livingstone, 8.11.07
7   *Times*, 1.1.01
8   *Daily Mail*, 30.6.03
9   See Chapter 22
10 BBC News Online, 'Labour rejects Livingstone's return', 23.7.02
11 Interview, Ken Livingstone, 8.11.07
12 BBC News Online, Labour choose Gavron for Mayor, 5.11.02
13 Interview, Simon Harris, 18.1.08
14 BBC News Online, 'Good news for Livingstone', by Nyta Mann, 6.11.02

15 Interview, Nicky Gavron, 22.2.08
16 *Tribune*, 'Livingstone: My new relationship', by Nicky Gavron, 17.5.02
17 *Today* programme, 15.12.03
18 BBC News Online, 'Livingstone back in from the cold', 6.1.04
19 *Daily Mail*, 2.2.04
20 BBC News Online, 'Livingstone sacks transport chief Norris', 22.11.01
21 Ken Livingstone's manifesto, 'KEN4London, A manifesto 4 London', London Mayoral and London Assembly elections, 2004
22 Results: www.londonelects.org.uk
23 *Dispatches*, Channel Four, 21.1.08
24 Email to Atma Singh from policy@ken4London.org, 24.5.04
25 *Today* programme, 24.1.08; Mayor's press conference, 22.1.08
26 *Daily Telegraph*, 9.4.04
27 Ibid.
28 BBC News Online, 'Talks hope to avert a Tube strike', 25.6.04
29 *Guardian*, 2.7.04
30 *RMT News*, Issue No. 6, volume 5, article by Bob Crowe, August 2004
31 Tony Travers, *The politics of London, Governing an Ungovernable City*, p95
32 BBC News Online, 'Livingstone accused of "cronyism"', 27.3.02
33 *Guardian*, 'Livingstone answers "cronyism change"', 28.2.02
34 BBC News Online, 'Livingstone accused of "cronyism"', 27.3.02
35 *Today* programme, 24.1.08
36 Mayor's press conference, 22.1.08
37 *Independent*, 10.4.02
38 Interview, Atma Singh, 27.1.08
39 Off-the-record briefing, senor GLA source, 18.2.08
40 Interview, Simon Harris, 18.1.08
41 Off-the-record briefing, 1.2.08; See chapter 23
42 Interview, Simon Harris, 18.1.08
43 Off-the-record briefing, senior advisor, 1.2.08
44 Website of the Mayor and Greater London Authority, 24.1.08
45 Interview, Brian Coleman, 4.12.07
46 Interview, Simon Harris, 18.1.08
47 Mayoral press conference, 22.1.08
48 Interview, Ken Livingstone, 3.1.08
49 See Chapter 15
50 *Tribune*, 'Livingstone: my new relationship', by Nicky Gavron, 17.5.02
51 Interview, Neale Coleman, 1.8.07
52 Off-the-record interview, 24.1.08
53 Author interview, 1.11.07
54 *Evening Standard*, 'Time to fire the GLC?' by Roland Freeman, 24.9.79
55 *Observer,* 'GLC press on with the Olympics', 26.5.79
56 Feasibility study on 1988 Olympic Games, by Peat, Marwick and Mitchell, June 1979, p161
57 Ibid., p103
58 Ibid., p107
59 Ibid., p109
60 GLC meeting, report of proceedings including Question Time, 26.2.80

61 *Guardian*, 'Athletics stadium will cost £100 million', 20.1.01; Culture, Media and Sport Select Common's Committee, 20.11.01
62 Ibid.
63 Interview, Neale Coleman, 1.8.07
64 *Guardian*, 2.11.02
65 Mike Lee, *The Race for the 2012 Olympics, The Inside Story of How London Won the Olympics*, Virgin Books, 2006, p12
66 Ibid., pp13-14
67 Ibid.
68 Ibid., pp10-11
69 Letter of clarification to the *Evening Standard*, by Mike Lee, 29.11.06
70 Interview, Ken Livingstone, 26.11.07
71 *Guardian*, 2.11.02
72 Project Raven, meeting note, 29.11.04
73 Interview, Ken Livingstone, 26.11.07
74 Ibid.
75 Report of the IOC Evaluation Commission for the Games of the XXX Olympiad in 2012, 18.5.04.
76 Ibid.
77 Interview, Simon Harris, 18.1.08
78 Mike Lee, *The Race for the 2012 Olympics*, p16
79 Interview, Ken Livingstone, 26.11.07
80 Mike Lee, *The Race for the 2012 Olympics*, p30
81 Report by the IOC Candidature Acceptance Working Group/Games of the XXX Olympiad in 2012 – General Infrastructure, 18.5.04
82 Ibid.
83 *Guardian*, 'Why Cassani had to call time, gentlemen please', 20.5.004
84 Interview, Ken Livingstone, 26.11.07
85 BBC News Online, 'What makes London a world beater?', February 2005
86 Interview, Neale Coleman, 11.1.08
87 Interview, Ken Livingstone, 26.11.07
88 Interview, Neale Coleman, 11.1.08
89 BBC News Online 'Voting error gave London Games', 23.12.05
90 Mike Lee, *The Race for the 2012 Olympics*, pp194-195
91 Interview, Nick Raynsford, 20.12.07

Chapter 25

Ken in an age of terror, 7 July 2005

The attacks by Islamist terrorists against London on 7 July 2005 were terrible and shocking, but they were not a surprise. Since the attacks on New York and Washington on 11 September 2001, and subsequently in Bali and particularly Madrid, it had always been a matter of time before it was London's turn. When the blow came, as Evelyn Waugh once said, it fell on a bruise.

On the evening of 6 July 2005, there had been many parties to celebrate the Olympics triumph. Ken Livingstone attended one in Singapore but he did not stay up late. On the following morning, 7 July 2005, he was up bright and breezy. Simon Harris, of ITN *London Tonight*, interviewed him. 'Everyone else was feeling jaded and hung over and tired,' remembers Harris, 'and he [Ken Livingstone] was as sharp as a pin. He was one of the few people who seemed capable of pulling a sentence together the next day.'[1]

The time difference was an important factor: Singapore was eight hours ahead of Greenwich Mean Time. Mohammed Sidique Khan, the chief conspirator, blew himself up and murdered six innocent people at 8.50 a.m. on 7 July as his train pulled out of the Circle line Tube station at Edgware Road. Two other bombs detonated within a minute of each other on two other Tube trains. At 9.47 a.m. a fourth suicide bomber attacked a double-decker bus in Tavistock Square. On the day, 52 people were murdered by the four terrorists. The expected attack had happened, but unlike the atrocities conducted by foreign terrorists in New York and Madrid, London had been assailed by Muslims who were British.[2]

◆

Ken Livingstone was out buying presents for his children around the famous Orchard Road shopping malls in Singapore when he received calls from Joy Johnson saying there had been reports of a 'power surge' on the Tube. But Johnson, an experienced former journalist, feared the worst and called Livingstone. 'It's something to do with the electrics, isn't it?' he said. 'I think it's more serious than that,' replied Johnson. 'I think there's going to be fatalities.'[3] Livingstone shared a cab back to his hotel, the Stamford, with an Australian journalist[4] and received a second call from Johnson who had just received confirmation from the Met that London had indeed been attacked. Mike Lee, who handled the press and media, described the scenes at Livingstone's hotel: 'As the full extent of what was happening became clear, a mood of helpless desperation and gloom descended. Athletes such as the Olympic triple jump champion Jonathan Edwards walked around the hotel lobby looking desolate at the way their emotions had gone from one end of the scale to the other.'[5]

Neale Coleman spent that traumatic day with Livingstone. 'We had all been in a euphoric mood,' says Coleman, 'and we had all been up to the wee hours of the morning getting totally pissed. And we woke up the next morning in the same mood except we were very hung over.'[6] Initially Coleman thought, 'Oh God! We've just been awarded the Olympics and we can't run the Underground. What are we going to say to the IOC? After 20 minutes, it became obvious that this was an attack and you began to get information.' The team crowded around the television to keep up with developments back in London while maintaining contact with the Met and TfL as well as Simon Fletcher and Redmond O'Neill at City Hall. There had been four bombs within an hour. Three were on Tube trains: on the Circle line between Liverpool Street and King's Cross; also on the Circle line at Edgware Road and on the deep-level Piccadilly line between King's Cross St Pancras and Russell Square. The fourth and last device exploded on a number 30 double-decker bus in nearby Tavistock Square. 'We were being mercilessly harassed by the media for a statement,' says Coleman. To collect his thoughts, Livingstone went for a swim in the hotel pool.

The hotel lobby was the only place available for Livingstone to give his reaction to the vast media scrum. Without a note, Livingstone delivered a heartfelt and moving speech, in which he said: 'I want to say one thing specifically to the world today. This was not a terrorist attack against the mighty and the powerful. It was not aimed at presidents or prime ministers. It was aimed at ordinary, working-class Londoners, black and white, Muslim and Christian, Hindu and Jew, young and old. It was an indiscriminate attempt to slaughter, irrespective of any considerations for age, for class, for religion, or whatever.'[7] At the end of his statement, Livingstone immediately turned on his heel and got back in the lift with Coleman and Ross. As the lift doors closed, Livingstone burst into tears.[8]

◆

After the 9/11 attacks, it was immediately obvious that London had no effective civil defence strategy to deal with a similar outrage. Until the collapse of communism in Eastern Europe, it had focused primarily on dealing with a nuclear attack. The emergency services also planned for the threat posed by the IRA and other republican paramilitary groups. But there was little in place to deal with this new sinister development in international terror. David Blunkett was clearly concerned about Livingstone and any role he might play in London's defence. He appointed Nick Raynsford, the former minister for London, to plan for the worst. In his diaries, Blunkett reveals that he talked to the Metropolitan Police Authority and other senior police officers 'because we are trying to make sure that we get a grip of what Ken Livingstone is up to'.[9]

Nick Raynsford says, 'David Blunkett was nervous about Ken being in charge of London's defence coordination for a variety of reasons to do with his past record [on Ireland and police].' The new group to coordinate defence for London was called London Resilience. Raynsford chose Livingstone to be his deputy on the group. 'I had a very interesting series of discussions with David about Ken's role,' says Raynsford. 'David accepted my recommendation that we should invite Ken to be my deputy with a clear understanding that he would be the public voice in the event of any incident. And actually it worked out very well because he was tied into the arrangements.'[10] Livingstone gave Raynsford the impression that he found meetings of the London Resilience team rather tedious, but after the so-called '7/7' bomb attacks in 2005, he acknowledged that 'every second had been well spent'.[11] Blunkett considered Raynsford the perfect man for the job. After all, he had designed the mayoralty and the new system of governance for London and he had a reputation for quiet and effective competence. He was the ideal choice to coordinate the emergency services and other groups which would have to handle an attack when it came.

On Sunday, 7 May 2003 the government and emergency

services sealed off the heart of the capital's financial district for an exercise based on a poisonous gas attack on Bank Station in the City. According to press coverage at the time, the exercise highlighted some serious shortcomings. 'Although response times were not being tested,' reported the *Guardian*, 'the fact that supposedly stricken passengers were still underground three hours after the exercise began will cause some concern.'[12] According to Nick Raynsford, Livingstone was against the exercise being carried out. 'We had real difficulty getting him to agree that that should take place,' says Raynsford. 'Because he was nervous, and I understand that – that this would be seen particularly by American tourists as worrying and it might deter people coming to London. By the time of the exercise, he was on side and he never publicly criticised it.'[13]

◆

On 11 March 2004, al-Qaeda terrorists attacked the rail network in Madrid, killing 191 people and injuring more than 1,700. On 16 March 2004, Livingstone and the then Met commissioner Sir John Stevens held an extraordinary press conference to warn people of the increasing likelihood of an attack not only against the Tube but also pubs and nightclubs. 'There are people out there who want to take lives, in the hundreds and the thousands,' Livingstone told reporters. 'These are people who celebrate death. We would be fools to assume we will always be able to stop terrorists.'[14] Blunkett was furious about the press conference and had what he described as a 'bit of a spat' with Stevens. He thought the press conference was 'likely to scare Londoners, rather than gain their confidence and provide reassurance'. He told Stevens, 'We've got enough problems with franchised terrorism (the al-Qaeda network) without franchised anti-terrorism.'[15]

After Madrid, Livingstone began to think seriously about the words he would use when it was London's turn. 'Whenever I'd be swimming or gardening,' says Livingstone, 'I would be going over in my head what I would say and how to handle it.'[16] Shortly before the May 2004 mayoral election, Livingstone received a significant amount of intelligence[17] warning about an imminent strike on London. It had always been a question of when.

◆

On 7 July 2005, Livingstone also had to decide how soon to restart the Tube and bus services. To many people's surprise, the buses were running within hours of the attack and most of the Tube network, excluding those lines worst affected, was almost back to normal within 24 hours.[18] The manager responsible for buses was Peter Hendy, one of Livingstone's most impressive managers. He was a graduate trainee for London Transport where he learned to drive a bus and helped lead a management buyout of part of the bus service for £27 million. Three years later in 1997, he was forced to sell what was then called Centrewest Buses for £54 million.[19] Hendy made a personal fortune of £4 million while remaining resolutely down to earth. In 2006, he would succeed Bob Kiley as transport commissioner.

Hendy, who was the managing director of surface transport for TfL on 7 July 2005, says, 'I was in charge of the bus service and Tim O'Toole (managing director of London Underground Ltd) was in charge of the Tube. You're never going to know whether the people you employ are up to dealing with something like that until it happens. You can practise all you like but nothing prepares you for that kind of stuff.'[20] TfL managed to evacuate 200,000 commuters[21] as the attacks started and both Tube staff and emergency services interacted well under the circumstances. It had been 'an awful day', O'Toole said later, but the staff did 'a magnificent job'.[22]

However, there were serious problems on 7 July, thanks mainly to the dilapidation into which successive governments had allowed the Tube to fall. O'Toole told a subsequent inquiry by the Greater London Assembly about the serious communication problems caused by the Tube's radio systems which were 'antiquated' and 'sometimes fail us'. As part of the PPP, £2 billion is being invested in a new digital radio system, but it will not be complete for another 20 years.[23]

◆

After his speech at the Stamford Hotel, Livingstone and his team started packing. The Singapore authorities provided an armed convoy to take Livingstone, Tessa Jowell and the others to the airport. 'There was no sign of life anywhere,' remembers Livingstone, 'they had cleared every vehicle and person from the roads because they certainly were not going [to allow anything to happen] to me and Tessa Jowell. At that stage, no one knew what the nature of the conspiracy was or if it was something that might involve strikes in other cities, so they took no chances.'[24]

On arrival in London, Livingstone was rushed to a meeting at New Scotland Yard with the recently appointed Met commissioner, Sir Ian Blair, for a briefing. Livingstone had other concerns aside from the overriding one of security. 'The most important thing was that there should be no backlash,' says Livingstone. 'Once it was known they [the bombers] were British-born, there was the question of just making sure you didn't get a breakdown in community cohesion in London.'

Livingstone drafted in his ad man Harry Barlow to help design an advertising campaign aimed at countering racism and Islamaphobia. The advertising industry contributed £3 million worth of free advertising including banners and cinema screens. The *Evening Standard* reprinted Livingstone's speech in full and many people put it up in their front windows. 'It was to show that we were all in it together,' says Barlow. 'It was about creating a feel-good factor about living in London and not to start to push the blame to a particular community. It worked well from that point of view because it wasn't preachy.'[25]

Livingstone and his team organised a big rally in Trafalgar Square for 14 July 2005. He nearly broke down in tears during the speech which was aimed at community harmony: 'Pericles who was the first mayor in Athens over 2,000 years ago said in time all great things flow to the city and the greatest of those is the people who come.'[26] He added: 'Those who came here to kill last Thursday had many goals but one was that we should turn on each other like animals trapped in a cage, and they failed.'

Peter Hendy says, 'It was a most extraordinary occasion. He spoke with such feeling and so deeply from the heart that you couldn't not be moved by it... and I remember looking at him and he looked absolutely drained.' Hendy said to Livingstone, 'You look tired.' Livingstone replied, 'I'm emotionally exhausted.'[27] At 12.00 BST, there was a two-minute silence for those who had died.[28]

Exactly one week later, came the four failed suicide attacks on London; three against the Tube – shortly after midday – at Shepherd's Bush, Warren Street, and Oval stations. A fourth failed to explode on a bus in Shoreditch. A fifth bomber dumped his device. By some miracle, the bombs were duds. Only the detonator caps fired but the bombs themselves did not go off. But now there were five suicide bombers on the loose.

◆

By 29 July 2005, all five suspects were arrested but the police blundered terribly the day after the attacks on 22 July 2005 by shooting dead a 27-year-old innocent electrician called Jean Charles de Menezes at Stockwell Tube station in south London. He was mistaken for one of the so-called 21/7 bombers and was shot seven times in the head and once in the shoulder.[29] The tragedy would embroil Sir Ian Blair and Livingstone in controversy for the next two and a half years and result in the Met being successfully prosecuted under health and safety legislation.[30] Around five and a half hours after the shooting, Blair falsely informed a press conference: 'The information I have available is that this shooting is directly linked to the ongoing and expanding anti-terrorist operation. Any death is deeply regrettable, I understand the man was challenged and refused to obey.'[31] That was simply not true. The question remains: did the Met deliberately peddle lies in the aftermath of the shooting?

In November 2007, the Independent Police Complaints Commission published its so-called Stockwell 2 Inquiry Report into allegations that the Met had supplied inaccurate information to the public, by suggesting that the victim was a terrorist suspect while knowing they had shot an innocent man. It revealed how Deputy Assistant Commissioner Brian Paddick had been convinced that Blair had been told on the day. Paddick was emphatic that he had been told by Blair's staff officer, Chief Superintendent Moir Stewart, 'We've shot a Brazilian tourist...'

The Stockwell 2 report says: 'Shortly before the 15:30hrs press conference DAC Paddick was with the commissioner's staff when he says he was told by Chief Superintendent Stewart that a Brazilian tourist had been shot. DAC Paddick states that the commissioner walked by about the same time, he presumed on his way to the press conference, but without saying anything and without anything being said.'[32]

De Menezes' wallet containing his driving licence and other forms of identification had been recovered from the Tube train where he was shot at 2.47 p.m., almost three quarters of an hour before the press conference.[33] At 3 p.m. this entry was made in the police log: 'The wallet examinations suggest that the deceased is Jean Charles de Menezes, born 07.01.78. A Brazilian born in São Paulo.'

At 4.30 p.m., the police briefed crime writers that the dead man was not thought to be one of the suspects, and shortly after 5 p.m. BBC TV *News 24* reported: 'A line just in about the shooting in Stockwell earlier. The man shot dead at the Tube station is not thought to be one of the four men shown in CCTV pictures released this afternoon.'[34] Over the next 24 hours, the Met issued a series of press releases suggesting that de Menezes had been shot after having been 'challenged' and that his 'clothing and behaviour' added to suspicions.'[35] None of this was true; de Menezes, as you would expect of an innocent man, behaved normally. The Met also issued other false information including statements that de Menezes had leapt over a ticket barrier after being challenged and was wearing a heavy jacket with wires protruding from it.[36] Blair maintained he did not know his officers had shot an innocent man until the following day, Saturday, 23 July 2005.

Later, he would tell the *News of the World*, 'The key component was, at that time, and indeed for the next 24 hours or so, I and everybody who advised me, believed that the person who was shot was a suicide bomber (or a potential suicide bomber) and either one of the four for whom we were looking, or even worse than that, someone else.'[37]

The Stockwell 2 report concluded that neither the Met nor Sir Ian Blair had deliberately misled the public and that the information released was 'believed at the time'.[38] Blair maintained de Menezes' identity was not confirmed to him until 10.30 a.m. on Saturday, 23 July 2005. Livingstone also says he was not told until lunchtime that day. Livingstone believes Blair's assertions that 24 hours went by before he knew the Met had shot an innocent man. 'I have worked with Sir Ian Blair for seven and a half years,' says Livingstone, 'and never once have I felt that he wasn't telling the whole truth.' Blair had been commissioner for only five months at the time of the shooting. 'I never have the slightest doubt that something he tells me is something I would have to question,' he adds.[39]

But serious doubts still linger. In November 2007, following the Met's conviction for the death, Richard Barnes, the Conservative leader on the London Assembly, called for Blair's sacking for his handling of the affair.[40] He remains convinced there was a cover-up: 'I find it incredible that the two most important people in London, as far as police and policy are concerned, did not know until the Saturday when police officers watching cricket knew, the Muslim Safety Forum knew and the crime reporters had been briefed.'[41]

After 9/11, government policy was geared to preventing attacks on British soil. But from late 2003 onwards, there was disagreement at City Hall about how to establish contacts with the Muslim community and whether to engage with the representatives of radical Islamist organisations. Again Livingstone would court controversy by forging links with individuals and groups which some people considered to be both extreme and dangerous.

Atma Singh, Livingstone's policy advisor on Asian affairs for seven years, claims he became slowly estranged from his colleagues at City Hall, a process which began with his decision to resign a second time from Socialist Action after attending a meeting of its central committee 'editorial board' on 23 June 2001 in the King's Cross Community Centre. Singh says, 'They were controlling my personal life as well as my political life. It just meant going to lots of meetings and spending my time on those things instead of developing my career and earning money.'[42] But his relationship with Livingstone and his senior advisors deteriorated when they wanted to reach out to controversial Muslim figures and groups.

Long before the 2005 bombings in London, debate raged in government circles and the security services about how best to counter the al-Qaeda threat and which groups to engage in dialogue. Livingstone had already made contacts with Islamist groups through his opposition to the 2003 Iraq invasion and his participation in the Stop the War Coalition whose key component was the Muslim Association of Britain, or MAB. Singh claims he had qualms about getting close to MAB, but he was overruled by Livingstone's more senior advisors. 'Political Islam was very heavily centred on the Middle East,' says Singh. 'And they could see it as a political force within the UK through the Muslim Association of Britain.'[43]

Established in November 1997, the Muslim Association of Britain has become a powerful voice for some sections of the Muslim community in Britain, but by no means all. Its objectives are to 'promote and propagate the principles of positive Muslim interaction with all elements of society to reflect, project and convey the message of Islam in its pure and unblemished form.'[44]

What that would mean in practice is Sharia law and Islamist theocratic government. MAB condemned the 7 July attacks on London[45] but it has many critics. Louise Ellman, the Labour MP for Liverpool Riverside and a member of the Labour Friends of Israel group, described the MAB as an 'extremist organisation'.[46] The writer Nick Cohen, one of the journalist hate figures at City Hall, has also been a prominent critic of the MAB.[47]

Livingstone wrote: 'There has undoubtedly been increased political mobilisation of Muslim communities in Britain over the last couple of years,' adding: 'This however has been driven, not by an Islamist conspiracy to reconquer Rome or impose Sharia law in Britain, but by opposition to the invasion of Iraq, the perceived double standards applied to the Palestinian/Israeli conflict and issues of equal rights in this country.'[48]

To some Special Branch officers working in counter-terrorism, Livingstone's high-profile opposition to the Iraq War and his willingness to talk to MAB and similar groups was extremely helpful. Former Detective Inspector Bob Lambert headed the Metropolitan Special Branch Muslim Contact Unit, which was set up in 2002 to prevent the mistakes made by the Met during the IRA campaign in alienating Irish people in London.[49] The unit's role was to work with credible Muslim figures to isolate and counter those prepared to support terror attacks. Lambert says, 'It became clear that most of the Muslim groups we were working with – those groups which were proving to be effective at the grassroots and in persuading young people not to get involved in dangerous activity – held City Hall and the mayor in very high regard.

'When at times they felt that other national politicians were not so supportive, it always appeared that the mayor enjoyed consistent support and that became most notable around 2003, with the Stop the War campaign. Often the campaign would be dismissed as being critical without being constructive; in reality it often did provide an outlet for young Muslims who were angry about foreign policy and in many instances, a useful safety valve.'[50]

The inspiration for the Muslim Association of Britain came from what is broadly considered to be the world's most influential international Islamist organisation, the Muslim Brotherhood, originally founded in Egypt in 1928. Its spiritual leader is widely seen as the Qatar-based Egyptian Muslim scholar, Sheikh Yusuf al-Qaradawi.

In July 2004, Livingstone was roundly criticised in some quarters for sharing a platform with al-Qaradawi at a conference in City Hall mainly hosted by the Muslim Association of Britain. The conference was held to discuss the potential impact of the ban on Muslim women in France wearing the hijab headscarf. On the day he arrived in Britain, the *Sun* carried the headline, 'The evil has landed, terror fan cleric invited to London.'[51]

Livingstone's interest in al-Qaradawi is obvious: he was one of the most influential voices in the Muslim world. Although he condemned the 9/11 attacks and those in Madrid, al-Qaradawi spoke repeatedly in support of suicide bombing by Palestinians, even against women and children. In 2004, al-Qaradawi told Peter Marshall, a reporter on *Newsnight*: 'It is not suicide; it is martyrdom in the name of God. Islamic theologians and jurisprudence have debated this issue, referring to it as a form of jihad under the title of jeopardising the life of the mujahideen. It is allowed to jeopardise your soul and cross the path of the enemy and be killed.'[52]

According to emails leaked later to Martin Bright, the political editor of the *New Statesman*, there was powerful support in government and security circles for al-Qaradawi to be allowed into the UK. Although Special Branch certainly did not condone or support al-Qaradawi's position on Palestinian suicide bombers, detectives considered the Sheikh's visit important in their primary task of preventing al-Qaeda recruiting young British Muslims and tackling the terrorist threat to London. Before changing its mind about al-Qaradawi, the *Sun* had praised him shortly after the New York attacks in 2001 for his call to Muslims to unite 'against those who terrorise innocents'.[53] In an internal Foreign Office memo written a year after the visit, the view of the Special Branch Muslim Contact Unit was briefly summarised: 'Sheikh al-Qaradawi has a positive Muslim community impact in the fight against al-Qaeda propaganda in the UK. His support for Palestinian suicide bombers adds credibility to his condemnation of al-Qaeda in those sections of the community most susceptible to the blandishments of al-Qaeda terrorist propaganda.'[54]

The unit would be criticised for appeasing radical Islam but this is rejected by its former boss.[55] 'Who were we worried about?' asks Bob Lambert rhetorically. 'We were worried about young London Muslims who in some cases could have become al-Qaeda terrorists and supporters. Ken is part of an alliance that says to the same young people, look we can empathise with your grievances, the same grievances that al-Qaeda exploits for terrorist recruitment – we have the same grievances; you don't have to go down that road.'[56]

Lambert believes the media 'rather misrepresented' the al-Qaradawi visit in July 2004. 'Where the mayor was useful was with his record of support for minorities,' he adds. 'I think potentially, if anyone can, he is well placed to broker dialogue. Clearly there are some very unacceptable views attributed to al-Qaradawi and they shouldn't be swept under the carpet but dialogue in the way the mayor recommends is often the way of getting rid of a lot of misconceptions. What is said is taken out of context and where you still have very difficult positions – you have to work on it. Only through engagement can you hope to move people forward.'[57]

Atma Singh claims he spoke out against the al-Qaradawi visit to City Hall. He was also against cosying up to the Muslim Association of Britain.[58] 'MAB has very close links with Hamas,' says Singh, 'it has some links with the Muslim Brotherhood and political Islam... I had very big doubts about what was going on.' But he clearly did not make his views clear to Ken Livingstone at the time, as the mayor later made clear to a press conference.[59] According to Singh, matters came to a head in February 2005. A senior Special Branch officer approached Singh and asked him to pass on to the mayor details of a visit by the controversial Muslim scholar, Professor Tariq Ramadan, and to request his support.[60] Singh admits he failed to pass on the information. 'Tariq Ramadan had been refused a visa by the US and this was public knowledge,' says Singh, 'and there were very serious doubts about him in France expressed by the security agencies. I knew that from informal contacts and this was also fairly public knowledge.'

After hearing nothing back, the Special Branch officer bypassed Singh and went straight to Redmond O'Neill. As the advisor with overall responsibility for community relations, O'Neill was taken aback that Singh had not reported the approach by the anti-terrorist squad to senior management as would be standard practice. 'When I asked Mr Singh about this, he did not suggest he had any objection to what had been suggested, rather it seems to be a simple issue of competence – he had forgotten about it,' said Mr O'Neill. 'Some considerable time later, I was contacted by the police as his manager and asked what were we intending to do about this matter. I said I hadn't heard anything about it and was absolutely flabbergasted. From any point of view, it was totally unacceptable. We are the government of London and the people in charge of protecting London from terrorists approached us for our help and somebody doesn't even take the trouble to tell the authority that he's received such an approach.'[61]

◆

Ramadan attended the July 2004 al-Qaradawi/hijab conference as well as a later symposium held by the mayor in 2007.[62] Livingstone would make it clear he was 'very keen to engage with Tariq Ramadan'.[63] As for Atma Singh, he fell chronically ill from a painful back condition called lumbar spondilitis in February 2005 and was unable to go to City Hall on the day of the 7 July attacks.[64] Livingstone would criticise Singh's failure to rush to City Hall at a later press conference.[65] Singh's colleagues were also furious. A senior Livingstone advisor says, 'We didn't hear a single word throughout the entire period from the person who was responsible for our relations with the Asian networks and in particular with the Muslim communities.'[66] But the debate on how to deal with people like al-Qaradawi would always remain a moveable feast. In 2005, the Foreign Office recommended that al-Qaradawi be allowed entry to the UK despite knowing his views on Palestinian suicide bombers; in 2008, the British government changed tack and denied al-Qaradawi a visa for what he had said to *Newsnight* about Palestinian suicide bombers.[67]

After an absence from City Hall of almost two years due to ill health, Atma Singh initially declined the offer of a goodbye package through a compromise agreement in late 2006. He was summarily dismissed in February 2007 before City Hall allowed him to leave by agreement, along with decent references, on 19 July 2007. In January 2008, he would be the star witness in the Channel Four *Dispatches* programme speaking out against Livingstone's City Hall.[68] But by welcoming al-Qaradawi, Livingstone had done himself few favours with the communities on which he had always been able to count for support. The gay community had little time for the old cleric's regular denunciations of homosexuality. This was most angrily expressed by the gay rights campaigner Peter Tatchell who condemned al-Qaradawi's visit in an article for the *New Statesman* headlined 'An embrace that shames London'.[69] In his article, he included al-Qaradawi's bizarre claim that the 2004 tsunami had killed people mainly in South East Asian beach resorts because of the 'alcohol consumption' and 'acts of abomination', his code for homosexuality. According to Tatchell, al-Qaradawi had asked, 'Don't they deserve punishment from Allah?'[70] But nothing could change Livingstone's mind about the cleric. Months after Tatchell's outburst, he would even compare al-Qaradawi to his great papal hero, John XXIII.[71]

'It's all very well people slagging Ken off about al-Qaradawi,' says one of Livingstone's most senior advisors, '...he was right. Al-Qaradawi has more influence with Muslims across the world than almost anybody. Ken says he's like the Pope. That doesn't mean Ken agrees with everything he says. He doesn't agree on some things, particularly on Palestinian suicide bombers. He's against all forms of violence.'[72] But as with Sinn Féin more than 20 years earlier, Livingstone was playing a dangerous game. It would help fuel what became one of the biggest crises of his mayoralty.

Notes

1   Interview, Simon Harris, 18.1.08
2   *Guardian,* 'British suicide bombers carried out London attacks, say police', by Duncan Campbell, 13.7.07
3   Off-the-record briefing, senior Livingstone aide, 1.2.08
4   Interview, Ken Livingstone, 26.11.07
5   Mike Lee, *The Race for the 2012 Olympics,* p201
6   Interview, Neale Coleman, 31.10.07
7   Context of speech in Singapore, issued by the Mayor and Greater London Authority, 7.7.05
8   Interview, Neale Coleman, 31.11.07
9   David Blunkett, *The Blunkett Tapes: My Life in the Bear Pit,* Bloomsbury, 2006, p298
10   Interview, Nick Raynsford, 20.12.07
11   Ibid.
12   *Guardian,* 'The day the City stood still... and Britain's defence against terror was put to the test', by Hugh Muir, 8.9.03
13   Interview, Nick Raynsford, 20.12.07
14   *Guardian,* 17.3.04
15   David Blunkett, *The Blunkett Tapes: My Life in the Bear Pit,* p623
16   Interview, Ken Livingstone, 26.11.07
17   Interview, Ken Livingstone, 26.11.07
18   Statement, Board of TfL, 13.7.05
19   Interview, Peter Hendy, 13.12.07
20   Ibid.

21 Minutes, TfL Board meeting, 13.7.05
22 Ibid.
23 Report of the 7 July Review Committee of the Greater London Assembly, published by the Greater London Authority, June 2006
24 Interview, Ken Livingstone, 26.11.07
25 Interview, Harry Barlow, 20.11.07
26 Speech, Ken Livingstone, 14.7.05, YouTube, (www.youtube.com/watch?v=6BSIBPsbL9c)
27 Interview, Peter Hendy, 13.12.07
28 BBC News Online, 'London falls silent for bomb dead', 14.7.05
29 BBC News Online, 'Police shot Brazilian eight times', 25.7.05; Stockwell 1 report, Independent Police Complaints Commission, November 2007
30 BBC News Online, 'Police guilty over Menezes case', 1.11.07; Stockwell 1 report, by IPCC, chronology
31 Stockwell 2 report, Independent Police Complaints Commission, November 2007
32 Ibid.
33 Ibid.
34 Ibid.
35 Metropolitan Police Service press release no. 8, issued at 6.13 p.m., 23.7.05
36 Stockwell 2 report, IPCC
37 *News of the World*, 19.8.05
38 Stockwell 2 report, IPCC, conclusions
39 Interview, Ken Livingstone, 26.11.07
40 BBC News Online, 'Blair resignation calls intensify', 2.11.07
41 Interview, Richard Barnes AM, 20.11.07
42 Interview, Atma Singh, 28.1.08
43 Ibid.
44 Muslim Association of Britain website, http://www.mabonline.net/content
45 *The Londoner*, 5.8.05
46 *Daily Mail*, 'Terror link of "moderate" Muslims at London rally', 11.2.06
47 Nick Cohen, *What's Left? How the Left Lost Its Way*, HarperPerennial, 2007, pp305-311
48 Report: 'Why the Mayor of London will maintain dialogues with all of London's faiths and communities: A reply to the dossier against the Mayor's meeting with Dr Yusuf al-Qaradawi', GLA, January 2005
49 *Guardian*, article by Seamus Milne, 14.2.08
50 Interview, Bob Lambert, 22.2.08
51 *Sun*, 5.7.04
52 *Newsnight*, 7.7.04
53 *Sun*, 13.10.01
54 Email, Mockbul Ali, Islamic Affairs advisor, the Foreign Office, to John Sawyer, director-general-political, Foreign Office, 14.7.05: first published in *When Progressives Treat With Reactionaries: The British State's Flirtation With Radical Islam*, the pamphlet by Martin Bright for Policy Exchange, Heron, Dawson and Sawyer, July 2006
55 *Guardian*, article by Seamus Milne, 14.2.08
56 Interview, Bob Lambert, 28.2.08

57 Interview, Bob Lambert, 22.2.08
58 Interview, Atma Singh, 27.1.08
59 Mayor's press conference, 22.1.08
60 Chronology supplied by Atma Singh, 28.1.08
61 Interview, Redmond O'Neill, 20.2.08
62 Clash of civilisations conference, City Hall, 20.1.07
63 www.somethingjewish.co.uk, interview with Ken Livingstone, 17.11.05
64 Chronology supplied by Atma Singh, 27.1.08
65 Mayor's press conference, 20.1.08
66 Interview, 20.2.08
67 BBC News Online, 'Muslim cleric not allowed into UK', 7.2.08
68 Channel Four *Dispatches, The Court of Ken*, 21.1.08
69 *New Statesman,* 'An embrace that shames London', by Peter Tatchell, 24.1.05
70 Ibid.
71 *Times Online*, 'Livingstone likens bomb apologist to reformer Pope John', 14.9.05; Also see Chapter 3
72 Off-the-record interview, senior advisor, August 2007

Chapter 26

London evening standards,
February 2005–March 2006

On 8 February 2005, Oliver Finegold left his home in the Finchley Road and travelled by Tube to the offices of the *Evening Standard* for the start of the unpopular 5 p.m. to 1 a.m. shift. Aged 29, he was being 'tried out' as a freelancer by the *Evening Standard* after stints working for local papers like the *Camden New Journal*. Staff jobs were hard to come by and 'shifting' for big papers like the *Evening Standard* was the only way to get on.

The general view of Finegold at the *Evening Standard* was that he was a nice guy, very polite but all in all 'a nervous little reporter'. He was not working out. A senior *Evening Standard* journalist says, 'To some degree, he was probably for the high jump. He had had a few months' try-out. He had done OK but not brilliantly and now it was time to say "Sorry mate, it hasn't quite worked out. We'll try somebody else now."'[1] But soon, Ken Livingstone was going to make Oliver Finegold indispensable to the *Evening Standard*, at least for the next 18 months.

The only item of marginal interest for the late shift reporter that night was a party at City Hall to celebrate the twentieth anniversary of the 'coming out' of the gay former Labour cabinet minister, Chris Smith. Ross Lydall, the *Evening Standard*'s City Hall editor, had planned to cover the event but could not make it. Lydall had spoken to Ben McKnight, one of Livingstone's press officers, and asked him who was on the guest list. 'As usual', the response was negative. Lydall said, 'We're probably going to send somebody along to stand outside and take some pictures.'

'We thought it was going to be quite glitzy,' says Lydall, 'because at these gay events you get these "right-on" politicians coming out for an event like that. It's a typical thing the *Evening Standard* might do for a page three the following morning. It's just like you'd go to a film premiere or something. You get a picture of someone in a fancy frock, write 200 words, and that's your page.

'Also, we liked Chris Smith because he had done something for the paper a week or two before. In fact I had known him, when I covered Islington [as a local newspaper reporter] because he was one of the Islington MPs. The paper liked Chris Smith and it was good on gay issues as well.'[2] For example, the *Evening Standard* had once asked its long-standing and openly gay theatre critic Nicholas de Jongh to write a piece about the Gay Pride march through Hyde Park in July 2003.[3]

◆

By the time Oliver Finegold arrived at City Hall on the evening of 8 February 2005, the Chris Smith story was being downgraded to a short diary item. To make matters worse, it was dark, cold and miserable. Finegold wrapped up warm, put on his gloves, got out his mini tape recorder and hung around outside with the photographer Nigel Howard waiting for guests to emerge. He was only looking for a few quotes and called up McKnight in the press office to tell him, 'I'm outside, do you think I could get a few words with Chris Smith?' As he waited for a response, Finegold grabbed a few words with some of the guests who started to drift home around 8 p.m. Among those happy enough to pass a few fleeting seconds with the chilly Finegold were Stephen Twigg, the gay Labour MP for Enfield Southgate, and Adam Boulton and Anji Hunter, respectively Sky News political editor and Tony Blair's former director of government relations.[4] Then, just before 9 p.m. Livingstone emerged wearing his scarf and coat, arm in arm with Emma Beal.

Finegold approached the mayor, tape recorder whirring. Livingstone told the photographer, 'You've got one of me already.'[5] There then followed an unpleasant 35-second exchange which would plunge City Hall into a full-blown and entirely avoidable crisis:

OLIVER FINEGOLD: Mr Liv... *Evening Standard*. How did...
KEN LIVINGSTONE: Oh, how awful for you.
FINEGOLD: How did tonight go?
LIVINGSTONE: Have you thought of having treatment?
FINEGOLD: How did tonight go?
LIVINGSTONE: Have you thought of having treatment?
FINEGOLD: Was it a good party? What did it mean to you?
LIVINGSTONE: What did you do before? Were you a German war criminal?

FINEGOLD: No, I'm Jewish. I wasn't a German war criminal...
LIVINGSTONE: Ah right.
FINEGOLD: I'm actually quite offended by that. So how did tonight go?
LIVINGSTONE: Well you might be, but actually you are just like a concentration camp guard. You're just doing it 'cause you're paid to, aren't you?
FINEGOLD: Great, I've got you on record for that. So how did tonight go?
LIVINGSTONE: It's nothing to do with you because your paper is a load of scumbags –
FINEGOLD: How did tonight go?
LIVINGSTONE: ... It's reactionary bigots...
FINEGOLD: I'm a journalist. I'm doing my job...
LIVINGSTONE: ... and who supported fascism.
FINEGOLD: ... I'm only asking for a simple comment. I'm only asking for a comment.
LIVINGSTONE: Well work for a paper that isn't...
FINEGOLD: I'm only asking for a comment.
LIVINGSTONE: ... that hadn't a record of supporting fascism.
FINEGOLD: You've accused me...[6]

Then Finegold turned off his recording machine. The quotes were in the can, and so it turned out, was Ken Livingstone. A shaken Finegold returned to the *Evening Standard* and gave the tape to the night news editor, Neil Sawyer, who in turn called the news editor Ian Walker who rang the paper's deputy editor, Ian McGregor. The decision was made to hang on to the story and decide how to play it.[7] In the meantime, Finegold was told to transcribe the tape and write up an account of what happened.

The decision not to run the story was taken by the editor, Veronica Wadley. Ross Lydall says, 'Her view was that it was a bit of a barney between the journalist and Ken – a rumbustious exchange of no obvious relevance and journalists should be prepared to put up with the hard knocks. If we had just run it saying "bad old Ken", then it would have been inflammatory and there was no obvious public justification for it.'[8] There was particular anxiety not to ratchet up the long-running tension between Livingstone and the *Evening Standard*, particularly as the Hedges incident was considered by staff at the paper to have ended in a 'score draw'.

Finegold's transcribed account was placed in a common

newsroom computer file where every journalist with access could read it. On the morning of 9 February 2005, reporters started reading the account of the night before. Some, particularly two Jewish reporters, Mira Bar-Hillel and Ruth Bloomfield, were incensed.[9] It was pretty obvious that one of the journalists at the *Evening Standard* would leak the transcript and that is precisely what happened. The key place for stories about journalists was the media section of the *Guardian*, and the following morning, it duly appeared. Livingstone still believes the leaking was done deliberately at the behest of senior editorial staff to blow it up into a big story.[10]

♦

Unlike raising newts, Livingstone's hobby of insulting journalists has never made it into *Who's Who* but few politicians have ever been able to address the press as 'pubic lice'[11] and get away with it. But this time, he had gone too far. The story in the *Guardian* written by Chris Tryhorn, under the headline 'Livingstone attacks "scumbag" *Standard*', effectively sprayed paraffin on the dying embers of the Finegold incident. In particular, the fiercely aggressive rebuttal from City Hall could only have inflamed the situation. As a result, within days, two powerful long-term foes of Livingstone came together: the *Evening Standard* and the Board of Deputies of British Jews, the most important representative body of British Jewry.

Not only did Livingstone unleash a vituperative attack on the *Evening Standard* and its sister paper, the *Daily Mail*, but also on the integrity of Oliver Finegold. In his statement, Livingstone accused Finegold of saying 'fuck off' at the end of the exchange. Finegold has always vehemently denied saying it and it must be said there is not a scrap of evidence to support the allegation. In any case, that would only have justified Livingstone's comments if Finegold had sworn at the beginning rather than at the end. Later, Livingstone would also claim Finegold 'barked' his questions. But this too was rejected by a hearing in late 2005 of the Adjudication Panel of England which would demand Livingstone's one-month suspension for bringing the office of mayor into disrepute in February 2006.[12]

Livingstone's attack on the *Evening Standard* and the company, Associated Newspapers, which owned both it and the *Daily Mail* was an extraordinary escalation. He justified his comments about Finegold working for a paper with a record for 'supporting fascism' by waving the hoary old chestnut of the *Mail*'s former proprietor Lord Rothermere's well-known fondness for Adolf Hitler in the 1930s and his tacit approval of Britain's Hitler mini me, Oswald Mosley, best exemplified by the notorious headline 'Hurrah for the Blackshirts!' in January 1934.

But the *Evening Standard* did not become part of Associated Newspapers until 31 October 1980 when it was merged with Lord Rothermere's *Evening News*.[13] Up until then, it had been owned by Beaverbrook Newspapers, famously the owners of the *Daily Express* in its heyday. Also, as many people pointed out, Livingstone had been content enough to draw an income for three and a half years from Associated Newspapers as a restaurant critic.

When it came to dodgy Third Reich analogy, few had greater form than Ken Livingstone. Since the rate capping farce of 1985 when everyone was going to look like 'the biggest fucking liars since Goebbels',[14] Livingstone was on record as believing that the 'international financial system kills more people than World War Two';[15] the conservation quango English Heritage's opposition to his plans for skyscrapers was the 'biggest threat to the economy of London since Adolf Hitler';[16] Britain's record in Ireland was 'as bad in 800 years as what Hitler did to the Jews in six';[17] most post-war physical education instructors were 'rehabilitated Nazi war criminals';[18] the press had treated him like 'a Nazi war criminal'[19] when investigating his Localaction tax affairs;[20] and the government's voucher scheme for asylum seekers was 'like putting the yellow star on Jews'.[21] 'What is particularly distasteful,' observed Peter Riddell about Livingstone in *The Times* almost five years before the Finegold incident, 'is his free use of comparisons with Nazi Germany.'[22] The Board of Deputies branded his remarks about international finance as 'actually quite offensive'.[23] Livingstone must have known how insulting many Jews found these comparisons.

◆

But does that make Livingstone anti-Semitic, as alleged? Apparently like Don Corleone, Adolf Hitler is a regular reference point, although clearly a much more dangerous one. That, according to his advisors interviewed for this book, is the result of having been born in the immediate post-war period when

Hitler was still a raw and recent memory, and for Livingstone, someone who had torpedoed his father's convoy. 'Ken is not an anti-Semite,' says one advisor, 'he's just got this obsession about the Second World War.'[24]

But that does not explain why Livingstone continued with his insults after Finegold told him he was a Jew or why he refused point blank to apologise afterwards. Like the Hedges episode, it could have been diffused with a simple apology; instead, again, it blew up into a storm that threatened him politically and damaged his reputation. Intense pressure from the prime minister downwards was brought to bear on Livingstone to apologise but to little avail. In an interview on Channel Five, Blair said, 'A lot of us get angry with journalists from time to time, but in the circumstances in which the journalist was a Jewish journalist, yes he should apologise. He should apologise and move on.'[25] Furthermore, the row was brewing up at the time of the visit by the evaluation commission of the International Olympic Committee to assess London's bid.[26] Mike Lee, who handled the media for London 2012, wrote later that the Finegold saga was a 'problem given that many international reporters were in London to cover the visit,' adding, '...the story grew, threatening to overshadow the commission's visit.'

Lee said, 'We were not looking for an apology directly to the journalist because we knew Ken was not prepared to do that. We were looking for an apology directly to people who might have been offended.'[27] The people he offended included those who had been at the receiving end of the worst the Third Reich had to offer. A group of elderly Holocaust survivors watched in horror as Livingstone sat before the London Assembly and refused to apologise, citing the pain caused him over the years by the *Evening Standard* and its stable mates at Associated Newspapers: 'If I could in anything I say relieve any pain anyone feels I would not hesitate to do it but it would require me to be a liar... I could apologise but why should I say words I do not believe in my heart? Therefore I cannot. If that is something people find they cannot accept I am sorry but this is how I feel after nearly a quarter of a century of their behaviour and tactics. I cannot say to you words I do not believe in my heart.'[28] Livingstone believes his enemies on the Assembly had mischievously orchestrated the seating arrangements so that he had his back to the audience and therefore he did not know there were Holocaust survivors present.[29]

The survivors, who had presented a petition, clearly thought Livingstone was self-pitying and disingenuous. Gena Turgel, 82, who had been chosen to lead the Queen to her seat in Westminster Hall at the Holocaust Memorial Day ceremony, said: 'I am shocked. There is no comparison between what Mr Livingstone's family have gone through and what ours suffered.' Another, Josef Perl, who was 74, and had survived eight concentration camps, said: 'The mayor is a bigoted person. He made no attempt to meet us and does not deserve the position he holds.'[30] In the face of demands to apologise from the five parties making up the Assembly and even his own deputy, Nicky Gavron, herself the daughter of a Holocaust survivor, Livingstone refused to say sorry.[31]

◆

By 2005, it is clear that City Hall under Ken Livingstone had developed something of a siege mentality, particularly with regard to the press. The belief that there was a right-wing media campaign to 'get' the mayor would be stamped through his administration like words in a stick of rock. By 2007, a real hatred had developed in particular between City Hall and the *Evening Standard* with Livingstone actually concluding that the sole purpose of the paper was to bring him down.[32]

'In that circumstance, there was no question of an apology,' says Livingstone, 'here was a campaign where the Board of Deputies thought, "Make a big fuss and he'll be quiet about Israel and the Palestinians"; and the Tories were saying, "Here's a chance to try and damage Livingstone." With something like that, you can't give in. You've got to face it down or they've found your breaking point.'[33]

◆

Livingstone's animosity towards the *Evening Standard,* the *Daily Mail* and the papers' owner, Associated Newspapers, dates back to the early days of his leadership of the GLC. Both papers gave him a terrible press. In 1982, Illtyd Harrington was dined at the Ritz by the *Mail on Sunday* and was offered £30,000 to write four articles blowing the lid off the GLC. In relation to Livingstone, a newspaper executive told Harrington, 'We're out to get him.' It was a big offer for Harrington, who had about £1,000 to his name. Nonetheless, he turned them down. On returning to County Hall he told Livingstone about the offer and asked him what he would have done. 'I'd have taken it,' replied a laughing Livingstone.[34] Later that year, Livingstone banned advertising in the *Evening Standard* over the Jak cartoon.[35] Early in 1983, shortly before the widely expected general election, George Tremlett, the Tory's GLC housing spokesman, was called to a meeting at County Hall with one of his party's press officers and two journalists, one from the *Daily Telegraph* and another from the *Mail on Sunday*. The *Mail* reporter took Tremlett to La Barca restaurant near County Hall and asked him, 'Can you help us with some information about Livingstone?' 'What kind of information do you want?' asked Tremlett. 'We want to know about his sex life,' replied the reporter. 'we want to know if he's gay.' 'Sorry,' replied Tremlett. 'I don't do things like that.'[36] In an attempt to prove that Livingstone was anti-Semitic, the *Daily Mail* asked Tremlett to make applications for GLC funding on behalf of certain Jewish groups to see whether they would be rejected. 'I refused point blank,' says Tremlett. In his GLC days, Livingstone clearly felt sympathy for individual Associated journalists like Richard Holliday, a superb reporter whose talents were wasted for a time by the *Daily Mail* which insisted he ferreted about for the latest loony outrage at County Hall. But a man as sensitive as Livingstone was always going to find it hard to forgive the company for the hurt it caused his family and him, despite outward appearances at the time and a lucrative restaurant column some time later. He prides himself on being able to 'move on' but clearly he is also a man who can bear grudges.[37]

◆

Aside from the odd contemptuous reference or article, Associated Newspapers appears to have taken relatively little notice of Livingstone during his parliamentary wilderness years. In the late 1990s, there was a truce of a kind when Livingstone started writing restaurant reviews for the *Evening Standard*'s magazine, netting him £32,500 in the period from June 1998 to January 2000 alone.[38] Livingstone enjoyed a good relationship with Max Hastings, the paper's editor, until February 2002.[39] But, despite their personal relationship, and the belief that he had the right to stand, Hastings made it clear he thought Livingstone would be 'the worst possible choice' and could prove to be 'a disastrous and embarrassing mayor'. The Tory candidate Steve Norris was 'overwhelmingly the best-qualified'.[40]

But things deteriorated rapidly under Hastings' replacement, Veronica Wadley, who Hastings once described as 'wonderfully focused and fiercely determined'.[41] Within hours of her appointment, Livingstone invited Wadley for lunch.[42] But she turned him down on the grounds that she was too busy. A little later, Livingstone again invited her, this time to a lunch he was hosting for New York mayor, Rudolph Giuliani, at Sir Terence Conran's restaurant, Pont de la Tour, on 14 February 2002.[43] Again citing pressure of work, Wadley declined. 'I think this put Ken's nose out of joint,' says the *Evening Standard*'s City Hall editor, Ross Lydall. 'And then came the party incident when he thought "she's out to get me."'[44] 'I didn't like his behaviour after a party punch-up at which a member of my staff was pushed over a wall,' Wadley conceded more than two years later.[45]

◆

In the 2004 mayoral election, the *Evening Standard* under Wadley gave Livingstone its extremely qualified support. Steve Norris had written himself out of the paper's affections by refusing to give up his chairmanship of the construction company Jarvis which had only recently accepted liability for claims emanating from the train crash at Potters Bar.[46] This time the *Evening Standard* made it clear that Livingstone was the least worst choice, adding: 'We remain wary of Mr Livingstone's empire-building, his impatience with opposition, and above all the enormous debts on his transport budget. But behind his cheeky chappie persona he is an effective operator.'[47]

In January 2005, a month before the Finegold encounter, war broke out again. Ken Livingstone made it clear he was prepared to threaten Associated Newspapers' business. Until then, the company had a virtual monopoly in the distribution on the London Underground of a free newspaper called *Metro* filled with yesterday's news which commuters picked up on their way through their Tube station. Livingstone started to make noises about allowing proprietors such as Richard Desmond, the owner of the *Express*, to distribute an afternoon freesheet, directly threatening the *Evening Standard*.[48] Although the Desmond paper came to nothing, it was enough to ratchet up tensions between City Hall and London's only evening newspaper at the time.

A few days after the threat to the *Evening Standard* became clear, Veronica Wadley assailed Livingstone through the columns of the *Spectator*. She highlighted some successes, but laid into his profligacy and 'financial recklessness': his number of staff had more than doubled from 287 to 682 in four years; his empty buses were 'clogging up the city'; and his proportion of the Council Tax for those on the middle band D had almost doubled from £123 to £241.[49]

Livingstone responded by baiting Wadley on the freesheet issue: 'Ms Wadley seems to have a particularly thin skin when it comes to my announcement that TfL will now seek to bring about the distribution of free afternoon newspapers on the Tube. But it is precisely because I regard the original contract with her sister paper the *Metro* as such poor value to the London tax- and fare-payer that I have acted.'[50] Oliver Finegold might have chosen a better time to have approached the mayor.

◆

It was not Finegold who lodged the official complaint but another of Livingstone's long-term foes, the Board of Deputies of British Jews. The complaint was first taken to the Committee on Standards in Public Life which passed it on to the Standards Board for England, the investigators of the 2002 Hedges incident.[51]

Ken Livingstone had long attracted the ire of the Board of Deputies for his outspoken and radical views on Israel and the Palestinians. The plight of the Palestinians following the 1982 invasion of Lebanon by Israel became a great cause célèbre for many on the Left and particularly for Ken Livingstone. Beginning in September 1982, Livingstone published his three-part history of Israel in the *Labour Herald*.[52]

A particular hate figure for Livingstone was the then Israeli prime minister, Menachem Begin. In one article on Israel called 'Creature of Terror', Livingstone argued that there was a 'feeling of guilt throughout the Western world' as the details of the Holocaust became known which was 'skilfully exploited in the demand for a Jewish homeland'.[53] Livingstone described the murderous campaign of the Irgun, also known as the Stern Gang after its founder Avraham Stern, to force the British to end its Mandate in Palestine and allow the Jews to establish Israel. This campaign, led by Menachem Begin, included the hanging of two British sergeants and the 1946 bombing in Jerusalem of the King David

Hotel, HQ of the Mandate's Secretariat, which killed 91 people. This terror campaign was often credited as having brought about Britain's withdrawal in 1948.

Livingstone says his attitudes towards Israel were also particularly influenced by an extraordinary document discovered after the war in the files of the German embassy in Ankara and published later by the Bar-Ilan University near Tel Aviv. Dated 11 January 1941, the document lists the Irgun's proposals for closer links with Nazi Germany to help end the Mandate and it is called 'Concerning the solution of the Jewish Question and the participation of the National Military Organisation (Irgun) in the War on the side of Germany'.[54] This document was drawn up just a year before a group of Nazi officials met in Wannsee on the outskirts of Berlin to discuss a wholly different 'solution' to the 'Jewish Question'.

It was this which apparently prompted Livingstone's decision to publish a shocking cartoon in the *Labour Herald* on 25 June 1982 portraying Begin in black SS uniform with arm outstretched in a Hitler salute and standing on a pile of Palestinian skulls above the words 'The Final Solution? Shalom? Who needs Shalom with [President] Reagan behind you?'[55] At the weekly *Herald* editorial conference, Ted Knight expressed doubts about the cartoon, but not Livingstone. 'No,' said Livingstone. 'I think it should run, I think it's true, I think Begin is a monster.' 'It was my decision specifically that that cartoon should run,' says Livingstone.[56] Six months or so later, around the time of the Jak cartoon row, Livingstone was accused of hypocrisy by a Labour Party member who had been outraged by the Begin cartoon. Peter Bradley, the future Labour MP for Wrekin, claims Livingstone replied, 'You Zionists are everywhere!'[57] The Board of Deputies reacted to the cartoon by making a failed attempt to get the *Herald* prosecuted under the Race Relations Act.[58] In April 1983, as described more fully in an earlier chapter, while defending Gerry Healy against the *Money Programme*'s story on the Libyan money, Livingstone attacked a 'campaign' orchestrated by 'Zionists' and 'agents of the Begin government'.[59]

There was further anger in December 1984 when the Israeli trade union newspaper *Davar* carried an interview with Livingstone in which he denounced the Board of Deputies as being 'dominated by reactionaries and neo fascists'. He went on, '…progressive

Jews support me: only Jews who hold extreme right-wing views oppose me.' He also suggested that some Jews traditionally supported Labour 'not necessarily because they are socialists but because the Conservative Party was anti-Semitic'. Peter Bradley, also a member of Poale Zion, the Jewish socialist society affiliated to the Labour Party, wrote: 'Nothing could have been calculated to offer greater insult to Labour's Jewish activists...'[60]

According to Atma Singh, there was already hostility at City Hall towards the British Board long before the Finegold incident, not only because of its occasional run-ins with Livingstone, but also because of its unequivocal support of Israel. 'Anyone who supports this "terrorist state" and criticises Muslims are their enemies almost,' claims Singh. 'Zionism is seen as an enemy.' Singh also points to the views expressed by Socialist Action on the Internet. Since the distant days in the 1980s when it dissolved its 'public face',[61] Socialist Action had achieved a rather ethereal state, of existing but at the same time not existing, of people being members and yet not, and holding 'editorial board meetings' for a non-existent newspaper. But there were always the Socialist Action printers in Stoke Newington and the website where anyone can read the group's views on Israel. As late as August 2006, at the time of the Lebanon conflict, Socialist Action described Israel as 'a terrorist state'.[62] The aggressive action by Israel was affirmation of 'the terrorist character of the Israeli state'.[63]

Socialist Action believes: 'The terrible atrocities committed by the Nazis against the Jewish people in the Holocaust were cynically used by imperialism to establish Israel in 1948... the plan of the imperialist powers was to create a state in the Middle East completely dependent on and loyal to Western imperialism. Thus Israel came into being, and is today armed to the hilt by the US.'[64] Before the 2003 Iraq invasion, Socialist Action went as far as to suggest, 'If the US administration's motive was to attack a country in the Middle East with weapons of mass destruction, its number one target would logically be Israel — of which, on the contrary, the US is the biggest supporter.'

But a number of Livingstone's senior advisors interviewed for this book insisted that Atma Singh was a discredited witness and an embittered former employee whose claims about City Hall wanting to confront the British Board are 'totally untrue'. One advisor, long associated with Socialist Action, points to the close ties between important Jewish organisations and the mayor's office. Not only has he consulted regularly with leading members of the Jewish community, Livingstone has also funded and actively supported important Jewish festivals in Trafalgar Square including the Simcha[65] and the Hanukkah 'Festival of lights.'[66] 'There are different opinions about the Middle East as you would expect,' says the advisor who did not want his comments attributed. 'There are very different views in the Jewish community. So it's perfectly possible to have radically different views about the Middle East and not merely oppose anti-Semitism but sense and celebrate the gigantic Jewish contribution to human civilisation and culture. And that's what we have set out to do.'[67] Livingstone has always been consistent in his belief that there must be a two-state solution to the Middle East but he has antagonised Jewish leaders with his outspoken criticism of Israel, and at public expense.

◆

In January 2005, Livingstone published a 26-page dossier defending his decision to welcome Yusuf al-Qaradawi to City Hall. It contains many criticisms of Israel and its backers, the United States, as well as articulating the Sheikh's views on suicide bombing in Israel. Livingstone wrote: '…like many people in the Middle East, he is a strong supporter of the rights of the Palestinians. He takes the view that in the specific circumstances of that conflict, where Israel is using modern missiles, tanks and planes in civilian areas to perpetuate the illegal occupation of Palestinian lands, it is justified for Palestinians to turn their bodies into weapons.'[68] In his foreword, Livingstone condemned 'all violence in Israel and Palestine', but added, 'It would be impossible to refuse to speak to a person like Dr al-Qaradawi who has no personal involvement in violence of any kind, but at the same time speak to an Israeli government, which kills Palestinian civilians with modern weapons every week.'[69]

While not unequivocally condemning al-Qaradawi's views on suicide bombers in Israel, the dossier draws attention to Israel's infamous role in the 1982 massacres of Palestinians at the Sabra and Shatila refugee camps in Lebanon carried out by a Christian militia allegedly with Israeli collusion. The camps were supposedly under the protection of Ariel Sharon, the Israeli prime minister at the time of the al-Qaradawi visit. The GLA dossier continues: 'In all consistency, therefore, the authors of the dossier should also be calling for supporters of the Sharon government to be excluded from City Hall.' It is hardly surprising that Livingstone's relationship with London's Jewish community remains the most problematic.

For nearly a year, Livingstone stubbornly refused to make an apology which would have ended the matter. Writing later in the *Evening Standard*, the journalist Jonathan Freedland accused Livingstone of 'playing a dangerous game', adding, 'Plenty of Jews cannot believe that if the mayor were confronted by, say, a black or Muslim or gay reporter who said they were similarly hurt, he would not have made amends immediately. This is a man who prides himself on his sensitivity to London's minorities – and yet, on that night outside City Hall, he trampled on a very raw Jewish nerve, for which he has never straightforwardly apologised.'[70]

◆

As with the Police and the Crown Prosecution Service, the role of the Standards Board for England was to investigate allegations of misconduct; meting out punishment was the job of another government quango called the Adjudication Panel for England, or rather unfortunately, the APE. In August 2005, the Standards Board referred the Finegold complaint, case number SBE10001.05, to the APE which met on 13 December 2005 to decide whether the mayor had breached the official Code of Conduct by bringing his office into disrepute.[71]

Livingstone turned up for the first morning of the hearing looking distinctly unimpressed, if not bored, and listened as the Finegold tape was played out with a slightly bemused calm. The following day witnessed the submission on Livingstone's behalf by his lawyer, Tony Child, who, as the solicitor for the Audit Commission, was best known for his forensic investigation into the Shirley Porter gerrymandering scandal. Child mainly argued that the Code of Conduct could involve 'infringement' of Livingstone's right to 'free expression' under Article 10 of the European Convention on Human Rights and his right to be free of interference in his private life under Article 8. The Adjudication Panel met again on 23 February 2006 and on the following day, ruled that Livingstone had apparently 'failed, from the outset of this case, to have appreciated that his conduct was unacceptable, was a breach of the Code and did damage to the reputation of his office'. The mayor had to take responsibility for matters having 'got as far as this' but he had 'started the matter and thereafter his position seems to have become ever more entrenched'.[72] Astonishingly, the APE, consisting of three unelected and obscure 'adjudicators' ruled that the first directly-elected mayor of London should be suspended from office for four weeks, starting on 1 March 2006.

There were some whoops at the *Evening Standard* and even some high fives[73] but elsewhere the widespread feeling of disbelief at the severity of the ruling was best expressed by Livingstone's deputy, Nicky Gavron, who said, 'This decision is absurd – and strikes at the roots of democracy.'[74] Artists and celebrities including Billy Bragg, the cartoonist Ralph Steadman and the comic Arthur Smith signed a letter protesting about the punishment, 'It is an outrage against democracy and it [the penalty] should be removed immediately.'[75] Livingstone appealed to the High Court against the ruling which resulted in the postponement of his suspension from office. It appeared his pursuers had, once again, overdone it. Livingstone reveals his own reaction to the decision: 'I was delighted because I realised they had guaranteed that in the end I would win. They had so overreached themselves. Hold your nerve until your opponents make a mistake or the tide turns.'[76]

Notes

1 Off-the-record interview, November 2007
2 Interview Ross Lydall, 16.11.07
3 *Evening Standard*, 'Pride blooms in Park', by Nicholas de Jongh, 28.7.03
4 Off-the-record briefing, 28.9.07
5 Judgment, High Court, Ken Livingstone vs The Adjudication Panel for England, 19.10.06
6 Ibid., transcript version used in High Court
7 Off-the-record briefing, *Evening Standard* reporter
8 Interview, Ross Lydall, 16.11.07
9 Off-the-record briefing, 3.2.08
10 Interview, Ken Livingstone, 3.1.08
11 Interview, Simon Harris, 18.1.08
12 Report of the Adjudication Panel for England, 15.12.05
13 *Evening Standard*, obituary of Louis Kirby, by Michael Leapman, 30.10.06
14 See Chapter 15
15 *The Times*, 12.4.00
16 *Evening Standard*, 14.9.01
17 *Evening Standard*, on remarks made by Livingstone in June 1983, 11.4.00
18 *Independent on Sunday*, 'The interview: Ken Livingstone', 31.8.03

19 *Independent*, 12.4.00
20 See Chapter 21
21 *Sunday Times*, 'Sunny Ken flies sky high on hot air', 16.4.00
22 *The Times*, 12.4.00
23 *Independent*, 12.4.00
24 Off-the-record briefing, 2.2.08
25 Channel Five, *The Wright Stuff*, 16.2.05
26 See Chapter 24
27 Mike Lee, *The Race for the 2012 Olympics*, pp120-121
28 Press Association, 'Livingstone refuses to say sorry for Nazi jibe', 14.2.05
29 Interview, Ken Livingstone, 3.1.08
30 Press Association, 'Livingstone refuses to say sorry for Nazi jibe', 14.2.05
31 Ibid.
32 Interview, Ken Livingstone, 28.12.07
33 Interview, Ken Livingstone, 3.1.08
34 Interview, Illtyd Harrington, 4.7.07
35 See Chapter 13
36 Interview, George Tremlett, 26.6.07
37 Interview, Ken Livingstone, 1.11.07
38 *Sunday Times*, 23.1.00; *Times*, 16.3.00; See Chapter 21
39 Off-the-record briefing, senior journalist, *Evening Standard,* November 2007
40 *Evening Standard,* 'A disaster in the making', 3.5.00
41 Max Hastings, *Editor: An Inside Story of Newspapers*, Macmillan, 2002, p25
42 *Spectator*, 'Diary', by Veronica Wadley, 22.1.05
43 Press release, Mayor of London, 'Livingstone and Giuliani join forces to promote tourism and trade'
44 Interview, Ross Lydall, 16.11.07
45 *Spectator*, 'Diary', by Veronica Wadley, 22.1.05
46 *Guardian* Unlimited, 'Jarvis admits liability for Potters Bar crash', 28.4.04
47 *Evening Standard*, 9.6.04
48 *Media Week*, 18.1.05
49 *Spectator*, 22.1.05
50 *Spectator*, 5.2.05
51 See Chapter 23
52 See Chapter 10
53 *Labour Herald*, 'Creature of Terror', by Ken Livingstone, p15, 1.10.82
54 David Yisraeli, 'The Palestine Problem in German Politics, 1889-1945', Bar-Ilan University, Tel Aviv
55 *Labour Herald*, Begin cartoon, by Tony, 25.6.82
56 Interview, Ken Livingstone, 25.10.07
57 Interview, Peter Bradley, 28.1.07
58 Tony Greenstein, 'Holocaust analogies: Repaying the mortgage', March 1990 www.iahushua.com/Zion/zionrac13.html
59 See Chapter 10; *News Line*, 9.4.83
60 *Times*, 'Why Labour is losing its Jews', by Peter Bradley, 7.3.85
61 See Chapter 18
62 www.socialistaction.org.uk

63 Ibid.
64 Ibid.
65 Simcha in the square, 14.10.07, www.simcha.org.uk
66 Press release, Mayor of London, 'Hanukkah', 11.12.07
67 Off-the-record briefing, 20.2.08
68 Report, 'Why the Mayor will maintain dialogues with all of London's faiths and communities', GLA, January 2005
69 Ibid.
70 *Evening Standard*, 'Stop playing with fire', by Jonathan Freedland, 2.3.06
71 Standards Board for England, summary
72 The Adjudication Panel for England, Notice of Decision, case number APE 0317, 24.2.06
73 Off-the-record briefing, former Standard reporter, 28.9.07
74 *Daily Mail*, 28.2.06
75 Ibid.
76 Interview, Ken Livingstone, 3.1.08

Chapter 27

The City State, 2008

On 4 February 2008, something significant happened in the long history of London. Until then, people were scarcely aware of entering the metropolis; just a gradual realisation of absorption into the suburban drabness of the outer London boroughs. After 4 February, they knew exactly when they crossed into the new low emission zone and if they were driving a filthy old lorry, they knew they would be £200 the poorer for the privilege. Ken Livingstone had tried to mark out the borders of Greater London before by declaring it a nuclear free zone, but the government still cheerfully carted nuclear waste in and out of the capital and the Soviet Union, had it been so inclined, would have flattened it with nukes. Now for the first time, there was a heavy tax for some on entry. Mayor Livingstone welcomes you to his domain of Londonland. No passport required – for the moment. Enjoy your stay.

◆

It is becoming increasingly clear that in reality the United Kingdom is made up of five not four constituent countries: England, Scotland, Wales, Northern Ireland and London. Like Wales and Northern Ireland, it even has an Assembly. At one time, London's nationhood was regularly debated in the Islington pub conclaves of Socialist Action. The theory that London is a 'City State' was often put forward by John Ross, the mayor's director of economic and business policy. Ross's former colleague and comrade Atma Singh says, 'The other concept he used to talk about was "London nationalism". It was similar to Scottish nationalism in that you had to appeal to people as Londoners. He said that London has a different pattern of economic activity in terms of the rest of the UK and that London's economic pattern is similar to other countries.' Livingstone once said, 'I'm in favour of an independent nation state. We would have European summer time and people could come over the border at Surrey to change their watches and their currency.'[2] He was only half-joking. Livingstone thinks there is too much central government and wants 'proper regional government'. After all, what is the point of low emission zones to deter polluting lorries if you cannot prevent the remorseless expansion of Heathrow Airport and check the apparent obsession with filling every spare piece of sky above the capital with planes?

Reporters covering City Hall often talk about Livingstone's constant use of the term 'Londoners'. 'No one really did that before Ken,' says Simon Harris of ITN *London Tonight*.[3] In his report 'The Case for London' for the Greater London Authority, Ross did argue that London was a special case, contributing between £9 to £15 or even £20 billion more in taxes than it receives in spending, yet with its own unique problems such as its transport infrastructure, child poverty and the cost and availability of decent affordable housing.[4] Tony Blair once warned Livingstone: 'I am running foreign policy,'[5] but the Kenocracy has developed its own with its positions on everything from Israel to China. It's even set up its own offices abroad, or 'Ken's embassies' as they would be described by contemptuous Tory Assembly members. City Hall would even enter into pacts with foreign countries, including, controversially, Venezuela and 'Kenbassies' have sprung up as far afield as Caracas, Beijing, Mumbai and Delhi. But Mayor Livingstone's era will be judged on his achievements, or otherwise, in London.

The mayor is responsible for a budget of £11 billion, much of it going on the salaries of bus drivers, firemen and police officers. It sounds a lot for one mayor but then the sheer scale of London inspires awe, all 609 square miles of it. It produces 17 million tons of rubbish each year; three million passengers use the Underground each day – a similar number to the entire national rail network; London's buses carry nearly six million passengers a day – a third of all bus passengers in England and Wales;[6] it has a population of more than 7.5 million,[7] about the same as Switzerland. The Statue of Liberty may exhort other nations to give up 'your huddled masses'; London would add 'and your plumbers, your doctors and your builders.' It is literally a capital of the world, and according to a survey in the *Independent* in December 2007, the 'best capital in the world'.[8] Livingstone's preoccupation is to keep London in pole position in this particular race, as he put it in 2008: 'Londoners' comparison now is whether

London is ahead of New York. The contest for number one city in the world, with only two in the race. Currently London is ahead. I believe London can increase its lead. But there is no room for complacency. We must continue further down the path London has followed if we are to enhance our position as the world's number one city.'[9]

But he is talking about the number one financial centre in the world; London is certainly not at the top of every list. For quality of life, London is number 39 in the world, according to the Cost of Living Index run by human resource consultants Mercer. In Mercer's health and sanitation section, London does not even make the top 50.[10] But despite all this, Mercer still makes London the second most expensive city to live in. During the course of a year, London moved from the fifth most expensive city in the world to number two due to soaring property prices combined with what has been described as the most expensive transport system in the world.[11] Transport in London costs three times that in New York or Sydney and six times taking a journey in Athens. What is the betting that the capital will one day head the list for the world's most expensive place to live while its inhabitants wonder why they cannot get their child into a decent school or spot a policeman out on the beat? Londoners are paying more but for what?

◆

Unquestionably, a success story has been the buses. When Livingstone became mayor in 2000, there were roughly 6,500 buses. In 2008, London could boast 8,500 – an increase of more than 35 per cent.[12] During 2006/07, bus passenger numbers reached their highest level since 1965. In the same year, London's 100 night bus routes carried 34 million people, more than double the number in 2000.[13]

Despite the detractors and the critics of bendy buses and empty buses, and often empty bendy buses, this form of public transport has been revolutionised under Livingstone's tenure. Of course, it did mean pensioning off one of London's iconic friends: the old red double-decker Routemaster. In 1998, Livingstone wrote: '...we must retain the Routemaster until a modern Routemaster can be designed. Not only is the Routemaster the bus that Londoners wish to use, it is also a symbol of London recognised the world over.'[14] In 2001, Livingstone had said, 'Only some ghastly dehumanised moron would want to get rid of the Routemaster,'[15] and yet only four years later, the day he said would never come dawned foggy and chill.

◆

At 6 a.m. on the morning of 9 December 2005, the *Today* pro-gramme dispatched its reporter Sanchia Berg to Westminster to report on the last day of the Routemaster.[16] There she met up with Stephen Pound, the Labour MP for Ealing North, to talk about his experiences as a conductor on the Routemaster. 'To ask what's special about the Routemaster is like asking what's so special about the London phone box or Big Ben,' says Pound. 'The point is that the Routemaster was the perfect engine. It was horrible to drive in many ways, but it was staggeringly reliable. When I was on the buses, all the mechanics at all the garages, every mechanic at Willesden garage or at Westbourne Park, were all ex-Army people who had learned driving during the war and you could actually learn to maintain a Routemaster in two weeks. It was the perfect urban transport. There is a place for saccharin and sentiment in the twenty-first century and there was some-thing about that great red galleon looming through the mist that was wonderfully reassuring whereas when you see a bendy bus coming around the corner, you think you're about to get your phone jacked .'[17]

But the Routemaster had to go. There were just too many acci-dents with people hopping on and off and too few disabled people able to climb aboard. On 9 December 2005, the last Routemaster chugged along the 159 route from Marble Arch to Brixton, its way lined by people waving Union Jacks. The last crew were from the West Indies: Winston Briscoe, born in Jamaica, at the wheel; Lloyd Licorish, originally from Barbados, churned out the last tickets which instantly became treasured souvenirs.

The other problem which tends to be overlooked is that no one makes Routemasters anymore. 'Ken was remarkably pragmatic on Routemasters,' says Peter Hendy, transport commissioner. 'We said to him, "Look we have bought all the old Routemasters from farmers, from bus preservationist societies and restaurants we can get, which is about 50 or 60. That's the most you are ever going to buy."'[18]

The answer was low-floor buses which would allow easier access for people in wheelchairs or with prams. More controversially, it was the end for the conductors. But people were wrong if they thought conductors deterred muggings and vandalism on buses. 'It's absolute bloody garbage,' says Hendy. 'In fact on route 12 the trade union was threatening to go on strike because the conductors were assaulted so often. The person most likely to be assaulted on a Routemaster is the bloody conductor.'[19] Instead, money was put into getting police to pop on to buses, now and then. But Stephen Pound is convinced the only answer to crime on buses is a permanent presence. 'You wait and see,' he says. 'We'll have conductors back and they'll be called something like "Passenger Escort Ushers" or something, but we will have them back because you can't get away with a hundred people on a bendy bus and not have some presence at the back.'[20]

◆

On 5 June 2002, Ken Livingstone launched the 'bendy bus' on to the streets of London.[21] At 18 metres long, this half-tram half-bus could carry up to 140 passengers, at least 60 more than a double-decker. Also known as the articulated bus, the bendy was not loved when it first appeared – nor may it ever be – and there was ill-disguised joy when the 130-strong fleet had to be withdrawn temporarily in March 2004 after three caught fire in a short period.[22] Boris Johnson, the Tories' mayoral candidate in the 2008 election, pledged to get rid of them and buy modernised Routemasters.[23] Some have claimed the bendys cause twice as many accidents as all other types of buses put together[24] but that overlooks the huge increase in the number of passenger journeys.[25] You will not hear too many complaints from people with babies, but there have been criticisms by some with disabilities.[26]

Revenue from the congestion charge has helped buy many of the buses. Unquestionably, its introduction was Livingstone's bravest decision and on 17 February 2007, in the teeth of local opposition,[27] he extended it westwards almost doubling its original size. Still, there have been calls for its abolition on the grounds that it is not working. Before its introduction in 2003, there were delays of 2.3 minutes per kilometre; four years later it was not much different at 2.27. 'What's the point of paying £8 for something you used to get for free?' asked Angie Bray, one of the Assembly Tories.[28] Was the congestion charge simply a charge for the honour of sitting in congestion? But according to Hendy and Livingstone, much of this congestion was mainly due to utilities digging up the road.[29] But TfL insisted there were still many fewer cars entering central London than was the case in 2003.[30]

On the rails, Livingstone has had some success, or luck, depending on your point of view. In October 2007, the government gave the go-ahead at long last to Crossrail, a £16 billion railway line passing under central London and linking Berkshire to Essex.[31] But below ground, the story is not good. By any criteria, the London Underground represented lousy value for money. Compared with other systems in cities like Paris and Berlin, it was dilapidated, overcrowded and expensive and was likely to stay that way for years to come. In 2008, Lionel Barber, the editor of the *Financial Times*, declared London could not claim to be the world's number one city given the poor state of the Underground, 'The Tube is a disgrace. It's maybe not as safe as some Tubes around the world. It's overcrowded. It doesn't work, and it's Victorian in the worst sense of the word.'[32] A 20-year programme to upgrade the network suffered a serious setback with the collapse in July 2007 of Metronet, one of the two PPP consortia and the biggest. Ruth Kelly, the transport secretary, told MPs that it was 'a terrible failure'[33] but it was one that had long been feared by Bob Kiley and Ken Livingstone during their doomed struggle against PPP.

Much of the blame for the debacle would be laid at the door of Gordon Brown who as chancellor, insisted on the PPP, as MPs would state in 2008: '... HM Treasury may be irritated and embarrassed by the Metronet administration – since they promoted and were instrumental in concluding the London Underground Ltd PPPs in the first place – but little more.'[34] It is now feared that the public may have to pick up the tab – to the tune of £1.9 billion.[35] In January 2008, the Commons Transport Committee was censorious: 'The government should remember the failure of Metronet before it considers entering into any similar arrangement again. It should remember that the private sector will never wittingly expose itself to substantial risk without ensuring that it is proportionally, if not generously, rewarded. Ultimately, the taxpayer pays the price.'[36] It was exactly what Bob Kiley said in 2000.

But Livingstone did revolutionise the way Londoners paid to travel around the capital with the introduction of the electronic pre-paid Oyster Card on 30 June 2003.[37] By 2008, few people would pay for their bus and Tube travel with cash. Buying paper

tickets was made almost prohibitively expensive and forced people to take up the Oyster. Since their introduction, 10 million
Oysters have been issued and they now account for more than
three quarters of all Tube journeys.[38] Tube and bus travel is also
free for 11- to 18-year-olds.

◆

On 10 February 2004, Livingstone published the so-called
London Plan, which sets out the future plans and policy of the
mayor. In it, there was much talk of regenerating run-down areas
of town, as well as addressing one of London's biggest problems:
the availability of affordable housing, particularly for the critical
'key' workers like nurses and teachers.[39] Britain's housing short-
age is a scandal which was gravely exacerbated by the Tories'
insistence on selling council homes through schemes like Right
to Buy – 1.7 million have been sold since 1979. But since Labour
came to power in 1997, the building of social housing has actually
fallen by 45 per cent.[40] Nearly 100,000 households in England will
have woken up in temporary accommodation – more than twice
as many as in 1997.[41] In London, rising house prices have made
the crisis far worse and is one of the main reasons why in 2004,
it was calculated that 35 per cent of London's children, rising to
48 per cent in inner London, live in poverty, statistics that would
shame most other western European nations.[42]

In the London Plan, Livingstone pledged to help bring about
the building of at least 30,000 new homes in the capital each year,
with as much affordable housing as possible, and despite the brick
bats, he appears to have made progress. According to the Greater
London Authority, more than 33,000 new homes were built in
London during 2007 – the largest annual figure since 1977. Of
that, a total of 11,980 affordable homes were also provided – an
increase of more than 70 per cent since 2000.[43] Although much
of the affordable housing is built by housing associations and the
like, Livingstone has tried to force private developers to include
social housing as part of their schemes. Ideally, he wants privately
developed housing schemes to include 50 per cent affordable
housing.

Here, again, there is a debate about just how successful
Livingstone has been. Mira Bar-Hillel, property and planning correspondent for the *Evening Standard*, says the mayor has failed to
hit the often-touted 50 per cent target and points to the official

figures which show that in the last seven years, affordable housing has not accounted for more than 30 per cent[44] of all housing
built in London.

Bar-Hillel adds, 'The mayor's headline policy is to require
50 per cent of all new homes to be "affordable". It is catchy and
superficially attractive – but it is also completely phoney, as he
applies it very selectively. In September 2007 Ken said he would
compulsorily purchase land belonging to Southwark Council
to help the Berkeley Homes company build a scheme with 374
homes – although only 114 of them will be affordable. He also
approved Arsenal's Highbury redevelopment, although only 25
of the homes will be "affordable". In Highbury Square itself, the
jewel in the crown, only seven per cent of flats will be "affordable". But then football is football…'[45] Neale Coleman, the may-
or's director of business planning and regeneration, says that 'a
lot of the criticism is silly criticism which isn't based on a proper
understanding of what we're trying to achieve and what we're
trying to do.

'Some schemes will never be able to have anything like 50 per
cent for a whole range of reasons. Perhaps they've got very dirty
land, maybe they're paying for a lot of essential transport which
we would prefer. So to pick out any individual scheme doesn't
make sense. Anyway that isn't what our policy says. Our policy
says we should aim for 50 per cent across London. You should
aim to get the most you can out of developers. In 2006, Croydon,
a Tory council, did get 50 per cent, and took pride in it. Ken congratulated them.'[46] In 2008, London was set to receive an additional £1 billion subsidy for new homes which Coleman was
confident would help Livingstone achieve the 50 per cent target
by 2010, at the earliest.

◆

Ken Livingstone has links to another fanatical group known as
the 'Militant Developer Tendency,'[47] as he once jokingly described
the builders of tall buildings. Livingstone's belief that London
needs more skyscrapers has puzzled some and angered others.
In January 2008, Prince Charles went on the offensive. Twenty-
four years after he attacked a proposed extension to the National
Gallery as 'a monstrous carbuncle', the Prince warned of: 'Not
just one carbuncle, ladies and gentlemen, on the face of a much
loved old friend, but a positive rash of them that will disfigure

precious views and disinherit future generations of Londoners.'[48] There will be 15 new skyscrapers over the next 20 years,[49] and furthermore, in April 2008, Livingstone received extra powers allowing him to overrule local borough councils on major planning applications.[50]

Livingstone courted controversy early on as mayor by supporting plans for the 202-metre-high Heron Tower in the City of London, close to St Paul's. In July 2002 the then deputy prime minister John Prescott approved the plans, as he would almost three years later for another contentious tower backed by Livingstone – the 181-metre Vauxhall Tower near Westminster Palace.[51] Livingstone is determined to give London the extra nine million square metres of office space it needs to compete with other world capitals.[52] 'London must continue to grow and maintain its global pre-eminence in Europe,' he wrote in 2001. 'London must continue to reach for the skies.'[53] Five of the proposed new towers will be higher than London's first proper skyscraper at Canary Wharf.

It is not just the buildings themselves, but the historic views which some people say may be defaced by the skyscrapers, whether it is the magical sight of St Paul's framed by trees from Richmond Park or of Westminster from Primrose Hill.[54] 'I don't particularly like or dislike tall buildings,' says Ken Livingstone. 'I like well-designed buildings... in terms of these things you have to ask, what do they replace? The London Bridge Tower was another one I supported. It takes down [replaces] the middle one of those three ghastly blocks between Guy's and the others. But 15 towers over the next 20 years? The idea we're going to turn London into Manhattan's absolutely rubbish. All of them are subject to a much more rigorous standard of quality than most of what else gets put up here.'[55]

'Livingstone has gone from Trotskyite to raw capitalist without an intervening phase of civilisation,' wrote Simon Jenkins in January 2008, as he complained how ugly London was becoming under the first executive mayor. In comparison with Paris, London was 'a shambolic, careless, sluttish hag', adding that Livingstone's towers were 'the planning equivalent of private equity capitalism, emblems of a city whose governance is corrupt and whose leadership is philistine. They will be plain ugly.'[56]

◆

Londoners' main concern is down at street-level: crime, not architecture, has always lost votes. Here Livingstone has claimed success with falling crime and rising numbers of police officers. But again, as with the congestion charge, it often does not feel that way. In January 2008, the home secretary Jacqui Smith drew hoots of derision and gave away the game a bit on crime by saying she would not feel safe walking around London late at night.[57] A YouGov survey in August 2007 showed that 46 per cent of Londoners did not feel safe in their neighbourhoods after dark.[58]

In February 2007, the Met revealed that there were 169 gangs in London, responsible for a fifth of all crime.[59] 2007 also witnessed a disturbing new trend, children murdering children. Each tragic shooting or stabbing would be followed by an explosion of press interest, which would gradually fade before the next seemingly inevitable murder.

In 2008, the killings had become an election issue. Livingstone's opposing candidates placed the apparent failure to tackle the problem at the feet of the mayor. 'We cannot allow 2008 to be as bad as 2007, when 27 London teenagers were murdered,' wrote Tory candidate Boris Johnson. 'It is time we got a grip on the culture of the gangs and gang-related killings – and the first step is for City Hall to stop treating the problem as though it were strange news from another planet.'[60]

Policing was part of the problem, but Livingstone thinks there is not enough for young Londoners to do and is pouring £78 million into youth facilities. He says, 'One of Thatcher's little horrors was to remove the statutory duty of councils to make youth provision for evening clubs. Wherever I go, kids and parents say there's nothing to do and that is absolutely true. Sometimes the only thing a kid can get involved in is a local gang.'[61]

◆

At the previous mayoral election in 2004, Livingstone was wildly over-optimistic about what he could achieve: 'I would be disappointed if, by the end of the rollout of the entire neighbourhood policing programme – which is going to take four years – we hadn't cut crime by 50 per cent.'[62] Simon Hughes, the Lib Dem candidate in 2004, scoffed, 'Even Batman would struggle to reduce a city's crime rate by 50 per cent in four years.'[63] How right he was.

Livingstone did reverse the long-term decline of police numbers. London has 35,000 officers including the 'community support officers', 10,000 more than in 2000, with plans to hire another 1,000 in 2008.[64] He also claimed that crime in London fell for the fifth consecutive year in 2007. He said the rate of decline is significantly accelerating: crime fell by 6.1 per cent last year, 4.4 per cent in 2006, 1.9 per cent in 2004 and 2.2 per cent in 2003. There may be 'lies, damn lies and statistics', but Livingstone would always say it was hard to rig the figures for murders,[65] for example, which, despite headlines, he insisted had fallen by 28 per cent since between 2003 and 2007.[66]

◆

On the issue of the day, climate change, few politicians can beat Livingstone on taking the initiative. There has been the low emission zone and the congestion charge. In 2008, despite threats of judicial review from the Porsche car company,[67] gas guzzling cars faced the prospect of a £25 fee to enter central London,[68] a draconian and punitive measure if ever there was one. On the other hand, cleaner small engine cars would be allowed in free, fuelling the argument that the charge was less about cutting congestion and more about the environment. Since 2004, Livingstone has needed the support of the London Assembly's two Green members, Darren Johnson and Jenny Jones, to get his budget passed. Sian Berry, the 2008 mayoral Green candidate and a leader of the Alliance against urban 4 × 4s, claims the Greens have been able to use their influence with Ken Livingstone, including getting action taken against the polluting gas guzzlers. 'We've had quite a lot of success,' she says. 'There are quite a lot of initiatives being launched that we can take credit for.'[69]

◆

As with the GLC, Livingstone is not master of all he surveys: he has no say in very many of the critical things like schools and hospitals which are central to the lives of Londoners. He has little control over the City of London, whose traders and bankers have pushed up house prices, jeopardised the economy with their credit crunch and forced the government to nationalise the Northern Rock bank. But in an age where people question the achievements of New Labour, Livingstone is seen by many as someone who takes risks and decisions, however unpopular, and gets things done. He still burns with resentment at the failures of Wilson and Callaghan, and he clearly also feels that Tony Blair and Gordon Brown have failed to take the advantage of the unparalleled opportunities so generously offered them by the British people in 1997.

◆

There is much déjà vu about Livingstone. At the GLC, he also ran a paper called the *Londoner*, got mixed up with some allegedly dubious characters, faced accusations of cronyism and was forced to face criticisms that he had handed public money out to cranks and toadies. He also broke new ground when it came to recognising the rights of minorities.

On 5 September 2001, just a week before the attacks in the US, two gay men, Alex Cannell, a 62-year-old former nurse manager, and his partner, Ian Burford, a 68-year-old actor and writer, arrived at the mayor's HQ in Romney House. At the time, neither the law nor the government legally recognised gay relationships. But Ken Livingstone did and invited Cannell and Burford to be the first to sign the London Partnership Register. Burford says, 'I think people thought, "Oh God, Ken Livingstone's doing one of his stunts! He's going to have a gay wedding thing." They always get that wrong and it drives me mental. It's never been anything but a *civil* partnership.

'We thought, "Well, we'll take it". The thing was that instead of two old leather queens with rings in their noses, the press saw two rather respectable middle-aged gentlemen with nice suits who were very articulate and who put the case very clearly that we were disadvantaged in certain things: tax, hospital visiting, death duties, and all sorts of things people never thought about.'[70]

Burford and Cannell, who had by then been together for 40 years, made their way through the press pack to be welcomed by Livingstone. 'He gave us a big hug and a kiss and said, "Congratulations and welcome",' remembers Cannell, 'he was so pleased to see that we had actually arrived.'[71] During the brief civil partnership ceremony, Livingstone wept.[72]

Within three years, the 2004 Civil Partnership Act came into force, giving gay couples rights and responsibilities identical to civil marriage, including inheritance tax, social security and pension benefits.[73] 'Nobody else thought of anything like that except for Ken,' says Burford. 'He has profound views on equality in every sense, racially, sexually, gender whatever. Now they are the buzz words and it's really fashionable to go on about them. But it wasn't back then when the GLC was around. He was the lone voice and was persecuted for it. He had the courage to say what he thought, which I think has always been the hallmark of Ken.'[74]

◆

In the early years, when the Islington pub conclaves would meet regularly, there was talk of Ken Livingstone as the 'honest social democrat',[75] who would help bring about not the bloody proletariat uprising but the 'bourgeois democratic revolution'[76] – surely a cop-out if ever there was one for the true revolutionary on at least two fronts, but much better than no revolution at all. But in the first eight years of the new millennium under Livingstone, revolutionary things had undoubtedly happened. Londonland – they have always done things differently there and the rest of the world catches up.

Notes

1   Interview, Atma Singh, 29.1.08
2   *Guardian*, 'London calling', 20.2.08
3   Interview, Simon Harris, 18.1.08
4   GLA report, 'The Case for London', by John Ross, published by the Greater London Authority, March 2004
5   See Chapter 24
6   Ibid.
7   Office for National Statistics, 2006
8   *Independent*, 22.12.07
9   *Evening Standard*, 'London's booming and it's all down to me', by Ken Livingstone, 22.1.08, (Headline not chosen by Livingstone!)
10 Website, Mercer Human Resources Consulting, www.mercer.com/knowledgecenter/
11 *Daily Telegraph*, 19.6.07
12 Interview, Peter Hendy, 13.12.07
13 Factsheet, 'London buses', published by TfL, 2007
14 'A mayor and Assembly for London' (A response to the government's White Paper), by Ken Livingstone, 1998, p2
15 *Times* Online, 9.12.05
16 Interview, Sanchia Berg, 1.2.08
17 Interview, Stephen Pound MP, 1.2.08
18 Interview, Peter Hendy, 13.12.07
19 Ibid.
20 Interview, Stephen Pound, 1.2.08
21 BBC News Online, 'London transport – with a twist', 5.6.02
22 BBC News Online, 'Bendy-buses withdrawn after fires', 24.3.04

23 *Evening Standard*, 'Scrap the bendy bus and bring back Routemasters, says Boris', 7.2.08

24 *Evening Standard*, 'Bendy buses – the fatal facts', 11.6.07

25 Report, 'Street management', published by TfL's road safety unit, February 2005

26 *Evening Standard*, 'Broken Ramps, lack of space... bendy buses fail the disabled, says charity', 5.3.08

27 *Times* Online, 'Livingstone takes charge zone farther despite opposition', 1.10.05

28 BBC News Online, 'Congestion charge "not working"', 23.11.07

29 See Chapter 23

30 BBC News Online, 'Congestion charge "not working"', 23.11.07

31 BBC News Online, 'Crossrail gets the green signal', 5.10.07

32 *Evening Standard*, Report of debate on London hosted by *Evening Standard*, 26.2.08

33 Report of the House of Commons Transport Committee, 'The London Underground and the Public-Private Partnership Agreements', Second report of session, 25.1.08

34 Ibid.

35 *Evening Standard*, 'Who'll pay £1.9 billion cost of Metronet collapse, ask MPs', 25.1.08

36 Report of the House of Commons Transport Committee, 'The London Underground and the Public-Private Partnership Agreements', Second report of session, 25.1.08

37 BBC News Online, 'Travelcards make way for "Oyster"', 30.6.03

38 Press statement, Mayor of London and Greater London Authority, 17.4.07

39 The London Plan, 'Spatial Development Strategy for Greater London', published by Mayor of London, February 2004

40 Shelter, report, 'Why has it come to this?'

41 Shelter, report, 'The facts and figures'

42 GLA report, 'The Case for London', by John Ross, published by the Greater London Authority, March 2004

43 Press statement, by Mayor of London and the Greater London Authority, GLA/2008/079, 7.2.08

44 London Plan monitoring reports, Greater London Authority

45 Interview, Mira Bar-Hillel, 4.2.08

46 Interview, Neale Coleman, 11.1.08

47 Mayor's press conference, 22.1.08

48 *Evening Standard*, 'This rash of carbuncles', 31.1.08

49 Interview, Ken Livingstone, 28.12.07

50 *Evening Standard*, 'Towers of London', 18.7.07

51 Ibid., 18.4.05

52 The London Plan, February 2004, p89

53 GLA report, 'Interim strategic planning guidance on tall buildings, strategic views and the skyline in London', October 2001

54 Ibid.

55 Interview, Ken Livingstone, 28.1.08

56 *Evening Standard*, 'Ken's towering ambition will forever scar our city', by Simon Jenkins, 28.1.08
57 *Sunday Times*, 'Home Secretary Jacqui Smith scared of walking London alone', 20.1.08
58 Ibid.
59 BBC News Online, 21.2.07
60 *Evening Standard*, 'Why is the Mayor still silent on these killings?', by Boris Johnson, 7.1.08
61 Interview, Ken Livingstone, 3.1.08
62 *Evening Standard*, 20.1.04; Ross Lydall's blog, 10.1.08
63 Ibid.
64 Press statement, Mayor's press office, 'Mayor's budget provides 1,000 more police for London', 30.1.08
65 Mayor's press conference, 8.1.08
66 Press statement, Mayor's press office, 'Mayor's budget provides 1,000 more police for London', 30.1.08
67 *Evening Standard*, 'Porsche threatens legal action over £25 C-charge', 19.2.08
68 Press release, TfL, the Greater London (central zone) congestion charging order, 2007
69 Interview, Sian Berry, 27.11.07
70 Interview, Ian Burford, 8.2.08
71 Interview, Alex Cannell, 8.2.08
72 Ibid.
73 Civil Partnership Act, 2004, www.opsi.gov.uk/acts/acts2004
74 Interview, Ian Burford, 8.2.08
75 Interview, Atma Singh, 29.1.08
76 Ibid.

Chapter 28

A little local difficulty, March 2006–2008

During the last half of his second term, Mayor Livingstone emerged increasingly as an international figure. His role during the terror crisis of 2005, the Olympics and the congestion charge attracted increasing interest from across the world. In 2007, he even brought the Tour de France to London. But, as he rubbed shoulders with the likes of Nelson Mandela and Bill Clinton, more unwelcome attention was paid to the way he ran City Hall and in particular, some of the people around him.

That is not to say everything was statesman-like on the international front. Roughly 50 foreign embassies refused to pay the congestion charge and yet could not be pursued in the courts – rather diplomatic impunity than immunity. The worst offender was, naturally, the US, with around a million pounds of unpaid charges and fines. On 28 March 2006, Livingstone, naturally, turned his ire on one Robert Holmes Tuttle, US ambassador to the Court of St James and friend of President George W. Bush: 'It would actually be quite nice if the American ambassador in Britain could pay the charge that everybody else is paying and not actually try and skive out of it like some chiselling little crook.'[1] A year later, the embassy's unpaid bills stood at £1.5 million.[2] In contrast, Livingstone did have an extremely high regard for some of America's enemies, particularly those within its direct sphere of influence, and despite their record on human rights.

Ken Livingstone has always loved Cuba. Down the years, there have been sightings of him amidst the romantic ruins of old Havana nursing a cold mojito while no doubt like most tourists, fending off the lithe jineteras and the tedious cigar-sellers. He has often praised Fidel Castro and the island's public services, and denounced the US embargo.[3] When he was leader of the GLC, he would even receive a bottle of rum each Christmas, courtesy of the Cuban embassy. He always remembered to thank the chargé d'affaires, Señor Rolando Álvarez.[4] A favourite tipple is Havana Club rum, and he is partial to the odd cigar.[5]

But nonetheless, it was a surprise to see the mayor in Cuba on Friday, 3 November 2006. BBC News reported that Livingstone was 'keeping his visit to Cuba low key' and that 'British diplomats in Havana admit they have been largely kept in the dark as to his plans'.[6] Then more strange things started to happen. Livingstone was joined by his chief of staff, Simon Fletcher, fresh from his honeymoon, while a short hop across the water, other senior figures from the mayor's office flew into Venezuela's capital, Caracas. At first, the story appeared to be that Livingstone had been invited to attend the Eleventh World Sport for All conference in Havana, an event sponsored by the International Olympic Committee.[7] But Havana was just a stop-off. The real purpose was a visit to Venezuela and a meeting with the Left's new hero of the hour, President Hugo Chávez,[8] with whom he hoped to sign a highly controversial oil deal to help subsidise bus travel for London's poor.

◆

Tim Donovan, BBC London's political editor, was in Cuba to greet Livingstone; Simon Harris, political correspondent for ITN *London Tonight*, hot footed it to Venezuela, where Chávez was campaigning to be re-elected. Both journalists thought they would be covering a high profile and controversial trip; instead they found themselves contemptuously dismissing an expensive shambles.

In Caracas, Harris met Livingstone's most senior press aide, Joy Johnson, and Redmond O'Neill, to discuss Livingstone's itinerary. Harris remembers, 'The big question was: Would he do an appearance at a Chávez election rally? All the time, there was a growing storm over his Cuba trip. The Assembly were furious. Back in London, there was a huge row about his trip at council taxpayers' expense to Cuba. At the same time, in Venezuela, the opposition were being publicly critical of the oil deal, making quite a bit of the fact that London, a developed city, was taking oil from a Third World country, and the argument that it was being used to help the poor in London cut very little ice with the opposition in Venezuela.'[9]

◆

On Saturday, 4 November 2006, Livingstone took in a cricket match at Havana at the invitation of Lord Moynihan, chairman of the British Olympic Association, while trouble brewed on both sides of the Atlantic. Angie Bray, the Tory Assembly member, expressed the anger of many of her colleagues: '…given the well documented far left socialist past of some of the mayor's closest advisors, is this not just an excuse to visit the last remaining bastion of twentieth-century Marxism, and maybe also the gravely ill Fidel Castro – no doubt an ideological hero to some of his inner circle – all conducted at our expense?'[10]

Meanwhile, in Cuba, Livingstone was being asked 'relentlessly'[11] by Tim Donovan of the BBC whether he had any plans to see Fidel Castro. Of course, he had planned to see Hugo Chávez, but he ended up seeing neither. After filming some of the worst slums Caracas had to offer, Simon Harris received a call from Joy Johnson with a short statement announcing the cancellation of Livingstone's trip to Caracas and his return to London. Clearly, Chávez had concluded it was not a good time to be seen with the mayor of London. 'We were furious,' says Harris. 'International travel on a regional television news programme budget is a luxury and Ken Livingstone had led us up the garden path and we were particularly angry because of the smokescreen put up over the Cuba trip and then we were dumped on in Venezuela.' Harris went to confront Johnson but she and the entire City Hall team had already cleared out, apparently not wanting to be filmed as the entourage of Livingstone's aborted trip.[12] Harris and his cameraman Kevin O'Mahony were left marooned and filled their remaining few days in Caracas filing reports detailing the debacle.

Donovan, who had been led to believe that Livingstone would even address the Venezuelan National Assembly, ended up filming Livingstone wandering around the old town of Havana, curiously inspecting national flags in a museum.[13] Shortly after, the mayor returned to London's Gatwick, to be pestered by a film crew.[14] His only response to the reporter's questions was a low tuneless hum. All in all, including Livingstone, nine people from City Hall had been sent to either Caracas or Havana; the total bill was roughly £29,000.[15]

◆

Chávez had initiated contact with City Hall through the Venezuelan embassy in London after learning of the support his regime had received from the mayor and others. He expressed the desire to stop off in London for an unofficial visit on his way back from a conference in Vienna.[16] The visit would lead to close ties between City Hall and Caracas, a relationship that was all the more extraordinary given Venezuela's poor human rights record. Figures released by Venezuela's own authorities and published in official reports show that between 2000 and 2005 the number of victims of murders committed by agents of Venezuela's security forces came to 6,377, in which a total of 6,110 police officials were involved. Of these cases, 3,346 were killings thought to have been committed by agents of state police forces; a further 2,116 were attributed to other organisations of policing or state security.[17] A report on Venezuela by Amnesty International in 2007 said that journalists, human rights workers and others are routinely murdered or intimidated by security services. Amnesty International states: 'Human rights violations, including torture, extrajudicial executions and enforced disappearances perpetrated by members of the security forces remained unpunished.'[18] According to figures published by Venezuela's own public prosecutor's office, of the 6,034 officials allegedly involved in cases of human rights violations, only 87, a pathetic 1.44 per cent, were convicted.[19] Livingstone's advisors say that Chávez is not personally behind the killings and is not in control of some sections of state security.[20] They also point to Chávez's regular referenda and elections. But the state of Venezuela's judiciary, its political independence, or the lack of it, as well as the large number of temporary judges and the ease with which they are hired and fired, has been a constant source of 'particular concern' to the Organisation of American States and can be laid at his door.[21]

Hugo Chávez is eulogised by many on the left in Britain for his apparent redistribution of his country's huge oil wealth, away from the Swiss bank accounts of the country's corrupt former rulers and into schools and hospitals for the poor. He is also admired for his aggressive opposition to the United States. When Chávez visited London in May 2006, Ken Livingstone hosted an event for him at City Hall. Tony Benn observed: 'The whole Left was there in force.' Benn thought Livingstone had done 'terribly well as mayor of London', adding: 'It's an extraordinary story really, quite extraordinary.' Livingstone introduced Chávez to Benn who gave the veteran left-winger a big bear hug and mentioned him in his speech.[22] During his visit to London, it was clear from Chávez's speeches that he shared many of Livingstone's values from virulent opposition to the Bush administration to women's rights and fighting racism. Chávez revealed how the mayor of Caracas – Juan Barreto – had erected a flag declaring the city a 'homophobia free zone'– pure Livingstoneism.[23] But Bob Neill, the leader of the Assembly's Tory group, turned down an invitation to meet Chávez, emailing Livingstone: 'President Chávez is well documented as having undermined pluralistic democracy, intimidated political opponents, rigged elections to Congress and packed the supreme court with his own supporters. He is an obstacle to good relations with ordinary Venezuelans rather than an assistance.'[24]

For Socialist Action, the visit was hugely important. On 17 May 2006, just two days after Chávez embraced Benn, the group's website said: 'What is taking place in Venezuela is the first self-defined and conscious attempt to create a socialist society since the Sandinista revolution in Nicaragua. It is therefore also the first offensive struggle at a state level for over 25 years.'[25] During his two-day visit, Chávez had first suggested a deal with London involving his vast oil reservoirs and shortly afterwards, on 18 May 2006, active negotiations began between the mayor's office and Venezuela.[26] Not only was the Chávez trip important to Socialist Action, the group had helped organise it.

Chávez's first speech was held on 14 May 2006 in the Camden Centre, hosted by the Venezuelan Information Centre, or the VIC.[27] The VIC was run by an economist called Professor Alan Freeman, a former City Hall employee and former editor of Socialist Action.[28] Ken Livingstone agreed to be the president of the VIC which has a website that portrays Venezuela and Chávez in a flattering light.[29] Like his mentor Fidel Castro, Chávez is fond of subjecting audiences to very long speeches. After two hours on his feet at Camden, Chávez turned to Livingstone and asked: 'Have I spoken too long, Mr Mayor?' Livingstone joked, 'No, no, you're only about halfway through.' The president pressed on for a further two hours.[30]

Chávez's initial suggestion of cheap heating oil for London's poor was rejected on the grounds that so few of them used it. But free petrol for the buses to subsidise bus travel would be welcome. In return, London would lend Venezuela its expertise in running public transport systems – Caracas could learn much from Peter Hendy – and on other issues including CCTV cameras and waste management.[31] However, a primary motivation for the Venezuelans was the propaganda value of any oil programme deal with London, as a memo in June 2006 from the ambassador, Alfredo Toro Hardy, to oil minister Rafael Ramírez, made clear. There would have to be: 'More visibility and public awareness of the programme, the advantage of which would benefit the image of the Venezuelan government.' The partnership could be advertised on and in buses: 'In addition, the mayor of London's office would undertake a well-articulated campaign outlining the partnership.' Hardy revealed: 'The representatives of the mayor's office declared that they were able to actively and effectively promote the image of Venezuela in the United Kingdom, highlighting the programme of cooperation and help with energy resources and the benefits of this for socially disadvantaged sectors. In this way, they indicated that they could use the bus network to promote Venezuelan tourism.'[32]

◆

On 20 August 2007, Livingstone announced half-price bus travel for poor Londoners funded with an annual tribute from Venezuela of £16 million, or $24 million petrodollars. The money would be used to help subsidise bus fares for up to 250,000 Londoners on benefits, including lone parents and sick and disabled people. To his critics, Livingstone was simply the latest beneficiary along with Cuba, Iran and even some US states, of Hugo Chávez's global oil diplomacy – buying goodwill and good publicity with black gold.[33] It is clear – aside from the financial benefits – the deal pleased those advisors who brokered it, particularly John Ross, Redmond O'Neill and Simon Fletcher, who undoubtedly saw it as much as an ideological success, forging closer links with a progressive socialist force in the world.

Others in the Labour Party were not impressed, particularly the former Labour government minister Nick Raynsford, who visited Venezuela for three weeks as a tourist in 2003 and learned of serious concerns about the Chávez regime from British diplomats and others in Caracas. 'There was quite a lot of evidence that there were corrupt practices,' says Raynsford. 'But the thing that above all shocked me was the incompetence with which the country was being run. You'd see a room labelled library in an indigenous area for tribal people and there would be no books or computers. The explanation was that the funds had been essentially siphoned off by party members who had taken their cut.'[34]

When Raynsford got to hear of Livingstone's dealings with Chávez, he told the mayor, 'Be very careful.' 'He just thought I was being anti-left wing,' says Raynsford, 'but I said it had nothing to do with politics; it had to do with corruption and Chávez's motives. I just think again that's a classic Ken error of judgement. He likes to be able to position himself as someone who is on the side of the leftists against Bush and the Establishment and he hasn't thought through the implications.'

◆

In May 2007, Ken Livingstone was the star turn of a conference in New York for the so-called C40 cities, the 40 cities around the world committed to cutting back carbon emissions and curbing the worst effects of climate change. After all, half the world's population live in cities and they consume three quarters of the world's energy and produce 80 per cent of its greenhouse gases.[35] London's mayor with his congestion charge, plans for the low emission zone and proposals to cut the emissions from public buildings by 20 per cent within three years[36] was seen as one of the few politicians leading the way and taking decisive action.

The event was hosted in New York by the city's mayor, Michael Bloomberg, and former US president, Bill Clinton. 'We have the tools,' said Livingstone, 'all that's lacking is the political will. It's in the cities where the battle will be won or lost.'[37] As chairman of the conference's C40 Cities Climate Change Leadership group, Livingstone encouraged other mayors, particularly Bloomberg, to go for congestion charging. At a dinner during the conference in the Time Warner building, Bill Clinton referred to Livingstone as 'our leader'. As the mayor rose to tumultuous applause, Joy Johnson bemoaned the absence of the domestic media.[38]

◆

On 23 August 2007, City Hall resounded to the sound of old negro spirituals sung by a group all dressed in white suits for Ken Livingstone's public apology for the slave trade on behalf of London. The year 2007 witnessed two anniversaries relating to slavery. The first, marked by Tony Blair, was the 200-year anniversary of the Slave Trade Act which received Royal Assent on 25 March 1807, following a 20-year campaign by William Wilberforce and others. Although Blair expressed his deep sorrow for slavery, he did not apologise. Writing in the *Guardian*, Livingstone described this refusal to apologise for the actions of long-dead ancestors as 'squalid', adding, 'Germany apologised for the Holocaust. We must for the slave trade.'[39]

In Livingstone's view, slavery was not ended by 'white philanthropy' but by the courageous rebellions of black slaves. To make his apology, he chose 23 August as the anniversary of the first great insurrection by slaves on Haiti in 1791. The United Nations Educational, Scientific and Cultural Organisation, UNESCO, had also suggested 23 August as the annual memorial day to commemorate the ending of trans-Atlantic slave trade. Livingstone astonished the assembled throng by weeping during his speech as he related the punishments and executions meted out to slaves by their cruel masters. He joined the Church of England Synod and the City of Liverpool in 'formally apologising for this monstrous crime'.[40] He received a standing ovation and a hug from Rev. Jesse Jackson. There was no mention of Wilberforce in the speech or the subsequent role played by the British navy in disrupting the slave trade.

◆

A week later and Livingstone was again in the international spotlight, with Prime Minister Gordon Brown, unveiling a statue of Nelson Mandela in Parliament Square. The ceremony held on 29 August 2007 in Mandela's presence marked the end of a long-running battle between Livingstone and Tory-controlled Westminster City Council. A statue of Mandela in London had been originally proposed by Donald Woods, the journalist and anti-apartheid campaigner, but the City Council vehemently opposed putting it in Trafalgar Square, as Livingstone and Woods wanted, because 'it would create an obstruction on the [north] terrace'[41] and instead gave the nine-foot statue made by the late sculptor Ian Walters permission for Parliament Square.[42]

◆

On the home front, 2006 had ended happily enough with the decision by the High Court to quash the Adjudication Panel's decision to suspend Livingstone over the Finegold incident.[43] The main reason given by the judge Mr Justice Collins: Livingstone was technically off duty when he abused Finegold, who in turn had not deserved such treatment. Collins also sympathised with Livingstone's arguments about how he had fared down the years at the hands of Associated Newspapers.[44] But the judge was clear, 'He could and in my view should have apologised for any particular hurt occasioned, not only to him but to others.'[45] As for Finegold, he decided journalism was not for him and became a press officer for Westminster Council. The *Evening Standard* had taken him off the road and given him a short-term contract with the lowliest job on the news desk – foreign planning. 'He was never one for the party scene or the pub scene,' says Ross Lydall, the paper's City Hall editor, 'he wasn't one who mixed socially that much. When he went off to get married – no one knew. The day he left, he just shuffled out the door and that was him gone. He didn't have a leaving do. I don't know if he felt his career had come off the rails through what happened but he was the real victim in all of this.'[46] Finegold always maintained his career change had nothing to do with Livingstone.[47]

While waiting for the court's judgment, Livingstone had faced further allegations of anti-Semitism and misconduct over remarks he made about two Jewish businessmen called David and Simon Reuben. The Reuben brothers were businessmen with a 50 per cent stake in a business consortium developing a site for the Olympic Games at Stratford.[48] Livingstone had heard that the brothers had been making a nuisance of themselves by shouting and screaming at meetings with Newham's mayor, Sir Robin Wales, to discuss the unsatisfactory progress of the development. Wales described the brothers' behaviour as 'worse than children' and both mayors feared they were more interested in asset-stripping than getting on with the work.[49] Asked at a press conference on 21 March 2006 about the risks posed to the development and the Olympics as a whole, Livingstone laid into the brothers, 'Perhaps they are not happy. Perhaps, if so, they can always go back to Iran and see if they can do better under the ayatollahs.' Livingstone told a later inquiry by the Greater London Authority that he was under the false impression that the Reubens were Muslims from Iran when, in fact, they were Indian by birth and their parents were Jews who had emigrated from Iraq to India. In June 2006, the GLA rejected the allegations of misconduct against Livingstone.[50]

◆

During 2007, the media and particularly the *Evening Standard* would start to take a long hard look at some of the people around

Livingstone, starting first with Bob Kiley, who at 72 was ill and had lapsed into alcoholism. Around the time of the 2004 mayoral elections, he underwent a serious operation for a chronic problem before getting tangled up in a power struggle with Jay Walder, former Harvard professor and TfL's prickly managing director of finance and planning.

Walder thought he was going to succeed Kiley but the commissioner 'showed no inclination' to let that happen. 'Bob actually enjoyed running the organisation,' says one senior TfL manager, 'and he was a great bloke to work for. Jay was getting itchy [feet] and thought he was the heir apparent and Bob decided that he wasn't.'[51] After a regrettable 'either he goes or I go' session with Kiley, Livingstone evidently took the view that neither should be commissioner and eventually plumped for Peter Hendy.[52] Walder left the organisation in November 2006[53] and Kiley was retained as a consultant to Livingstone on £700,000. Soon the *Evening Standard* picked up rumours that Kiley had hit the bottle and was not doing much for his huge salary. A reporter from the paper went to the off-licence nearest to Kiley's Belgravia home with a photo of Kiley and the former commissioner was immediately identified as a regular customer.[54] In March 2007, David Cohen, one of the *Evening Standard*'s feature writers approached Kiley and was rewarded with an interview of searing honesty.

Kiley admitted he did not do much for the money and added, 'I'm an alcoholic. But I'm not going to make excuses and say the reason is because I lost my family[55] because, [the] facts are, I always liked a drink. It is true, though, that things have got worse now that I'm not exactly overworked. I've always had high-pressure jobs that kept me extremely busy; now that I've got time on my hands, I start drinking.'[56] In June 2007, there was much flapping of gums from the Assembly about Cohen's revelations which Livingstone imperiously dismissed, '…neither do all of you do the work you're paid for given you're paid £50,000 a year to come in and do a full day's work… frankly that's almost fraudulent on the council tax payer.'[57]

◆

For Ken Livingstone, the political climate seemed to become chillier with the Tories' decision to field Boris Johnson, the 43-year-old MP for Henley, in the 2008 mayoral elections; he was formally selected on 27 September 2007.[58] Early on, it was clear that an important part of Livingstone's strategy was to depict his opponent as a racist for ill-advised comments and poor jokes he had made in the past. Even before his selection, the left-wing think tank Compass published a glossy leaflet detailing all the many embarrassing episodes in Johnson's blunder-strewn past, including his oft-quoted use of the word 'piccaninnies' to describe black people and his comment about Africans' 'water melon smiles'.[59] But despite the bumbling demeanour, Johnson was, like Livingstone, an aggressive maverick who seemed popular with some voters and one of the few politicians to be known simply by their first name. Undoubtedly, he represented the biggest electoral threat yet to Livingstone.

◆

On 1 November 2007, the Met was convicted on health and safety grounds for the shooting of Jean Charles de Menezes,[60] and six days later the Liberal Democrat and Tory members of the London Assembly joined forces to pass a vote of no confidence in the Met commissioner Sir Ian Blair.[61] The Tories' national home affairs spokesman David Davis demanded Blair's sacking.[62] The commissioner refused to go and was supported by Livingstone, who again defended Blair to the hilt and described the Assembly members as 'second-rate politicians who no one has ever heard of'.[63]

◆

Towards the end of 2007, a much harsher spotlight was to fall on a third key figure in the mayor's orbit. Eventually Ken Livingstone would be forced first to suspend and then accept the resignation of his policing and equalities director, Lee Jasper.[64] Livingstone acted after a two-month media blizzard of allegations of corruption, fraud and cronyism. This was close to home: Livingstone and Jasper were long-standing political allies.

The seeds of the storm lay in the growing unease felt by some members of the London Assembly about the London Development Agency (LDA), the so-called 'mayor's piggy bank', and some of the cultural projects funded by it. They commissioned the accountants Deloitte to undertake a short investigation into some of the start-up firms that received grants totalling millions in public money. The report, finally published on 12 November 2007, raised a number of serious concerns. There had been an 'inconsistent' approach to paperwork, said the Deloitte auditors, adding that the LDA had adopted 'an inconsistent approach to monitoring, evaluation and audit, a lack of appropriate evidence for internal and external reviews, a lack of detailed evidence considering project risks...'[65]

It soon became clear that the LDA had not handed over all the paperwork necessary for a more thorough inquiry, leading some Assembly members and others to question the validity of the Deloitte report.[66] It confirmed the fear of some that the LDA, a body responsible for billions of pounds of spending, was 'about as transparent as a medieval secret society'.[67] A second more-focused investigation was commissioned.[68]

Meanwhile, on 5 December 2007, the *Evening Standard* began publishing a series of articles alleging that large sums of money received by projects linked to Jasper had gone missing. All of the projects were run by black organisations. Off the record, senior aides to the mayor will concede that this assault caused the biggest crisis of Livingstone's two terms as mayor bringing together the sensitive areas of money and race.[69] The paper's reporter Andrew Gilligan stated that Jasper was at the 'centre' of a network of companies and organisations which had received at least £2.5 million from the mayor's London Development Agency, 'while appearing to do little or no work of public benefit in return.'[70] The sums involved were said to represent just 0.07 per cent of the £3.6 billion spent by the LDA since 2000.[71] If fraud is found, it is likely to be a fraction even of that amount.

The issues exposed by the *Evening Standard* were clearly serious and raised important questions of probity and competence. But, as yet, by no stretch of the imagination do the sums involved justify the claims made by Richard Barnes, the Tory leader on the London Assembly, of 'a real tide of corruption'.[72] However, coming so close to an election, the *Evening Standard*'s stories caused severe palpitations at City Hall.[73] The mayor's office issued a series of furious rebuttals and denials and on 13 December 2007, Livingstone called on the newspaper's editor, Veronica Wadley, to dismiss Gilligan for his 'dirty and mendacious campaign' adding: 'It is clear the *Standard* must apologise.'[74] The *Evening Standard* saw no reason to apologise and stood by its story and its reporter.

Livingstone was always convinced that people could never believe he personally was corrupt – all they had to do was look at his house and the clothes he wore. 'This campaign has been about the people around me,' says Livingstone.[75] He became convinced that the *Evening Standard* was out to destroy him. In particular, John Ross, the mayor's director of economic and business policy, advised Livingstone that Associated Newspapers was only keeping the *Evening Standard* afloat for the 2008 election, a suggestion laughed off as paranoia and self-delusion by reporters interviewed for this book. But Ken Livingstone insists: 'The *Standard*'s doomed. What I'm saying [is that] they're only keeping it going to see if it can bring me down. They think it's worth continuing to run that loss if at the end of the day, they can get rid of me. No one has any doubt Rupert Murdoch has his political objectives but his primary objective is making money. That isn't the case with Associated. Its primary role has always been setting a political agenda, going right back to the days of the first Lord Rothermere.

'Therefore, for them the fact [is] that I'm still here after all they've done over 25 years and still setting a lot of the political agenda of where we're going on Green politics and multiculturalism. They're batting away relentlessly against multiculturalism and City Hall is standing out as the last real layer of the state defending multiculturalism. That may very well prove to be a decisive factor in the election. Boris is running his election against multiculturalism; I'm supporting it.'[76]

An intriguing aspect of the saga was the sudden phenomenon of the leaked confidential email, something that was unheard of in Livingstone's tightly-controlled and tight-knit City Hall. The *Evening Standard* started to publish emails purporting to show Jasper interceding aggressively on behalf of at least two apparently failing organisations that had received hundreds of thousands of pounds in funding from the London Development Agency. For example, in April 2006, the LDA chief executive Manny Lewis had written to one of Jasper's associates, Joel O'Loughlin, to express his 'deepest possible concern' that his company, Diversity International Ltd, was about to go into liquidation despite having received more than £350,000 in LDA funds.[77] Lewis was inclined to 'sever relationships'.[78] Yet by 1 May 2006, following emails from Jasper, Lewis had agreed to pay Diversity a further £250,000.[79] The payment was not made, but only because Diversity went into liquidation and the company's liquidator allegedly forbade it.[80] Lewis also sought advice from Jasper about what to do with Brenda Stern, a lawyer on secondment to the LDA from the law firm BLP. She had expressed grave reservations about O'Loughlin and Diversity. 'Send her back to BLP,'[81] was Jasper's curt advice, and so she was. It seems more than likely that this correspondence and other incriminating material fell into the 'wrong hands', as a result of astonishing carelessness by Jasper. A person with access to City Hall, almost certainly an employee, went up to the eighth floor used by Livingstone and his senior aides and logged into one of the computers using Jasper's password which he would stick up near the computer of his latest temporary secretary for everyone to see.[82]

◆

By 31 January 2008, the LDA had reported six projects to the police, among them the European Federation of Black Women Business Owners, the Deshbangla Foundation, and Brixton Base, a youth project devised by Lee Jasper which owed the LDA hundreds of thousands of pounds in unpaid rent.[83] Diversity International and Ethnic Mutual were also referred to the police over apparent financial irregularities and a fourth, the Green Badge Taxi School, to HM Customs and Excise, over 'some unresolved issues'.[84] There were some dawn raids by the police, including one on a company in south-east London that had direct links to Lee Jasper.[85] On 15 February 2008 came the news that Jasper himself had been temporarily suspended by the mayor 'at his own request' and had asked Livingstone to refer the matter to the police because he was 'being prevented from clearing' his name.[86] But less than three weeks later, on 4 March 2008, Jasper resigned. Earlier in the day, the *Evening Standard* had published more of his leaked emails, this time of a more lethal and embarrassing nature. In June and July 2006, he had sent a series of apparently intimate messages to a married mother of three, Karen Chouhan, who was involved with organisations, including the 1990 Trust, in receipt of funding from City Hall. In one, Jasper, a married father with nine children, expressed a desire to 'honey glase' [*sic*] Chouhan before 'a torrid and passionate embrace'. He signed the note 'General Jasper'.[87] The pair vehemently denied an affair, but the damage was done.[88] In his letter of resignation, accepted by Livingstone, Jasper said he and his family had been placed under 'an intolerable strain' by 'the racist nature of a relentless media campaign'.[89] The resignation saved Jasper the ordeal of facing London Assembly hearings on 5 March 2008, and it broke Livingstone's golden rule of never giving in to media pressure, but at least it drew a line under the affair before the election.

Although some at City Hall have questioned his judgement, no evidence has yet emerged of any criminal wrongdoing by Lee Jasper, or indeed, by his friends and associates. As of April 2008, inquiries were ongoing.

Further allegations against Livingstone were made on 21 January 2008 by a Channel Four *Dispatches* investigation.[90] Atma Singh, initially dismissed by City Hall for alleged incompetence in 2007 and then allowed to leave after a compromise agreement,[91] appeared on the programme to allege that some of Livingstone's advisors had broken the rules governing their conduct during the 2004 mayoral election. This allegation was strenuously dismissed by City Hall.[92] Again, Jasper was accused of participating with Livingstone in a covert attempt to prevent Trevor Phillips being appointed to head a new government body.[93] Livingstone was also accused of drinking whisky during the day which he insisted was used for warding off bronchitis and sore throats.[94] On 22 January 2008, there was further embarrassment when Jasper's deputy, Rosemary Emodi, was forced to resign after a BBC London investigation showed she had lied about a visit to a holiday resort in Nigeria.[95]

Following the *Dispatches* programme, Professor Tony Travers, the leading expert on the capital's government at the London School of Economics, warned Livingstone to 'refresh his team and provide grounds for a belief that his administration is clean and competent', and referring to the current media onslaught further observed: 'Martyr status has worked for Livingstone in the past, but one day it won't.'[96]

◆

In 1998, Ken Livingstone himself told the government to 'reconsider its decision not to have term limits for the mayor,' adding: 'So much of the American experience of directly-elected mayors shows it gets progressively more difficult to defeat a well-dug-in incumbent who has been able to establish extensive systems of patronage... corruption tends to flourish the longer an incumbent is able to hold on to power.'[97] The May 2008 mayoral election will be Livingstone's third and should he beat Boris Johnson, he has made it clear he will stand again in 2012 when he will be nearly 67. As Livingstone often says, consistency in politics is greatly overrated, or at least, that is what he has said until now.

Livingstone has always polarised public opinion: some will point to incidents like Jasper-gate for evidence of hubris and corruption, others to his road-pricing policies, the Olympics and other successes as reasons to vote him back in. Many people have voted for Livingstone essentially because they always felt instinctively that he was one of them, the 'people's Ken', as former backbench MPs call him, fondly or otherwise. Lance Price, one of the Number 10 spin doctors who tried and failed to defeat Livingstone in 2000, says, 'He's got that knack that certain politicians have got of being an "anti-politician politician", of being a politician but at the same time talking the sort of language and having the sort of body language that they're giving the impression that they're prepared to stick two fingers up to politics. Mo Mowlam could do the same thing and so could Clare Short. It's something you've either got or you haven't.

'It's the appearance, and it's not always true, but it's the appearance of being honest and straightforward and anti-spin and saying exactly what you think about things even if it's unpopular. People like that and that works and Ken's always had that.'

Perhaps, at last, after eight years in City Hall, and thirty on the national stage, the penny may have dropped that Ken Livingstone is what he has always been – a politician; and, love him or loathe him, one of the best political operators in the country. He has survived, and thrived, despite all the odds and political risks; he still manages to appal, anger and delight both friends and enemies in equal measure. *Newsnight*'s political editor, Michael Crick, says, 'The most skilful politicians in this country operate outside Westminster. You've got Ken Livingstone, Alex Salmond (Scotland first minister), George Galloway and one or two from Ireland. There is a certain sterility about Westminster that drives some of the maverick types who are nonetheless brilliant exponents of power.'[98] In 2008, many people started to point at Livingstone and say, they are all the same, aren't they? But surely even his most bitter enemies would have to concede, well since you ask, not really.

Notes

1 ITN *London Today*, 28.3.06; *Times* Online, 28.3.06
2 Channel Four News Online, 22.7.07
3 *Sun*, 'Ken Livingstone in US rant', 6.11.06
4 Letter, Ken Livingstone to Rolando Álvarez, London Metropolitan Museum, file no. GLC XX/01/27, 7.1.86
5 Off-the-record briefing, 10.2.08
6 BBC Radio News report, by Stephen Gibbs, 3.11.06
7 BBC News Online, 'Livingstone's surprise Cuba trip', by Tim Donovan, 2.11.06
8 Mayor's Question Time, London Assembly, 15.11.06
9 Interview, Simon Harris, 18.1.08
10 BBC News Online, 'Livingstone's surprise Cuba trip', by Tim Donovan, 2.11.06
11 Mayor's Question Time, London Assembly, 15.11.06
12 Interview, Simon Harris, 18.1.08
13 BBC London, 6.11.06
14 ITN *London Tonight*, 8.11.06
15 Letter, 'GLA visits to Cuba and Venezuela', Anthony Mayer, chief executive of GLA, to Brian Coleman AM, 13.11.06; Mayor's Question Time, 15.11.06
16 Off-the-record briefing, senior advisor, February 2008
17 Annual Report of the Inter-American Commission of Human Rights, Organisation of American States, based on speech by the Venezuelan Prosecutor General on the occasion of the presentation of the 2005 Performance Report. 25.4.06
18 Report, 'Venezuela, Bolivarian Republic of Venezuela', published by Amnesty International, 2007
19 Letter from Amnesty International to the candidates in Venezuela's 2006 presidential election, file no. AMR 53/008/2006, 7.11.06
20 Off-the-record briefing, senior advisor, February 2008
21 Annual Report, Inter-American Commission on Human Rights, Organisation of American States, 2006
22 Tony Benn, *More time for politics: 2001–2007*, (see 15.5.06)
23 www.socialistaction.org.uk, 'Venezuela and 21st century socialism', 17.5.06,
24 Email from Bob Neill to Ken Livingstone, 10.5.06
25 Ibid.
26 Memo from Alfredo Toro Hardy, Venezuela ambassador, to Citizen Rafael Ramirez, Venezuela minister of Energy and Petroleum, June 2006
27 Email from Bob Neill to Anthony Mayer, GLA chief executive, 11.5.06
28 Socialist Action File, University of Warwick
29 VIC website, www.vicuk.org/index.php
30 Off-the-record briefing , senior advisor, February 2008
31 Memo from Alfredo Toro Hardy, Venezuela ambassador, to Citizen Rafael Ramirez, Venezuela minister of Energy and Petroleum, June 2006
32 Ibid.
33 *Financial Times*, 21.8.07
34 Interview, Nick Raynsford MP, 20.12.07

35 Website, C40 Cities, www.c40cities.org/
36 *Environmental Finance News*, 17.5.07
37 *Toronto Star*, 'Miller's green plan cool', 15.5.07
38 Off-the-record briefing, 1.2.08
39 *Guardian*, 21.3.07
40 Speech by Ken Livingstone, City Hall, 23.8.07
41 Press release, Westminster City Council, 27.9.05
42 Press release, Westminster City Council, 19.4.07
43 See Chapter 26
44 High Court judgment, Ken Livingstone vs Adjudication Panel for England, before Mr Justice Collins, 19.10.06
45 Ibid.
46 Interview, Ross Lydall, 16.11.07
47 Off-the-record briefing, 28.9.07
48 Report of local investigation, Greater London Authority, 78331/3/PKL, by Peter Keith-Lucas, 14.6.06
49 Ibid.
50 Ibid.
51 Off-the-record briefing, December 2007
52 Ibid.
53 Press release, 'Transport for London, Jay Walder to leave Transport for London', 22.11.06
54 Off-the-record interview, *Evening Standard* reporter, 14.11.07
55 See Chapter 22
56 *Evening Standard*, '£3k a day Tube Chief Admits: I'm an alcoholic', by David Cohen, 28.3.07
57 Mayor's Question Time, London Assembly, 13.6.07
58 *Guardian*, 'Boris Johnson to be Tory candidate for London Mayor', 28.9.07
59 Report: 'Boris Johnson, a member of the Tory hard right', published by Compass, August 2007
60 Press Association, 1.11.07
61 *Times* Online, 'Sir Ian Blair defies no confidence motion', 7.11.07
62 Letter, David Davis MP to Jacqui Smith MP, Home Secretary, 2.11.07
63 Sky News, 7.11.07
64 *Evening Standard*, 'Ken calls in police over key aide', 15.2.08
65 Report: 'The London Development Agency (LDA)'s funding of cultural projects', 12.11.07
66 Evidence of Manny Lewis, The London Assembly Economic Development, Sport and Tourism Committee, (EDSCT), 12.11.07
67 *Dispatches*, 'The Court of Ken', 21.01.08
68 Report, Executive Director of Secretariat, The London Assembly Economic Development, Sport and Tourism Committee (EDSCT), 4.11.07
69 Off-the-record briefing, senior advisor, 1.2.08
70 *Evening Standard*, 16.12.07
71 Information, Greater London Authority, 5.2.08; See Chapter 22 for a brief explanation of the GLA
72 *Evening Standard*, 13.12.07
73 Off-the-record briefing, senior advisor, 1.2.08

74 Press release, Mayor's office, 'Mayor – "Evening Standard must sack Gilligan after falsehoods proved"', 13.12.07
75 Interview, Ken Livingstone, 28.12.07
76 Interview, Ken Livingstone, 28.12.07
77 Letter, Manny Lewis to Joel O'Loughlin, Diversity International, 27.4.06
78 Email, Manny Lewis to Lee Jasper, 22.4.06
79 Ibid., 1.5.06
80 *Evening Standard*, 17.12.07
81 Email, Lee Jasper to Manny Lewis, 25.6.06
82 Off-the-record briefing, 18.2.08
83 Briefing for Assembly members provided by secretariat for meeting on 7 February
84 Report, 'Review of *Evening Standard* allegations', published by LDA, inquiry by Andrew Travers, Group Directors, Resources and Risk, 11.1.08
85 *Evening Standard*, 'Mayors aide: police move in', 28.1.08
86 Press release, Mayor of London and GLA, 'Lee Jasper requests Mayor to immediately refer all allegations against him in the *Evening Standard* to full police investigation', 15.2.2008
87 Email, Lee Jasper to Karen Chouhan, 23.6.06. Reproduced in the *Evening Standard*, 4.3.08
88 *Evening Standard*, 'Mayor aide's £100,000 for his "darling"', article by Andrew Gilligan, 4.3.08
89 Letter of resignation, Lee Jasper to Ken Livingstone, 4.3.08
90 *Dispatches*, 'The Court of Ken', 21.1.08
91 Press release, GLA, 'The Greater London Authority and Mr Singh', 20.1.08; GLA statement, 'Statement from the Greater London Authority, following allegations in the *Sunday Times*', 20.1.08.
92 See Chapter 24
93 See Chapter 20
94 Mayor's press conference, 22.1.08
95 Press release, statement on Rosemary Emodi, 22.1.08
96 *Guardian*, 'Mud sticks to martyrs too', by Professor Tony Travers, 22.1.08
97 'A Mayor and Assembly for London' (A Response to the government's White Paper), by Ken Livingstone, 1998, p4
98 Interview, Michael Crick, 18.1.08